THE WORLD OF LEONARD COHEN

Leonard Cohen's artistic career is unique. Most poets and novelists do not become rock stars. No other rock star's career peaked in their eighth decade as Leonard Cohen's did. Cohen's popularity is still growing five years after his death. In *The World of Leonard Cohen*, a team of international scholars and writers explore the various dimensions of the artist's life, work, persona, and legacy to offer an authoritative and accessible summation of Cohen's extraordinary career. His relation to key themes and topics – Judaism, Buddhism, Christianity, Zen and the East, the Folk tradition, Rock & Roll, Canadian and world literature, film – are all addressed. *The World of Leonard Cohen* offers a comprehensive, uniquely informed and wholly fresh account of this iconic songwriter and artist, whose singular voice has permanently altered our cultural landscape.

David R. Shumway is Professor of English, and Literary and Cultural Studies. He is the author of *American Narrative Realism: The Novel, Film, Television, and Theater*, to be published by Cambridge University Press in 2026. He wrote *Rock Star: The Making of Musical Icons from Elvis to Springsteen* (2014) and contributed to *The World of Bob Dylan*, *The Cambridge Companion to Bob Dylan*, and *The Cambridge Companion to the Singer-Songwriter*.

THE WORLD OF LEONARD COHEN

Edited by

David R. Shumway

CAMBRIDGE
UNIVERSITY PRESS

Shaftesbury Road, Cambridge CB2 8EA, United Kingdom

One Liberty Plaza, 20th Floor, New York, NY 10006, USA

477 Williamstown Road, Port Melbourne, VIC 3207, Australia

314–321, 3rd Floor, Plot 3, Splendor Forum, Jasola District Centre, New Delhi – 110025, India

103 Penang Road, #05–06/07, Visioncrest Commercial, Singapore 238467

Cambridge University Press is part of Cambridge University Press & Assessment, a department of the University of Cambridge.

We share the University's mission to contribute to society through the pursuit of education, learning and research at the highest international levels of excellence.

www.cambridge.org
Information on this title: www.cambridge.org/9781009350594

DOI: 10.1017/9781009350549

© David R. Shumway 2026

This publication is in copyright. Subject to statutory exception and to the provisions of relevant collective licensing agreements, no reproduction of any part may take place without the written permission of Cambridge University Press & Assessment.

When citing this work, please include a reference to the DOI 10.1017/9781009350549

First published 2026

Printed in the United Kingdom by CPI Group Ltd, Croydon CR0 4YY

A catalogue record for this publication is available from the British Library

A Cataloging-in-Publication data record for this book is available from the Library of Congress

ISBN 978-1-009-35059-4 Hardback

Cambridge University Press & Assessment has no responsibility for the persistence or accuracy of URLs for external or third-party internet websites referred to in this publication and does not guarantee that any content on such websites is, or will remain, accurate or appropriate.

For EU product safety concerns, contact us at Calle de José Abascal, 56, 1°, 28003 Madrid, Spain, or email eugpsr@cambridge.org

In memory of David Yaffe

Contents

Notes on Contributors *page* x
Acknowledgments xvii

Introduction: You Don't Know Leonard Cohen 1
David R. Shumway

PART I: CREATIVE LIFE

1 The Life of a Troubadour 13
   Ira B. Nadel

2 The Poetry and Prose: "Almost Like the Blues" 29
   Julian Stannard

3 Songwriting: Hymns of the Heretic 47
   Alan Light

4 Assembling Albums in the Tower of Song 61
   Anthony DeCurtis

PART II: MUSICAL CONTEXTS

5 Folk Music 77
   Gillian A. M. Mitchell

6 Singer-Songwriters 97
   David R. Shumway

7 Unrocking Rock & Roll: Hiding Songs, War Horses,
   and Cabaret Blues 109
   Eric Weisbard

CONTENTS

PART III: RELIGIOUS CONTEXTS

8 Judaism: At the Peripheral Center 125
   Elliot R. Wolfson

9 Zen and the East: Leonard Cohen as Buddhist Monk and
   Bodhisattva Poet 138
   Christophe Lebold

10 Christianity: The Little Jew Who Wrote the Bible and Much
   about Jesus 151
   Marcia Pally

PART IV: CULTURAL CONTEXTS

11 Canadian Literature 167
   Ian Rae

12 World Literature 181
   Francis Mus

13 Cohen's Cinematic Appeal 195
   Laura Cameron and Jim Shedden

14 Neurotic Affiliations: Montreal and Belonging 209
   Erin MacLeod

15 Boudoir Poet: A Thousand Kisses Deep with Leonard Cohen 223
   David Yaffe

16 For the Matriarchy: Women and the Music 235
   Heather S. Arnet

17 The Counterculture 249
   Sarah Hill

18 Politics: Insincerely L. Cohen 263
   David Boucher

PART V: RECEPTION AND LEGACY

19 "You Know Who I Am": From Writer to Rock Star 285
   Loren Glass

20 Documentary (Re)presentations: "You Know Who I Am" . . 300
   Robert de Young

21 "I'll Wear a Mask for You" 313
   Lucy J. Boucher

CONTENTS

22   How to Be an Aged Rock Star 327
     David R. Shumway

23   Covers: Six Hundred and Forty-Nine Broken "Hallelujah"s . . 340
     Ray Padgett

24   The Archives: "I Hope You're Keeping Some Kind of Record" 353
     Robert de Young

Further Reading   366
Index   370

Notes on Contributors

Heather S. Arnet, gender equity advocate, writer, and artist, is former CEO of the Women and Girls Foundation (2004–22), who has written and directed several plays and films, including *Madame Presidenta: Why Not U.S.?* and *YoMama!* Currently CEO/Executive Director of the Heckscher Museum of Art in Huntington, NY, Arnet contributed to new art historical scholarship and exhibition catalogs for Courtney Leonard (2023), George Grosz (2024), and Emma Stebbins (2025); served as Co-Chair of the Council of Feminist Art, Brooklyn Museum, and Chair of the Ms. Foundation for Women; and has a BA from Carnegie Mellon University in English and Drama, and an MA from Harvard University, Extension School, in Museum Studies.

David Boucher is Professor Emeritus of Political Philosophy, and Director of the Collingwood and British Idealism Centre, Cardiff University. He is a Distinguished Visiting Professor, University of Johannesburg, South Africa. He has published widely on history, politics, philosophy, and culture. He is the author of *Dylan and Cohen: Poets of Rock and Roll* (2004) and *Bob Dylan and Leonard Cohen: Deaths and Entrances* (2021, with Lucy J. Boucher). Among his recent edited books are *Language, Culture and Decolonisation* (2022), *Decolonisation: Revolution and Evolution* (2023) and *Reappraising The Life and Legacy of J C Smuts* (2024).

Lucy J. Boucher has a PhD in Creative Writing and English Literature from Brunel University, UK, and has been a visiting researcher at the University of Johannesburg, South Africa. She is currently researching ideas of the "healthy" body in nineteenth-century physical culture at the University of Texas at Austin. She is the coauthor of *Bob Dylan and Leonard*

NOTES ON CONTRIBUTORS

Cohen: Deaths and Entrances (2021). She has published articles on physical culture in leading journals in the field, and is waiting patiently for Kanye West to write a poem about Leonard Cohen.

Laura Cameron holds a PhD in English from McGill University, where she wrote a dissertation on twentieth-century Canadian poetic careers. She has published on writers including Phyllis Webb, P. K. Page, and Leonard Cohen, and she has taught numerous courses in Canadian and American literature. Laura worked for several years as an editor at the Art Gallery of Ontario, and she is presently completing a law degree at the University of Toronto.

Anthony DeCurtis is a contributing editor for *Rolling Stone* and a Distinguished Lecturer in the Creative Writing Program at the University of Pennsylvania. He is the author of, among other books, *Lou Reed: A Life* (2017) and coauthor of Clive Davis's autobiography *The Soundtrack of My Life* (2013). He was awarded a Grammy for his liner notes accompanying the Eric Clapton box set *Crossroads*. His interview with Leonard Cohen ran in *Rolling Stone* in 1993, and he has written liner notes for several of Cohen's albums. He holds a PhD in American literature from Indiana University and lives in New York City.

Loren Glass is Professor and Chair of English at the University of Iowa, specializing in twentieth- and twenty-first-century literatures and cultures of the United States, with an emphasis on book history and literary institutions. He is the author of *Counterculture Colophon: Grove Press, the Evergreen Review, and the Incorporation of the Avant-Garde* (2013), republished in paperback under the title *Rebel Publisher: Grove Press and the Revolution of the Word*, and is the editor of *After the Program Era: The Past, Present, and Future of Creative Writing in the University* (2016). His most recent book is a study of Carole King's *Tapestry* for Bloomsbury's "33 1/3" series. He is a member of the Post45 collective and coedits their book series. He is currently working on a history of creative writing at the University of Iowa.

Sarah Hill is Associate Professor of Popular Music and a Fellow of St. Peter's College, University of Oxford. She is Coordinating Editor of the journal *Popular Music*, and has published on popular music historiography, popular music and politics, and popular music and cultural identity, particularly as it relates to the Welsh language. Her most recent books are the monograph *San Francisco and the Long 60s* (2016) and the edited collection *One-Hit Wonders: An Oblique History of Popular Music* (2022).

Christophe Lebold is Associate Professor at the University of Strasbourg (France), where he teaches literature, performance studies, and rock culture. After a PhD on the voices and masks of Leonard Cohen and Bob Dylan, he has published extensively on both poets and other songwriters. A friend of Leonard Cohen in his later years, he has travelled extensively in the poet's tracks and spent time with him in Los Angeles. His critically acclaimed biography-cum-monograph *Leonard Cohen, The Man Who Saw the Angels Fall* (2024, originally published in French) was awarded the National Jewish Book Award for "best biography of 2024." Also a theater actor and student of Zen, he likes poets, cats, and – when in a good mood – all sentient beings.

Alan Light is an Emmy Award–winning music journalist, a bestselling author, and the co-host of the music news podcast "Sound Up!" The former Editor-in-Chief of *Vibe* and *Spin* magazines, and a former Senior Writer at *Rolling Stone*, he is a frequent contributor to the *New York Times*, the *Wall Street Journal*, and *Esquire*, among other publications. Alan's books include *The Holy or the Broken: Leonard Cohen, Jeff Buckley, and the Unlikely Ascent of "Hallelujah"* (2012), which was adapted into the acclaimed documentary *Hallelujah: Leonard Cohen, a Journey, a Song*, as well as biographies of Prince, Johnny Cash, Nina Simone, and the Beastie Boys.

Erin MacLeod is the author of *Visions of Zion: Ethiopians and Rastafari in the Search for the Promised Land* (2014) and coeditor with Moji Anderson of *Beyond Homophobia: Centering LGBTQ Experiences in the Anglophone Caribbean*. She holds a PhD in Communications from McGill University and a Master's in English Literature from the University of Toronto, and has taught and lectured at both college and university levels in Ethiopia, Canada, and Jamaica. Her writing has appeared in international publications such as the *New York Times*, *Guardian*, *NPR*, *Pitchfork*, *Rolling Stone*, and many others. Erin teaches at Vanier College in Montreal, Canada, and works as a consultant in international development.

NOTES ON CONTRIBUTORS

Gillian A. M. Mitchell is a senior lecturer in History at the University of St Andrews in Scotland, UK. She specializes in the sociocultural history of popular music and popular culture in Britain and North America from the 1950s to the 1970s. Her most recent books are *Adult Responses to Popular Music and Intergenerational Relations in Britain, c. 1955–1975* (2019) and *The British National Daily Press and Popular Music, c. 1956–1975* (2019).

Francis Mus is Assistant Professor of French and Translation Studies at the University of Ghent and an affiliated researcher at the University of Antwerp, Belgium. Among his research interests is the Canadian and international reception of Cohen's works, including in translation. His monograph *The Demons of Leonard Cohen* (2020) was awarded the Literary Prize of the Province of East Flanders and was a finalist for the Foreword INDIES Book of the Year Awards.

Ira Nadel is Professor of English Emeritus at the University of British Columbia. His biography of Leonard Cohen, *Various Positions*, first appeared in 1996. He subsequently published lives of Tom Stoppard, David Mamet, and Philip Roth. Two recent critical studies are *Love and Russian Literature* (2023) and *The Business of Ballet, Diaghilev's Ballets Russes between Profit and the Avant-garde* (2024). In March 2023 he chaired the Leonard Cohen symposium "In My Secret Life" on the Cohen archive at the Art Gallery of Ontario in Toronto.

Ray Padgett is a music writer based in Burlington, Vermont. He is the author of the "33 1/3" series book *I'm Your Fan: The Songs of Leonard Cohen* (2020), as well as *Pledging My Time: Conversations with Bob Dylan Band Members* (2023) and *Cover Me: The Stories behind the Greatest Cover Songs of All Time* (2017). He writes the Substack newsletter *Flagging Down the Double E's*, about Bob Dylan in concert, and is the founder of the cover-songs blog *Cover Me*. His writing has appeared in the *New Yorker*, *SPIN*, *Vice*, and *MOJO*.

Marcia Pally teaches at New York University and held the Mercator Guest Professorship in the Theology Department at Humboldt University-Berlin, where she is an annual guest professor and member of the Center for Interreligious Theology and Religious Studies and the

Berlin Institute for Public Theology. In 2019–20 she was a fellow at the Center for Theological Inquiry (Princeton). Her most recent books are: *From This Broken Hill I Sing to You: God, Sex, and Politics in the Work of Leonard Cohen* (2021); *White Evangelicals and Right-Wing Populism: How Did We Get Here?* (2022); and *Commonwealth and Covenant: Economics, Politics, and Theologies of Relationality* (2016), selected by the UN Committee on Education for Justice for worldwide distribution.

Ian Rae is Chair of the Department of English, French, and Writing at King's University College at Western University in Canada. He completed studies at Queen's University (Canada), the University of Oslo, the University of British Columbia (Governor General's Gold Medal for MA Thesis), and McGill University (SSHRC and Max Bell Postdoctoral Fellowships) before accepting Visiting Assistant Professorships at the University of Bonn and the McGill Institute for the Study of Canada. He is the author of the monograph *From Cohen to Carson: The Poet's Novel in Canada* (2008) and editor of *George Bowering: Bridges to Elsewhere* (2010), a special issue of *Open Letter*.

Jim Shedden is the Curator, Special Projects, and Director, Publishing at the Art Gallery of Ontario. He coedited *Leonard Cohen: Everybody Knows* for the AGO in 2022. Shedden is the author of numerous articles on film, popular music, and visual culture. Shedden has made documentary films on Stan Brakhage and Michael Snow, as well as more personal documentaries on addiction and recovery, and popular music and everyday life, and co-curates the AD HOC experimental film series. Shedden hosts the podcast 1000 Songs, and co-programs a series of salons and concerts, "Tavern of Song," with his daughter, Meredith Shedden.

David R. Shumway is Professor of English, and Literary and Cultural Studies at Carnegie Mellon University. His most recent book is *Rock Star: The Making of Musical Icons from Elvis to Springsteen* (2014). He has also written *Michel Foucault* (1989), *Creating American Civilization: A Genealogy of American Literature as an Academic Discipline* (1994), *Modern Love: Romance, Intimacy, and the Marriage Crisis* (2003), and *John Sayles* (2012). *American Narrative Realism; The Novel, Film, Television, and Theater* will be published by Cambridge University Press in 2026, and he is currently working on an institutional history of theory in literary studies.

Juian Stannard is a Reader in English Literature and Creative Writing at the University of Winchester. He previously taught American and English Literature at the University of Genoa. His academic writing includes *Fleur Adcock in Context: From Movement to Martians* (1997), *The Poetic Achievements of Donald Davie and Charles Tomlinson: Expanding Vision, Voice and Rhythm in Late Twentieth Century English Poetry* (2010), and *Basil Bunting* (2014). He has published nine collections of poetry, including *Sottoripa: Genoese Poems* (2018), a bilingual publication, and *New and Selected Poems* (2025). In 2024 he published a campus novel, *The University of Bliss*. In 2010 he won the International Troubadour Prize for Poetry, and in 2024 he was awarded the Shelley Prize for his contribution to Anglo-Ligurian poetry.

Eric Weisbard is Professor of American Studies at the University of Alabama. His books as an editor and author include *Spin Alternative Record Guide* (1995), *This Is Pop*, *Use Your Illusion I* and *II* (2007), *Top 40 Democracy: The Rival Mainstreams of American Music* (2014), *Songbooks: The Literature of American Popular Music* (2021), and *Hound Dog* (2023). He cofounded the Pop Conference, coedited the *Journal of Popular Music Studies*, and was *Village Voice* music editor. He is currently editing the *Oxford Handbook of Pop Music*.

Elliot R. Wolfson, a fellow of the American Academy of Jewish Research and the American Academy of Arts and Sciences, is the Marsha and Jay Glazer Endowed Chair in Jewish Studies and Distinguished Professor of Religion at University of California, Santa Barbara. He is the author of many publications, including most recently *The Duplicity of Philosophy's Shadow: Heidegger, Nazism and the Jewish Other* (2018); *Heidegger and Kabbalah: Hidden Gnosis and the Path of Poiēsis* (2019); *Suffering Time: Philosophical, Kabbalistic, and Ḥasidic Reflections on Temporality* (2021); and *The Philosophical Pathos of Susan Taubes: Between Nihilism and Hope* (2023).

David Yaffe was the author of three books, including *Reckless Daughter: A Portrait of Joni Mitchell* (2017), a *Washington Post* Notable Book of the Year, winner of the ASCAP/Deems Taylor/Virgil Thomson Award, and the Association for Recorded Sound Collections Award for Excellence in Historical Recorded Sound Research. He also wrote *Fascinating Rhythm* (2006) and *Bob Dylan: Like a Complete Unknown* (2011). His writings appeared in the *New York Review of Books, New York Magazine, Harper's Magazine, New York Times, The Nation, Slate, The Paris Review,* and *Air Mail,* where he was a regular contributor starting in 2021. He is a professor of Humanities at Syracuse University. He died in 2024.

Robert de Young holds a master's degree and doctorate in literary studies and has taught widely in literature, popular music, and media theory and practice. He worked as a writer, director, and producer with ABC Radio National and ABC Television for over a decade before working as an independent documentary filmmaker (credits on IMDb). Most of his films revolve around Hollywood history and popular music. From July 2017 until November 2023 he was an archivist and creative producer with the Leonard Cohen Family Trust.

Acknowledgments

Many people have contributed to the making of this volume. My research assistants Shourya Mohaniya and Megan Hamilton helped me with library work, manuscript preparation, and much more. Sean Latham, the editor of the first book in this series, *The World of Bob Dylan*, shared many useful tips. The four readers for Cambridge University Press were enormously perspicacious in their reports. Leonard Cassuto discussed the project with me on numerous occasions, always to my benefit. Ray Ryan, my editor at Cambridge University Press, was a consistent source of support and encouragement. Finally, I need to thank the contributors for writing such a stellar group of essays and for their patience with a process that took longer than any of us expected.

Introduction

You Don't Know Leonard Cohen

David R. Shumway

WHO IS LEONARD COHEN? AS THE CHAPTERS IN THE present volume demonstrate, this remains a question despite his enormous following. That Cohen remains a mystery may be surprising given that in many respects he was remarkably unchanged over the course of his career. His appearance, for example, changed little, his well-tailored suits and short hair apparent in 1967 and 2009. The themes and concerns of his songs – sex, love, death, religion – are also consistent from start to finish. While his voice deepened as he aged, his singing style remained largely the same. Moreover, a strong part of Leonard's appeal was that we as his audience felt that he was baring his soul to us. There is an intimacy in his self-presentation that made us feel that we knew him. And yet, more than Dylan or anyone else in popular music, he remains a mystery because he doesn't fit any of the usual categories. Almost any statement you can make about him must immediately be qualified or be met with a contrary. He is so multifaceted that it is almost as if he were many different people all at the same time. The many sides of Leonard Cohen are on display in the essays that follow. While we cannot claim to have solved his mysteries, we do offer a starting place for understanding this enormously complex and powerful artist.

Cohen's anomalies begin with the fact that he grew up in an upper-middle-class household, but rebelled by running off to become a writer. Yet unlike many other young rebels of the period, he retained much from his upbringing, including his conservative dress and religion, as Ira Nadel's chapter on Cohen's biography explains. He was already a poetry star in Canada and an accomplished fiction writer when he launched his career as a songwriter and singer. While the link between lyric poetry and song lyrics is very old, going back at least to the troubadours of the late Middle Ages, the gulf between poetry and popular song has been largely unbridgeable since the nineteenth century. Some songwriters, including Dylan and Joni Mitchell, published a few poems after they became established musically, but not stand-alone books of poetry. Cohen continued to publish poetry, and those books of poems typically include his song lyrics, sometimes slightly modified, sometimes not. As Julian Stannard makes clear in his chapter on poetry and prose, Cohen's writing constitutes a significant achievement apart from this songwriting. And he wasn't just a poet, having also published two novels, one of which, *Beautiful Losers*, was treated by Linda Hutcheon as foundational to Canadian postmodernism.[1] Stannard places Cohen's poetry in the context of modernism and a longer poetic tradition, but he also shows how the themes of Cohen's poems and novels are consistent with those of his songs. Stannard also suggests that "his status as a singer-songwriter eclipses the poetry" in the late collections *Book of Longing* and *The Flame*.

If most of Cohen's fans may not be familiar with his poetry and prose, they probably think they know his musical output well. Cohen is certainly best known today as a songwriter, with "Hallelujah" having become nearly ubiquitous in contemporary culture. But I suspect that most people focus on Cohen's lyrics, and don't give a lot of thought to the music. In his chapter on Cohen's songwriting, Alan Light reminds us of the importance of Cohen's tunes, insisting that Cohen's greatness rests on more than just his deservedly celebrated lyrics and noting that Cohen said, "Usually, the tunes were completed before the lyric." Cohen is much better recognized as a maker of songs than of albums, as Anthony DeCurtis acknowledges in his chapter, noting how many of Cohen's album titles incorporate the word "songs." But DeCurtis shows that many of the albums are much more successful works than is usually recognized. For example, he calls *Songs of Leonard Cohen* "one of the most stunning debut albums in history."

When Cohen first began writing and recording songs, he was associated with folk music. Gillian Mitchell shows how Cohen's music is related to this genre, asserting that "his early career as a professional musician

---

[1] Linda Hutcheon, *The Canadian Postmodern: A Study of Contemporary Canadian Fiction*, xvi, 230 (Oxford: Oxford University Press, 2012).

certainly illustrated the lingering, complex and pervasive influence of folk – as a musical form and as a set of broad artistic ideals – upon the wider popular music world of the later 1960s." Folk music provides the context for Cohen's early reception, but he would soon be connected with an emergent group of performers known as singer-songwriters. In my chapter on that musical formation, I observe that Cohen is not only the earliest artist to be considered a part of it, but also a major influence on its most representative figure, Joni Mitchell. Yet despite being there at the creation, Cohen is not typical of the singer-songwriters because he is not, in the main, confessional. If Cohen's music doesn't fit the definitions of folk or singer-songwriter exactly, then his connection to rock & roll must seem even more remote. And yet, as Eric Weisbard notes, he was a "rock icon." Cohen's musical career began at a moment when rock was the dominant form of popular music, and he willy-nilly found himself in it. But Weisbard asserts a more essential role: "With 'Avalanche' and other songs like it, Cohen created classic examples of a form unknown to 1950s rock & roll but central to post-Dylan rock: war horses."

Cohen's impact has been felt beyond the world of popular music. His songs, poems, and novels have a significant presence as literature. While Dylan's fans understood his lyrics as poetry in the 1960s, among the literary establishment popular songs were long regarded as subliterary. Dylan's winning the Nobel Prize for Literature in 2016 has called that long-standing prejudice into question. And because Cohen continued to publish books of poetry after he became a singer and songwriter, he is better suited even than Dylan to break down this hierarchy. Ian Rae and Francis Mus in their contributions place Leonard's work in the context of Canadian literature and world literature respectively. Rae observes the artist's continuing connection to his homeland and hometown expressed in his writing despite his having lived much of his life elsewhere. These connections are literary rather than merely personal, and Cohen continued to the end of his life to acknowledge his mentors and friends of the Montreal literary world. Mus points out that Cohen's career in music, which was from quite early on international, is what has made his poems and novels of interest beyond the anglophone world. Mus also demonstrates that Cohen's work is itself influenced by the work of writers from Europe such as Lorca and Baudelaire.

While Leonard Cohen did not write film scores, and he did not compose a song specifically for use in a movie, he did have a significant impact on cinema. We are not mainly here talking about Cohen's actual creation of movies, although he did cowrite and star in *I Am a Hotel* (1983), a Canadian television production based around his music. But more important, his songs have played major roles in important films since the early 1970s. While the compiled score has become increasingly common and much popular music has found its way onto soundtracks, Cohen's music has usually been more than just background. Robert Altman's *McCabe & Mrs. Miller* (1971), as Laura Cameron and Jim Shedden discuss in their chapter, features a number of cuts from *Songs of Leonard Cohen*, and Altman remarked that it was as if the songs and script were written together, the songs having been etched in the director's subconscious. Many other directors have made prominent use of Cohen's songs, and in one case, John Cale's cover of "Hallelujah" in Andrew Adamson and Vicky Jenson's *Shrek* (2001), the use seems to have propelled the song into the cultural firmament. But the song, as Cameron and Shedden show, also adds an important dimension to the film, likening it to a *deus ex machina*, which does "what the dialogue, action, and mise-en-scène of the film cannot: it makes space for feeling and holds us there with the characters."

Cohen's deep roots in Canada and Montreal in particular are apparent, but his relationship to the city of his birth is more complicated than it might at first seem. This relationship is explored movingly by Erin MacLeod here, using her own experience of the city as a lens through which to view Montreal's embrace of Cohen and his more ambivalent feelings about it. As she argues, "It is not that Cohen's songs are about or set in Montreal, but rather his relationship to the city seems paramount, as does the city's relationship to him." She notes that for Montreal, Cohen is a "selling point," a kind of tourist attraction even if he himself is no longer one of its residents. Montrealers are fond of quoting Cohen's famous assertion that that he had to keep "coming back to Montreal to renew my neurotic affiliations," but MacLeod demonstrates that that statement is even more ambivalent when its source, a blurb from *The Spice-Box of Earth*, is quoted in full. On Montreal's side, its strong embrace of Cohen as "a great uniter" obscures both the history of colonialism (French and English) and a history of virulent anti-Semitism.

Several chapters in this volume quote boygenius's song "Leonard Cohen," a track on their album, *The Record* (2023), which describes Cohen as "an old man ... writing horny poetry." This raises the question about why Cohen's reputation as a "ladies' man" didn't seem to be a problem during the "Me Too" era. Two chapters in the volume throw light on this conundrum from different angles. One could argue that Cohen expressed the world through sex, which figures more prominently in his songs than in those of most of his contemporaries. As David Yaffe puts it in his chapter, "coitus was half of his grand theme ... the thing that haunts you when you don't meditate, or ponder the abyss, or seduce, or fail to seduce, or still feel the hunger when the body inevitably fails." It's not, as Yaffe notes, that Cohen's lyrics are particularly explicit, "Don't Go Home with Your Hard-On" being the exception that proves the rule. Rather, it's that "wanting is everywhere ... Desire is where a poem begins."

We have usually thought of popular music stars as appealing either to preadolescent girls or postadolescent boys, perhaps the original distinction in the Beatles–Stones opposition, usually understood as soft versus hard expressions of male sexuality. But who do girls like after they grow up? All of the evidence seems to suggest that many of them liked Leonard Cohen. Perhaps Leonard's focus on desire, on wanting rather than having, enhanced his appeal to women. Heather Arnet, in her chapter titled "For the Matriarchy," explains Leonard's appeal to women in other ways. She thinks that it's Cohen's representations of women's desire that make his songs so appealing to female listeners. Arnet's title comes from something Cohen said in 1968, "I wish the women would hurry up and take over ... I really am for the matriarchy." She shows that his songs express this point by giving us female characters who have agency. Arnet notes the way numerous great women artists, from Judy Collins, to Nina Simone, to Tori Amos, have recorded Cohen's songs and in various ways made them their own.

Cohen emerged as a recording artist in 1967, the year of the "summer of love," and yet no one looked less like a hippie than he did. As Sarah Hill shows, the 1960s counterculture is an important context for understanding Cohen and his songs. She notes that even though Cohen was thirty-three when *Songs of Leonard Cohen* appeared, he was younger than other leading figures such as Allen Ginsberg and Timothy Leary. Hill observes that the counterculture was strongly identified with changing consciousness: "The ultimate countercultural text, however, was *The Psychedelic Experience* (1964), written by Timothy Leary, Ralph Metzner, and Richard Alpert, a guide to the process of ego loss and spiritual rebirth associated with an acid trip. Although for many people acid consumption was simply recreational, for many other people it was the first step on a quest for higher consciousness." Hill shows that Cohen was pursing these ends on the island of Hydra, where he seems to have first learned something of Eastern modes of thought, and where he lived the hippie life *avant la lettre*. While Cohen's poetry was self-consciously traditional, his novel, *Beautiful Losers*, reflects the changes in literary form and social reality of that cultural moment: "Eschewing any traditional sense of storyline, narrative voice, or structural coherence, in *Beautiful Losers* Cohen explores many of the themes that later emerged in his songwriting – love, ecstasy, spiritual connection ... It was an experimentation in form and style, written in two intensive periods with the aid of amphetamines." In other words, appearances to the contrary, Cohen's concerns rhyme with those of the counterculture, even if they also are not contained by it.

While the politics of the counterculture were debatable in the 1960s – those in New Left organizations such as Students for a Democratic Society sometimes finding this new consciousness not productive of the changes they hoped to see – the counterculture is typically associated with the anti-war movement and other left-leaning political manifestations of the 1960s. Unlike Bob Dylan or Joni Mitchell, Leonard Cohen didn't write protest songs, but he did write some songs, such as "Everybody Knows" and "Democracy," that seem to articulate a left critique of the social order. David Boucher's chapter, however, makes us wonder if these interpretations are correct. "In his public persona, and to a considerable degree with his friends and lovers, Cohen refused to express strong political opinions, or he would equivocate to the extent that it wasn't clear which side he was on." Boucher observes, as I have been emphasizing here, that Cohen was a man of many contradictions, and that these are nowhere more apparent than in his politics. In his politics, at least, Cohen is in Boucher's view insincere, the opposite of what he seemed in almost every other aspect. Indeed, it is hard to think of another popular musician who embodies authenticity as Cohen does.

Issues of sincerity and authenticity are also raised in several of the chapters in the volume's last section, on reception and legacy. We normally look askance at artists who seem to be overly concerned with image, something that we take to compromise their authenticity. Cohen's consistency of self-presentation and his seriousness mitigate against us paying much attention to any active shaping of his image, but he was acutely conscious of the way he appeared to the public and was actively engaged in defining how he would be represented in the media. Chapters 19 and 20 call attention to Cohen's subtle mastery of the machinery of celebrity. After movie stars, rock stars, and social media influencers, we may forget that literary celebrities came first. At the turn of the twentieth century, Mark Twain might have been the biggest celebrity on earth. Thus, we shouldn't dismiss the fact that Leonard Cohen was presented to Canada as a celebrity before he had begun his music career, as Loren Glass details in his chapter. The documentary *Ladies and Gentleman, Mr. Leonard Cohen*, released in 1965 by the National Film Board of Canada, "profiles Cohen on the brink of his transition from marginal Canadian writer to major international rockstar, in the process both revealing and constructing the celebrity persona that would facilitate the shift." Glass suggests that the persona of celebrity poet allowed for an almost seamless transition to the role of rock star. Both Glass and Robert de Young, in his chapter on documentaries, call attention to the way in which Cohen is carefully managing his representation in *Ladies and Gentleman* and elsewhere. Both mention the following scene, as described by Glass:

> The film concludes in a screening room, with Cohen sitting beside director Don Brittain watching a scene of himself pretending to sleep in the hotel bed, and then taking a bath. "A man has invited a group of strangers to watch him cleaning his body," Cohen says. And then, as we watch alongside him, he writes on the bathroom wall in soap above the bathtub: "CAVEAT EMPTOR." Asked by Brittain to explain what he means he answers that he's acting as a "double agent for the filmmakers and the public ... This is not entirely devoid of the con." This sly combination of

intimacy and misdirection, of "confidence" in its multiple meanings, crystallizes Cohen's emerging sense of his public persona as a complex confluence of sincerity, sexuality, and sleight of hand.

De Young reads the scene as revealing "Cohen's skillful and playful management of his textualized life ... Cohen is already, very early in his career, exercising a complex agency in the service of an equally complex persona." He goes on to show that Cohen would take an active role in the making of other documentaries, especially *Bird on a Wire* (1974), which Cohen spent six months re-editing, and in the end still felt it did not present him as he wanted to be seen. It is perhaps ironic that the documentary that best represents the artist, *Hallelujah: Leonard Cohen, a Journey, a Song*, is one that he could not directly control, since it was largely produced after his death.

This introduction began with the observation about how Leonard Cohen seemed to have remained largely the same throughout his career. In "I'll Wear a Mask for You," Lucy J. Boucher calls that assumption into question by detailing three successive personae that Cohen adopted over the course of his career. Boucher is not really arguing that Cohen's persona changed radically but rather that, at different moments, different elements came to the fore. The first persona Boucher identifies, "The Poet of Rock 'n' Roll," fits nicely with the trajectory Glass describes. The second one, which itself has two aspects, the "Ladies' Man" and "Depressive Lothario," Boucher associates with Cohen's struggles in achieving critical and commercial success in the 1970s. It isn't so much a rejection of the first persona, as it is a specification of it, bringing out elements that had long been lurking. The final mask, the "High Priest of the Heart," emerges as dominant in the 1990s and, in Boucher's view, remains so through the end of Cohen's life. It relies in part on his becoming a Buddhist monk, a role seemingly at odds with that of a "Lothario," but which also relies on continuities that go back as far as his early 1960s poetry. My own chapter, "How to Be an Aged Rock Star," argues for a different conception of Cohen's late-life persona, though one that is not necessarily incompatible with Boucher's. I describe this late persona as simply "Old Leonard Cohen," calling attention to the fact that Cohen embraced his age during his triumphant late tours and on his prolific late recordings. While most rock stars do their best to appear not to have lost their youth, Cohen looked every one of his seventy-four years when he took the stage again after a long hiatus from live performance. This persona worked in part because Cohen had been calling attention to his aging at least since 1988's "Tower of Song," and death had always been one of his concerns. By openly performing as an old man, Cohen challenged the ageism that remains the last acceptable prejudice in our culture.

The many important recordings by other artists of Leonard Cohen's songs represent one of the most important parts of his legacy. Ray Padgett discusses this phenomenon in his chapter on "Covers." He details the enormous number of these recordings – 649 of "Hallelujah" alone – but also their reach and their impact. Cohen's career as a songwriter began with Judy Collins recording "Susanne," which wasn't a cover, since Cohen himself had not yet recorded his own version. While "Susanne" and other early Cohen songs were covered, the cover phenomenon really takes off later in his career. "Hallelujah" was first released on *Various Positions*, the album Columbia declined to distribute, and thus was hardly heard in its original form. John Cale's cover, which was used in part in the movie *Shrek*, was key in making this song widely known. Bob Dylan likened Cohen to Irving Berlin, and even though Dylan does not give a reason for this, the comparison does seem apt, given the range of people who have performed Cohen's songs. Finally, Robert de Young, who was at the time he wrote the chapter on the Leonard Cohen archives the film and audio archivist for the Leonard Cohen Family Trust, makes us aware of the wealth of unpublished and unreleased materials that Leonard left behind. This includes the notebooks that he had been keeping his entire life. These contain germs and early drafts of his poems and songs, but also random jottings and images, often Cohen's own drawings. Besides the notebooks, there are video and audio materials, loose manuscript pages, and correspondence. The archives promise to be a major resource for scholars and fans alike. As they are explored, they may resolve some of the questions raised here, but they may also generate more. In any event, Leonard Cohen will remain a compelling figure in part because he cannot be pinned down.

PART I

CREATIVE LIFE

CHAPTER 1

The Life of a Troubadour

Ira B. Nadel

LET US COMPARE MYTHOLOGIES

"I always had a background of distress, ever since I was young . . . I didn't have a sense of operational ease."[1] These opening words of suffering and dismay resonate throughout the life and career of Leonard Cohen, who grew up in the Westmount section of Montreal, very much in the mold of a Jewish middle-class boy who would become a courtly poet, Zen priest, and world-renowned singer. Outwardly Cohen had all the trappings of a secure life, but inwardly he faced emotional challenges, partly caused by his father's death in 1944 when he was nine and his mother's psychological instability.[2] On the day of his father's funeral, Cohen wrote his first poem, stuffed it in one of his father's bow ties and buried it in the backyard, confronting unhappiness with creativity.[3] This would become his artistic practice.

Cohen's middle-class arc continued at Westmount High, where his school yearbook lists his ambition to be a world-famous orator, with photography his hobby. He became president of the students' council and a member of the board of publishers, also joining the menorah club

---

[1] Leonard Cohen, in Sarah Hampson, "Leonard Cohen: Life of a Ladies' Man," *Globe and Mail* (May 26, 2007), www.theglobeandmail.com/arts/music/from-the-archives-leonard-cohen-life-of-a-ladies-man/article32811791/.

[2] At one point, she had to be institutionalized. "'She laughed and wept deeply'," he remarked to the biographer Sylvie Simmons. See Simmons *I'm Your Man: The Life of Leonard Cohen* (Toronto: McClelland and Stewart, 2012), 5.

[3] See Ira B. Nadel, *Various Positions: A Life of Leonard Cohen* (New York: Pantheon 1996), 5–6. A version of the incident appears in chapter 14 of Cohen's first novel, *The Favourite Game*. Leonard Cohen, *The Favourite Game* (New York: Bantam Books, 1971 [1963]), 23.

and the art club, and chairing the drama club. Athletics also had a place, whether cross-country skiing, sailing, or even hockey. With the encouragement of his English teacher, Cohen began to write poetry and short stories. But art and a conventional life soon clashed.

One enclosure surrounding Cohen at this time was his synagogue, the Orthodox Shaar Hashomayim, founded in 1846. Moving to Westmount in 1921, Cohen's grandfather, Lyon Cohen, laid the new cornerstone.[4] The poet-to-be regularly attended Shabbat services and had his bar mitzvah there in 1947. His involvement with elements of Jewish spirituality prepared him for his later understanding of Christianity and acceptance of Rinzai Zen Buddhism as taught by his teacher, Roshi Kyozan Joshu Sasaki. A further impediment to an artistic life was the Freedman Company, manufacturer of men's suits and coats with a reputation for style and durability, and which was run by Cohen's uncle Horace – his own father (who enjoyed dressing formally) was too ill to play an active part. Cohen worked at the Freedman Company in the late 1950s after McGill University, either in the office or hanging finished suits and coats on racks; it then had over 650 employees and could manufacture upwards of 3,500 garments a year. But Cohen disliked the drudgery and repetitiveness. Nonetheless, the company made a financially secure life possible even after the death of Cohen's father in January 1944. A photo of a smiling Leonard Cohen standing between two executives of the Freedman Company shows the well-dressed singer-to-be in a suit with a pronounced striped tie.[5]

Music entered this well-framed world when, at fifteen, Cohen heard a young Spaniard playing a guitar and saw how he impressed the young women in Murray Hill Park behind his home. He knew at once he had discovered a secret. He urged the young Spaniard to give him lessons,

---

[4] Simmons, *I'm Your Man*, 7.
[5] See Nadel, *Various Positions*; the photo appears between pages 118 and 119.

  Originally founded in 1887 as S. Freedman Sons and Co., it was bought in 1906 by Lyon Cohen, industrialist, who in 1913 also took over Friedman Bros., an early pioneer in men's clothing. On the death of Lyon Cohen in 1937, his son Horace became the managing director. From 1941 to 1947, Horace Cohen was also the Federal Administrator of Fine Clothing for the Canadian government. His company soon became the largest manufacturer of officers' uniforms in Canada. It was dissolved in 1982. Corporate records can be found at Queens University, Kingston, Ontario.

and after three he knew the six chords and flamingo guitar pattern that Cohen later called "the basis of all my songs and all my music."[6] The life of the troubadour, the singer of courtly love, had begun.

A guitar quickly became Cohen's talisman as his repertoire rapidly expanded: at a Jewish community camp where Cohen was a counselor in 1950, the twenty-seven-year-old director was a folksinger and socialist who knew a large range of workers' songs from Europe and beyond. Another friend introduced Cohen to *The People's Song Book*, songs of protest and affirmation which taught him the political and social impact of singing. Folk music became his first love and, through that, literature: "I discovered what a lyric is and that led me to a more formal study of poetry."[7] He even managed to play the clarinet in the high school band. From music to poetry, and then back to music again, became Cohen's pathway out of Westmount.

At McGill, he discovered an even newer identity, that of a poet, the university reinforcing the clash between the artistic and the bourgeois. He began university in September 1951 on his seventeenth birthday and graduated in October 1955 shortly after his twenty-first. A semester at McGill law followed, but he disliked it; in fact, his overall academic achievements were modest, but he excelled in extracurricular activities, becoming president of the debating society and of his fraternity, ZBT, where he often led meetings with songs. He also joined Hillel, the on-campus Jewish student organization, and formed a Hillel band. Before the start of his second year, he formed the Buckskin Boys, which performed at high school dances and community square dances, and in church basements. He enjoyed performing but was always nervous appearing onstage.

Stabilizing his vacillating interests at McGill – law, teaching, even police work at one point– were three critical teachers: the poet Louis Dudek, the novelist Hugh MacLennan, and the poet and constitutional lawyer, F. R. Scott. And there was a fourth, the poet, bon vivant, and "Lion of Canadian Literature," Irving Layton. More Judaic prophet than timid Canadian poet, Layton was an artistic powerhouse and would be a formative influence on Cohen's development.

---

[6] Simmons, *I'm Your Man*, 518.   [7] Cohen in Nadel, *Various Positions*, 26.

In 1954, Cohen took Dudek's modern poetry course and began to show him some of his writings. In a second batch, Dudek spotted a five-stanza work, "The Sparrows." As they walked down a corridor of the arts faculty building, Dudek ordered Cohen to kneel. With his manuscript, Dudek knighted him "poet" and bade him rise: a medieval knight–courtier replaced the Westmount prodigy. "The Sparrows" went on to win the 1954 Literary Contest sponsored by the *McGill Daily*, which printed the poem on its front page of December 7, 1954. During this time, Cohen was also taking the writer Hugh MacLennan's course on the modern novel, where he read Joyce's *Portrait of the Artist* for the first time.

The *CIV/n* literary magazine, where Cohen published his early poems, attempted to revolutionize Canadian poetry; it was a mimeographed work established by four recent graduates led by Aileen Collins, later to marry Dudek. Dudek and Layton were editorial advisers. The goal was a new, colloquial style. Cohen's work appeared in volume IV, which had contributions from Robert Creeley, Layton, Phyllis Webb, Dudek, and Ezra Pound (with whom Dudek had been corresponding). Most important was Cohen's exposure to the *CIV/n* literary circle of older writers, including F. R. Scott, Eli Mandel, Creeley, and Charles Olson. He often brought his guitar to their gatherings, which became workshops for poems shifting Canadian poetry away from that shaped by narrative and history towards a fresh, modern lyricism. No longer should Canadian poets write "with maple syrup on birch bark," as Aileen Collins complained.[8]

This coincided with the start of a series of serious relationships for Cohen with young women who provided creative inspiration for his work not only in song but also poetry, fiction, and later drawing. This began with Yafa Lerner, a student at McGill from Montreal interested in dance; Freda Guttman, an art student he met when he was sixteen, followed, a relationship fueled by artistic as much as sexual intensity. His early poem "The Fly," appearing in his first book, *Let Us Compare Mythologies* (1956), is about Freda, who in fact provided the cover and five interior sketches. When they broke up, he wrote a short, unpublished essay about her and love in which he explains that love has many alternate paths.[9]

[8] Ibid., 37.   [9] Ibid., 29.

The title of a notebook of Cohen's from the mid 1950s containing poems of desire and fear of loss reads "Leonard Cohen/ Poems Written/ While dying of love." Like a medieval courtly lover – Leonard fashioned himself very much in that tradition in his songs and writing – he dies multiple times, as do lovers in his poetry. Yet he was a hesitant lover, explaining that one should love generally but resist a particular love. Protect your heart, keep your guard. Yet despite the need for love, one's very resistance to it creates an alluring figure. The more he (Cohen) denied individual love, the more others wanted to give it.

The role of the courtly lover would not only identify Cohen's relation to women but also to song. Asked if he began a song with a lyrical idea, he answered, "It begins with an appetite to discover my self-respect. To redeem the day. So the day does not go down in debt. It begins with that kind of appetite."[10] The song is his love, and he is the chivalrous lover.

The new union of song and poetry meant the cultivation of a modern, bohemian persona in contrast to his bourgeois Westmount past. This very contradiction became the origin of his intriguing appeal. A photo makes the contrast clear: while he types out a poem, scattered papers, two ashtrays (one with an extinguished cigar), a newspaper, and a general disarray envelop him. Yet he wears a properly tailored suit and tie with a white pocket square, and a copy of his first novel, *The Favourite Game*, nearby, as well as a work by Baudelaire.[11] There is even an empty shot glass and a box of matches. This is the mid 1960s Canadian poet at work.

Earlier, in the mid 1950s after McGill, Cohen landed in New York, supposedly to attend Columbia University's School of General Studies. He enrolled in various English courses but found the absence of rigor in the literary program disheartening and quit. But he discovered the counterculture life in Greenwich Village and a new girl, Anne Sherman. The former showed him that jazz and poetry could work together (which he took back to Montreal, reciting poetry accompanied by jazz), while the latter brought beauty and discipline to his life and

---

[10] Leonard Cohen, interview, in *Songwriters on Songwriting*, ed. Paul Zollo, 2nd ed. (New York: Da Capo Press, 2003), 333. For this exceptionally valuable interview, see ibid., 329–49.

[11] The copy is that published in London by Secker & Warburg, 1963, the first UK edition.

work; she appears as the divorcée Shell in his first published novel, *The Favourite Game*. Her beauty made "every room original," and her guiltless love was something he did not find in any other women.[12] But the relationship could not continue: she wanted a stability Cohen could not provide, although in 1960, when he moved to the Greek island of Hydra, he wanted her to join him. She declined but continued to infuse his writing for the next five or six years.

Women, in fact, quickly became the inspiration for almost all of Cohen's books and albums, beginning with Freda Guttman for *Let Us Compare Mythologies* and Anne Sherman for *Beauty at Close Quarters*, the unpublished version of *The Favourite Game*. Other women who inspired his books and records include Marianne Ihlen, dedicatee of *Flowers for Hitler* and whose beguiling image appears on the back cover of Cohen's second album, *Songs from a Room*; Suzanne Elrod, the mother of his two children and pictured on the album cover of *Death of a Ladies' Man* (with Leonard and Eva LaPierre, a French Canadian model); and Dominique Issermann, French photographer and dedicatee of his album *I'm Your Man*.[13] Others included Sharon Robinson, songwriter and backup singer on *Ten New Songs*; Rebecca De Mornay, dedicatee and coproducer of his album *The Future*; and then Anjani Thomas, songwriter and lover. Additional women appear scattered throughout his songwriting: "Suzanne," "So Long, Marianne," "Alexandra Leaving," and "Dear Heather" are only four of myriad examples. Janis Joplin is the center of "Chelsea Hotel No. 2," Nico the focus of "Take This Longing." He believed that such identifications, especially of women, reinforced the authenticity of his writing.

Cohen's treatment of women underscored his role as a courtly lover. Drawing a naked woman from a photograph became for him a courtly act: in an interview, he explained that he would actually "rescue her. I put her back in the 12th century, where she belongs," half-jokingly adding that "you know, I couldn't get anyone to undress." And when asked what

---

[12] Nadel, *Various Positions*, 54.
[13] Elrod, met in New York in 1969, was fifteen years his junior and the later inspiration for "I Tried to Leave You" on his album *New Skin for the Old Ceremony* (1974). Issermann did a black-and-white video for "First We Take Manhattan."

did you learn from women, he answered, "You learn everything ...."[14] Leonard, as his friend Eric Lerner noted, was "courtly in all things," and was nothing less than the "master of manners."[15]

VARIOUS POSITIONS

By 1965, and after the start of his literary career with the publication of *Let Us Compare Mythologies* (Contact Press, 1956), *The Spice-Box of Earth* (McClelland and Stewart, 1961) and *Flowers for Hitler* (McClelland and Stewart, 1964), plus his first novel, *The Favourite Game* (Viking Press, 1963), Cohen expanded his presence through a widely shown 1965 National Film Board documentary *Ladies and Gentlemen, Mr. Leonard Cohen*. Directed by Donald Brittain and Don Owen, the film traces Cohen's habits in hotel rooms and poetry readings where, in a leather jacket, markedly not a coat and tie, he responded to receptive audiences, who were fascinated by the courteous rebel poet. Young and old listeners absorbed his language, cadence, and imagery.

But during these early creative years, he remained unsettled, combatting depression, intensified by the struggle between his desire to be an artist and what he felt were the obligations of a middle-class Montreal Jew. His early experiences destabilized any emotional security. He, himself, began to display signs of manic-depressive behavior as early as eighteen or nineteen, in which periods of intensity and hypercreativity would be offset by periods of depression and anxiety, often expressed through a drive for orderliness. He became fixated on detail, especially the right word, the right note. Order and neatness dominated; discipline and precision were essential, habits confirmed by the principles of Rinzai Zen Buddhism and transferred to his extended labor on songwriting. To complete a song often took years, "Anthem" supposedly taking ten to fifteen years. But as he wrote in a 1967 notebook entry, "it is only in regard to details that success is still to be achieved."[16]

---

[14] Hampson, "Leonard Cohen."
[15] Eric Lerner, *Matters of Vital Interest: A Forty-Year Friendship with Leonard Cohen* (New York: Da Capo, 2018), 22, 29.
[16] Nadel, *Various Positions*, 50.

Adding to the romantic image of the poet was a trip to Cuba in 1961 during what turned out to be the aborted Bay of Pigs invasion. He was actually arrested but befriended his captors and managed to leave. Not only did the adventure result in his popular poem, "The Only Tourist in Havana Turns His Thoughts Homeward," but it supplemented his dashing, almost Byronic image extended by his statement on the book jacket of what would become his first Canadian hit, *The Spice-Box of Earth*. It partly reads:

> I shouldn't be in Canada at all. Winter is all wrong for me. I belong beside the Mediterranean. My ancestors made a terrible mistake. But I have to keep coming back to Montreal to renew my neurotic affiliations.[17]

Hydra became Cohen's new creative center. On that isolated Greek island not only did he find new love with the Norwegian Marianne Ihlen, but he also discovered the creative freedom to express his conflicted views of his Montreal past and his artistic present. He continued with his poetry but also, in two intense eight-month periods, wrote the radically structured *Beautiful Losers* set in Quebec, an unorthodox novel that mingles sex, mysticism, drugs, and excess in a fragmented style. Critics declared it was one of the most troubling Canadian novels ever to appear but also one of the most fascinating and a must-read. Reviews were appropriately mixed, Robert Fulford damning the book as "the most revolting book ever written in Canada"; at the same time he claimed that it was also "'probably the most interesting Canadian book of the year."[18]

Cohen explained that he sought a "liturgy, a big confessional oration, very crazy but using all the techniques of the modern novel" in his effort to radicalize Canadian fiction.[19] But completing the novel led to a breakdown caused by amphetamines, fasting, and sunstroke, all three elements, he believed, collectively sanctifying the self. He also continued to write songs and moved to New York to pursue, or at least begin, a singing career. Being a poet or novelist did not come close to paying the bills. His goal was Nashville, but New York, where he found a folk renaissance with new fame for Judy Collins, Joan Baez, and Phil Ochs,

---

[17] Ibid., 98. [18] Ibid., 138. [19] Ibid., 128.

diverted him. His residence became the Chelsea Hotel, populated by singers, writers, and composers, the very space evoking a kind of romantic decay. Dylan, Jimi Hendrix. Allen Ginsberg, Kris Kristofferson, and Janis Joplin all stayed for various periods during his residence. He often retold his encounter with Joplin in an elevator, the source for "Chelsea Hotel No. 2" written after her death. Even Marianne and her son, Axel, visited.

Cohen's manager at the time, Mary Martin, arranged an introduction to Judy Collins in the fall of 1966. At first, he had little to offer, but several months later he sang "Suzanne" to her over the phone from Montreal. Within weeks, she recorded it for her album *In My Life*. Her next album, *Wildflowers* (1967), included three of his songs. His career was underway, marked by his first major singing engagement on April 30, 1967: a town hall rally in New York. It was at first a failure: he walked out, sang a few bars of "Suzanne," and froze before leaving the stage. He returned to finish the song only after shouts from the crowd and Collins's encouragement. As he later admitted, performing is a great opportunity to "test your courage."[20]

By 1967 Cohen had a contract with Columbia records signed by John Hammond, who had signed Dylan. *Songs of Leonard Cohen* (1967) appeared with "Suzanne," but he was thirty-three, considered too old to start a singing career. In New York, however, he found a community of artists who valued his work and encouraged him to do more, and in 1969 he released his second album, recorded in Nashville, *Songs from a Room*. The producer was Bob Johnston, who had done Dylan's *Nashville Skyline*, also in 1969. Johnston was agreeable to Cohen's wish for a spartan sound, the recording emphasizing the lyrics rather than the arrangements, with "Bird on the Wire" stressing the words over the music, which contributed to its popularity. The song was Cohen's response to new phone lines on Hydra, just when he thought he had escaped civilization: "I wasn't going to be able to live this 11th century life that I thought I had found for myself," he confessed.[21]

In 1969, he also won Canada's prestigious Governor General's Award for Literature for *Selected Poems*. But he created a controversy by refusing

---

[20] Cohen in Zollo (ed.), *Songwriters on Songwriting*, 339.   [21] Ibid., 346.

to accept the prize, claiming, in a telegram to the committee, that "the poems themselves forbid it absolutely."[22] The radical poet acted in a radical manner. He also went on his first tour, with Bob Johnston as his musical director. In preparation, he asked Mort Rosengarten to make him a performance mask to protect himself and the songs from "contamination." The mask was of Cohen himself, but in the end he chose not to wear it, although he kept it for decades.[23] And the tour? Fueled by LSD and Mandrax, and with Cohen dressed in a safari suit, it was mayhem, seared by the May 4, 1970 Hamburg concert where Cohen started the second half by clicking his heels and giving the Nazi salute. A near riot followed.

When not touring, Cohen returned to the edges of the New York artistic scene, frequenting the Chelsea Hotel, and drifting in and out of Andy Warhol's orbit at the silver-foil-lined Le Dom, befriending Nico and, through her, Lou Reed (who in 2008 would induct Cohen into the Rock & Roll Hall of Fame).

Soon, a moderately successful European tour took place in 1972, which also included Israel, where he would return in 1973 supposedly to fight in the Yom Kippur War. Instead, he ended up singing for the troops at the front. For the next decade, Cohen was finding his voice – discovering in objects of love and regret material for his songs and poetry. From the beginning, he carried a stylish, self-regarding sense of abjection possibly summarized as moody love. He once claimed that there is confusion between depression and seriousness, explaining that "I happen to like the *mode* of seriousness. It's peaceful and relaxing to me to be serious."[24] Periods of depression still occurred, and his later involvement with drugs was one of the ways he confronted his darkness. Songwriting was another, his early albums known for their lugubrious tone and melodies. Rinzai Zen Buddhism, focusing on one's inner development through discipline, was a further means of combatting and ultimately defeating the despair.

By 1977, with the release of the album *Death of a Ladies' Man* (Phil Spector producer) and the volume of poems entitled *Death of a Lady's Man*, he began to realize that a light could penetrate the gloom. "Anthem"

---

[22] Simmons, *I'm Your Man*, 223.   [23] Ibid., 228–29.   [24] Nadel, *Various Positions*, 2.

(1992) said it clearly: "There is a crack in everything/ That's how the light gets in." In the early 1980s, he sidestepped the music scene, although there were two tours. He focused on his writing, publishing the prayer-like *Book of Mercy* (1984) and then releasing the album *Various Positions* (1984), featuring "Dance Me to the End of Love" and a little-recognized song, "Hallelujah," on the Passport label. Columbia actually decided not to release the record, the company president famously telling Cohen, "we know you're great, but we don't know if you are any good."[25]

Undaunted, he continued to record and produced *I'm Your Man* (1988). Drawing on a Euro-disco sound, it reflected a more mature Cohen, with synthesizers offering a more modern style that propelled his music to a larger, international audience. Hits from the album included "First We Take Manhattan," "Tower of Song," "Ain't No Cure for Love," and "I'm Your Man." Despite American hesitation over the album, Europe loved the record: "I'm Your Man" was Number 1 in Norway for sixteen weeks. His relationship with the French photographer Dominique Issermann during this time was a catalyst for the new writing. Four years later, it was *The Future*, co-produced with his new flame, Rebecca De Mornay (rumors had them engaged at one point). Three of the songs were featured in Oliver Stone's *Natural Born Killers* (1994), while "Anthem," "Democracy Is Coming to the USA," and "Closing Time" became hits.

Los Angeles had by then become the center of Cohen's world. He had moved there after Suzanne left for France with his children and because his roshi (Zen master) lived and practiced at the Cimarron Zen Center. Purchased in the summer of 1979 at a probate auction, the duplex on Tremaine was only a ten-minute drive from Sasaki Roshi's Zen Center. Cohen bought the home with two fellow students, one of them Eric Lerner, with whom he kept a forty-year friendship.[26] On the upper level in the front was his music room or "Tower of Song." Lerner and his young family lived on the first floor, but after seven years Lerner left and Cohen's daughter, Lorca, moved in. In time, Adam Cohen and his family would move to the same block.[27] Years later, a studio would be

---

[25] Ibid., 151. [26] Simmons, *I'm Your Man*, 315; Lerner, *Matters of Vital Interest*, 20.
[27] Lerner, *Matters of Vital Interest*, 33–35.

built above the garage where Sharon Robinson and Leanne Ungar produced a variety of new songs.

But after his 1993 tour, Cohen retreated to Mt. Baldy above Claremont, California, where his roshi, Kyozan Joshu Sasaki, had moved; in 1994, to cure himself of his excesses he decided to devote himself full time to the life of a Buddhist monk, working in the kitchen and as Sasaki Roshi's secretary. But it was not all serenity. "They're not saints, and you aren't, either," he said of his fellow monks.[28] For almost five years he renounced the music scene, seeking freedom from drugs, alcohol, and women. But after his intensive study with Sasaki Roshi, he was ready to return to music full time, which he hoped would further ease his earlier depression and anxiety. He left Mt. Baldy in the late 1990s not because he could not find what he sought, but because "I had completed that phase of my training."[29]

He also had a new partner, Anjani Thomas from Hawaii, originally a backup singer on his 1985 tour. She herself had given up music for a while but at thirty-nine decided to return, moving back to LA from Austin, Texas, about the same time Cohen returned from Mt. Baldy.

Anjani and Cohen met, and he admired her songwriting; they soon became musical collaborators and lovers. He also approached his former backup singer Sharon Robinson with material he had composed at Mt. Baldy, asking her to fashion melodies for his verses. *Ten New Songs* (2001) was the result, entirely recorded in a studio above his garage. During this period, he also managed to return to Mumbai, where he had been studying Vedanta with Ramesh Balsekar, which somehow alleviated his depression.[30]

Columbia, however, continued to release albums, often of earlier concerts and work. But again, he reached a new plateau, a new style, with *Ten New Songs*. In 1993, his collection of poems and song lyrics *Stranger Music* had appeared; at 432 pages, it was his largest collection–anthology to date, with an iconic cover: moody, thoughtful, mysterious. By 2006, his first new book of poems in twenty-two years, *Book of Longing*,

---

[28] Hampson, "Leonard Cohen." [29] Ibid.
[30] Simmons, *I'm Your Man*, 433; John Zeppetelli and Victor Shiffman, *Leonard Cohen: A Crack in Everything* (Montreal: Musée d'art contemporain de Montréal, 2018), 25.

was published, soon to be transposed into a song cycle by the composer Philip Glass. The work mixed singers, Cohen's spoken word, and music.

But the embezzlement of a sizeable amount of funds by his manager, Kelley Lynch, necessitated a readjustment to his "program."[31] His finances became perilous, and in 2004 he had to remortgage his home to pay lawyers, the legal and financial quagmire nearly overwhelming him. At that point, Anjani introduced Cohen to her former husband, Robert Kory, a music industry lawyer who would also become his new manager. He began to shape a plan that had as its foundation Cohen touring.

The idea at first had no appeal for Cohen: it had been fifteen years since he was onstage, and he was unsure he could do it. And would anyone want to see him? The enthusiasm of a UK concert promoter reassured Cohen and Kory that it would work, and between 2008 and 2010 he hit the road, travelling relentlessly under the guidance of Kory with a new band led by his experienced musical director, Roscoe Beck. After four months of rehearsals, the tour began on May 11, 2008 in a 700-seat theater in Fredericton, New Brunswick, and ended on December 11, 2010 at the 4,000-seat Colosseum at Caesar's Palace, Las Vegas, where Dylan had played four months earlier. A highlight was his 2009 London concert, forming the basis of *Live in London* (2009). From Cohen's perspective, every concert became an act of mutual generosity: he to the audience, and they, in their response, to him.

Throughout the arduous schedule, he remained fit, energetic, and eager to perform, and released *Songs from the Road* in 2010, a live album. *Old Ideas* appeared two years later as he began another world tour (2012–13). To mark his eightieth birthday, he produced his thirteenth studio album *Popular Problems* (2014). His final album would be *You Want It Darker*, released on October 21, 2016. Almost three weeks later, on November 7, 2016, he died unexpectedly at his home after a fall.[32] The Quebec flag flew at half-mast over the National Assembly in Quebec City. Fans mourned his passing worldwide; the *New York Times* printed his obituary on the front

---

[31] For an account of his discovery of the missing funds and its impact, see Simmons, *I'm Your Man*, 445–55.

[32] Returning from the bathroom, he fainted and hit his head on the floor. He climbed back into bed but was unaware of a cranial bleed and passed away in his sleep.

page of its November 11, 2016 issue with the editorial board publishing a special statement celebrating his creative vitality.[33]

STRANGER MUSIC

Cohen's passing did not halt his art. Several posthumous works appeared, notably *The Flame* and *A Ballet of Lepers*. *The Flame* (2018) contains sixty-three poems, song lyrics from his last four albums, notebook passages, emails, and a text message sent hours before his death. It repeats earlier themes but through new forms, as in these lines from a notebook: "I pitched my tent/ wher'ere love led/ the troubles followed/ bed to bed."[34]

A Ballet of Lepers (2022) is his formerly unpublished novel of the same name, written between 1956 and 1957, plus fifteen short stories and an additional work, "Trade." Most of the short stories were written in Montreal, with two composed on Hydra. One of the stories, the fourteenth, imitates a Hebraic text: it has no title, capital letters, punctuation, or accents. All of this material resides in the Thomas Fisher Rare Book Library at the University of Toronto. He tried repeatedly to have these works published but failed, possibly because of narrative self-doubt: "I do not know if I will be able to make believable the rest of the story which I must tell you" is the opening of chapter 5 of *Ballet*.[35]

Posthumous Cohen has also seen new exhibitions and films, notably the Musée d'art contemporain de Montréal's immensely popular "Leonard Cohen: A Crack in Everything" (November 9, 2017–April 9, 2018) and the Art Gallery of Ontario's (AGO) "Leonard Cohen: Everybody Knows" (December 10, 2022–April 10, 2023). The former focused on innovative artistic interpretations of Cohen's life and art, the latter displayed, for the first time, items from his archive. Canada Post honored Cohen with a set of stamps issued on what would have been his eighty-fifth birthday, September 21, 2019.

---

[33] Editorial board, "Leonard Cohen, Vital to the End," *New York Times* (November 11, 2016), www.nytimes.com/2016/11/12/opinion/leonard-cohen-vital-to-the-end.html.

[34] Leonard Cohen, *The Flame: Poems and Selections from Notebooks*, ed. Robert Faggen and Alexandra Pleshoyano (Toronto: McClelland and Stewart, 2018), 192.

[35] Leonard Cohen, *A Ballet of Lepers: A Novel and Stories*, ed. Alexandra Pleshoyano (Toronto: McClelland and Stewart, 2022), 23.

Recent films have narrated his romantic and musical life. *Marianne & Leonard, Words of Love* (2019) is a documentary directed by Nick Broomfield concentrating on Hydra. *Hallelujah: Leonard Cohen, a Journey, a Song* (2022), directed by Dayna Goldfine and Dan Geller, tells the story of the song's creation and Cohen's creative process. *Thanks for the Dance*, released November 22, 2019, was his last studio album, most of the songs prerecorded but finished by Adam Cohen, who had discussed the instrumentation and melodies with his father before his death. The album earned four stars from *Rolling Stone* and was a Juno Award nominee in 2020.

Some twenty-one books on Cohen appeared between 2014 and 2022, with two standouts: Eric Lerner's *Matters of Vital Interest* (2018) and Matti Friedman's *Who by Fire* (2022).[36] A screenwriter and novelist, Lerner originally met Cohen at a Zen retreat in April 1977, and in his book offers a close account of their forty-year friendship, a personal record of their shared enterprise in pursuit of *sila* or "right conduct." Their attachment, he writes, "was a bond of affirmation," and he offers such insights as Cohen's enjoyment of rituals "not out of any sense of belief but for the simple pleasure of performing them."[37] Lerner also provides important details on Sasaki Roshi and his teaching, and a moving description of Leonard's funeral in Montreal on November 10, 2016, three days after he died.[38]

Who by Fire: War, Atonement and the Resurrection of Leonard Cohen by Friedman is a carefully researched account of Cohen's October 1973 visit to Israel during the Yom Kippur War. In Israel Cohen found himself entertaining the troops, moving around the front with a guitar and a set of local musicians, at one point crossing the Suez Canal and performing in a hangar on an Egyptian airfield. In a notebook, he wrote: "Feeling good in the desert. War is ok. People at their best."[39] More importantly, his music spoke emotionally to the soldiers, expressing "feelings and meanings for

---

[36] For a full accounting, see www.leonardcohenfiles.com, a remarkable repository of Cohen's works and writings.
[37] Lerner, *Matters of Vital Interest*, 38, 50.   [38] Ibid., 285–7.
[39] Cohen in Matti Friedman, *Who by Fire: War, Atonement and the Resurrection of Leonard Cohen* (Toronto: McClelland and Stewart, 2022) 146. For the impact of the war on Cohen, see ibid., 185.

which words fall short," as Friedman writes. "'We didn't understand all the words, but it penetrated the heart,'" a pilot remarked. Cohen later admitted to a reporter that "I came to raise their spirits, and they raised mine."[40]

Friedman not only reprints a set of never-before-seen photos but is able to draw from an unpublished forty-five-page manuscript by Cohen on his Israel trip. Before his journey, he had announced the end of his musical career; upon his return, he wrote a series of new songs, reconnected with Suzanne Elrod, had a second child, and went on to release *New Skin for the Old Ceremony* in 1974, which included "Lover, Lover, Lover" (written during his Israeli visit), "Chelsea Hotel No. 2," "Field Commander Cohen," and "Who by Fire."

But what remains? In a word, the Cohen archive, a vast collection of writings, audiotapes, film, and notebooks that in themselves total more than 3,000 pages. The collection includes the eighty-four original verses to "Hallelujah" in addition to hundreds of letters to and from friends and ex-lovers. It promises to reveal new aspects of Cohen's life from his lasting commitment to writing to his determination to find the right note, or chord, or phrase.

Artistic and personal restlessness defined Leonard Cohen's career from the start, a life constantly ensnared by art. "Poetry is a verdict, not an occupation," Breavman announces in *The Favorite Game*, expanded in Cohen's late confession to Lerner: "we were mostly interested in life as material for the line, the verse, the story."[41] Art consistently triumphed over experience, although often with regret. As he put it in "I Came So Far for Beauty," he left his patience and family behind, and "My masterpiece unsigned."[42] Like a courtly lover, he never completed his quest.

---

[40] Ibid., 81. Cohen in Diane Cole, "In 1973, Leonard Cohen Hated His Life. Then He Went to a War Zone," *Washington Post* (April 15, 2022), www.washingtonpost.com/outlook/2022/04/15/1973-leonard-cohen-hated-his-life-then-he-went-war-zone/.

[41] Cohen, *The Favourite Game*, 180. Cohen in Lerner, *Matters of Vital Interest*, 153.

[42] Leonard Cohen, "I Came So Far for Beauty," *Recent Songs*, 1979.

CHAPTER 2

The Poetry and Prose

"Almost Like the Blues"

Julian Stannard

"ELEGY" IS THE OPENING POEM OF LET US COMPARE Mythologies (1956), Cohen's debut collection.[1] He was twenty-two at the time of publication, yet he wrote many of these poems as a teenager. In "Tradition and the Individual Talent," Eliot argues: "Tradition ... is not inherited, and if you want it you must obtain it by great labour. It involves, in the first place, the historical sense, which we may call nearly indispensable to anyone who would continue to be a poet beyond his twenty-fifth year."[2]

Young poets, by this reckoning, are allowed some kind of hormonal fillip, or free run before the real work begins – at twenty-five! No little glamour or spiritual value in the idea of the boy-poet, the young poet. Difficult not to think of Thomas Chatterton, whose brief life became the poster boy for the Romantics. Difficult not to consider Wordsworth's "The child is father of the man." Difficult not to remember John Keats's early death, gone at twenty-five. In the nineteenth century Arthur Rimbaud hammered out the prototypes of European modernism. By the age of twenty he'd brought his precipitous career to an end, slipping off to the Horn of Africa. Rimbaud's call for the "disordering of all the senses" would be heeded by an older Cohen whose experimentation with drugs, not least on the island of Hydra, was part of the zeitgeist.[3]

---

[1] Leonard Cohen, *Let Us Compare Mythologies* (Edinburgh: Canongate Books, 1956), 1.
[2] T. S. Eliot, "Tradition and The Individual Talent," *Selected Essays* (London: Faber, 1999), 14.
[3] Leonard Cohen, *Book of Longing* (London: Penguin, 2006): "if you are young and you don't happen to be Arthur Rimbaud, we would prefer not to hear from you, and if you do happen to be Arthur Rimbaud, we definitely do not want to hear from you," 59.

Fortunately, Cohen lived long and wrote long, even if intimations of mortality informed his writing from the beginning. "Elegy" looks forward as well as backwards. *Let Us Compare Mythologies* is dedicated to the memory of his father, Nathan B. Cohen, who died in 1944 when Cohen was only nine. The poem "Rites" deals with his father's death.[4] The thirteen-line piece portrays the family at a death-bed scene. His father's heart "half-rotted" and "his throat dry with regret." The uncles' prophesies and promises of life stopped only "after he had died/ and [the boy-poet] had begun to shout." The death of the father has, from the beginning, bled into what Francis Mus calls "the myth of [Cohen's] artistry."[5] Sylvie Simmons comes back to the story, which has become part of that mythology. After the funeral the boy took a bow tie from his father's bedroom, cut it open, and put a message inside.

> The next day, in his own private ceremony, the boy dug a hole and buried it in the garden under the snow. Leonard has since described this as the first thing he ever wrote. He has also said he has no recollection of what it was and that he had been "digging in the garden for years, looking for it. Maybe that's all I'm doing, looking for the note."[6]

In the beginning was the word. A promissory note, a chthonic gesture. His father's death is taken up again in the "Story of Isaac" (1969), the track which conflates the Old Testament with personal history. The boy is nine years old, and his father enters the room and builds an altar. The poem tells us, "You who build these altars now/ To sacrifice the children/ You must not do it anymore," in lines that some read as a protest against the Vietnam War.

No one, they say, becomes a man until his father has died. Cohen's father had been in poor health for years. "I didn't feel a profound sense of loss," Cohen explained in 1991, "maybe because he was very ill throughout my entire childhood. It seemed natural that he died. He was weak and he died. Maybe my heart is cold."[7] Yet this memory is

---

[4] Cohen, *Let Us Compare Mythologies*, 7.
[5] Francis Mus, *The Demons of Leonard Cohen* (Ottawa: University of Ottawa Press, 2020), 58.
[6] Sylvie Simmons, *I'm Your Man: The Life of Leonard Cohen* (London: Vintage, 2013), 16.
[7] Ibid., 16–17.

tempered by his father's warrior status in World War One, and photographs of his father in uniform. Nathan Cohen was one of the first Jewish commissioned officers in the Canadian army. He kept his gun in the bedside cabinet – a .38, whose barrel was engraved with name, rank, and regiment. For the boy, the father's weapon was totemic. From the posthumous track "Happens to the Heart" (2019), we learn: "I was handy with a rifle, my father's 303/ I fought for something final, not the right to disagree." No doubt the memories of his father – the sick man and the man of action – created a dichotomy which nurtured future projects, not least Cohen's reckless trip to Cuba in 1961, later remembered in the track "Field Commander Cohen" (1974), which proclaims him "our most important spy," who was wounded and parachuted "acid into diplomatic cocktail parties."

His father's death was an opportunity. Breavman – the protagonist in Cohen's autobiographical first novel – has a friend called Lisa: "Had she ever been called a Dirty Jew?" he asks. She replies: "What was it like to have no father?"

> It made you more grown up. You carved the chicken, you sat where he sat. Lisa listened and Breavman, for the first time, felt himself dignified, or rather, dramatized. His father's death gave him a touch of mystery, contact with the unknown. He could speak with extra authority on God and Hell.[8]

"Elegy" is another thirteen-line piece; the poem is within touching distance of a sonnet, or a quatorzain, reaching out for hallowed space. The sacred, from the beginning, informs much of Cohen's writing, and the elegiac offers up crepuscular notes and poetic tropes. "Elegy" begins with an imperative not to look for him in mountain streams because the water is "too cold for any god." The "god" is both mythological, quasi-Poundian, yet by the poem's end the "snow-bruised body" in the "fluttering winding sheet" points to the heightened language of the King James Bible. The unnamed "god" is Christ-like. The half-rhyme "god/ blood" implies sacrifice deferred (Abraham and Isaac) or sacrifice enacted (crucifixion), and the description of the wounded god creates a form of Pietà. "Do not look for him," the poem begins, because there will be

---

[8] Leonard Cohen, *The Favourite Game* (London: Blue Door, 2009), 26.

nothing in the tomb.[9] And the "hovering ... fish," that Christian symbol, will build "their secret nests/ In his fluttering winding-sheet": namely, resurrection, life in death, Biblical typology. The elegiac, in this poem, is about manifold possibilities. Fish are transformed into the sparrows of the eponymous poem.[10] The young poet is drawn to Judeo-Christian narratives of suffering which in part acknowledge the sickness of his father and which also provide self-dramatizing, neo-Romantic, self-elegizing potential. In "Final Examination," Cohen – now in his forties – says he is ninety, and "Everyone I know has died off/ Except Leonard."[11] Not yet the *poète maudit* of *Flowers for Hitler* and *Beautiful Losers*, Cohen embraces narratives redolent with sorrow, ironic self-aggrandizement, myth, savagery, damnation, salvation, longing. In the track "Almost Like the Blues" (2014), he reaches for that hallmark bathos, the story of the gypsies and the Jews "was good, it wasn't boring/ It was almost like the blues." The tone is altogether different in the later track "You Want It Darker" (2016): "A million candles burning/ For the help that never came."

Breavman is described, self-deprecatingly, if knowingly, as "a kind of mild Dylan Thomas, talent and behaviour modified for Canadian tastes."[12] In *The Energy of Slaves* (1972), where Dylan Thomas and Bob Dylan have become one, the poet imagines himself "lying there with the books ... among the dead and future Dylans."[13] The imagery is more visceral in "So Long, Marianne" (1967): "You held on to me like I was a crucifix."

Notwithstanding the youthfulness of the author, *Let Us Compare Mythologies* is neither Rimbaudian nor Ginsbergian.[14] It's a savvy debut, even if the writing is, at times, weakened by abstractions. The writing can appear brittle or formulaic; there are too many adjectives. From the beginning, in effect, Cohen is negotiating the numinous and the luminous, and

---

[9] In "Show Me the Place" (2012), Cohen sings, "Help me roll away the stone/ I can't move this thing alone."
[10] Cohen, *Let Us Compare Mythologies*, 10–11.
[11] Cohen, *Death of a Lady's Man* (London: Black Spring Press,1995), 212.
[12] Cohen, *The Favourite Game*, 122.
[13] Leonard Cohen, *The Energy of Slaves* (London: Jonathan Cape, 1972), 71.
[14] Allen Ginsberg's "Howl" was published in 1956.

this movement between the abstract and the tangible image runs through later work. The writing, nevertheless, is intelligent and reflective, a form of cultural stock-taking, as if the poet were exploring the possibilities and the limits of poetry in both a technical and emotional sense.

Let Us Compare Mythologies leans into the conversations of Eliot, Pound, Yeats, Joyce, et al., yet positions itself in a postwar context. Ezra Pound was still languishing in St. Elizabeth's, incarcerated for his radio broadcasts during World War Two, and Theodor Adorno had made his much talked-of declaration regarding the barbarity of writing poetry after Auschwitz.[15] Reviewing Joyce's *Ulysses*, Eliot argues, "In using the myth, in manipulating a continuous parallel between contemporaneity and antiquity, Mr. Joyce is pursuing a method which others must pursue after him."[16] If the mythopoeic was integral to modernist creativity, the horrors of the Second World War questioned the rationale of poetry. Greco-Roman mythology and Judeo-Christian mythology, for Cohen, become points of reference, comparison, and exegetical possibility: Jew, Christian, people of the book, post-Nietzschean, sacred, profane. Accordingly, we find poems in Cohen's first collection whose titles are freighted with religious-mythological significance: "The Song of the Hellenist," "Prayer for Messiah," "City Christ," "Exodus," "Just the Worst Time," with its nod to Eliot's "The Journey of the Magi." In "Lovers," Jewish history, recent and distant, is made explicit in the reference to "pogrom" and "hot oven" and "furnace."[17] "For Wilf and His House" begins with Christians claiming "we pinned Jesus/ Like a lovely butterfly." The poem ends by contracting centuries of anti-Semitism. Here the imagery is sharp: thorns, bat, barn, ravens, yellow sign (the Star of David), all part of an "elaborate lie."[18]

In "The Song of the Hellenist" Cohen sets up a hierarchy in which Jews are presented as a lesser race: "I tell you, my people, the statues are too tall./ Beside them we are small and ugly." In the third stanza, Cohen turns on Eliot: the speaker observed "my landsmen in museums" and "jested on

---

[15] Theodor Adorno, "Cultural Criticism and Society" (1949), republished in *Prisms*, trans. Samuel and Shierry Weber (Cambridge, MA: MIT Press, 1967).
[16] T. S. Eliot, "Ulysses, Order, and Myth," *The Dial* (November 1923): 480–83.
[17] Cohen, *Let Us Compare Mythologies*, 22.   [18] Ibid., 2–3.

the Protocols... quoted 'Bleistein with a Cigar'."[19] The language is knowing. "Landsmen" speaks to Jewish emigration, and the "Protocols" refer to the *Protocols of the Elders of Zion* (1903), that infamous document which purportedly set out the Jewish project for global domination. "Bleistein with a Cigar" references Eliot's malicious poem "Burbank with a Baedeker: Bleistein with a Cigar" (1920). The protagonist is skewered with Jew-hating contempt; the location, "the Rialto," evoking *The Merchant of Venice*. Let us compare mythologies. Let us – after World War Two – consider the genocide of the Jewish people: "The rats are underneath the piles./ The Jew is underneath the lot." The philistine Bleistein, whose "lustreless protrusive eye/ Stares from the protozoic slime,"[20] is transformed, in Cohen's poem, into a gatekeeper of culture: "landsmen in the museums/ the brilliant scholars." Cohen's critique of Eliot is simultaneously a critique of modernist poetry, whose ideological range harbours the fascistic and the anti-Semitic. The young poet, by means of intertextual maneuvering, demonstrates a cultural capital which nourishes his writing until the end: "I was always workin' steady but I never called it art/ I got my shit together meeting Christ and reading Marx."[21]

Eliot argues that tradition is not inherited, that you must obtain it by great labor, that it involves a historical sense. But whose tradition are we celebrating? Arguably, in the case of Cohen, a great deal of Jewish and European culture *was* inherited. He was born in Montreal in 1934, on the right side of the tracks, into an educated Jewish family; his grandfather on his father's side had cofounded the *Jewish Times*; his grandfather on his mother's side was Rabbi Solomon Klonitsky-Kline, formerly the principal of a school for Talmudic study in Lithuania. I had a "Messianic childhood," Cohen says of his early years, and "he was well aware that he was a *kohen*, one of a priestly caste, descendent of Moses' brother, Aaron, and born to officiate," all of which gave him access to the liturgy, the psalms, arcane shibboleths, a quest for the sacred.[22] Cohen also had a keen sense of Montreal's history: First

---

[19] Ibid., 4–5.
[20] T. S. Eliot, "Burbank with a Baedeker: Bleistein with a Cigar," *Collected Poems 1909–1962* (London: Faber, 1974), 32–33.
[21] From the track "Happens to the Heart" (2019). [22] Simmons, *I'm Your Man*, 16.

Nation Canadians (colonial history informs *Beautiful Losers*, his second novel), French-speaking Catholics, Anglo-Saxon protestants, Jews from diverse backgrounds.

In "Making It Mainstream: Montreal and the Canadian Jewish Poetic Tradition," Norman Ravvin considers Jewish emigration to Canada in the twentieth century and recognizes the writer A. M. Klein, born in Ukraine in 1909, as a father figure – in *The Spice-Box of Earth* Cohen writes "Song for Abraham Klein."[23] Many poets came from Eastern Europe, including J. I. Segal (1896–1954), Melech Ravitch (1893–1976), Rachel Korn (1898–1982), and Chava Rosenfarb (1923–2011), who survived Auschwitz and emigrated to Montreal in 1950. She speaks of a community of Yiddish writers whose lives "often merged with the drama of Eastern European Jewish life in the first half of the twentieth century."[24] In fact, Rosenfarb argues "a Yiddish writer ... arriving here from Europe, already possessed a rich cultural baggage ... He felt that he had a superior degree of sophistication, of worldliness, even though he may have just recently stepped out of the *shtetl*."[25]

The Spice-Box of Earth (1961), Cohen's second collection, provides a title spilling over with possibilities. The spice-box is used to mark the end of the Sabbath and is therefore integral to Jewish custom. The collection, however, transcends Jewish ritual and marks the acquisition of a more luxurious voice: "Our rabbi dances up the street,/ Wearing our lawns like a green prayer-shawl."[26] The fragrance of the spice-box hovers over the collection. Louis Dudek, Cohen's tutor at McGill University, had described *Let Us Compare Mythologies* "as a ragbag of classical mythology" and "a confusion of symbolic images," yet his response to the second collection was enthusiastic.[27] The language of religion, which not infrequently comes with an erotic charge, creates a heightened effect. "I Have Not Lingered in European Monasteries," for example, takes its cue from

---

[23] Norman Ravvin, "Making It Mainstream: Montreal and the Canadian Jewish Poetic Tradition", *Literature and Theology* 24, no. 2 (June 2010): 121–36.

[24] Ibid., 122.

[25] Ibid. NB Important to mention Irving Layton (1912–2006), born in Romania, who was Cohen's lifelong friend, fellow poet, and mentor–teacher.

[26] Leonard Cohen, *Selected Poems* (London: Jonathan Cape, 1969), 71–72.

[27] Simmons, *I'm Your Man*, 71.

the title. The ineffable and the gnomic are inscribed in lines such as, "I might hear the breathing of G-d," yet the imagery quickens in "I have not become the luminous trout," and a habitual register shift is evident in the last stanza, where the all-gesturing "I have not been unhappy for ten thousand years" slips into the quotidian "My favorite cooks prepare my meals."[28]

"Isiah" is an example of poetry as devotion: "In the sculptured temple how many pilgrims ... kneeled before the glory of the ritual?"[29] The gorgeousness of the writing, evoking *The Song of Songs*, anticipates the *Book of Mercy*. Images and motifs from *Let Us Compare Mythologies* – flesh, thighs, fish, birds – are redeployed and reworked, becoming part of Cohen's lexicon. The "secret nests" from "Elegy" have opened up to "rising flocks of ravens" ("Isiah"), or "the upturned bellies/ Of breathing fallen sparrows" ("Beneath My Hands"). And, for Cohen, the mouth enjoys an emblematic charge. The "corners of my mouth" ("The Hellenist") and "the smallest movement of your mouth" ("These Heroics") become "all her flesh is like a mouth" ("You Have the Lovers"). The mouth is vessel and oracle, and organ and orifice, and the mouth delivers song. The image is amplified in "Take This Waltz" (1986), Cohen's translation of García Lorca's "Pequeño Vals Vienés": "There's a concert hall in Vienna/ Where your mouth had a thousand reviews."[30]

"The thick glove of words" which nourishes much of the collection also gives way to an economical mode which not only prefigures Cohen's movement into songwriting but also the sharper trajectory of his third collection.[31] "I Have Two Bars of Soap," for example, uses a shorter line, as well as a simpler diction: "And here's a jar of oil,/ Just like in the Bible./ Lie in my arms,/ I'll make your flesh glisten."[32] Cleanliness, spiritual preparation, is also readiness for sex. Mus asks, "Is this anointing oil or massage oil for the poet's lover?"[33] In "Celebration," the hieratic and the sexual converge, creating a more literary version of those well-known lines from

---

[28] Cohen, *Selected Poems*, 45. [29] Ibid., 73–75.
[30] Cohen's enthusiasm for Lorca is demonstrated again in "Lorca Lives" from Cohen, *Book of Longing*, 90.
[31] Simmons, *I'm Your Man*, 100. [32] Cohen, *Selected Poems*, 60.
[33] Mus, *The Demons of Leonard Cohen*, 150.

the "Chelsea Hotel No. 2":[34] "When you kneel below me and ... hold my manhood like a sceptre."[35]

In 1959 Robert Lowell published *Life Studies*, in which a more elaborate poetic gave way to a simpler, prosier style revealing Lowellian "secrets," both familial and personal. Cohen's "confessional" writing might be better explored in the novels. Yet inevitably there are poems which draw on personal experience. "The Cuckold's Song" is a good example of Cohen employing a more colloquial style, eschewing the temptations of the "cosmic poet," or poetry with a capital P, and embracing the poetry of "5 Mackewan Ales."[36] If the title has a Chaucerian ring, the poem is a single block piece full of line-length variation (using lower case at the beginning of the line) in which the poet as "cheated" lover steps into the limelight, the poet is now a wounded troubadour, part of Cohen's growing playlist of romantic trysts: "I'd crawl to you baby and I'd fall at your feet/ And I'd howl at your beauty like a dog in heat."[37]

Cohen, "one of a priestly caste," or, conversely, that "lazy bastard/ Living in a suit"[38] takes pleasure in laying it down: "I repeat: the important thing was to cuckold Leonard Cohen./ I like that line because it's got my name in it." Rather than Lowell, this self-referentially has something of Frank O' Hara about it. Useful, perhaps, to think of the New Yorker's poem "Katy," in which we find "One day I'll love Frank O' Hara." Cohen's declaration is turned into an alchemic triumph, putting one's name in lights, a solipsistic flourish: "The fact is I'm turning to gold, turning to gold." He's become a knight errant. Not gold yet, the final line declares, but "[he's] already turned to clay." He's become a Talmudic golem, shrouded in magic, sacred, a little sinister.

Flowers for Hitler (1964) is, arguably, his most audacious collection. It demonstrates continuation and gear-change. The title is provocative, Baudelairean, reminding us of Frederick Seidel's controversial *Final*

---

[34] "I remember you well in the Chelsea Hotel/ You were talking so brave and so free/ Giving me head on the unmade bed" (1974).

[35] Cohen, *Selected Poems*, 61.

[36] Inter alia, I refer to this poem in "Audacious Troubadour: The Early Poetry of Leonard Cohen," in *Spirituality and Desire in Leonard Cohen's Songs and Poems: Visions from the Tower of Song*, ed. Peter Billingham (Newcastle-upon-Tyne: Cambridge Scholars Publishing, 2017), 115–26.

[37] From the track "I'm Your Man" (1988). [38] From the track "Going Home" (2012).

Solutions (1963), or even A. M. Klein's *The Hitleriad* (1944). It addresses Adorno's post-Holocaust declaration and resonates with Alvarez's Beyond the Gentility Principle, which he laid out in the introduction to *The New Poetry* (1962), calling for "a new seriousness" and, in the light of World War Two, a recognition of "mass evil" where concentration camps were "run scientifically as death factories."[39] The publisher of *Flowers for Hitler* included an excerpt from a letter by Cohen on the dust jacket: "This book moves me from the world of the golden-boy poet into the dung pile of the front-line writer." N. David Greyson argued: "Leonard Cohen vomits on the street, and then bids us gaze at his vomit."[40]

Flowers for Hitler employs an epigraph from Primo Levi: "Take care not to suffer in your own homes what is inflicted on us here." The collection is not uniquely about Nazi atrocities, yet there are poems whose titles are emblematic: "Goebbels Abandons His Novel and Joins the Party," "Hitler the Brain-Mole," "Opium and Hitler," "Hitler," and "All There Is to Know about Adolf Eichmann." The unconscionable trauma of the Holocaust hangs over Cohen's writing. In this third collection, however, the delivery is sharper, shucking off the "thick glove of words." "Hitler the Brain-Mole" begins: "Hitler the brain-mole looks out of my eyes/ Goering boils ingots of gold in my bowels."[41] If, in "Daddy," Sylvia Plath juxtaposes the sing-along rhythm of the nursery rhyme with unflinching brutality, Cohen creates a *faux* pastoral in "Folk." The poem describes a little village with a school, a church, and "doggies making love." The insistent lower case is in a paradoxical relationship with the enormity of Nazi crimes, and the absence of a final full stop implies that butchery isn't tucked away in the past:

> the flags are bright as laundry
> flowers for hitler the summer yawned[42]

A touch of Cohenesque levity here, which both attenuates and underscores the horror of history. *Flowers for Hitler* is also a dialogue about style, register, voice. In "The Cuckold's Song" he writes, "I don't want to turn anything

---

[39] A. Alvarez (ed.), *The New Poetry* (Harmondsworth: Penguin, 1986 [1962]), 21–32.
[40] Natalia Vesselova, "'The Past Is Perfect': Leonard Cohen's Philosophy of Time," unpublished PhD thesis, University of Ottawa (2014), 108.
[41] Cohen, *Selected Poems*, 98.   [42] Ibid., 134.

into poetry." In "Style" he says, "I will forget my style/ I will have no style."[43] The quest for song – oftentimes Cohen's poems have "song" in the title or are called "Song" – competes with silence.[44] Do I take up the lyre?, the poet asks, or do I hunker down in some three-dollar hotel?[45] "All There Is to Know about Adolf Eichmann" is less a poem and more a withering piece of bureaucracy, the ultimate response to Adorno's declaration. Habitual poetic tropes are bled dry, and the poem/non-poem reconsiders what Hanna Arendt, in the coverage of the Eichmann trial in 1961, called the banality of evil in a chart that lists eyes, hair, weight, height, and intelligence as "medium," and "distinguishing features" as "none."[46]

The contours of Cohen's poetic are, in effect, laid out in the first three collections and the two novels. In the ten years from *Let Us Compare Mythologies* (1956) to his controversial second novel *Beautiful Losers* (1966) he explored the sacred and the profane, the heightened and the banal, the lyrical and the demotic, the effusive and the laconic, the exclamatory and the deadpan, the serious and the humorous (so many jokes "told in the dark").[47] He continued, in different ways, to pick at these binaries. "I've Stepped into an Avalanche," from *Parasites of Heaven* (1966), later the eponymous track (1971), begins "I stepped into an avalanche/ It covered up my soul." Yearning is hardwired into Cohen's poetry, and spiritual thirst is all-important, as we shall see later, in the *Book of Mercy* (1984).

Cohen's poetry is often a form of metapoetry. Breavman (the bereaved man?), the Cohenesque character in *The Favourite Game*,

> never described himself as a poet or his work as poetry. The fact that the lines do not come to the edge of the page is no guarantee. Poetry is a verdict, not an occupation. He hated to argue about the techniques of verse. The poem is a dirty, bloody, burning thing that has to be grabbed with bare hands.[48]

---

[43] Ibid., 95–6. [44] See "Gift"; ibid., 39.
[45] See the documentary *Ladies and Gentlemen, Mr. Leonard Cohen* (1965), www.youtube.com/watch?v=_GvTeMdmdCI.
[46] Cohen, *Selected Poems*, 122.
[47] Leonard Cohen, *Book of Mercy* (Edinburgh: Canongate Books, 2019), 76.
[48] Cohen, *The Favourite Game*, 197.

"On the Sickness of My Love" (1964) begins: "Poems! break out!/ Break my head!/ .../ I need you!,"[49] while, from *The Energy of Slaves* (1972), "The poems don't love us anymore/ They don't want to love us/ They don't want to be poems."[50] From the beginning of his oeuvre, prose poetry (open form) lies down with more traditional poetry (closed form), thereby interrogating the very dynamic of poetry. Cohen, in fact, argued, "I always describe myself as a writer rather than a poet."[51] This conversation between prose and poetry is seen in *Death of a Lady's Man* (1978), where poems converse with adjacent commentaries, where the manifesto-like "How to Speak Poetry" tells us, "Never close your eyes and jerk your head to one side when you talk about Death."[52]

Poetry inhabits both novels in various ways. Lawrence Breavman enjoys a first name which nods to and withdraws Lawrentian possibilities, and the strategies of the poet are all over *Beautiful Losers*: repetition, anaphora, listing, grammatical and syntactical dislocation, a variety of forms, symbolism, making strange, surrealism. Cohen's second novel is historical/postcolonial, Joycean at times, discombobulating, profane. The opening section of the tripartite narrative focuses on the virginal, seventeenth-century Algonquin–Mohawk saint, Catherine (or Kateri) Tekakwitha. She becomes the novel's essential historical figure. Born in 1656, she converted to Catholicism, thanks to France's colonizing missionaries, and she took a vow of perpetual virginity. Contemplation of her chastity provides a constant source of fantasy. The narrator – unnamed – wants to deflower her: "Fuck a saint, that's how, find a little saint and fuck her over ... get right into her plastic altar,"[53] or "All parts of the body are erotogenic. Assholes can be trained with whips and kisses ... Pricks and cunts [are] monstrous!,"[54] and, again, "What is this fucking of a dead saint?"[55] In *Beautiful Losers*, demotic language becomes a sonic mantra: blasphemous, scatological, predatorial, provocative.[56]

---

[49] Cohen, *Selected Poems*, 113. [50] Cohen, *The Energy of Slaves*, 117.
[51] Simmons, *I'm Your Man*, 98. [52] Cohen, *Death of Lady's Man*, 196.
[53] Leonard Cohen, *Beautiful Losers* (New York: Vintage Books, 1993), 12. [54] Ibid., 32.
[55] Ibid., 35.
[56] Tim Falconer argues in his essay "Beautiful Losses": "When I'd first read *The Favourite Game*, its eroticism already seemed tame. But *Beautiful Losers* is still a dirty book; I can't

Beautiful Losers might be described as Rabelaisian or Sadeian or even, at moments, Nabokovian. In 1964, Cohen was awarded the Prix Littéraire du Québec for *The Favourite Game*; the reception of his second novel was rather more complicated. The *Globe and Mail* dismissed it as "verbal masturbation"; the *Toronto Daily Star* described it as "the most revolting book ever written in Canada."[57] The narrator suffers from constipation, one of the novel's in-jokes. "Will I be able to shit," "Will my bowels churn?" he asks.[58] The antidote to this blockage is an unleashing of priapic ambition:

> Let cocks again rise and twine like ivy round the gold projector beam, and cunts yawn under gloves and white paper bags full of candy, and no naked flashing breasts lure the dirty laundry of our daily lives into the movie palace ... I speed down my zipper and out falls dust and rubble. Hard cock alone leads to Thee.[59]

While Cohen said of *Flowers for Hitler* that the book removed him from "the world of the golden-boy poet into the dung pile of the front-line writer," *Beautiful Losers* created a more glorious dung-heap. Breavman, who was described in that innocent, if picaresque, bildungsroman as "a kind of mild Dylan Thomas, talent and behavior modified for Canadian tastes," is now a distant figure.[60] Yet the jury remained out as to whether this second novel took him nearer to the front line or whether he had crossed the line of reason and embraced a narcotic mysticism, fueled with fetishism. "The Jews," we are told, "didn't let young men study the Cabala. Connections should be forbidden citizens under seventy."[61] The codes, symbols, and games, all part of *Beautiful Losers*, reveal a transgressive poet thumbing his nose at the patriarchs. The narrator and F – the other male protagonist – create their own religious and/or liturgical text, at times drug-fueled and incantatory, yet hungry for gnostic breakthrough: "God is alive. Magic is afoot. God is alive, Magic is afoot. God is afoot. Magic is alive.

think of another novel I've read in which a woman's vagina is referred to as a cunt so frequently," https://hazlitt.net/feature/beautiful-losses.
[57] Simmons, *I'm Your Man*, 134.   [58] Cohen, *Beautiful Losers*, 6.   [59] Ibid., 22.
[60] Cohen, *The Favourite Game*, 122.   [61] Ibid., 18.

Alive is afoot. Magic never died ... Magic never weakened. Magic never hid."[62]

In *The Demons of Leonard Cohen*, Mus dedicates a chapter to *Beautiful Losers*. Accordingly, we learn Sylvia Söderlind described the book as "the essential Canadian postmodern novel";[63] Christian Bourgois called it "one of the craziest and most dazzling books of the sixties";[64] Stan Dragland argued the book "broke so successfully with traditional form, showing outrageous new possibility for fiction to a rather staid Canadian scene, it is one of the most important novels written in this country."[65] Jack McClelland, Cohen's publisher, found it "appalling, shocking, revolting, sick," yet he also found it "wild and incredible and marvellously well written."[66] The Dutch critic Gerrit Komrij, on the contrary, didn't pull his punches: "imagination *nil*, structure *nil*, originality *nil*, style *nil*, self-control *nil*, premise, *nil*."[67]

Readers today, no less, might find the male fantasies and the detailed descriptions of sex troubling and gratuitous. Cohen's "pornography," nevertheless, is full of purpose. The celebration of sex, in a number of guises, is central to the work and folds in a colonial dimension. After Cohen had spent two amphetamine-fueled years on the island of Hydra, the novel was published. According to Cohen, *Beautiful Losers* is "a love story, a psalm, a Black Mass, a monument, a satire, a prayer, a shriek, a road, a map through the wilderness, a joke, a tasteless affront, a hallucination, a bore, an irrelevant display of diseased virtuosity" and "a disagreeable religious epic of incomparable beauty."[68]

Beautiful Losers is iconoclastic, hubristic, and quintessentially Canadian. The sexual content has its own peculiar architecture, allegorical as well as graphic. The novel has a schema *sui generis*, and there are examples of poetic–typological experiment: the use of micro-chapters; the forgoing of punctuation at various moments; the varying use of upper and lower case; the employment of both English and French in macaronic display and/or "a multilingual game";[69] the incorporation of adverts into the text (including "Water from the Miraculous Fountain

---

[62] Ibid., 157. [63] Mus, *The Demons of Leonard Cohen*, 131. [64] Ibid., 135. [65] Ibid.
[66] Simmons, *I'm Your Man*, 134. [67] Mus, *The Demons of Leonard Cohen*, 144.
[68] Simmons, *I'm Your Man*, 130. [69] Mus, *The Demons of Leonard Cohen*, 139.

at Lourdes");[70] the use of motifs, intertextual allusions, jazz-like fugues, riffs, and luminous fish, no less.[71] All of which might be said to amplify the literary quality. There are moments of humor, cartoonish or otherwise, as well as interludes of distilled lyricism and aphoristic bravura. And the novel, significantly, cuts across time, becoming "a re-write of Canadian history," as well as a history of the defeated.[72] It is, in effect, a book about losers. F lays it down clearly enough: "The English did to us [French] what we did to the Indians and the Americans did to the English what the English did to us. I demand revenge for everyone."[73] The language of sexual predation can therefore be seen as inscribing the brutality of colonial exploitation.

To write a meaningful synopsis of *Beautiful Losers* – an inherently unstable text – is tricky.[74] The tripartite novel inscribes the trinity or some mystical-religious order. The narrator, his wife Edith of First Nations heritage, and the mysterious F have sexual relations with each other at differing moments: straight sex, gay sex, sometimes throwing a "Danish Vibrator" into the mix. The narrator discovers that F has been sleeping with Edith, reminding the reader of Cohen's poem "The Cuckold's Song," with its quasi-triumphant "the important thing was to cuckold Leonard Cohen."[75] And both the narrator and F are obsessed with Saint Catherine Tekakwitha in what is tantamount to a *ménage à trois* across time. Book one, "The History of Them All," is recounted by the nameless anglophone scholar who is studying an indigenous tribe. Book two, "A Long Letter from F," comes from the narrator's boyhood orphan (francophone) friend writing from a psychiatric hospital.[76] Not only is he suffering from syphilis ("my prick rotten and black"), he has also been

---

[70] Cohen, *Beautiful Losers*, 108.
[71] Motifs and images from Cohen's poetry find their way into the novel, including fish, often seen as a Christian symbol.
[72] Mus, *The Demons of Leonard Cohen*, 133.   [73] Cohen, *Beautiful Losers*, 187.
[74] Cohen describes the novel "more [as] a sunstroke than a book" and says, "May I suggest you skip over the parts you don't like? Dip into it here and there"; Mus, *The Demons of Leonard Cohen*, 143.
[75] Cohen, *Selected Poems*, 56.
[76] At the beginning of the film *Ladies and Gentlemen, Mr. Leonard Cohen*, a suave-looking Cohen tells a joke about visiting a friend in a mental hospital in Montreal.

locked up as a terrorist, responsible, inter alia, for blowing up the statue of Queen Victoria.[77]

"A Long Letter from F" opens with Wordsworthian panache: "My Dear Friend, Five years with the length of five years. I do not know exactly where this letter finds you,"[78] but the language quickly rediscovers its habitual modus operandi:

> I followed women into the world, because I loved the world. Breasts, buttocks, everywhere I followed the soft balloons. When women hissed at me from brothel windows, when they softly hissed at me over the shoulders of their dancing husbands, I followed them and I sank down with them, and sometimes when I listened to their hissing I knew it was nothing but the sound and the collapse of their soft balloons.[79]

The third book, "Beautiful Losers: An Epilogue in the Third Person," reveals that F has fled the asylum. It reminds us of the political tension in 1960s Quebec, a period sometimes referred to as the Quiet Revolution, as well as the longer trajectory of Canada's colonial history. First Quebec:

> They could all sense it as they closed in on the Main: Something was happening in Montreal history! ... Every man who was a terrorist in his heart whispered, At Last ... Poets arrived hoping to turn the expected riot into a rehearsal ... Androgynous hashish smokers rushed in for a second chance to fuck ... It was the Revolution![80]

And on the penultimate page of the novel, in circular manner, we are told: "The end of this book has been rented to the Jesuits. The Jesuits demand the official beatification of Catherine Tekakwitha!"[81] The histories of Canada, Quebec, Montreal, and Leonard Cohen are improbably conflated in this improbable novel.

According to Simmons, Cohen began hallucinating once he had finished the manuscript and suffered a breakdown. On his recovery, Cohen announced he was going to Nashville to become a songwriter.[82]

---

[77] On July 12, 1963, the Front de Libération du Quebec (FLQ) blew up a statue of Queen Victoria in Quebec City.
[78] Cohen, *Beautiful Losers*, 145. [79] Ibid., 146. [80] Ibid., 240.
[81] Ibid., 242. Tekakwitha was beatified in 1980 and canonized in 2012.
[82] Simmons, *I'm Your Man*, 129.

Beautiful Losers was the end of Cohen's career as a writer of fiction. The writing of this drug-fueled book had brought about a drowning and a resurrection, unexpected transcendence, and a change of direction. In a piece of writing crammed with allusions and references, it's worth noting the somewhat oblique presence of the musician Ray Charles. The epigraph name-checks the musician. Cohen wrote *Beautiful Losers* listening to *The Genius Sings the Blues*. At the end of the novel, the protagonist (is he a conflation of the un-named narrator and the enigmatic F?) "reassembled himself into ... a movie of Ray Charles."[83] In 1967 the writer began his new career with the *Songs of Leonard Cohen*.

The *Book of Mercy*, Cohen's seventh collection, is unapologetically a book about nourishing the soul. Cohen was now fifty, and the book is made up of fifty prose-poems, fifty meditations. If *Beautiful Losers* was like a hospital for the insane, even a form of post-Holocaustic writing, an oblique response to Adorno, the *Book of Mercy*, some twenty years later, offers spiritual compensation. If "Elegy" edges towards the grace bestowed by a sonnet, the *Book of Mercy* is soused with Biblical language. The writing is hieratic, Hasidic, kabbalistic, evoking Donne's love poetry, and drawing on the Sufi poets Rumi and Atta. We read, for example: "YOU HAVE SWEETENED your word on my lips,"[84] and "Bless The Lord, O MY soul [...] who has given you a tongue like the wind, and a heart like the sea,"[85] and "YOU WHO POUR MERCY INTO hell."[86] Cohen described the book as a conversation with eternity. Out of the "affliction of disbelief" – the cloud of unknowing – it has "the chutzpah to speak to G-d." The only way "to reconcile with the butcher shop of history, the veil of suffering," Cohen argues, "is to glue your soul to prayer."[87] Four years later he released "Hallelujah."

Cohen describes himself "a civilian of the spiritual."[88] He brings this qualification to his later writing, even if the poetry is something of a mixed bag. His status as a singer-songwriter eclipses the poetry in *Book*

---

[83] Cohen, *Beautiful Losers*, 242.   [84] Cohen, *Book of Mercy*, 13.   [85] Ibid., 45.
[86] Ibid., 43.
[87] Cohen talks about the *Book of Mercy*, interview by CKUA's Tony Dillon Davis (1984), www.google.com/search?q=loeobard+cohen+on+Book+of+mercy+Youtibe&rlz=1C1GCEO_enGB970GB970&oq=loeobard++cohen.
[88] Ibid.

of Longing (2006) and, posthumously, *The Flame* (2018). Too often the poems are bereft of a necessary tension. "Something from the Early Seventies" argues "If I strain too easily to push a pun into a profundity, it is only because I am at the end of my tether."[89] The balance between profundity and banality often comes down on the side of the latter.[90] Much of his later work, with some notable exceptions, are riffs, jokes, koans, squibs, doggerel, variations on a theme, Buddhist musings, and "scraps," self-deprecating and solipsistic in equal measure.[91] "You Are Right, Sahara" continues to address spiritual matters: "The Seeker become the Passionate Lover, and The Passionate Lover becomes The Beggar, and The Beggar becomes The Wretch."[92] Poetry continues to make its stringent demands. Of the thousands of would-be poets, we are told, only one or two are real: "The rest are fakes/ .../ I am one of the fakes/ And this is my story."[93] If Cohen's poetry, from the beginning, is fueled with the elegiac, these late poems contemplate last things, accompanied by sardonic sketches, self-portraits, "death masks."[94] The trajectory of his writing, in effect, evokes Eliot's line from the *Four Quartets*: "In my beginning is my end."

---

[89] Cohen, *Book of Longing*, 125.
[90] See William Logan's withering review: "Leonard Cohen's Posthumous Collection of Poems, Lyrics and Sketches," *New York Times* (January 2, 2019).
[91] See editorial note in Leonard Cohen, *The Flame*, ed. Robert Faggen and Alexandra Pleshoyano (Edinburgh: Canongate Books, 2019).
[92] Cohen, *Book of Longing*, 44.   [93] Ibid., 73.
[94] Mus considers "Masks, Mirrors, and Demons," in *The Demons of Leonard Cohen*, 17–23.

CHAPTER 3

Songwriting

Hymns of the Heretic

Alan Light

LEONARD COHEN OFTEN MADE SONGWRITING SEEM LIKE agony. He spoke frequently of the painful rigor and emotional cost of his work, the years he spent polishing a single lyric. It was so recurrent as a theme that it sometimes felt like schtick, or a bit of a humblebrag, but the evidence was also there – in the drafts and revisions, even after a song came out – that he certainly wasn't kidding about the effort his material demanded. Cohen often referred to the act of writing as "blackening the pages." ("I blacken pages. I'm not a writer," he told the *Guardian* in 1970. "The writing is the ash of the experience.")[1] The glimpses we have gotten into his legendary notebooks illustrate that this "blackening" wasn't purely metaphorical, nor was it simply a matter of scrawling out words, but also of adding, crossing out, moving sections around, revealing the traces of a writer's restless, unsatisfied mind in action. And certainly, it slowed down his output – Cohen put out just fourteen studio albums in his career (three of which were recorded during the last five years of his life), a fraction of Bob Dylan's forty or Neil Young's forty-five releases.

"The process of songwriting for me is arduous and painful because I have to go to the place where the song is," Cohen told Thom Jurek of Detroit's *Metro Times* in 1993. "I have to inhabit it and allow it to have its way with me. I have to write perfectly many verses that get thrown away because they are

---

[1] Hugh Hebert, "From the Archive, 29 August 1970: An Interview with Leonard Cohen," *Guardian* (August 29, 2013), theguardian.com/theguardian/2013/aug/29/leonard-cohen-interview-1970.

imperfect for a particular song, and it takes time and patience and tears to get there."[2]

It's important to remember, though, that pursuing songwriting as his medium was a choice Cohen made at a certain point in his life, that he was on a path as a different kind of writer – and with this decision came specific requirements and modifications in his work. His shift away from his early ambitions as a celebrated young poet and novelist to become a songwriter ultimately revealed strengths that few could have anticipated, and that remain underappreciated.

"All great literature begins at the level of the line," said Salman Rushdie in his speech honoring Cohen with the inaugural PEN Award for Song Lyrics of Literary Excellence in 2012:

> If you can't write a good line, you can't write a good paragraph, you can't write a good page, you can't write a good book. At the level of the line for all these years, Leonard Cohen's work has been amazing us again and again. This is work of great beauty and depth, and to put it simply, if I could write like that, I would.[3]

Line by line, Cohen's songs stand next to anybody's – and really, his efforts are even more granular than that. His true target seemed to mirror a striking line in "Hallelujah," his 1984 composition that became a global anthem: "There's a blaze of light in every word." He burnished his writing to the level that each and every word could indeed blaze, with a precision and a concision unmatched in pop songwriting. "I have to discard versions of myself, and versions of the songs, until I can get to a situation where I can defend every word, every line," he told Jurek.[4] But Rushdie's words of praise could apply to pure poetry, and that's not what Leonard Cohen's songwriting is. It has a different intent, involves a different execution, and derives from a different set of sources.

---

[2] Thom Jurek, "The Prophet of Love Looks into the Abyss: A Conversation with Leonard Cohen," *Metro Times* (August 18, 1993).

[3] Salman Rushdie, "Literary Excellence in Song Lyrics: Leonard Cohen," www.youtube.com/watch?v=s5Hd8ocgEvs.

[4] Jurek, "The Prophet of Love."

Cohen's early life led him to the point where these miraculous songs could materialize. Groomed to take over his family's successful clothing business, Cohen instead set his sights on being a writer, devotedly reading poetry as a teenager. Attending McGill University, Cohen was embraced by the poetry community – particularly the prominent personality Irving Layton, who would become a mentor – and published his first poem, "Satan in Westmount," at age nineteen. Cohen graduated in 1955, and his first book of poetry, *Let Us Compare Mythologies*, was published the following year. Cohen's 1966 novel *Beautiful Losers* was perhaps his best-known work, partly because of the book's explicit sex scenes. "James Joyce is not dead. He is living in Montreal under the name of Cohen,"[5] wrote the *Boston Globe*, while the *Toronto Star*'s Robert Fulford called *Losers* "the most revolting book ever written in Canada … an important failure. At the same time it is probably the most interesting Canadian book of the year."[6]

Still, the book only sold a few thousand copies, and Cohen had never abandoned his early interest in music. In a 2011 speech accepting the Prince of Asturias Award in Barcelona, he recounted a transformational moment in his life's direction. "I was an indifferent guitar player," he said. "I banged the chords. I only knew a few of them. I sat around with my college friends, drinking and singing the folk songs, or the popular songs of the day, but I never in a thousand years thought of myself as a musician or as a singer." But one day in the early 1960s, he visited his mother's house, beside which sat a park with a tennis court. There he found a young man playing flamenco guitar. "I loved the way he played," Cohen said. "There was something about the way he played that captured me. It was the way I wanted to play – and knew that I would never be able to play." He persuaded the guitarist to give him lessons; they had three sessions, in which Cohen learned a sequence of chords. When the young teacher didn't show up for their fourth lesson, Cohen learned that he had taken his own life. But in that short time, everything had changed. "It

---

[5] Alan Light, *The Holy or the Broken: Leonard Cohen, Jeff Buckley, and the Unlikely Ascent of "Hallelujah"* (New York: Atria, 2012), 6.
[6] Ibid.

was those six chords, it was that guitar pattern, that has been the basis of all my songs and all my music," he said.[7]

Frustrated by his lack of success as a writer, in 1967 Cohen decided to take his shot at music. Still enamored of country music, he headed for Nashville, but stopped in New York City to meet with Mary Martin, a fellow Canadian who had been working with Bob Dylan's manager, Albert Grossman. Martin introduced Cohen to Judy Collins, and he sang her "Suzanne." She quickly recorded it, in what would turn out to be the first of many versions of this composition.

Leonard Cohen's future as a songwriter was off and running. But there was no guarantee that the shift from poetry to songwriting was going to be so seamless. The two formats are very different animals, which is what makes the common conception that great lyrics are "good enough to be poetry" so condescending. Cohen has been of at least two minds in considering the relationship between writing poems and writing songs. Sometimes he has said things like, "My songs are poems with a guitar behind them,"[8] and "I never made a big distinction between that which we call a poem and that which we call a song."[9] Elsewhere, though, he maintained that "I never did set poetry to music … I got stuck with that. It was a bum rap. I never set a poem to music. I'm not that hopeless. I know the difference between a poem and a song."[10]

At risk of overstating the obvious, songs are meant to be heard, not read. Though rhythm and meter can of course be crucial elements of poetry ("I think of poets in the twentieth century who have had a real relationship with meter and rhyme," said Rushdie in his PEN speech, "and I think of W. H. Auden and James Fenton, and I think that the kind of playfulness of those rhymes in 'Hallelujah,' for example, is something that an Auden or a Fenton would respond to very immediately because

---

[7] In Leonard Cohen, *The Flame: Poems Notebooks Lyrics Drawings*, ed. Robert Faggen and Alexandra Pleshoyano (New York: Farrar, Straus, and Giroux, 2018), 268–69.

[8] Ray Connolly, "Leonard Cohen," *Evening Standard* (July 1968), www.rayconnolly.co.uk/leonard-cohen/.

[9] Christian Fevret, "Comme un guerrier," *Les Inrocks* (1991), online translation, https://allanshowalter.com/2020/01/02/three-characteristics-that-make-a-song-a-leonard-cohen-song-3-artistic-design-sacred-mechanics/#footnote_3_25469.

[10] Adrian Deevoy, "Porridge? Lozenge? Syringe?," *Q Magazine* (1991), www.leonardcohenfiles.com/qmag.html.

it's the kind of language play that you find in their poetry"),[11] creating songs also involves melody and harmony, arrangement and hooks, an overarching impact on a listener. As tempting as it is with a wordsmith of Cohen's caliber to put too much weight on the lyrics, it is imperative to look at his songwriting in its totality. No matter how impressive the imagery, if nobody wants to hear a song, if the words and the music don't work together to create something bigger than the both of them, a song is a failure.

It is only fair, then, to first consider Cohen's musical work, since he pointed out that this is where his songs often began. "Usually, the tunes were completed before the lyric," he said. "Then, there's that long process of uncovering the lyric, and fitting it to the melody."[12] "He is a much more savvy musician than you'd think," Bob Dylan said to the *New Yorker*'s Remnick. In granting a rare interview for this profile of Cohen, Dylan spoke almost exclusively about the musical skills of one of his few peers. "When people talk about Leonard, they fail to mention his melodies, which to me, along with his lyrics, are his greatest genius," Dylan said. "Even the counterpoint lines – they give a celestial character and melodic lift to every one of his songs. As far as I know, no one else comes close to this in modern music."

"His gift or genius is in his connection to the music of the spheres," Dylan went on. "In the song 'Sisters of Mercy,' for instance, the verses are four elemental lines which change and move at predictable intervals . . . but the tune is anything but predictable. Leonard's always above it all." He offered specific examples of Cohen's harmonic aptitude. "'Sisters of Mercy' is verse after verse of four distinctive lines, in perfect meter, with no chorus, quivering with drama," said Dylan:

> The first line begins in a minor key. The second line goes from minor to major and steps up, and changes melody and variation. The third line steps up even higher than that to a different degree, and then the fourth line comes back to the beginning. This is a deceptively unusual musical theme, with or without lyrics. But it's so subtle a listener doesn't realize

---

[11] Rushdie.
[12] "The John Hammond Years: Interview with John Hammond and Leonard Cohen," BBC TV, September 20, 1986, www.leonardcohenfiles.com/jhammond.html.

he's been taken on a musical journey and dropped off somewhere, with or without lyrics.

Finally, Dylan offered an unexpected comparison:

> He's very much a descendant of Irving Berlin, maybe the only songwriter in modern history that Leonard can be directly related to ... Both of them just hear melodies that most of us can only strive for. Berlin's lyrics also fell into place and consisted of half lines, full lines at surprising intervals, using simple elongated words. Both Leonard and Berlin are incredibly crafty.[13]

(Cohen included a boozed-up, eight-minute cover of Berlin's "Always" on *The Future*.) Maybe all of this focus on Cohen's musical side was a typical Dylan feint, a way to dodge expectations or avoid being forced into a compare–contrast between two writers who are so often linked that there was a "Cohen and Dylan" app comparing their recordings and set lists.

But Dylan is not the only musician who insists that Cohen's greatness rests on more than just his deservedly celebrated lyrics. Jake Shimabukuro is a Hawaiian-born ukulele virtuoso; *Guitar Player* magazine tagged him "the Jimi Hendrix of the ukulele." He has built a huge online following through such mind-blowing, fleet-fingered performances as solo uke arrangements of "Bohemian Rhapsody" and "While My Guitar Gently Weeps," but one of his most popular performances and live staples is his instrumental rendition of "Hallelujah" – a song he was drawn to quite unrelated to the words. "To me, it's not about the lyrics at all," said Shimabukuro when I interviewed him for my book *The Holy or the Broken: Leonard Cohen, Jeff Buckley, and the Unlikely Ascent of "Hallelujah."* "I really think that it has a lot to do with the chord progression in the song. There are these very simple lines that are constantly happening," and, though we were seated in the restaurant of a midtown Manhattan hotel, he stopped to get his instrument out of its case and demonstrate. As he ran through the song's chords, he said, "What I like about it is it picks me up. It's very uplifting, and I think it's the way that the melody moves, the way that the chords move. This is the line that made me want to cover this

---

[13] David Remnick, "Leonard Cohen Makes It Darker," *New Yorker* (October 10, 2016), www.newyorker.com/magazine/2016/10/17/leonard-cohen-makes-it-darker.

song" – he played the melody for the second half of the verse, like the lines "It goes like this: the fourth, the fifth/ The minor fall, the major lift;/ The baffled king composing Hallelujah!" – "that ascending line just does something to me internally that makes me feel good."[14]

"The way the melody is structured is quite genius," said David Miller of the popular classical crossover group Il Divo (who are also among the hundreds of artists who have recorded and performed "Hallelujah" over the years). "It builds, it lifts, then there's always the one word coming back down. It's almost like sex – it builds, it builds, there's that moment, and then the afterglow. To go on that journey, the whole thing taken as an experience, is wonderful."[15] Simply put, for people to want to hear these songs, much less want to sing them, they have to respond to the totality of the composition. They're listening, not reading. They hear a hook, a melody, a phrase before they even have the chance to absorb the words. And those handful of flamenco chords clearly served Cohen well. But then, oh, those words.

When it comes to Leonard Cohen's lyrics, to talk about writing is to talk about rewriting. There's a story that Cohen told on various occasions over the years, to illustrate the contrast between his own process and Bob Dylan's. He said that he and Dylan once met for coffee when they both found themselves in Paris in the mid 1980s. Dylan expressed admiration for Cohen's then obscure composition "Hallelujah" and asked how long it took to write. Cohen replied that it took him a couple of years ("I lied, actually. It was more than a couple of years"). Cohen responded by praising a song of Dylan's on his recent album *Infidels* called "I and I," and inquired how long he needed to write that one. "Fifteen minutes," Dylan responded.[16]

However apocryphal this anecdote is, or how literally we are to take either of their answers, the stark difference between Dylan's desire for creative immediacy and Cohen's painstaking craft is real and significant. "Sometimes I think that I would go along with the old Beat philosophy, 'First thought, best thought'," Cohen once said. "But it never worked for

---

[14] Light, *The Holy or the Broken*, 27. [15] Ibid., 28.
[16] Paul Zollo, "Leonard Cohen: Inside the Tower of Song," *SongTalk* (April 1993).

me. There hardly is a first thought. It's all sweat."[17] The endless revision and perpetual editing, drafting, and altering lyrics that defined Cohen's work remained with him until the end. In 2011, he told *Mojo*'s Sylvie Simmons of one unfinished song that he had been working on for years. "I've got the melody, and it's a guitar tune, a really good tune, and I have tried year after year to find the right words," he said. "The song bothers me so much that I've actually started a journal chronicling my failures to address this obsessive concern with this melody. I would really like to have it on the next record, but I felt that for the past two or three records, maybe four." Cohen played another melody for Simmons on the synthesizer, saying it had been kicking around for "five or ten years." He added that "The Treaty," one of the songs on the *Old Ideas* album, had been in play "easily for fifteen years," while he had been working on another, "Born in Chains," since 1988. "It's not the siege of Stalingrad," he said, "but these are hard nuts to crack."[18]

Ultimately, it is this sense of control and economy, more than anything stylistic, where Cohen's study of and training in poetry impacted his work. He seemed to have a passion for order and discipline – from his fascination with the military to his devotion to the grueling program of meditation during his years at the Zen monastery in Mt. Baldy, California. Cohen claimed that the reason he enjoyed touring later in his life was because he liked having a daily routine. As far back as 1966, he spoke of the focus and patience his writing demanded. "It takes a fantastic inner compulsion [to write]," he said to Jon Ruddy for the Canadian magazine *Maclean's*. "Nobody writes who doesn't really drive himself. I feel secretly that I am much more highly disciplined than anybody I meet."[19] After years of laboring over his poetry, from the beginning his songwriting language seemed fully formed. The clarity of the images – the tea and oranges in "Suzanne," the martyr being seduced by the fire in "Joan of Arc" – scarcely felt like the efforts of a rookie. And over the decades the

---

[17] In *Hallelujah: Leonard Cohen, a Journey, a Song*, dir. Dayna Goldfine and Dan Geller (Sony Pictures Classics, 2022).

[18] Sylvie Simmons, "Bringing It All Back Home," *Mojo* (March 2012).

[19] Jon Ruddy, "Is the World (or Anybody) Ready for Leonard Cohen?," *Maclean's* (October 1, 1966), in *Leonard Cohen on Leonard Cohen: Interviews and Encounters*, ed. Jeff Burger (Chicago: Chicago Review Press, 2014), 9.

specificity of his word choices only sharpened; by the time of 2016's *You Want It Darker*, the album released just days before his death, his lyrics were practically Zen koans (Leonard Koan?) in their sparseness.

Beyond the actual construction of the lyrics, this mastery truly emerged in Cohen's high-wire balance of tone, especially when it came to his twin obsessions – religion and sex. On the one hand, no doubt his themes could be bleak – his songs were tagged "music to slit your wrists by," and he was given the ironic nickname "Laughing Lenny." In 1993, his friend Leon Wieseltier, the literary editor of the *New Republic* and a National Book Award finalist, memorably labelled Cohen "the Prince of Bummers."[20] Trent Reznor worked several Cohen songs into the soundtrack to Oliver Stone's brutal 1994 film *Natural Born Killers*. But Cohen always dismissed the perception of his work as being dour. "I never thought of myself as a particularly solemn person, and I don't think my friends think of me that way," he said. "I understand over the years I acquired this reputation for being a somber chap, and of course we all go through periods where, you know, it's not that funny. But I think there's always been a perspective of letting a little light in somewhere."[21] Actual humor took a while to surface: "I was born like this, I had no choice/ I was born with the gift of a golden voice" in 1988's "Tower of Song," for example (though rhyming "hallelujah" with "what's it to ya?" is actually pretty funny). But the flip from formal or even Biblical language to something more undercutting and earthy was one of Cohen's signature moves. "Who by Fire," from 1974's *New Skin for the Old Ceremony* album, adapts the Yom Kippur prayer "Unetanneh Tokef," which lists all the ways in which members of the congregation standing together at this holy moment might perish in the coming year. Both song and prayer include the lines "Who by fire/ And who by water," and Cohen follows the liturgical structure while straying further from the specifics ("Who in her lonely slip/ Who by barbiturate"). But then each verse lands on the punch line "And who shall I say is calling?"

---

[20] Leon Wieseltier, "The Prince of Bummers," *New Yorker* (July 18, 1993).
[21] Light, *The Holy or the Broken*, 9.

"There has always been something anthemic, something hymn-like about Leonard Cohen's greatest songs," said Salman Rushdie, "though when you start listening closely, you hear his wit and his jaundiced comedy and sometimes his disillusion undermining those hymnal qualities ... There is only one man who writes like this, exploring melancholy and exaltation, desire and loss, as nobody else can."[22] This tension between high and low, sacred and profane, somber and comedic – all achieved in few words, none of them wasted – is something that other songwriters in particular treasure about Cohen's work. "The melody is conversational, the lyrics are Shakespearian" is how Mark Eitzel of the American Music Club described the title track of 1988's *I'm Your Man* album. "'I'd crawl to you baby, and I'd fall at your feet/ And I'd howl at your beauty like a dog in heat' ... He's very casually describing the truth of carnality, of the mortality of mating, of life itself, which is Leonard fucking Cohen. And it's overtly, unapologetically sexual."[23] "It was the way he wrote about complicated things," said Suzanne Vega.

> It was very intimate and personal. Dylan took you to the far ends of the expanding universe, eight minutes of "one hand waving free," and I loved that, but it didn't sound like anything I did or was likely to do – it wasn't very earthly. Leonard's songs were a combination of very real details and a sense of mystery, like prayers or spells.[24]

Shane MacGowan, hard-bitten frontman of the Pogues, expressed admiration for Cohen in his own distinctive way, singling out "Sisters of Mercy" from Cohen's 1967 debut *Songs of Leonard Cohen* as a particular favorite. "What I like about him as a songwriter is the fact he's so vile and cynical," he told UK music magazine *Uncut*. "With pretty tunes. He is a craftsman. I don't respect him at all. But I like his songs ... It's a really hard fucking target, 'Sisters of Mercy.' It's about prostitution, but he manages to make it moving."[25] In that same *Uncut* story, Hal Willner, the longtime *Saturday Night Live* sketch music producer, mastermind of

---

[22] Rushdie.
[23] "Leonard Cohen's 20 Best Songs," *Uncut* (April 3, 2015), www.uncut.co.uk/features/leonard-cohens-20-best-songs-67539/.
[24] Remnick, "Leonard Cohen Makes It Darker." [25] "Leonard Cohen's 20 Best Songs."

acclaimed tribute albums, producer of albums – by Lou Reed, Lucinda Williams, Marianne Faithfull, and many more – and a friend and confidante of Cohen's, talked about the apocalyptic title track to the 1992 album *The Future*. "What a brilliantly bleak song!," he said. "Bring back the Berlin Wall, give us crack and anal sex, Hiroshima and Charles Manson. How can you get more pumped than that? It's sophisticated, but it's also got the power and the emotion you get in the best of his songs." Willner noted that he spent time with Cohen as he was working on this album and observed the duality that he presented within this set of songs. "We often met at a bar and drank strange concoctions of tequila and cranberry juice," he said.

> He was very happy. He was in love, I believe, and he had a lot to say. He was like that cartoon character where the angel appears on one shoulder and the devil on the other. 'The Future' is desperately bleak, but 'Anthem,' on the same album, might be the most uplifting song ever written. It's an amazing mind that can do that.[26]

"Anthem" is undoubtedly one of Cohen's masterpieces, a perfectly nuanced exploration of disappointment and renewal and moral engagement, seamlessly moving from intimate, dirge-like verses to soaring chorus. It's the source of his beloved, oft-quoted line "There is a crack in everything/ That's how the light gets in," which can come off a bit sappy when it's quoted in isolation but really offers defiance and the resistance of survival. It's also one of the songs he wrestled with for an extended period of time; he told Paul Zollo of *Song Talk* that "Anthem" took a decade to write and was recorded multiple times for his previous albums, and that he had been "recycling" lines from his efforts into many other songs. "There was something wrong with the lyric, there was something wrong with the tune, there was something wrong with the tempo," he said. "There was a lie somewhere in there. There was a disclosure that I was refusing to make."[27]

The Future was largely inspired by a time of global chaos and conflict – the First Gulf War, Tiananmen Square, the Los Angeles

---

[26] Ibid. [27] Zollo, "Leonard Cohen."

riots (Cohen could see the fires burning from his house) – and the tracks that got the most attention at the time were "The Future" and the even more jaded "Everybody Knows" ("Everybody knows the war is over/ Everybody knows that the good guys lost"). But it was "Anthem" that would prove sturdiest. It's hopeful but scarred, wise with experience but not cynicism. In the face of injustice, he promises action: "The killers in high places say their prayers out loud/ But they've summoned up a thundercloud/ They're going to hear from me." It's no surprise that in the miasma of the 2020s, references to "Anthem" continue to appear, most recently in songs by Lana Del Rey and by indie supergroup boygenius. "I think it is one of the best songs I have written, maybe the best," Cohen told the *Los Angeles Times* in 1995. "I knew that song was everything that my whole work and life had somehow gathered around."[28]

Many Cohen fans would offer "Anthem" as their favorite of his songs (forced to answer, most days I'd probably go for "Tower of Song" myself), but of course the one that defines him to most of the world is "Hallelujah." Ignored when it was first released, it has become one of the best-loved, best-known, most-performed songs around the world. When Cohen died, his obituary ran on the front page of the *New York Times*; the headline identified him as "Writer of 'Hallelujah' Whose Lyrics Captivated Generations." "Hallelujah" is sung at weddings and at funerals, on televised singing competition shows (endlessly) and in religious services, at official state functions, and heavy metal shows. It has, for reasons not entirely clear, become a popular Christmas song. These occasions aren't always a comfortable fit for a complex and ambiguous set of lyrics. The verses touch on the Biblical figures King David and Samson, but offer such charged language as "I remember when I moved in you,/ And the holy dove was moving too," and "all I ever learned from love/ Is how to shoot at someone who outdrew you." Yet the song also returns and lands, each time around, on the reassurance and celebration of the title, which serves as a repeated, single-word chorus.

---

[28] Robert Hilburn, "Telling It on the Mountain," *Los Angeles Times* (September 24, 1995).

The focus given to the hymnlike incantation of "hallelujah," in contrast to the romantic and spiritual challenges evoked by the verses (along with the fact that the song was so obscure in its initial release), has given it a unique malleability. It's acceptable, even commonplace for verses to be dropped or moved – Cohen himself started changing the lyrics onstage immediately after the original recording came out – and, unlike such comparable, monumental songs as "Imagine" or "Bridge over Troubled Water" or "A Change Is Gonna Come," there is no truly definitive version.

The mysterious, even opaque imagery of "Hallelujah" has rendered the song something of a musical Rorschach test. Singer-songwriter Brandi Carlile, who does not hesitate to refer to "Hallelujah" as "the greatest song ever written," said that it provided her with the key for reconciling her Christian faith and her homosexuality. "To me, it really outlined how people tend to misconstrue religion versus faith," she said.

> I felt that this song was, in a really pure, realistic way, describing what "hallelujah" actually is. "It's not a cry that you hear at night,/ It's not somebody that's seen the light" – "hallelujah" is not something that you shout out on Sunday in a happy voice; it's something that happens in a way that's cold and broken and lonely. And that's how I was feeling at the time.[29]

But for Alexandra Burke, who won the 2008 season of *X Factor* in the UK with a version of the song that went to Number 1 in the charts, "to anyone who's a Christian, that word *hallelujah* – full stop, that's what you're going to hear."[30] To the acclaimed, offbeat singer-songwriter Regina Spektor, Cohen is "using traditional Jewish stories and history, and having gone to yeshiva and studied those stories, all the biblical things are an extra place for my mind to go."[31] For Rabbi Ruth Gan Kagan, who has included "Hallelujah" in the Yom Kippur service at the Nava Tehila congregation in Jerusalem, "it's a hymn of the heretic, a *piyut* [liturgical poem] of a modern, doubtful person."[32] Other responses are more secular. "I got the sexuality in the song right

---

[29] Light, *The Holy or the Broken*, xxxv.   [30] Ibid., xxxvi.   [31] Ibid.   [32] Ibid.

away," said Jon Bon Jovi. "The chorus is like the climax, the rest is like foreplay."[33] For some, it's this very ability of "Hallelujah" to contain multitudes, to embrace contradictions, that gives it such power. "The interesting thing that Leonard Cohen is able to do," said Justin Timberlake, who performed "Hallelujah" at the 2010 benefit telethon following the earthquake in Haiti, "which equates to some of my favorite actors, is that he never makes you choose what to feel. He just gives you, like, a three-pronged road, and you can take whichever path you like. That's the beauty of all of his work."[34]

Well, maybe not all. The circumstances surrounding "Hallelujah" are specific, allowing Cohen's plea for hard-fought perseverance to adapt and adjust and evolve in a way that no other pop song has done before. This one time, the nuance and shading and complex imagery constructed by Cohen became untethered from its creation, enabling the song to assume infinite meanings for millions of listeners. Assigning meaning to songs is a tricky business, anyway – ask Bruce Springsteen about "Born in the USA" or R.E.M. about "The One I Love." Once a song is released into the wild, it's not the artist's any more: it belongs to the audience to do with and make of what they will.

With his Zen training, Cohen seemed to accept the unprecedented trajectory of "Hallelujah" with some amusement. But his own faith in his songwriting, with all its hard-fought intention, its elegance and clarity, never wavered, whether the result was the harrowing "Dress Rehearsal Rag," the merciful "Come Healing," the bittersweetly romantic "So Long, Marianne." The torment of his process, the pain associated with creation, was rewarded with each particular truth he wished to convey. "I've only learned one thing from writing songs," he said, "and that is, if you stay with it long enough, the song will yield. You burn away those versions of yourself, your courage, and your modesty until you get something irreducible."[35] Cohen put it more succinctly in a 1988 radio interview. "I had to revise my work," he said, "until it became the only possible song I could sing."[36]

---

[33] Ibid.   [34] Ibid.
[35] Tom Moon, "Painstaking Effort Pays off in Leonard Cohen's Future," *Philadelphia Inquirer* (January 4, 1993).
[36] Kristine McKenna, "Eight Hours to Harry," KCRW-FM (October 1988).

CHAPTER 4

Assembling Albums in the Tower of Song

Anthony DeCurtis

"LEONARD COHEN ONCE SAID/ 'THERE IS A CRACK IN everything/ That's how the light gets in'," Lucy Dacus sings on "Leonard Cohen," a track on *The Record*, the 2023 debut album by boygenius. "And I am not an old man having an existential crisis/ At a Buddhist monastery writing horny poetry," she continues, "But I agree." A collaboration by three young female songwriters – Dacus, Phoebe Bridgers, and Julien Baker – the group boygenius is, in part, a send-up of self-regarding male artists who, in the view of the trio, have been taught never to question their genius. (The girls even take the stage to the roar of Thin Lizzy's "The Boys Are back in Town.") The reference to one of Cohen's best-known lines from his song "Anthem" is, fittingly, both admiring and a dig. Setting aside whether Cohen, indeed, wrote "Anthem" at the California Zen retreat he frequented on Mt. Baldy (unlikely, since it took ten years to write and he cowrote it with his girlfriend, the actress Rebecca De Mornay), boygenius punctures the seriousness and spiritual ambition of Cohen's writing while simultaneously paying tribute to it. No doubt, everyone recalls Kurt Cobain's wish in his 1993 song "Pennyroyal Tea" for a "Leonard Cohen afterworld/ So I can sigh eternally."

Among other meanings, however, boygenius's reference to "Anthem" (from Cohen's 1992 album *The Future*) in the song that bears his name is a telling example of precisely how Cohen's admirers, young and old, hold him in their esteem: by citing specific songs and quoting specific lyrics. The most dramatic examples of that, needless to say, are the innumerable versions, interpretations, and references to his song "Hallelujah," from his 1984 album, *Various Positions*. But perhaps more so than with any major artist of his generation, Cohen's albums tend to be lost in comparison to the regard for his songs. That may well have to do with his career as a poet or what, for want of a better term, we might call his perfectionism. "The song will yield if you stick with it long enough," he explained to me one time. "But long enough is way beyond any reasonable idea you might have of what long enough is. It takes that long to peel the bullshit off."[1] If every song requires that degree of literary and psychological commitment – we're all well aware of the dozens of verses, for example, that he wrote for "Hallelujah" over the course of years – it's difficult, not to say impossible, to conceive of entire albums as a whole and then write in accordance with whatever concept you've devised. "I always experience myself as falling apart, and I'm taking emergency measures," he said.

> It's coming apart at every moment. I try Prozac. I try love. I try drugs. I try Zen meditation. I try the monastery. I try forgetting about all those strategies and going straight. And the place where the evaluation happens is where I write the songs, when I get to that place where I can't be dishonest about what I've been doing.[2]

Cohen himself seemed indirectly to acknowledge this struggle with the very titles of his albums, which often defined themselves as collections of individual songs rather than as larger, cohesive statements with an overarching theme. That began with his debut *Songs of Leonard Cohen* in 1967. After that came, intermittently, *Songs from a Room* (1969), *Songs of Love and Hate* (1971), *Recent Songs* (1979), and *Ten New Songs* (2001). Beyond that, Cohen regularly released live albums that drew on songs from throughout his career, and artists like Judy Collins and Jennifer Warnes, among others, recorded entire albums dedicated to his songs from various different albums. Finally, Cohen's ongoing impact on other artists, particularly younger ones, manifested in a series of tribute albums, on which performers ranging from the Pixies to Trisha Yearwood, from R.E.M. to Nick Cave and the Bad Seeds, chose specific songs of his to interpret.

---

[1] Anthony DeCurtis, "No Mercy: Leonard Cohen's Tales from the Dark Side," in his *Rocking My Life Away: Writing about Music and Other Matters* (Durham, NC: Duke University Press, 1998), 89. (Originally published in *Rolling Stone* [January 23, 1993].)

[2] Ibid., 87.

You could argue that such titles employing the word "Songs" are typical Cohen deflections, a characteristic method of diminishing expectations in order, conversely, to have the songs themselves hit with undiminished power. And it's certainly not to suggest that Cohen did not occasionally create albums of quite extraordinary mastery. It's more a function of the consistency of Cohen's writing, the way in which his entire career unfurls like one long, ever-evolving song. There are variances, of course, and shifts in direction, in instrumentation, in literary style. And certainly his writing, like his voice, deepened as he aged. But more remarkable is the stability and regularity of his writing over the course of a nearly five-decades-long career.

In subtle ways, each of his albums reflects the times and personal circumstances in which they were created. But would we know that if we didn't have the contextual knowledge of his interviews and the biographies and memoirs written about him? How far removed is "A Thousand Kisses Deep," which appears on *Ten New Songs*, from "One of Us Cannot Be Wrong," from his debut? "You Want It Darker" from "Last Year's Man"? Any discerning listener can parse the differences among those songs, but what exactly makes one early and another mid or late period?

Cohen was already a recognized poet and novelist when, at the age of thirty-three, he released *Songs of Leonard Cohen*. That album came out in the year of the "summer of love," a time when no self-respecting young person was supposed to trust anyone over thirty. But at that age and with his refined literary experience, Cohen did not need to search for his voice. His themes and his concerns, his approach, and his ideas had already been defined. The songwriting struggles he talks about were the battles of an artist desperate to create work that met his own rigorous standard, a standard he had already fully established. His concerns always reflected the concerns of a fully grown adult. He once said, "it's wonderful to hear from a guy who's talking about his first love – especially, if it's Rimbaud. If it isn't Rimbaud, it's not so interesting as you get older."[3] His interests, really, were never the stuff of pop songs.

That accounts for the authority that's so evident on *Songs of Leonard Cohen*, one of the most stunning debut albums in history. It's an album

---

[3] Ibid., 92.

that's lost none of its aesthetic force over the years. In liner notes I wrote for the album in 2007, I remarked upon "how thoroughly this album maps the territory that Cohen would explore throughout his career. There are songs about women, and songs about love; songs about power and the illusion of power; songs about the body and songs about the spirit; songs about finding what you think you want, and songs about endless searching."[4] In ways that no one could have known at the time, Cohen provided a template for all the work that would come after.

For that reason, even if Cohen had stopped recording after that debut, he would still be regarded as among the greatest songwriters of our time. "Suzanne," "Sisters of Mercy," "So Long, Marianne," and "Hey, That's No Way to Say Goodbye" all would still have taken their place among Cohen's best-loved standards – and the best-loved standards of their time. But the mystery that resides at the heart of all of Cohen's work is perhaps most evident in "The Stranger Song," which was partly inspired by the 1955 film *The Man with the Golden Arm*. Despite – because of? – the startling imagery that runs through the song – "He was just some Joseph looking for a manger"; "while he talks his dreams to sleep, you notice there's a highway that is curling up like smoke above his shoulder" – its meanings shift in complicated ways. The references to "dealers" in the song suggest both drugs and gambling, two addictions that, while denoting need and unreliability, seemingly offer deliverance from the quotidian tedium of life in a conventional committed relationship.

What is so extraordinary about Cohen, however, is that the song's brilliant lines and striking imagery manage both to be indelible and conversational, as if they had just occurred to the singer at the instant of performance as the inevitable way that a particular thought or observation needed to be expressed. "It's hard to hold the hand of anyone who is reaching for the sky just to surrender," Cohen sings. At another moment he sings, "Like any dealer he was watching for the card that is so high and wild he'll never need to deal another." The limitations of Cohen's voice, needless to say, contribute to that conversational quality he manifests so naturally. He sings with force and clarity, never attempting vocal effects – at

---

[4] Anthony DeCurtis, liner notes for the reissue of *Songs of Leonard Cohen* (Legacy Recordings, 2007).

least in part because he is incapable of them – with the intention of selling the meaning of what he has to say. His melodies are simple and beautiful, but he means for his words to do all the necessary work. And that they do.

As for what the song is ultimately about, it makes sense that it's not easy to figure that out. It's "The Stranger Song," after all – a song about a stranger, or a series of strangers, or the nature of strangers, or the quality of strangeness itself. It is also "The Stranger Song," the song that is stranger than other songs, a song that revels in its own mysteries. It is another example of Cohen's emphasis on "song" in the very title: the song is a work of art, a story, not a piece of autobiography or pages from a journal. Finally, though, the song is not only about the difficulty of truly knowing another person, but the difficulty of knowing yourself. After exploring a series of her failed relationships with the woman whom he is addressing in the song, relationships with men who would forever remain strangers to her, men whom she could never come to know, Cohen unsentimentally turns the focus on her and declares, simply, "It is you, my love, you who are the stranger."

So much of what Cohen would do for the next half century was fully established in "The Stranger Song," and on *Songs of Leonard Cohen*, in general: the lyrics that achieve an incomparable degree of literacy, an obsessive fascination with complexity; a conviction to explore the furthest reaches of both erotic desire and spiritual aspiration; a voice that intimates truths and insights, but never certainty, never the knowingness that ends a conversation. That voice, so unaffected, direct, and masculine, is routinely accompanied by gentler, more beautiful female voices in a sung dance that is both sensual and elegant. If his words in his own voice convey his meanings, the female voices transport the listener to a realm of suggestiveness and pleasure beyond literal meaning. While Cohen complained endlessly about the "sweetening" that producer John Simon employed to provide texture to his sparse songs, Cohen would employ similar effects throughout his career, though always according to his own dictates.[5]

---

[5] Stephen Deusner, "Alienated Old Man Creates Some Sad Music," *Los Angeles Review of Books* (July 1, 2014), https://lareviewofbooks.org/article/alienated-old-man-creates-sad-music/.

Such was the template created on *Songs of Leonard Cohen*, to the degree that, with a few notable exceptions, every one of his subsequent albums could have shared that name. *Songs from a Room* sets out, in its way, to correct the problems that Cohen believed afflicted his debut, and in that regard it stands fully in its predecessor's shadow. Working with producer Bob Johnston, Cohen kept the album as spare-sounding as possible, a strategy that led to some questioning reviews. "Well, it looks like Leonard Cohen's second try won't have them dancing in the streets either," *Rolling Stone* announced. "It doesn't take a great deal of listening to realize that Cohen can't sing, period."[6] The album's sparseness also solidified the early – and, admittedly, philistine – impression of Cohen as a doom-obsessed depressive.

The album's opening song, "Bird on the Wire," however, quickly took its place among Cohen's classics, inspiring many covers. Kris Kristofferson famously declared that he wanted to use the song's opening lines ("Like a bird on the wire/ Like a drunk in a midnight choir/ I have tried in my way to be free") as his epitaph.[7] Its place at the top of the album seemed designed to reassure anyone who wondered if he could live up to the standard of the handful of masterpieces on *Songs of Leonard Cohen*. But the album's darkness is undeniable. The agonizing suicide in "Seems So Long Ago, Nancy" and the casual, plainspoken drug references in "The Butcher" ("I found a silver needle/ I put it into my arm/ It did some good/ Did some harm") recall the roughly contemporaneous album *Berlin* (1973) by Lou Reed, one of Cohen's great admirers. (Reed, in fact, would induct Cohen into the Rock & Roll Hall of Fame in 2008.)[8]

Indeed, "the European blues," the description that Cohen applied to his third album, *Songs of Love and Hate*, suits *Berlin* just as accurately.[9] The

---

[6] Alec Dubro, review of *Songs from a Room* by Leonard Cohen, *Rolling Stone* (May 17, 1969), www.rollingstone.com/music/music-album-reviews/songs-from-a-room-98486/.

[7] Jim Beviglia, "Behind the Song: Leonard Cohen, 'Bird on the Wire'," *American Songwriter*, 2019, https://americansongwriter.com/behind-the-song-leonard-cohen-bird-on-a-wire.

[8] Lou Reed, induction speech for Leonard Cohen, Rock & Roll Hall of Fame Induction Ceremony (March 10, 2008), "Induction of Leonard Cohen," www.youtube.com/watch?v=t9IZfiHEgd8.

[9] Harvey Kubernik, "Cohen's New Skin," *Melody Maker* (March 1, 1975), https://wearecult.rocks/leonard-cohen-archive-interview-cohens-new-skin-1975.

album's title, once again, could equally apply to any of Cohen's albums, as long as it was understood that love and hate were not perceived as opposites but as emotions inextricably entwined and coexisting in every relationship. Cohen attempted to broaden his sound on the album, with Paul Buckmaster providing string and horn arrangements. He also included a live track, "Sing Another Song, Boys," which he had performed in front of more than half a million people at the Isle of Wight Festival in 1970. Like his previous two albums, *Songs of Love and Hate* failed to significantly broaden Cohen's audience, particularly in the United States. Still, as usual, a number of specific songs emerged to take their place in the Cohen canon. Most notable among these are "Avalanche," "Dress Rehearsal Rag" (which Judy Collins had recorded years before), and, in particular, "Famous Blue Raincoat," which became the title track of Jennifer Warnes' splendid album of Cohen's songs.

New Skin for the Old Ceremony (1974) introduced John Lissauer as Cohen's producer and attempted, once again, to expand Cohen's commercial appeal by broadening his sound and trimming the length of his songs. (Only two of the album's eleven songs edge slightly above four minutes, and the album itself runs just over thirty-seven minutes.) Despite being one of Cohen's strongest collections, the album failed to crack the Billboard 100, the first of his albums to do so. "Chelsea Hotel No. 2" soon became one of Cohen's best-known songs, not least due to its off-handed reference to his receiving oral sex ("giving me head on the unmade bed") from a woman he later revealed to be Janis Joplin. Cohen described the song as "an indiscretion." He further explained that:

> I don't know how it got out, but it did. I said it somewhere. I may have been juiced at a concert and spoken about it in a way that seemed appropriate at the moment – and I have regretted it. There's nothing I can do about it. If I could do it again, I would have kept my mouth shut.[10]

Interestingly, female artists, including Lana Del Rey and Meshell Ndegeocello, have countered the song's casual male bravado in the most effective way: by performing the song themselves.

---

[10] DeCurtis, "No Mercy," 91–92.

Given that, at least in part, Cohen had become interested in a career in music as a way to make money, his failing commercial prospects became a matter of some concern, both to him and those around him. As the 1970s progressed, the free-wheeling music industry of the 1950s and 1960s became more of a business, with record companies and music executives in general becoming much more aware of how much money record sales and live performances could generate. While he wanted success, Cohen was realistic about what he was likely to achieve – and he had no inclination to compromise the standards of his work.

Still, when his manager at the time concocted the deranged idea of his working with producer Phil Spector, Cohen went along with it, however reluctantly. The result, *Death of a Ladies' Man* (1977), is surely the strangest product of Cohen's lengthy musical career. Both Cohen and Spector were drinking heavily at the time, and along with characteristically using dozens of musicians on the sessions, unnerving Cohen, who typically liked to keep things tight in the studio, Spector regularly engaged in gun play, a terrifying harbinger of events to come later in his life. The two men cowrote the album's eight songs, and the album's bombastic sound and poorly recorded vocals (Spector ran off with the album's tapes before Cohen could redo what he regarded merely as guide vocals) doomed it to poor reviews and, yet again, nonexistent sales. One might have hoped that a Leonard Cohen session with Bob Dylan and Allen Ginsberg on hand to deliver background vocals would have yielded something more poetic than "Don't Go Home with Your Hard-On," but that hope would be disappointed. With the exception of "Memories," Cohen would rarely perform any songs from the album onstage, and it inspired few covers.

"It has its admirers," Cohen admitted, begrudgingly, about the album, while describing it as "a grotesque, eccentric little moment." Spector, he said:

> was in his Wagnerian phase, when I had hoped to find him in his Debussy phase ... I was holding on for dear life. My family was breaking up at the time – just to show up was rough. Then I'd have to go through this ninth-rate military film noir atmosphere. I've never forgotten Phil coming towards me with a bottle of Manischewitz in one hand, a .45 in the other

and putting his arm around my shoulder, shoving the gun into my neck, cocking it and saying, "Leonard, I love you." It wasn't that much fun.[11]

As its title would suggest, Cohen attempted a return to form with *Recent Songs* (1979), and largely succeeded. For production, he turned to Henry Lewy on the suggestion of fellow Canadian genius Joni Mitchell, with whom Lewy had previously worked. Like *Songs from a Room*, *Recent Songs* stands as much as an effort to correct the perceived excesses of its predecessor as an album in its own right. In opposition to the sonic chaos of *Death of a Ladies' Man*, Lewy crafts musical settings that are tasteful and discreet to the point of near-tedium. Cohen writes with typical brilliance, particularly on "Came So Far for Beauty" (cowritten with Jon Lissauer) and "Ballad of the Absent Mare," but none of these ten songs rise to his top tier.

Various Positions (1984) would ironically become one of Cohen's most celebrated albums, primarily due to Columbia's refusal to release it in the United States. That was an insult, of course, one that Cohen never forgot. People understandably mock Columbia president Walter Yetnikoff's casual dismissal of Cohen at the time: "Look, Leonard, we know you're great, but we don't know if you're any good."[12] Appalling, if hilarious, that remark needs to be understood as a frustrated record executive's response to a prestige artist who has failed to sell any records during what was quickly becoming the industry's commercial peak. "Hallelujah," one of the tracks on *Various Positions* and now the song for which Cohen is best remembered, only gained its notoriety through the extraordinary covers it inspired. Cohen's version is barely known, even today. Of course, "Dance Me to the End of Love" would become a Cohen classic, though in performances and arrangements far different from the one that opens *Various Positions*.

Interestingly, after that low point, Cohen released two of his most important and most cohesive albums: *I'm Your Man* (1988) and *The Future* (1992). *I'm Your Man* is suffused with sexual references that, while hardly

---

[11] Ibid., 92.
[12] Richard von Busack, "'Hallelujah' Traces the Arc of Leonard Cohen's Career via the Evolution of His Most Iconic Song," *San Francisco Standard* (July 4, 2022), https://sfstandard.com/2022/07/04/hallelujah-traces-arc-of-leonard-cohens-career-via-the-evolution-of-his-most-iconic-song/.

a departure for Cohen, capture the anxiety about the AIDS crisis that permeated society at that point. The tension that he had always located in love relationships (*Songs of Love and Hate*, indeed) found a perfect referent in the predominant anxiety of the times, as songs like "Ain't No Cure for Love" and "Everybody Knows" demonstrate. Released the year before the fall of the Berlin Wall, "First We Take Manhattan" channels the unease underlying the seeming triumph of capitalism. Finally, the album ends with "Tower of Song," a song so close to Cohen's heart that reciting its lyrics constituted his acceptance speech when he was inducted into the Rock & Roll Hall of Fame in 2008.[13] The song is a humorous, self-deprecating but deeply felt honoring of the songwriter's calling. It says a great deal about how he viewed himself.

As did *I'm Your Man*, *The Future* continued the modernization of Cohen's sound. Rhythmically, the album moves in sleek, contemporary ways, incorporating synthesized elements not merely as coloring but as driving parts of the rhythm. And again, like *I'm Your Man*, *The Future* takes big swings thematically – very much beginning with its title. Historically, Cohen had travelled deeper and deeper into his explorations of his characters' psychosexual lives. That focus did not relent on these two albums, but it's as if he had determined to examine the reality that those characters were living in a bigger world that was every bit as complex, dangerous, and shaky as any of the fault lines within their personal lives. "The record involved a four-year struggle; the songs, some of them, are eight, ten years in the works," he said about *The Future*. "The record is there for keeps. There's flesh and blood attached to it. I did what was necessary, and I sit here kind of wrecked."[14]

The Future was, in part, inspired – which hardly seems the appropriate word – by the riots in Los Angeles that followed the acquittals of the police involved in the beating of Rodney King. Fires raged in the city, many not far from where Cohen was living. He could see them and smell

---

[13] Leonard Cohen, acceptance speech at Rock & Roll Hall of Fame Induction Ceremony (March 10, 2008), "Induction of Leonard Cohen," www.youtube.com/watch?v=t9IZfiHEgd8&t=35s.

[14] DeCurtis, "No Mercy," 89.

the smoke from his balcony. "People seem to know what 'The Future' is about," Cohen said about the album's title track:

> It's humorous, there's irony, there's all kinds of distances from the event that made the song possible. It's art. It's a good dance track, it's a hot number. It's captivating – it's even got hope. But the place where the song comes from is a life-threatening situation. You've got to go to some risky terrain. That's why the record takes so long to make, and that's why you're shattered at the end of it.[15]

As always with Cohen, getting to that final point with the song was a harrowing journey. "'The Future' began as a song called 'If You Could See What's Coming Next.' That point of view was a deflected point of view. I didn't have the guts to say, 'I've seen the future, baby/ It is murder.' The song was more observational, on the edge of the action."[16] Along with "The Future," the songs "Waiting for the Miracle," "Closing Time," "Anthem," and "Democracy" all earned a hallowed place in the Cohen canon.

After *The Future* and until his death in 2016, Cohen returned to making albums that were more significant for individual songs than for their larger statements. He titled his album succeeding *The Future*, *Ten New Songs* (2001), a return to his tendency to emphasize his releases as collections of songs rather than cohesive albums. He wanted to title his next album *Old Ideas*, but at the urging of his record label opted for *Dear Heather* (2004) instead. He ended up using *Old Ideas* as the title of his 2012 album release, yet another indication of the degree to which he regarded his albums as, if not exactly interchangeable, consistent in their themes and focuses, like chapters in a long book rather than entirely independent works of their own.

During this final phase of Cohen's career, other factors conspired to emphasize individual songs rather than his albums. Of course, by this point "Hallelujah" was continuing its ascent to becoming one of the best-known songs of our time, enjoying hundreds of cover versions. When it became known that Cohen's manager had stolen virtually his entire life savings, he devoted himself to touring in order to make back some of the money he had lost. Those shows became legendary, often running longer

---

[15] Ibid., 90. [16] Ibid., 89.

than three hours and familiarizing fans both old and young with his extraordinary song catalog. Live albums and best-of collections satisfied the new demand of fans for work with which they may have been completely unfamiliar previously.

On tour and on the albums released during his final decades, he continued – and, indeed, extended – his collaborations with women as singers, cowriters, and producers, including Sharon Robinson (who appears with him on the cover of *Ten New Songs*), Rebecca De Mornay (to whom *The Future* is dedicated), Jennifer Warnes, and Anjani Thomas. Indeed, Cohen produced and cowrote all the songs on Thomas's 2006 album *Blue Alert*, and her haunting vocals render her a kind of psychosexual doppelganger for Cohen. Of course, during this period, Cohen also worked closely with Patrick Leonard, who is perhaps best known for producing Madonna, as well as with his son, Adam Cohen.

Cohen's most cohesive album during his final years is *You Want It Darker*, which came out fewer than three weeks before his death in 2016 at the age of eighty-two. Cohen was ill while making the record, and the album is rightly heard as a meditation on mortality. But then what album of Cohen's isn't? The album's music is quiet and haunting, and Cohen's voice, while still wonderfully expressive, is shaky, which suits the album's theme. The album's title could be read as Cohen's final, ironic challenge to listeners (very much including me, to be honest) who resisted any of his attempts at light-heartedness. It's a question delivered as a statement, and it captures a final note of defiance. A posthumous collection, *Thanks for the Dance*, appeared in 2019, under the guidance of Adam Cohen. Clocking in at under half an hour, it consisted of nine songs Cohen had worked on during and after the recording of *You Want It Darker*, and to that extent is an extension of that album.

If you wanted to make a point – a point along the lines, I suppose, of the one I've been making throughout this piece – you could argue that those final two albums could easily have come out earlier in Cohen's career. After all, which of his albums are not death-haunted, gripped by a raw sense of the simultaneous intensity and ephemerality of life? But that's hardly necessary. It displays a lack of respect for the degree to which Cohen maintained a supremely high standard in his work, even as he struggled with infirmity and neared death. *You Want It Darker* has often been compared to *Black Star*, the album David Bowie released two days before his death in 2016. Both men took their identity as artists with absolute seriousness and saw no need to relinquish their lives' purpose even as those lives drew to a close.

In Cohen's case, what matters more than the degree to which he should be celebrated for his songs than for his albums is that his recording career truly is like the creation of one long album with very few dips below the best work that has been done in the history of popular music. That was as he intended. "Those questions are hammered out in the workshop," Cohen said about the process of songwriting.

> They have urgency, because you really do see the years, you really see the end. I think as long as you can crawl into the workshop, you should do the work. I always saw those old guys coming down to work, whatever job I happened to be in. Something about that always got to me. I'd like to be one of those old guys going to work.[17]

---

[17] Ibid., 93.

PART II

MUSICAL CONTEXTS

CHAPTER 5

Folk Music

Gillian A. M. Mitchell

WHEN, IN THE LATE 1960S, LEONARD COHEN FIRST GARNERED significant attention for his musical work, he was frequently described as a "folksinger." In some cases, this categorization was entirely casual and based largely on the fact that his performance style broadly resembled those of the influential folk-style musicians who had dominated the music scene earlier in the decade. The perception that he was "the next Bob Dylan" became particularly prevalent as observers noted certain characteristics shared by the two performers – in particular, their profound lyrics and their unpolished vocal styles. Comparisons between the two artistes, however justified, persisted throughout their respective careers – as did the belief that both had originally been folk musicians.

Cohen, however, was a latecomer to the folk scene. His first album, *Songs of Leonard Cohen* (1967), was released after the folk revival had peaked, both artistically and commercially. The "great boom" in the popularity of folk music, particularly among younger, middle-class audiences, occurred in North America from the late 1950s to the early 1960s. "Folk," to this audience, broadly connoted music which embodied particular ethnic or community traditions, and which deployed acoustic and traditional instrumentation; the definition was inexact, and widely debated, but the term was generally applied to music which possessed (and to contemporary works which emulated) such qualities.[1] An earlier folk revival, straddling the war years, had,

---

[1] See Robert Cantwell's description of the revivalists' understanding of "folk" in "When We Were Good: Class and Culture in the Folk Revival," in *Transforming Tradition: Folk Music Revivals Examined*, ed. Neil Rosenberg (Urbana: University of Illinois Press, 1993), 35–36. The term "great boom" was coined by Neil Rosenberg. See Rosenberg,

among its most prominent figureheads, the folk-blues performer Huddie Ledbetter (Lead Belly), the Oklahoman writer-singer Woody Guthrie, and the Harvard-educated Pete Seeger. Using vernacular music styles to champion union causes, anti-fascism, and (increasingly) civil rights for African Americans, the early movement fell afoul of anti-communist forces in the 1950s, but, while Lead Belly had died in 1949 and Guthrie was increasingly debilitated by illness, Seeger, despite ongoing harassment from authorities, continued performing and became an inspiration to a younger generation of middle-class North Americans who sought meaningful alternatives to the conformism of contemporary society. The 1960s revival maintained its politically active stance – its association with civil rights growing particularly strong – and, while some young musicians devoted themselves to "pure" traditional styles which they considered uncorrupted by commercial influence, the revival, in reality, was a musically diverse movement, actively embracing a myriad forms of folk music, in keeping with its culturally inclusive ideals. Original songwriting in the folk vein, which reflected poetically the realities of contemporary politics and culture, became particularly prized by many revivalists, and, by the early 1960s, the young Bob Dylan, a protégé of Seeger's, was being lauded as "the most important new songwriter of the time," via his distinctive blend of complex, socially conscious lyrics and folk-style melodies.[2]

By 1965, the folk "boom" seemed, largely, to be waning. Dylan had increasingly disassociated himself from the organized folk movement, eschewing his status as its "spokesman" – his adoption of electric instrumentation was frequently considered a betrayal of anti-commercial folk ideals – and while, for some, this disavowal hastened the "death" of the revival, it is perhaps more accurate to state that the popular music scene, within which Dylan and his peers operated, merely continued to evolve,

"Introduction," ibid., 2. I originally explored many of the broader sociocultural aspects of the revival highlighted in this chapter in *The North American Folk Music Revival: Nation and Identity in the United States and Canada, 1945–1970* (Aldershot; Burlington, VT: Ashgate, 2007).

[2] Words of Robert Shelton, describing Seeger's opinion of Dylan, quoted in Benjamin Filene, *Romancing the Folk: Public Memory and American Roots Music* (Chapel Hill; London: University of North Carolina Press, 2000), 210.

just as the political and cultural climate altered around them.[3] Folk survived, becoming an integral ingredient of an increasingly experimental and diverse late 1960s rock scene.

Leonard Cohen emerged as a singer during this transitional phase of rock history; as his musical career gathered momentum in the early 1970s, the "folk" label which critics assigned to him tended, increasingly, to be replaced by that of "singer-songwriter" – a category into which many performers with links to the earlier folk revival (including Paul Simon, fellow Canadians Joni Mitchell and Gordon Lightfoot, and Dylan himself) found themselves placed as they continued to develop as perceptive and reflective composers. While political songwriting by no means disappeared, many former revivalists seemed more hesitant, amid the incendiary contemporary climate, to set their thoughts on current affairs straightforwardly to music, and, indeed, Cohen's songs seldom engaged overtly with politics. His tendency to reflect, instead, on personal and interior matters was more in keeping with the approaches taken by many of the songwriting veterans of the revival. However, the prizing of songwriting skills became essential to the "serious" later 1960s music scene, and Cohen's complex, poetic work played an integral role in furthering perceptions of popular music as an art form.

Nevertheless, while Cohen himself was hesitant to deploy labels to describe his work as he transitioned tentatively from poet–novelist to lyricist–composer, to consider him as a "folk" artist, particularly in the early stages of his musical career, is by no means erroneous. This chapter examines Leonard Cohen's relationship with folk music by considering, firstly, his formative interests in the genre and the manifestation of these in his earliest musical activities; secondly, by examining his tangible connections with the North American folk scene, as his singing career developed; and thirdly, by considering the ways in which his work could be, and was, considered "folk." While the frequent comparisons which were made between Dylan and Cohen were often simplistic and somewhat reductive, to consider the temporary construction of Cohen as "the Canadian Dylan" (a title to which Cohen allegedly once claimed to aspire, although he subsequently denied this) nevertheless provides

---

[3] Ibid., 212.

significant insights into the character of the later 1960s music scene, and the ways in which artistes like Cohen handled critical expectations and preconceptions as they sought to evolve their craft and hone their own distinctive musical personae. If Cohen was too late to contribute extensively to the folk "boom," his early career as a professional musician certainly illustrated the lingering, complex, and pervasive influence of folk – as a musical form and as a set of broad artistic ideals – upon the wider popular music world of the later 1960s.

EARLY INTERESTS IN FOLK MUSIC

Participants in the 1960s folk revival were, archetypically, young, middle class, well educated, and politically conscious, either as a reaction against their sterile, affluent upbringings, or via inherited familial allegiances. Jewish participants, often from politically left-leaning families, frequently played prominent roles within the revival. Many of these youngsters had first encountered folk-style music in the 1950s, via left-wing summer camps, such as Camp Kinderland or Camp Woodland, which promoted "progressive, secular Jewish" values for participants.[4] Folk-style music, with its leftist aura, frequently underpinned camp activities.[5]

Most Cohen biographies concur that the singer's first encounters with folk music occurred at such a camp. Cohen's privileged, relatively conservative, upbringing in the wealthy Jewish community of Westmount, Montreal, scarcely qualified him to be considered a "red-diaper baby," and he was somewhat older than the "average" revival participant; nevertheless, at fifteen, Cohen served as a counselor at Camp Sunshine in rural Quebec. This he identified as "a Jewish Community Camp for kids [who] ... couldn't afford the expensive summer camps," with an American socialist director named Irving Morton. "The socialists," according to Cohen, "were the only people who were playing guitar and singing folk songs [at that time]," and it was in this environment

---

[4] Mickey Flacks and Dick Flacks, *Making History, Making Blintzes: How Two Red Diaper Babies Found Each Other and Discovered America* (New Brunswick: Rutgers University Press, 2018), 15.

[5] Ibid., 24, 27, 435–41.

that Cohen first encountered *The People's Song Book*, a compendium of international folk songs that championed ordinary people's experiences and inspired left-wing sympathies.[6] Cohen revealed to his biographer, Sylvie Simmons, the profound impact which these songs – from "Solidarity Forever" to Guthrie's "Union Maid" – had made on his teenage consciousness, declaring that, even fifty years later, he could "sing the *Songbook* by heart from beginning to end."[7]

The work of folk pioneers, from Guthrie to Seeger and Lead Belly, clearly became integral to Cohen's inner world.[8] By the time he attended the camp, he was able to play the acoustic guitar, functionally if basically (he subsequently took several Spanish guitar lessons), and friends recalled the young Cohen's being a "natural," an enthusiastic amateur performer, eager to engage others in the communal music-making which typified informal folk gatherings.[9]

Equally significant in terms of formative folk influences, however, were Cohen's interests in country music. The Buckskin Boys, formed in 1952 while Cohen was studying at McGill University, Montreal, performed for square dances in local schools and church halls; a widespread trend for such events in the early 1950s was observed by Cohen, and, indeed, square dances played a significant role in the wider early folk revival.[10] Cohen's involvement with square dances undoubtedly enhanced his familiarity with vernacular music. Country music was perceived, by some 1960s folk practitioners, as antithetical to the ideals of the revival – at least in its most commercialized forms. Nevertheless, as Tim Footman notes, "British and American folk music ... formed the roots of Cohen's country songs," and these overlapping genres instilled in Cohen an interest in traditional lyrics which inspired his first

---

[6] Sylvie Simmons, *I'm Your Man: The Life of Leonard Cohen* (London: Vintage, 2013), 30–31.
[7] Ibid., 31.
[8] Michael Posner, *Leonard Cohen, Untold Stories: The Early Years* (New York; London: Simon & Schuster, 2020), vol. I, 53.
[9] Simmons, *I'm Your Man*, 42.
[10] On square dancing in the revival, see Ronald D. Cohen, *Rainbow Quest: The Folk Music Revival and American Society, 1940–1970* (Urbana; University of Illinois Press, 2002), 26 and 62.

explorations into poetry.[11] "[T]hat whole tradition touched me very deeply," he recalled.[12]

Cohen's early artistic aspirations were predominantly literary, and music remained, initially, a background interest as he honed his craft as a poet and novelist. There were, however, many aspects of Cohen's outlook and personality which displayed a certain broad empathy with folk revival ideals. While, as noted, his admiration for *The People's Song Book* did not inspire considerable political activism, Cohen, as a writer and a person, appears to have been curious and open-minded by nature, and accepting of cultural diversity.[13] Cohen attributed this trait, which became a key characteristic of the 1960s revival, to his exposure to different cultures in bilingual Montreal.[14] He maintained lifelong ties with Montreal's Jewish community and was keenly interested in Native North American cultures.[15] Nevertheless, although respectful of traditions, and despite his well-groomed outward appearance, Cohen also boasted an unconventional streak, rebelling against the "bourgeois ... expectations" of his upbringing.[16] His bohemian adventures on the Greek island of Hydra illustrated a desire to live a simple life, in harmony with nature – something with which many revivalists would have identified.[17] Arguably, even the more controversial of Cohen's youthful exploits – his prolific interest in women, or the intense candor of his literary style (as manifested in his scandal-generating 1966 novel *Beautiful*

---

[11] Tim Footman, *Leonard Cohen: Hallelujah: A New Biography* (New Malden, UK: Chrome Dreams, 2009), 57; Ira B. Nadel, *Various Positions: A Life of Leonard Cohen* (London: Bloomsbury, 1996), 26.

[12] Interview with Vin Scelsa, June 13, 1993, WXRK-FM, New York, in *Leonard Cohen on Leonard Cohen: Interviews and Encounters*, ed. Jeff Burger (Chicago: Chicago Review Press, 2014), 347–48.

[13] Cohen tended to be restrained when discussing his political views. During a visit to Cuba in 1961, Cohen was mistaken for a revolutionary, and he expressed some sympathy for the Black Power Movement when asked about this in 1974. However, despite showing some tentative support for several contemporary causes, Cohen ultimately stated, "I don't feel that my talents run in those directions." Interview with Robin Pike, September 15, 1974, *ZigZag* (UK magazine), in Burger (ed.), *Leonard Cohen*, 60–61. For more on Cohen's approach to political issues, see David Boucher in this volume (Chapter 18).

[14] See Simmons, *I'm Your Man*, 10, 22–23. [15] Nadel, *Various Positions*, 131–32.

[16] Ibid., 31. [17] Footman, *Hallelujah*, 35.

Losers) – demonstrated a striving for inner authenticity which broadly evoked revival ideals.[18] Therefore, both directly, through his love of traditional music, and indirectly, via his values, Cohen seemed attuned to crucial tenets of the folk revival, even prior to the launch of his singing career.

COHEN AND THE FOLK REVIVAL

Cohen was thirty-one years old when he began the serious pursuit of music and songwriting. Although already acclaimed as a writer in Canada, he found himself struggling by the mid 1960s; "beautiful reviews" did not bring economic gains.[19] If Cohen's motives for embracing songwriting were at least partly financial, however, his interests in music had clearly been long-standing – indeed, as Simmons notes, "gospels diverge" regarding the exact time period in which Cohen first declared himself a musician, and he had been casually performing and writing songs for some years before the metamorphosis became "official."[20] When asked about the career change, Cohen frequently articulated the imaginative linkages among different writing forms; "to take his poetry into music" seemed a natural progression.[21] "[T]he borders have faded between a lot of endeavors," he suggested to Adrienne Clarkson in a May 1966 television interview, as she queried his new status as a "writer of pop songs" – an identity-shift which perplexed, and even angered, some of those who had nurtured him as a writer.[22]

Arriving in New York in 1966 (having apparently initially planned, amid his frustration, to travel to Nashville to pursue his country-music

---

[18] On the reception of the novel, see Simmons, *I'm Your Man*, 133–36.

[19] See Jack Hafferkamp, "Ladies and Gents, Leonard Cohen" (interview), February 7, 1971, *Rolling Stone*, in Burger (ed.), *Leonard Cohen*, 20–21.

[20] Simmons, *I'm Your Man*, 136, 137–38.

[21] Words of Cohen's friend Henry Zemel, quoted in Posner, *Leonard Cohen, Untold Stories*, vol. I, 294.

[22] Quote from TV interview with Adrienne Clarkson, May 23, 1966, *Take 30*, CBC, in Burger (ed.), *Leonard Cohen*, 5. On reactions of the literary world to his career move, see Simmons, *I'm Your Man*, 195, and David Boucher, *Dylan and Cohen: Poets of Rock 'n' Roll* (London; New York: Continuum, 2004), 14.

interests), Cohen recalled "bump[ing]" into the so-called folk-song renaissance" on the city streets, specifically citing the names of Dylan, Joan Baez, Phil Ochs, Judy Collins, and Joni Mitchell as key folk practitioners.[23] Cohen had, of course, arrived too late to witness the city's folk "boom," the epicentre of which had been the bohemian neighbourhood of Greenwich Village. However, as Stephen Petrus and Ronald D. Cohen note, despite the prevalent perceptions that the revival had declined nationwide, and although the "Village" folk scene "diminished" as youngsters increasingly pursued amplified rock music, "many New York folk institutions, albeit in modified form, remained vibrant in the late 1960s and after."[24] Greenwich Village remained "the destination of talented folksingers," and it was among such musicians that Cohen would attain his first significant successes as a performer and songwriter.[25]

Although Judy Collins was not the first performer to promote Cohen's songs (the importance of the Stormy Clovers, a Toronto-based folk group, should be particularly acknowledged in this regard), she was, nevertheless, justified in asserting that her "endorsement" of his work established his musical career in earnest. "[H]e knew it and he always thanked me for it," she declared.[26] A classically trained musician with a mellifluous, expressive singing voice, Collins had been integral to the folk revival since the late 1950s, committing herself wholeheartedly to the promotion of traditional music and the political causes espoused by the movement. However, although remaining within the revival's infrastructures, Collins was not constrained by purist conceptions of what "folk" should be, and continuously sought to expand her repertoire.[27]

---

[23] Simmons, *I'm Your Man*, 140.
[24] Stephen Petrus and Ronald D. Cohen, *Folk City: New York and the American Folk Music Revival* (Oxford: Oxford University Press, 2015), 304, 293.
[25] Ibid., 299.
[26] Quoted in Posner, *Leonard Cohen, Untold Stories*, vol. I, 297. On the Stormy Clovers, see ibid., 301–04.
[27] In 2015, Collins told an interviewer that she wished to be remembered as an artiste who "always move[d] forward." Jim Sullivan, "Judy Collins," *Cape Cod Times* (November 2015), accessed at Rocksbackpages.com. See also David Dicaire, *The Folk Music Revival, 1958–1970: Biographies of Fifty Performers and Other Influential People* (Jefferson, NC; London: MacFarland and Company, 2011), 85.

She became particularly renowned as a champion, and interpreter, of the works of emergent songwriters, recording songs by, among others, Dylan, Phil Ochs, and Richard Fariña, and stimulating Joni Mitchell's career by attaining chart success with "Both Sides Now" in 1967. Transfixed by Cohen's early songs, which possessed the uniquely "unusual" qualities which she sought, she recorded "Suzanne" and "Dress Rehearsal Rag" for *In My Life*, released in 1966. Three more Cohen songs would feature on *Wildflowers*, her 1967 album.

Collins also enhanced Cohen's reputation by using her influence as a board member for the (at this time somewhat faltering) Newport Folk Festival to secure his inclusion on the 1967 programme, and by inviting him to appear as a guest artist at her concerts.[28] During his first major public performance – at a benefit event, headlined by Collins, for the radio station WBAI in New York's Village Theatre in February 1967 – Cohen was, reportedly, so nervous during a solo rendition of "Suzanne" that he walked offstage.[29] Persuading him to return and finish the song alongside her, Collins recalled that the audience responded ecstatically. "Because my recording [of 'Suzanne'] was out, and they knew it, and because of it, they knew him."[30]

The circumstances surrounding Cohen's entry to the professional music world, and his initial status as Collins's protégé, rendered him, effectively, "folk by association," and Cohen undoubtedly did form strong links with the folk scene, and with folk musicians, during his early career. These included Joni Mitchell, with whom he had shared the stage at Newport (the two subsequently had a brief romantic dalliance), the American folksinger Julie Felix, whom he had first met on Hydra (Felix recalled "trad[ing] songs" with him; while she had performed the works of Woody Guthrie and some Mexican songs, Cohen, in turn, sang "union songs"), and the eccentric folklore collector Harry E. Smith, whose

---

[28] On Collins's influence at Newport, see Posner, *Leonard Cohen, Untold Stories*, vol. I, 353. On Newport's difficulties in the late 1960s, see Cohen, *Rainbow Quest*, 273–74.

[29] Some biographers, as Simmons notes (*I'm Your Man*, 159), state that this turbulent debut took place in April 1967 at Town Hall, but Simmons highlights a letter concerning the concert which Cohen wrote to his lover, Marianne Ihlen, which seems to confirm the February date.

[30] Quoted in Posner, *Leonard Cohen, Untold Stories*, vol. I, 343.

Anthology of American Folk Music became a seminal musical reference source for revivalists.[31]

Cohen also became involved in the Canadian folk scene during this period. His appearance at Newport was followed by performances in Montreal, which, during that year (the centennial of the Canadian Confederation), was hosting Expo '67 to international acclaim, and at the Mariposa Folk Festival at Innis Lake, Ontario.[32] The Montreal folksinger Penny Lang recalled many local musicians performing "Suzanne" as it "passed down to the other singers around town."[33] Even before the recording of his albums, Cohen was, thus, significantly integrated into the folk scene, and his work was already becoming part of its repertoire. The writer Sandra Djwa described him, in February 1967, as "Leonard Cohen, the folksinging personality," and many of Cohen's activities during that year suggest that such a title was fitting.[34]

"CANADIAN DYLAN"? COHEN AND THE IMAGE OF THE FOLKSINGER

Despite being nurtured, initially, by representatives of the American folk scene, Cohen, like many artists in this period, was wary of labels, and quickly tired of the oversimplifications in which the press so often indulged, particularly where popular music was concerned. He later declared that, while he had encountered the "folk music renaissance" in New York, the experience had been akin to an "ambush"; it had never been his intention to join the movement into which he had "bumped."[35] In many respects, he was, as Boucher suggests, "in the American folk scene" but "not of it" – and, of course, when Cohen began performing in

---

[31] Felix quoted ibid., 196; on Smith's association with Cohen, see Simmons, *I'm Your Man*, 196–97.

[32] Simmons, *I'm Your Man*, 165–69.

[33] Ibid., 147.

[34] Sandra Djwa, "After the Wipeout, Renewal," interview, February 3, 1967, *The Ubyssey* (Vancouver, Canada), in Burger (ed.), *Leonard Cohen*, 13.

[35] Anthony Reynolds, *Leonard Cohen: A Remarkable Life*, 2nd ed. (London; New York: Omnibus Press, 2012), 57.

earnest, this "scene" had lost some of the cultural potency which it had possessed half a decade earlier.[36]

Cohen seemed also to dislike some of the connotations which the "folksinger" label had acquired by this point; the revival had generated certain perceptions, and stereotypes, concerning "folkies" and their viewpoints. He took issue, for instance, with those who assumed that "folk" musicians were invariably serious and anti-commercialist. He abhorred the "intellectual bag" into which he had been placed following his New York performances and indicated his support for commercial success by lauding Noel Harrison's 1967 hit recording of "Suzanne."[37] He also remained resistant to suggestions that his songwriting must have a political dimension. "If my passion was involved in those daily issues I would write about them," he declared in 1973; although maintaining that his songs "protest[ed] in their own way," he felt little affinity with musicians who effectively became political "slogan writers."[38] (David Boucher, in Chapter 18 of this volume, further highlights the ambivalence with which Cohen approached contemporary political issues.)

Cohen knew that many of the popular preconceptions concerning "the folksinger" were the legacies of Dylan – or at least of the image which he had acquired during the early 1960s, when he was considered to embody the persona of a politically aware, anti-materialistic musician. Whether or not he had ever consciously aspired to be Dylan's Canadian counterpart, Cohen certainly understood why the media so readily pronounced him the legendary singer's successor.[39] As Footman observes, it was commonplace for the press to perceive the music scene as "a complex relay race," with the "baton of influences" being passed around artists – Cohen was certainly not the only performer to be considered Dylan's heir.[40] In Cohen's case, however, there were, perhaps, particular

---

[36] Boucher, *Dylan and Cohen*, 111.
[37] "Intellectual bag" comment in Karl Dallas, "Leonard Cohen: Songwriter Who Got into Folk by Accident," *Melody Maker* (February 17, 1968), accessed at Rocksbackpages.com.
[38] Alistair Pirrie, "Cohen Regrets," *New Musical Express* (March 10, 1973), in Burger (ed.), *Leonard Cohen*, 43.
[39] On the background to the "Canadian Dylan" story, see Simmons, *I'm Your Man*, 137.
[40] Footman, *Hallelujah*, 215.

similarities – some superficial, but others more significant. Cohen seemed amused by some of the more simplistic comparisons which commentators had drawn between them, and at the folk caricatures which they implied. He joked that, while he shared Dylan's "emaciated" build and "terrible" singing voice, he already "play[ed] the guitar too well" to supplant him.[41] The voices of both singers were, certainly, relatively uncultivated, and both frequently set complex lyrics to unadorned, folk-style melodies. Dylan had, inadvertently, and via his own adaptations of the persona, image, and musical style of his idol, Woody Guthrie, helped to establish these qualities as archetypical 1960s folksinger attributes. Cohen's onstage stance, as a soloist accompanied by an acoustic guitar, also evoked the performance style of Dylan during his folksinging phase.

There were, however, more substantial similarities between them. Both had been profoundly shaped by their Jewish heritage (albeit differently – Cohen considered himself "demonstrably Jewish," compared with Dylan), and both had, effectively, rebelled against the communities which had first nurtured their talents (in Cohen's case, the literary world, and in Dylan's, the structured folk movement).[42] Cohen recognised the more significant parallels between his career and that of Dylan, but Boucher suggests that Cohen (Dylan's elder by some years, and no newcomer to the arts world), while "recognis[ing] Dylan's genius," wished not to follow his musical path, but to "emulate" his "role" as "the voice and icon of an age."[43] The fact that Cohen had entered the scene amid a rapidly changing musical (and cultural) climate also diluted the pertinence of the "Dylan's successor" designation, although the straightforward comparisons continued.

The idea of Cohen as "the *Canadian* Dylan" also carried significant connotations for critics north of the border. Robert A. Wright has noted that some commentators, filled with the nationalism of the Centennial

---

[41] Quoted in Boucher, *Dylan and Cohen*, 104.

[42] Ibid., 49. On Dylan's "complex relationship" with his Jewish heritage, see Elliot R. Wolfson, "Judaism: Saturnine Melody and Dylan's Jewish Gnosis," in *The World of Bob Dylan*, ed. Sean Latham (Cambridge: Cambridge University Press, 2021), 313–24.

[43] Boucher, *Dylan and Cohen*, 137.

era, observed that many Canadians – including Cohen, Gordon Lightfoot, Joni Mitchell, and Neil Young – were finding success as popular musicians. Ironically, these singers were pursuing recording careers in the United States (the Canadian music industry remained in a fledgling stage), and most were, as highly singular talents, reluctant to be considered as proof that Canadians were naturally predisposed to musical excellence, or that there existed a discernibly "Canadian" sound.[44] Cohen himself, while attached to, and frequently inspired by, his homeland and native Montreal, did not conceive of his artistic persona, which had been formed by experiences in many places, quite so narrowly.[45] Nevertheless, his increasing success as a musician certainly coincided with a tendency, in certain quarters, to perceive something innately "Canadian" about the style of poetic, reflective songwriting which he had espoused.

To be labelled so readily as "folksinger," or, indeed, "the next Dylan" seemed, therefore, frustratingly limiting for Cohen. Politely disputing Djwa's "folksinging personality" designation, his response to her also demonstrated awareness that the "folk" label, especially when applied unthinkingly, had grown rather limited, as the late 1960s counterculture, with its chaotic diversity and resistance to straightforward definitions, evolved. "I don't care what people call me," he told Djwa, "whether ... folksinging or ... a priestly function or ... revolutionary activity or acidheads see it as psychedelic revolution or poets see it as the popularization of poetry. I stand with all these people."[46] The folk world was not the only community with which Cohen interacted in New York; he may, in fact,

---

[44] Robert A. Wright, "Dream, Comfort, Memory, Despair: Canadian Popular Musicians and the Dilemma of Nationalism, 1968–1972," *Journal of Canadian Studies* 22, no. 4 (winter 1988): 27–43.

[45] As an artiste whose work had been shaped by his itinerant lifestyle, Cohen's feelings on this matter were certainly complex, but he maintained a warmth for his home city in particular, while tending to evade espousals of a more amorphous Canadian nationalism. For example, after buying a house in Montreal in 1972, Cohen told *Maclean's* magazine that, while this constituted a return to his "homeland," "it's not even Canada, it's Montreal. Not even Montreal, it's a few streets." Paul Saltzman, "Famous Last Words from Leonard Cohen," *Maclean's*, June 1972, in Burger (ed.), *Leonard Cohen*, 33.

[46] Djwa, "After the Wipeout," 13.

have felt "more comfortable" amid the city's vibrant bohemian scene.[47] Having lived in New York in the late 1950s, whilst attending Columbia University, Cohen had encountered Beat poetry, and, on his return to the city in 1966, he again expanded his artistic horizons via the countercultural underground as epitomized by Andy Warhol's "Factory" and the enigmatic artist–singer Nico, with whom he became infatuated, and whose "deep monoton[ous]" singing style undoubtedly influenced him, as significantly as did the work of any folksingers.[48] As a regular patron of the infamous Chelsea Hotel, Cohen also interacted with many of its hedonistic artistic clientele, and reportedly took hallucinogenic drugs frequently during this period.[49] Many considered such drugs to be incompatible with the core ideals of the folk revival. Neil Rosenberg suggests that its communitarian and politically focused aspects were weakened by the increasing prevalence of drug use by the mid 1960s, as "dropping out and getting stoned" often promoted introversion rather than activism.[50] Clearly, therefore, neither Cohen nor the artistic world within which he operated espoused one-dimensional identities, and he resisted narrow "pigeonholing" for this reason.[51]

FOLK INFLUENCES IN COHEN'S SONGS

Nevertheless, if Cohen generally disliked simplistic stereotyping of his work and persona as "folk," he was certainly not averse to discussing or acknowledging the folk influences within his music or the traditional artists who had inspired him.[52] This, arguably, constituted another more meaningful similarity with Dylan, who had also bridled at restrictive

---

[47] Boucher, *Dylan and Cohen*, 106.   [48] Simmons, *I'm Your Man*, 149, 150–55.
[49] Cohen had been experimenting with drugs before his time in New York. See ibid., 102–03, 128–29, and 171–72, and Footman, *Hallelujah*, 34.
[50] Neil Rosenberg in Ronald D. Cohen, (ed.), *"Wasn't That a Time!": Firsthand Accounts of the Folk Music Revival* (Lanham, MD; London: Scarecrow Press, 2002), 76.
[51] Liz Thomson suggested that to call Cohen a "folksinger" was "an inaccurate pigeonholing of his talent." "Songs from a Room: The Inside Story of Leonard Cohen," *The History of Rock*, 1983, accessed at Rocksbackpages.com.
[52] See, for example, comments on the New York scene in Paul Williams, "Leonard Cohen: The Romantic in a Ragpicker's Trade," *Crawdaddy* (March 1975), in Burger (ed.), *Leonard Cohen*, 91.

labelling, but who, nevertheless, retained deep interests in folk music and did not abandon "his allegiance to the folk song process [essentially a forward-looking and flexible approach to folk music] that [his former mentor] Seeger so treasured" – as evidenced by such "post-revival" albums as *John Wesley Harding* (1967).[53]

Cohen did not invariably reject the folk designation; when one interviewer suggested that "some [listeners] would [classify his] music as folk music," Cohen expressed the hope that it might "st[i]ck around long enough to become folk music," and (perhaps unwilling to enter another debate on the subject) conceded that folk was "as good a term as any" for his work.[54] Folk music had left an indelible imprint on his imagination. The fact that his second album, *Songs from a Room* (1969), included the wartime protest song "The Partisan," taken from *The People's Song Book*, testifies to this; his 1979 album *Recent Songs* also included the nineteenth-century Québécois song "Un Canadien errant" ("A Wandering Canadian"), which Simmons suggests encapsulated the "exile[d]" state with which the perpetually itinerant Cohen had become familiar.[55] The political consciousness associated with folk music was not entirely absent from Cohen's own songs. Cohen's apoliticism can, in fact, be overstated; he was never a self-professed "protest singer," but, as Boucher has argued, many of his complex, emotionally charged songs may still be considered "highly political in their imagery of the modern world" and in their explorations of "the depths of human experience and alienation."[56]

Cohen's first three albums certainly bore some of the hallmarks of "folk," as the term was understood by that time. Indeed, Cohen seems to have wished his albums to possess certain qualities which were generally associated with folk-style music. Both he and his listeners knew that the music scene had evolved significantly from the "folk boom" era – yet, as Boucher suggests, "there was a subtlety to the difference that did not make what he did jar with convention, but imperceptibly made listeners alert to a difference."[57] Cohen's desire to allow his lyrics to be heard, his wish to

---

[53] Filene, *Romancing the Folk*, 215. On Seeger's understanding of "the folk process," see ibid., 194.
[54] Pat Harbron, interview with Leonard Cohen, summer 1973, *Beetle*, in Burger (ed.), *Leonard Cohen*, 45–46.
[55] Simmons, *I'm Your Man*, 303.   [56] Boucher, *Dylan and Cohen*, 43.   [57] Ibid., 111.

keep accompaniments simple, and his preference for acoustic instruments in an increasingly amplified age rendered him broadly attuned to the ethos and legacy of the folk revival. The recording of his debut album, *Songs of Leonard Cohen*, grew challenging for him because his producers – John Hammond and, subsequently, John Simon – seemed inclined to overarrange the songs. Hammond had initially employed skilled session musicians; this intimidated Cohen, who felt musically limited, while Simon's plans for elaborate arrangements to underpin "Suzanne" caused him particular distress.[58] "[Simon] wanted a heavy piano syncopated, and maybe drums ... I didn't want drums on any of my songs." His own simple "guitar-picking" should retain prevalence.[59] However, following a chance encounter with Kaleidoscope, a West Coast "psychedelic folk group," Cohen sensed that this band might produce the sounds which he sought; "improvis[ing]," they ultimately accompanied several numbers, including the seminal "So Long, Marianne" and "Teachers."[60] The group's sensitive arrangements were devised organically, via Cohen's "t[elling] them when he liked something and if he wanted them to add another instrument." Kaleidoscope's inclusion of rare instruments, from various ethnic traditions, also helped to achieve the mysterious, sparser sounds which Cohen sought.[61]

Songs from a Room (1969) arguably betrayed the strongest allegiance to folk, in terms of its arrangements and content.[62] Recorded in Nashville and produced principally by Bob Johnston, this straightforwardly arranged album seemed to satisfy Cohen; among the most notable numbers were "Bird on the Wire," "The Story of Isaac," and "Seems So Long Ago, Nancy." All were characterized by Cohen's distinctive "guitar-picking," subtly and gently accompanied by other instruments at times (particularly notable is the Jew's harp, which added to the album's "roots" flavor). Cohen's inclusion of "The Partisan," which led to its wider rediscovery (both Baez and Buffy Sainte-Marie recorded it in the

---

[58] Footman, *Hallelujah*, 65–66.   [59] Quoted in Simmons, *I'm Your Man*, 178.
[60] Footman, *Hallelujah*, 65.
[61] The recording process is described in Simmons, *I'm Your Man*, 178–83.
[62] Nadel notes that it was on the strength of this album that Cohen was named "Le folksinger de l'année" by the French magazine *Le Nouvel Observateur*. See *Various Positions*, 169.

early 1970s), serves as further testament to the folk spirit with which this album was imbued. For Simmons, this "simple" and "stark" work constituted Cohen's "country album," but, particularly as Cohen understood them, country and folk were interlinked, and the overall effect of the somewhat barren, understated arrangements on this album of largely melancholy songs pleased him. *Songs of Love and Hate* (1971), again produced by Johnston, encapsulated the raw sound for which Cohen had aimed in his previous recordings (and certainly did little to challenge Cohen's reputation as one of the gloomiest songwriters on the scene).[63]

Whether the rather infamous grimness of Cohen's songwriting – which regularly explored death, depression, romantic failure, and suicide – betrayed folk influences in itself is debatable: tragic songs had been prominent within the revival's repertoire from its earliest days (the Kingston Trio's 1958 version of the murder ballad "Tom Dooley" had, after all, constituted the first introduction to folk music for many baby boomers).[64] The despair which often characterized Cohen's early work may perhaps have resonated with those who lamented the "death" of 1960s optimism and the failure of the counterculture to usher in more peaceful times.[65] He was certainly not alone in his introspection: *Time* magazine suggested in 1968 that the new generation of folk "troubadours" – including Cohen, Arlo Guthrie, and Richie Havens – was "turning away from [political] protest" to explore "the realms within."[66] However, in his capacity as a poetic writer of thoughtful, complex songs with candid, and often unsettling, lyrics, Cohen became a vivid illustration of one of the folk revival's most significant legacies. The movement's prizing of the artistry of the thought-provoking, skillful songwriter undoubtedly helped to pave the way for the so-called "singer-songwriter movement" of which Cohen could be considered part. Keir Keightley notes the ways in which the ideals of the revival – not merely its anti-commercialism and romantic ruralism, but also its promotion of original songwriting – survived within the wider rock scene from the late

---

[63] Simmons, *I'm Your Man*, 206, 233. [64] See Cantwell, "When We Were Good," 35–39.
[65] As early as 1967, hippies were declaring the failure of their mission to imbue the world with their ideals. See "Hippies: Death on a Sunny Afternoon," *Rolling Stone* (UK edition), 1 (November 9, 1967): 11, on a mock funeral for the counterculture held by a group of disillusioned hippies in Haight-Ashbury, San Francisco.
[66] Quoted in Cohen, *Rainbow Quest*, 278.

1960s onwards and helped to shape concepts of "authentic" rock artistry.[67] As Rosenberg suggests, despite its decline as a cohesive movement, the revival did not "fail" or "f[a]ll apart," but "really succeeded," infusing aspects of its character and outlook into many areas of the wider scene.[68] The embracing of songwriting constituted one crucial facet of this.

Cohen, of course, was far from being simply another introspective songwriter. Judy Collins had been drawn to his songs principally because "there was nothing like them around. Nobody, including Dylan" (who had probably set the benchmark for uniqueness, at least among his contemporaries) produced material like his, she declared.[69] While the dark tone of much of Cohen's work repelled some listeners, he was, nevertheless, admired by many within a generation which appreciated skillfully crafted lyrics and perceived "rock" as "poetry."[70] John Simon felt that, while Dylan had "paved the way," via his "thoughtful" lyrics, Cohen's songs had "more finesse" and "reveal[ed] a more educated, exposed, literate poet."[71] For the songwriter Steve Andrews, Cohen's performance at the 1970 Isle of Wight Festival proved more memorable, and "emotional", than any songs by the exponents of "loud music and freaky sounds." Many festival-goers, he believed, had felt "awe and reverence" for this "great poet and writer," whose set had seemed "almost a religious experience."[72] Cohen's "erudite and serious" songwriting was recognized by many for its highly distinctive contributions to an increasingly diverse, rich music scene.[73] Ruth R. Wisse, who studied with Cohen at McGill, observed that, while Cohen's songwriting ventures did not always please his original mentors, "his higher literary standards won him the awe of

---

[67] Keir Keightley, "Reconsidering Rock," in Simon Frith, Will Straw, and John Street (eds.), *The Cambridge Companion to Rock and Pop* (Cambridge: Cambridge University Press, 2011), 122, 134.

[68] Rosenberg in Cohen (ed.), *"Wasn't That a Time!,"* 76.

[69] Quoted in Simmons, *I'm Your Man*, p. 145.

[70] On this tendency, which was epitomized by the 1969 publication of Richard Goldstein's *The Poetry of Rock*, see Pete Astor, "The Poetry of Rock: Song Lyrics Are Not Poems But the Words Still Matter: Another Look at Richard Goldstein's Collection of Rock Lyrics," *Popular Music* 29, no. 1 (January 2010): 143–48.

[71] Quoted in Simmons, *I'm Your Man*, 182.

[72] Quoted in Reynolds, *Leonard Cohen*, 97.   [73] Footman, *Hallelujah*, 222.

music critics accustomed to thinner gruel."[74] It appears, in fact, that fame as a songwriter amplified Cohen's reputation as a poet and boosted sales of his books; he undoubtedly stirred literary interests within many young music fans in this period.[75] His poetic style constituted a particularly vivid, singular embodiment of the thoughtful, profound songwriting which the folk revival had bequeathed to the wider scene.

Though an adept lyricist, Cohen was self-deprecating about his musicianship – but, as John Simon observed, he was not simply "a poet who strummed a little."[76] His guitar-playing, though limited, was distinctive; while admitting to having "only one chop" (a Spanish-influenced triplet-picking) he asserted that "very few guitarists [could] emulate" it.[77] Cohen's sparing musical accompaniments were integral to the songwriting which had so impressed admirers in the late 1960s; the marriage of words and music constituted one of the principal attractions of his work for fans, and the deceptive simplicity of the arrangements highlighted his elastic, yet significant, ties to the folk revival.

CONCLUSION

Cohen, like many of his contemporaries, continued to develop his musical style, and his fourth album, *New Skin for the Old Ceremony* (1974), marked a more decisive change. By the time the album was issued, the folk "boom" seemed considerably distant, and its residual impact became less of a preoccupation for commentators. Yet folk music had exerted a profound influence on Cohen. He had explored folk traditions in his early musical ventures, and, although he had participated in the revival during its last days as a major sociocultural phenomenon, his folk connections remained tangible as he began songwriting and performing in earnest.

Pete Seeger, for whose "music and life" Cohen maintained a great admiration, believed that "the folk tradition could not remain healthy...

---

[74] Ruth R. Wisse, "My Life without Leonard Cohen," *Commentary* (October 1995): 29.
[75] Boucher, *Dylan and Cohen*, 14. [76] Simmons, *I'm Your Man*, 183.
[77] Quoted in Paul Zollo, "Leonard Cohen: Inside the Tower of Song," *SongTalk* (April 1993), in Burger (ed.), *Leonard Cohen*, 268.

unless it maintained strong connections to the contemporary world."[78] Cohen's status as an individualistic poet who had been profoundly influenced by the mysterious, elemental beauty of folk and country styles allowed him to develop a musical persona which was as "contemporary" as it was respectful of traditions. These qualities not only rendered him meaningfully akin to his alleged counterpart, Bob Dylan, but also allow him, today, to be considered as one of Seeger's true heirs.

---

[78] Filene, *Romancing the Folk*, 199. On Cohen and Seeger, see Boucher, *Dylan and Cohen*, 139.

CHAPTER 6

Singer-Songwriters

David R. Shumway

A ROUND 1970, A NEW MUSICAL FORMATION EMERGED IN THE United States as a part of the cultural practice of rock & roll. This music was connected to folk both stylistically and genealogically, but it differed significantly from that form. Where folk presented itself as the expression of the people, the music of the singer-songwriters was understood as the expression of an individual. Its defining characteristic is the claim of direct address, that the singer is writing and performing explicitly as him or herself without the invocation of an implied "speaker" or invented persona. Moreover, the most important current within this songwriting was autobiographical, the singer presenting the song as if it told the truth about his or her life. And where folk had stuck with acoustic instruments and generally avoided drums, the singer-songwriters were often backed by rock bands. Leonard Cohen was there at the start of this movement and, indeed, may be its earliest instance. Paradoxically, however, his music is not typical of the formation. Where the central figures of the early 1970s like James Taylor and Joni Mitchell were understood as confessional songwriters, Cohen's songs, even those that make use of autobiographical details, rarely seem to be about the singer. The goal of this chapter is to explore Cohen's relationship to the singer-songwriters, showing both how he paved the way for them and how his songs finally are best understood as distinct from the movement.

When Leonard Cohen began to imagine himself as singer and songwriter, there were two other musical formations that influenced him. One of them was country music, which was the first music he performed as a member of the Buckskin Boys, a trio he joined when he was an undergraduate at McGill University. According to biographer Sylvie Simmons, "By

Leonard's own account – in 1967 in the *Village Voice* and to any number of music journalists since, this biographer included – his intention was to write country songs."[1] And, after recording his first album in New York, Cohen would go to Nashville to record his second album, *Songs from a Room* (1969). Moreover, it should be noted that the one other singer mentioned in "Tower of Song" is country legend Hank Williams, whom Cohen describes as residing a hundred floors above him. So, we should not discount country music's influence on Cohen, but it is hard to find much direct evidence of its effect on either his music or his lyrics.

The first musical formation he became commercially involved with was folk, as Gillian Mitchell details in Chapter 5 of this volume. Cohen had actually sung folk songs at a Jewish summer camp before he played in the country band. He was introduced to *The People's Song Book*, a compilation of lefty songs like "Solidarity Forever" and "Joe Hill." It also included "The Partisan," which would be the first song he would record that he had not written himself.[2] The more direct link of folk to Cohen's songwriting begins with the story Ira B. Nadel tells in his biography of a party attended by a number of prominent Canadian poets in January 1966 and at which "Cohen played guitar, sang, and raved about Dylan. No one had heard of him, but [F. R.] Scott rushed out to buy *Bringing It All Back Home* and *Highway 61 Revisited*. He returned and to the chagrin of everyone put them on ... Only Cohen listened intently, solemnly announcing that *he* would become the Canadian Dylan, a statement all dismissed."[3]

Dylan was emerging as a rock musician on these two albums, but he was still strongly identified with folk, where his career began. Moreover, when Cohen started to write songs, the first singer to record them was Judy Collins, a central figure in the New York folk scene. She recorded two of Cohen's songs on *In My Life*, released in November 1966, and three more on her next release, *Wildflowers* (1967). Thus, when *Songs of Leonard Cohen* appeared in January 1968,[4] he was already associated with folk.

---

[1] Sylvie Simmons, *I'm Your Man: The Life of Leonard Cohen* (New York: Ecco, 2012), 142.
[2] Ibid., 27–28.
[3] Ira B. Nadel, *Various Positions: A Life of Leonard Cohen* (New York: Pantheon, 1996), 141.
[4] The album is copyrighted 1967, but it was not available until January 1968.

And yet, by the time Cohen's first album was released, folk as a commercial category was on life support. Starting in 1965, folk music experienced "a sharp commercial decline" in the wake of the rise of folk-rock.[5] Moreover, the music was changing. Previously, folk musicians had mainly performed and recorded traditional songs, and when they did occasionally write new material, it was traditional in the form. What folk music claimed was that it spoke for the collective. As Izzy Young, one of the chief proponents of the revival, asserted, "the minute you leave the people, or folk-based ideas, you get into a rarefied area which has no meaning anymore."[6] Young was commenting on Bob Dylan's move into what he saw as "introspective" songs such as "My Back Pages," released in 1964, but he would have much more to complain about in future years as folk moved in that direction.[7] You can see it in Judy Collins's career, which began with an album of traditional folk songs, *Maid of Constant Sorrow* (1961), but by 1967, with *Wildflowers*, it was now focused on contemporary songs, including some of her own composition. The singer-songwriter movement emerged out of these changes in folk, but took them much further. It explicitly took up rock, which was already an expanding category.

One can see from early issues of *Rolling Stone* how folk artists such as Collins and Joan Baez are included in this rock-oriented periodical, signifying that they are becoming absorbed in the cultural practice of rock & roll. Cohen's career depends heavily on this development, making Dylan's explicit move into rock & roll decisive, whether or not Cohen was consciously influenced.

The moment when Cohen began writing and recording songs was between the folk revival and the emergence of the singer-songwriter a few years later. There are other songwriters and performers who contributed to the new formation without actually being central to it. Paul Simon and Dylan, who wouldn't record a singer-songwriter album until 1974's *Blood*

---

[5] Ronald D. Cohen, *Rainbow Quest: The Folk Music Revival and American Society, 1940–1970* (Amherst: University of Massachusetts Press, 2018), 230.

[6] Izzy Young, *The Conscience of the Folk Revival: The Writings of Israel "Izzy" Young*, American Folk Music and Musicians Series, no. 18 (Lanham, MD: Scarecrow Press, 2013), 178.

[7] David R. Shumway, "The Emergence of the Singer-Songwriter," in *The Cambridge Companion to the Singer-Songwriter*, ed. Katherine Williams and Justin A. Williams (Cambridge: Cambridge University Press, 2016), 14–15.

on the Tracks, are important precursors. In 1968, Randy Newman, one of whose songs Collins recorded on *In My Life*, and Laura Nyro released albums of their own songs, *Randy Newman* and *Eli and the Thirteenth Confession*. The latter was a major critical and commercial success, while the former was not, but both songwriters' songs were widely recorded by others. These songwriters' songs were distinctive, but they do not have much in common with those that would characterize singer-songwriter music of the 1970s. They are not focused on the self, and their style owed more to American pop music than to rock & roll or folk. But it may be folksinger Tom Rush who was the most important transitional figure. As I have argued elsewhere, Rush's recording of songs by James Taylor, Joni Mitchell, and Jackson Browne on *Circle Game* (1968), together with his own "No Regrets," was a key moment in the emergence of the singer-songwriter formation.[8] Rush's introspective song is actually a closer to the confessionalism of the songs Mitchell would soon begin to write.

The singer-songwriter movement emerged with Mitchell's *Ladies of the Canyon* (1970) and *Blue* (1971), and Taylor's *Sweet Baby James* (1970). Taylor's earlier *James Taylor* (1968) had hardly reached any listeners until the success of the later album. Cohen was present at the start of this movement and may be as important to it as Rush or Collins. Collins, who was a member of the board of the Newport Folk Festival, fought against the resistance of the traditionalists to have a "singer-songwriter afternoon" in 1967 to include Cohen, Mitchell, and Janis Ian.[9] It was at that Newport Festival that Collins introduced Cohen and Mitchell to each other. They immediately became a couple, and, although the relationship lasted only a few months, Mitchell credited Cohen with being one of two peers who had influenced her – the other being Dylan. According to Mitchell's biographer, David Yaffe, theirs was "a romantic and creative friendship that would deeply influence both of their careers."[10] Cohen's influence on her seems undeniable, although the exact nature of it is harder to pin down. When they met, Mitchell had yet to record an album

---

[8] Ibid.
[9] David Yaffe, *Reckless Daughter: A Portrait of Joni Mitchell* (New York: Farrar, Straus, and Giroux, 2017), 45.
[10] Ibid., 53.

of her own, although Collins had recorded "Both Sides Now" on *Wildflowers*, and released it as a successful single the following year. That song was written before she met Cohen, as a recording of a live performance exists from 1966. Mitchell didn't record "Both Sides Now" until her second album, *Clouds*, released in 1969, which includes two songs said to be about Cohen, "That Song about the Midway" and "The Gallery." She is known to have written a song, "The Wizard of Is," which she never released, that is an imitation of "Suzanne."[11] Moreover, it is after meeting Cohen that her songwriting changes from the more traditional folk style of "Both Sides Now" and "The Circle Game" to one that was both more musically innovative and newly confessional.

We know that several of those songs were inspired by her relationship with Cohen, and they deal explicitly with it in ways the earlier songs did not. One of Mitchell's first confessional songs was "Rainy Night House," which is about their visit to Leonard's childhood home in Montreal where his mother still lived. The song's detailed description and clear narrative distinguish it from Leonard's songs, while the music illustrates Mitchell's move away from traditional folk melodies and arrangements. The piano accompaniment is closer to cabaret or even the art-song style, displaying both Mitchell's instrumental virtuosity and musical innovation. Mitchell tells of Cohen staying up all night to watch her sleep, while calling him a "holy man" on the radio and, perhaps most penetratingly, "a refugee from a wealthy family." The song seems to be about the quest to understand self and an intimate partner.

Cohen was also the inspiration for one of Mitchell's greatest songs, "A Case of You." The song's first verse recounts a conversation between Joni and Leonard in which he tells her "I am as constant as the northern star," and she replies, "Constantly in the darkness/ Where's that at?/ If you want me I'll be in the bar." Mitchell reports that Cohen actually said that to her, borrowing from Shakespeare's *Julius Caesar*, but the reply came to her only later.[12] The song's second verse quotes something Mitchell says Cohen's mother told her about Leonard, that if she stayed with him, she should "be prepared to bleed." While Cohen's name is not used here (or in "Rainy Night House"), and it was not until many years later that Cohen

[11] Ibid., 56.   [12] Ibid., 62.

was widely known to be its subject, the song makes use of words he and his mother said to Mitchell. Cohen apparently felt violated by Mitchell using his words, while Mitchell came to complain that Cohen's use of lines of other poets made him "unoriginal." What is significant here is not which songwriter is right, but how these judgments reveal their different conceptions of their art. As Yaffe puts, there was "a schism in their songwriting styles."[13] Mitchell recognized Cohen as a "word man," and when they first met, she asked him to provide her with a reading list because she hadn't read very much. Cohen's poems and songs are emmeshed in literature, taking allusion and reference to other works to be fundamental. Mitchell was already the far more advanced musician when she met Cohen, and her prodigious talent led someone to ask Leonard what it was like to live with Beethoven. But Mitchell's lyrics, especially after she left folk behind, are grounded in the particulars of her own experience rather than in any larger tradition, whether that be literary, religious, or philosophical. This makes her much more typical of the singer-songwriters than Cohen.

It is hard to say exactly how Cohen influenced Mitchell because even though her meeting him seems to be a watershed moment in her career, the songs that she becomes known for after their meeting are not much like his. Mitchell's songs, along with those of James Taylor, Jackson Browne, and Carole King, were associated in the 1970s with the confessional movement in poetry. The songs on these albums were called "confessional" because of their similarity to the confessional school of poetry that had emerged with Robert Lowell's *Life Studies* (1959), and included Lowell's students, Sylvia Plath, Ann Sexton, and W. D. Snodgrass, in addition to John Berryman. According to critic M. L. Rosenthal, who named the movement, confessional poetry is defined by way the self is presented in the poems, the poet appearing as him- or herself without invoking the convention of an invented "speaker."[14] Irving Howe elaborated, "The sense of direct speech addressed to an audience is central to confessional writing."[15] The key point here is

---

[13] Ibid.
[14] M. L. Rosenthal, *The Modern Poets: A Critical Introduction* (New York: Oxford University Press, 1960), 226.
[15] Irving Howe, *The Critical Point: On Literature and Culture* (New York: Horizon Press, 1973), 167.

that confessional poetry is defined by its form, not by whether the details are true. Confessional writing takes the form of autobiography, the author appearing to bare his or her soul. Like confessional poetry, the songs of Mitchell and Taylor feature direct address, and, like the poetry, these songs reveal personal pain and suffering. Taylor's "Fire and Rain," the first big confessional hit, as I have argued elsewhere, is remarkable for "the starkness of the pain and despair it reveals. Pop music had long featured laments about lost love, being pop, they seemed conventional rather than personal. 'Fire and Rain' advertises itself as autobiography."[16]

Cohen, who was born in 1934, was closer in age to some of those poets, including Plath (born 1932) and Sexton (1928), than he was to Dylan (1941), Mitchell (1943), or Taylor (1948), and he was a poet before he became a songwriter. But Cohen was not a confessional poet. As Julian Stannard shows in Chapter 2 of this volume, Cohen's work remains engaged with the modernism of Pound, Eliot, and Yeats.[17] And yet, as Stannard also shows, some of Cohen's poems draw explicitly on his private life, for example, his father's death when Cohen was nine. Still, even these poems do not take the form of autobiography, unlike his first novel, *The Favourite Game* (1963). While it's not clear whether most of these poems presume the convention of a speaker, they do not feel directly addressed by a self revealing itself to us. We have the sense that Cohen is telling us about his thoughts and emotions, but in forms that distance them from him as an individual.

Cohen's songs in general remain true to his poetry in this sense. They make use of autobiographical details, but they do not present themselves as confession. But paradoxically, the songs do rely on something like the convention of direct address that characterizes the confessional singer-songwriters. This has to do largely with the difference between songs and poems. We speak of poets having voices, but that's a metaphor. Singers have actual voices through which we hear the lyrics they sing, and if the singer has also written the lyrics, it is hard not to hear them as a form of

---

[16] David R. Shumway, *Rock Star: The Making of Musical Icons from Elvis to Springsteen* (Baltimore: Johns Hopkins University Press, 2014), 154–55.

[17] This engagement with modernism is something Cohen shares with Dylan, as I argue in *Rock Star*, but Dylan's obscurity and primitivism represent aspects of modernist poetry missing from Cohen's poems.

direct address. The effect is heightened when, as on most of Cohen's albums, the singer's voice is unambiguously meant to be the center of the listener's attention. On the stripped-down early albums, the production is designed to focus the ear on Leonard's voice and his lyrics. This may account for why what were heard as defects in his voice were so often mentioned in early reviews. As Liel Leibovitz put it, "Cohen wanted nothing standing between [his listeners] and his words, removing all distractions, from ornate arrangements to excessively impenetrable voices ... Dylan reveled in the playful and surreal. Cohen was sincere and direct."[18]

"Suzanne," the first song for which Cohen was known, illustrates these points well. It is now well-known that the eponymous Suzanne was the dancer and bohemian Suzanne Verdal whom Cohen knew in Montreal in the 1960s. She was, according to Simmons, something like his soulmate but not his lover, and the biographer confirms that she did indeed serve tea and oranges.[19] So, the song is about an actual person who was part of Cohen's life, but it is not directly about Cohen or even his relationship with this person. Verses one and three speak of Suzanne by name in relation not to a singing "I" but to an impersonal "you." Of course, it is not uncommon to speak of one's own experience using the second person, but its effect is to generalize that experience, to make it in principle available to the audience. The song as a result seems less a revelation of Leonard's private life than a more public account of a remarkable woman. The second verse, which begins "And Jesus was a sailor," takes the song even farther away from the singer's life. It points the song in the direction of the spiritual and mystical, and it makes us rethink the chorus. Following the first verse, the lines "For you've touched her perfect body/ With your mind" seem to be about unconsummated physical desire. After the second verse, the pronouns change such that Jesus has touched "your" perfect body, and, after the third, it is Suzanne doing the touching. These shifting pronouns further distance the song from the singer. And yet Cohen's recording of the song, in

---

[18] Liel Leibovitz, *A Broken Hallelujah: Rock and Roll, Redemption, and the Life of Leonard Cohen* (New York: W. W. Norton, 2014), 148–49.

[19] Simmons, *I'm Your Man*, 124–26.

which his voice and acoustic guitar dominate, makes it feel as though we are in direct communication with the singer. This description also shows how the song uses the folk convention of voice and acoustic guitar, but in the service of lyrics that have left folk conventions behind.

If we compare "Suzanne" to a song like Taylor's "Fire and Rain," we see how different Cohen's use of autobiography was. Taylor's song also mentions a Suzanne, yet the song is not about her but about his reaction to her death. As Heather Arnet puts it in Chapter 16 of this volume, "The thirty-three uses of 'I' and 'me' make it clear who is the central character of Taylor's song. The focus in Cohen's song is on the female character." Where Cohen's three verses point towards mysteries of relationships and the spiritual, Taylor's song is about his own emotional struggles, each verse alluding to a different one. As I have shown elsewhere, fans heard "Fire and Rain" as autobiographical, and there was intense interest in discovering what events had motivated it. In 1971, articles in both *Rolling Stone* and the *New York Times Magazine* revealed those events to be "a friend's suicide, Taylor's heroin addiction, and the break-up of his first band, the Flying Machine."[20] Musically, the spare accompaniment and Spanish guitar sounds on "Suzanne" reinforce the mysterious character of the lyrics, while "Fire and Rain" at first strikes the ear as a simple melody and folk-rock-style arrangement. While more careful listening reveals chords and an arrangement that borrows from a number of sources uncommon in rock, the appearance of simplicity corresponds to the apparent openness of the singer about his life.

"Suzanne" illustrates how Cohen's songs move away from those of the folk revival, treating spiritual or perhaps aesthetic concerns rather than the public issues or experiences of the earlier folk performers. The general pattern of an almost conversational and highly distinctive voice singing about diverse topics, but not openly about the singer, is consistent throughout Cohen's first three albums. Some of these songs do clearly make use of autobiographical details. Famously, "So Long, Marianne," was inspired by Marianne Ihlen, with whom Cohen had lived on the Greek island of Hydra. The song is clearly about the singer's ambivalence about the woman the song addresses – the chorus proclaims that they should both laugh and cry – but it

---

[20] Shumway, "Emergence," 15.

reveals very little about the singer. The verses tell us mainly about how Marianne affects the singer, but because of the song's ambivalence, even that is inconsistent. The song's mood is what makes it distinctive, distinguishing it from most love songs, which profess certain love or hate. That attitude does characterize the singer, making him more of an individual than someone singing, say, Cole Porter's "Every Time We Say Goodbye." "The Story of Issac" from *Songs from a Room* alludes obliquely to the death of Cohen's father by giving the narrator the age of nine, but the song is not about that event. "Famous Blue Raincoat," on *Songs of Love and Hate* (1971), is named for a Burberry coat Cohen himself had purchased in London when he first arrived there in 1959, and which was stolen from his New York apartment in 1968.[21] In the song, the coat is owned not by Cohen, who is identified as the speaker (or writer) of this letter, but to its addressee, "my brother my killer," a man who was also involved with "Jane." The song's description of the writer's situation – the time of day, where he is living, the weather – makes it sound personal, specific, and yet the song is defined by the ambivalence expressed in the dual attribution brother–killer. The letter seems to be almost thanking the addressee for the affair he had with Jane. This is a kind of confessionalism, but one very different in tone from the more straightforward expressions of "Fire and Rain" or "River."

Probably Cohen's most overtly autobiographical song is "Chelsea Hotel No. 2," with its account of a blow job at that location. It is presented as memoir, the song beginning "I remember you well in the Chelsea Hotel." Lines like "giving me head on an unmade bed" are what led the *Telegraph* in its obituary to remark:

> the overriding feature of Cohen's writing was what he described as "accuracy." It emphasized lyrics with the "qualities of a novel" and involved the compression of long pieces into song-sized bites … The realism of Cohen's lyrics brought sex into an arena more usually occupied by love – and their delivery had the air of the confessional.[22]

---

[21] Nadel, *Various Positions*, 73.

[22] "Leonard Cohen, Poet and Singer-Songwriter – Obituary," *Telegraph* (November 11, 2016): sec. Obituaries, www.proquest.com/docview/1838348761/abstract/C5A2 B387DECA4EEDPQ/1. For a better understanding of Cohen's sexual frankness, see Yaffe, Chapter 15 in this volume.

But "Chelsea Hotel No. 2" seems less like a confession than a combination of a boast and lament. This seems more the case after Cohen's revelation, which he later said he regretted, that the song is about Janis Joplin. Like "Suzanne," it is very much about the unnamed woman whom the singer remembers, but it does tell us more about the singer and his feelings, which are predictably ambivalent. The opening line is to some extent contradicted directly in the end by "I don't even think of you that often." The fact that the encounter was a one-night stand seems to be celebrated in the song's chorus, where the woman's never having said "I need you" is praised. Her assertion that he was not handsome is presented humorously, but one can imagine that the remark would have been wounding. Her untimely death is described as getting away and "turning your back on the crowd," as if it were her choice to overdose.

Compare this song to Mitchell's "River," in which the singer confesses "I'm selfish and I'm sad." Of this song, Mitchell said, "I have on occasion sacrificed myself and my own emotional makeup ... We all suffer for our loneliness, but at the time of *Blue*, our pop stars never admitted these things."[23] Mitchell clearly doesn't see this song as self-promotion, but as self-revelation. She called herself a "confessional poet" who became so "out of a compulsion to be honest with my audience."[24] Later she would reject that label and the idea of compulsion, holding that her songs were not confessions, because they were not forced out of her.[25] But like "Fire and Rain," and other songs by both Mitchell and Taylor, it is hard not to hear "River" as "self-therapeutic," one of the motives Rosenthal ascribed to confessional poetry. Moreover, the stated "compulsion to honesty" corresponds to the strong sense that the song is not about an invented "speaker," but Joni Mitchell herself. Indeed, as I have argued, the sense of direct address in the work of the singer-songwriters is stronger than it is in the poetry of Plath or Lowell.[26]

---

[23] Joni Mitchell quoted in Timothy White, "A Portrait of the Artist," *Billboard* (December 9, 1995): 15.

[24] Joni Mitchell, "The Rolling Stone Interview," *Rolling Stone* (July 26, 1979): 49.

[25] Joni Mitchell quoted in Stephen Holden, "The Ambivalent Hall of Famer," *New York Times* (December 1, 1996): 36.

[26] Shumway, *Rock Star*, 159.

There are no songs in Cohen's oeuvre that claim this kind of direct address. We know that Cohen, like Mitchell, suffered from depression and, like Taylor, from substance abuse, but there are no songs that tell us directly of these experiences. We don't have the sense that songwriting for Cohen was self-therapeutic, as he turned perhaps instead to the discipline of Zen. It is striking that, while Mitchell wrote at least two songs explicitly about her relationship with Leonard, he wrote nothing about that relationship. Indeed, even songs like "So Long, Marianne" are not about relationships in the way that Mitchell's are. Mitchell would continue after *Blue* to produce songs on *For the Roses*, *Court and Spark*, and *Hejira* that dissect the way intimate relationships succeed and fail. Cohen's songs, on the contrary, deal with love and with lust, but they regard these finally as mysteries. Mitchell's characterization of him as a "holy man" seems an accurate reflection of their differences, she having a profoundly secular vision that claimed to see through to the practical reality behind such mysteries.

Cohen, then, is both a key figure in the singer-songwriter movement, but his songs are not typical of it. His early recordings and personal connections helped to launch the movement. His songs moved away from those of the folk revival into more personal and introspective territory. He presented himself as sincere and direct with this audience, but he did not mainly sing about himself or his problems. This may be why Cohen's recordings were not as popular as those of the singer-songwriters like Mitchell, Taylor, and Browne who emerged a bit later, and for whom he partly paved the way. Their confessionalism may have allowed their listeners to feel closer to them, where Cohen remained for his audience a more remote and mysterious figure. And yet, if the number of covers tells us anything, in the long run, Cohen's songs seem destined to outlive those of all of the singer-songwriters, except Mitchell.

CHAPTER 7

Unrocking Rock & Roll

Hiding Songs, War Horses, and Cabaret Blues

Eric Weisbard

THE ICONIC AUSTRALIAN POSTPUNK, NICK CAVE, CONNECTS the transgressive nature of his music, the cataclysmic experiences in his personal life, and yet the relatively straightforward nature of his artistic career with a perfect antidote to the audacity of star text. He answers questions online, in the manner of an author rather than a rocker. Asked for his favorite pieces of music in 2019, he remembered an earlier poem, "The Sick Bag Song," which included his reaction to hearing Leonard Cohen as a boy:

> The boy will grow older, and over time there will be other songs – not many – ten or maybe twenty in a lifespan, that stand apart from the rest of the music he will discover. He will realize that not only are these songs sacred, they are "hiding songs" that deal exclusively in darkness, obfuscation, concealment, and secrecy. He will realize that for him the purpose of these songs was to shut off the sun, to draw a long shadow down and protect him from the corrosive glare of the world.

For this particular Red Hand Files, Cave elaborated on what some of these "hiding songs" might be, calling them "the essential pillars that hold up the structure of my artistic world." The first cited, preceding others by Karen Dalton, Neil Young, John Lee Hooker, Big Star, and Nina Simone, by Bill Callahan and Gun Club, was Leonard Cohen's "Avalanche."[1]

---

[1] Nick Cave, *Red Hand Files*, January 2019, www.theredhandfiles.com/10-most-favourite-pieces-music/.

Let's start there as we reckon with Cohen's relationship to rock & roll. Not with Bob Dylan embracing "Hallelujah" early. Not with Nirvana's Kurt Cobain pulling for "a Leonard Cohen afterworld, so I can sigh eternally." Not with indie supergroup boygenius, who in the months after I accepted this assignment released "Leonard Cohen," which quotes "Anthem" – "There is a crack in everything/ That's how the light gets in" – but protests "And I am not an old man having an existential crisis/ At a Buddhist monastery writing horny poetry."

Not with Lana Del Rey, also caught up with cracks in 2023, with "Kintsugi" and "Let the Light In," but for whom drawing long shadows down, to use Cave's language, beats feminist riposte any day. Not with latest pop sensation Sabrina Carpenter, putting down a lover: "Try to come off like you're soft and well-spoken/ Jack off to lyrics by Leonard Cohen." Not with Connor Roy on *Succession* performing "Famous Blue Raincoat" as his first-ever karaoke to corrosive glares from his siblings. Not with Big Thief's "Not," either, prime Cohen parataxis though it is ("not the end, not the beginning, not losing, not winning"); bandleader Adrianne Lenker has a Leonard Cohen tattoo.

Start with the avalanche. "I stepped into an avalanche, it covered up my soul," Cohen sang, his words dating to a poem in his earlier poetry collection, *Parasites of Heaven*. The lyrics make him out to be a Notre Dame troll, a stabbed Jesus, a beggarly cripple, a wearer of others' flesh. As his great biographer, Sylvie Simmons (findable on YouTube covering the tune), wrote:

> It is sung in the character of a hunchback, a grotesque creature with a mountain of gold lusting over women – a Nazi caricature of a Jew. Or from the depths of hell by a tormented man who longs for connection with the Divine. Or by a man who already has the woman but does not want her or the domesticity she offers. And/or it is sung by God – a gentle, New Testament Jesus, with the crumbs of the Last Supper on the table and a wound in his side, who turns out to be as hard as an Old Testament Jehovah.[2]

Perhaps, Genius.com speculates, the "golden hill" references Hindu mythology, too.

---

[2] Sylvie Simmons, *I'm Your Man: The Life of Leonard Cohen* (New York: HarperCollins, 2012), 248.

Though Cohen was the rare singer-songwriter with lyrics published as straight poetry, what made him a rock icon required music and singing. His "chop," as he called it, a set of flamenco chords learned in Montreal – as he told the tale – from a Spanish street musician who killed himself mid tutelage, proved perfect for his Lorca-themed poetry because it was a loop, confined like his vocal range, not some Fender eruption. As for those flattened melodies, Cohen sang with just enough of a mystery accent that they leavened. And enough of a chuckle, too: a masked actor's distancing rather than a method actor's reality invasion. That, combined with the strategic ways his downer lyrics always found space to register the absurdity of their gesturing, made sure he never turned into Jim Morrison.

With "Avalanche" and other songs like it, Cohen created classic examples of a form unknown to 1950s rock & roll but central to post-Dylan rock: war horses. Elongated songs in the manner of long poems, sequences that even on arrival, before they became festival rituals, or had every take reissued for added overkill, felt well-worn and epic. War horses refused to be power ballads of love, substituting instead the role, thematically useful to protopunks as much as postpunks, of pinnacles of anti-heroicism. They were failures told as boasts. Examples include Neil Young's "Down by the River," Richard and Linda Thompson's "The Cavalry Cross," Pere Ubu's "Thirty Seconds over Tokyo," the Velvet Underground's "Heroin," and seemingly Patti Smith's entire repertoire. Can't really leave out "Stairway to Heaven," "Hotel California," and "Free Bird," can we? "Hallelujah," then, must be namechecked too.

Cohen could not rage, instrumentally or vocally. Little rock & roll could erupt out of his cadences. When Nick Cave's second band, the Bad Seeds, performed "Avalanche," it sounded feral, as if revivified by Australians on the other side of the planet for a scene out of a *Mad Max* movie. Lou Reed would induct Cohen into the Rock & Roll Hall of Fame, marveling at his words, not his nonexistent position as a rock & roll animal. By contrast, when Reed took up Cohen's early "Stranger Song" in a 2006 Hal Willner tribute concert, he cracked his guitar over the thing like Warhol had once encouraged a Velvets crony to crack a whip.[3] The whole absence of rocking became something of a joke, like the time

---

[3] "Lou Reed: The Stranger Song," www.youtube.com/watch?v=5df2NXYZ8OE.

Cohen called back a woman who had advertised in the personals that she was seeking a man who combined "the raw energy of Iggy Pop with the elegant wit of Leonard Cohen."[4]

But the man from the family with the Montreal clothing factory money, born to wear a suit, could summon an avalanche. His keyword, dark, eventually became his testament, his *Blackstar*, with the no-question-asked title track of his final album: *You Want It Darker*. If Cohen could not rock, in the "Louie Louie" sense, he could compete in this category, the man who, as Cave attested, pulled down the shadows and shut off the sun, who created hiding songs. He belonged in the rock & roll pantheon to the extent that rock revised itself away from Chuck Berry and towards Hank Williams, away from Beatles and towards Nirvana, away from mass popularity provoking subcultural revolt and towards a permanent "indie" demographic of folks with his kind of raw–cooked taste and breeding.

To productively recast this argument, consider "Avalanche," too, as a song in the tradition of what Michael Denning, in his book *The Cultural Front*, called "cabaret blues."[5] Denning grappled with how the Popular Front, a communist effort to stem fascism worldwide in the 1930s, used American popular culture in the 1930s to further a left-wing European notion of revolution: a "Ballad for Americans" here, a *Cradle Will Rock* there. First, from the right, with the Red Scare purges of the 1950s, then from the New Left, with the counterculture of the 1960s, many of these works had been expunged as flimsy agit-prop. Denning responded by expanding the category: Orson Welles's undoubtedly great *Citizen Kane* was a "cultural front" work, however skeptical of revolution in tone. The cultural front's signature move was less political than formal, a termite assault on ruling ideology. This in part involved mocking, through the construction of grotesque parallels, verities of epic American pop-culture norms, the "genius of the system," from Hollywood genres to big bands. As important to Denning was the audience, a "cultural formation" of immigrants' children raised in America, Blacks from the Great

---

[4] Simmons, *I'm Your Man*, 355.

[5] Michael Denning, *The Cultural Front: The Laboring of American Culture in the Twentieth Century* (New York: Verso, 1996).

Migration, union stalwarts, and other city types. This formation, however, cracked with World War Two and beyond, as white southerners migrated north and nuclear family suburbs rose up like atom clouds.

Substitute Elvis Presley and rock & roll more generally for that last part. Add to the mix the kids playing in garage bands because their middle-class suburban Levittowns were outgrowing downtowns. In this span of rock & roll becoming rock, the older Cohen, with his ties to Montreal, Judaism, and the global cosmopolitanism of a home in Hydra, offered along with his dark courtliness a cultural front restoration of sorts within the rock formation. Denning, writing about the mixture of European cabaret ideals and jazzy blues at Café Society, one of the Popular Front's leading venues, develops his "cabaret blues" idea around "Strange Fruit," written by the left activist Abel Meeropol but shaped by Billie Holiday's authorial presence as a singer. For John Hammond, a leftist with serious popular music expertise who had been an early supporter, Holiday was ruined by "Strange Fruit," drifting from jazz standards to become "mannered" and "stylized." Denning responded by asking how a cabaret blues that led to "God Bless the Child," "Don't Explain," and other masterpieces could be dismissed. These Holiday "love songs" of a formally unorthodox type negated the pastoral South, the beaten woman of the torch song – they were blues, but darker and more European, what Denning called "songs of love and hunger."[6]

Cohen's *Songs of Love and Hate*, the final album in a trilogy ushered in by Hammond himself, who pushed Columbia Records to sign him and then got out of the way, were works in the cultural front tradition of cabaret blues. He was the opposite of Presley, rocking all blues away with an all-American YES in Greil Marcus's "Presliad" account.[7] You could hardly call him a hippie: as he once told a critic:

> From when I was coming of age in Montreal there was the bohemians, then the Beats, the beatniks, the hipsters – which was a group I liked – and then there were the hippies. By the time the hippies came along, they pulled

---

[6] Ibid., 347.
[7] Greil Marcus, *Mystery Train: Images of America in Rock 'n' Roll Music* (London: The Folio Society, 2020 [1975]), 157–231.

flowers out of public gardens. They left their campsites in messes. There seemed to be something flabby about the movement. No self-discipline.[8]

And notably, while he struggled to fill seats in American venues outside New York and Los Angeles, and could not even get a US release for the album that contained "Hallelujah," he was bigger than Dylan in Europe.

Rock needed cabaret blues to question the counterculture's arena bands and singer-songwriters. That was glam, Ziggy Stardust, as we usually tell the tale: a modernist rejection of organic hippie communalism, favoring the strange, especially regarding gender and sexuality. You can shoehorn the Leonard Cohen who sang "Avalanche" into this moment: the dissipated performer, touring the continent and Israel on drugs and red wine, captured in the headshot photo on the cover of *Songs of Love and Hate*. But hiding songs are a bigger lineage than glam, with room for a range of old-soul bohemians. Put the cabaret-blues Cohen on a playlist with the Neil Young who sang "Revolution Blues" or Lou Reed's *Berlin*, with Alex Chilton sliding down into the "Holocaust" of Big Star's tortured third album, Sly Stone's *There's a Riot* [Not] *Goin' On*, and jazzy Joni Mitchell, P-Funk's "Maggot Brain," and the Bowie of *Low*. If Popular Front culture was charged with agit-prop, these broken hallelujahs would be damned as self-indulgent. ("My person has been satirized as being suicidal, melancholy, and self-indulgent," Cohen told a *New York Times* writer in 1973.)[9] And as with *Citizen Kane*, or Holiday's modernist love songs, exiting the movement, crashing down iconography, proved useful; here, it gave rock & roll a new wing. An alternative, as we called it in my *Spin* days, putting an entry on Cohen, not Dylan, into the *Spin Alternative Record Guide*.

"EVERYBODY KNOWS": THE ALT-ROCK LEONARD COHEN

Hiding songs were half of Leonard Cohen's rock & roll legacy by the 1990s. For the other piece, Cohen as a symbolic leader for alternative

---

[8] Sylvie Simmons, "Leonard Cohen: Felonious Monk," *Mojo* (November 2001), accessed at Rocksbackpages.com.

[9] Mike Jahn, "I Have Been Satirized as Suicidal and Self-Indulgent," *New York Times* Special Features Syndicate (June 1973), in *Leonard Cohen on Leonard Cohen: Interviews and Encounters*, ed. Jeff Burger (Chicago: Chicago Review Press, 2014), 44.

rock, go to archive.org, of all unlikely places, and check out what, for reasons of commerce or clearances, is left of a former Hollywood teen movie. The first iteration of Leonard Cohen on screen had been Robert Altman's Western-puncturing *McCabe & Mrs. Miller*, using the songs to animate a work that paralleled "Avalanche," right through to Warren Beatty's gambler dying in the snow. *Pump up the Volume* claimed no such gravitas. It started, "You ever get the feeling that everything in America is completely fucked up?" We are experiencing just the voice of a DJ calling himself "Hard Harry" or Happy Harry Hardon, "a total sex maniac," says a high school girl passing around the tape of his pirate radio broadcast in her suburban Arizona high school the next day.

Yet Cohen's song "Everybody Knows," from the 1988 album *I'm Your Man*, is the first song we see Harry play, putting the needle directly on the vinyl album, no slip-cueing, just letting a scratchy plunk-down lead into an opening pulse that blends string section and cheap keyboard, homologically akin in its modern rock sonics to the Soundgarden, Camper Van Beethoven, the Pixies, and Henry Rollins tapes depicted holding up the DJ's radio clock. Gone from the Cohen mix is that flamenco guitar chop, replaced by what might be Cohen's version of Barry White's quiet storm, only anticipating Depeche Mode's "Enjoy the Silence." In another change, the lyrical message is more pointed: "Everybody knows that the dice are loaded ... Everybody knows the fight was fixed/ The poor stay poor the rich get rich." Cohen doesn't sound like a vocal hunchback now. Taking us through the opening credits, he's an MC of pomp and new circumstances, the equivalent of Aerosmith's Steven Tyler making an everlasting lozenge of "Sweet Emotion" in the opening sequence of *Dazed & Confused* or Bill Haley dotting the beat in "Rock around the Clock" to start *American Graffiti* like Morse Code delivering a telegram from the past. There's a scoff when Cohen gets to "everybody wants a box of chocolates and a long stem" – he lets that baritone take a proud bow for a moment – "rooooossssseee." The attribution, "Written and Directed by Allan Moyle," comes during the line that reverts social retrenchment back to sexual betrayal with a cuckold's bravado: "everybody knows that you've been faithful, give or take a night or two."

Hard Harry, played by Christian Slater (for a time the alternative rock era's Jack Nicholson), delivers an opening monologue about how everything has been done already, the great themes turned into theme parks. Some seventeen minutes in, he starts up his show on a different night, once more to the sound of Cohen's dice getting rolled. He talks about how much he hates the legacy of the 1960s, and plays "Wienerschnitzel" by the brilliant hardcore band Descendents, so why does a guy associated with the counterculture serve as his theme music? Clue: he also loves "Love Comes in Spurts," by Richard Hell and the Voidoids, loves Lenny Bruce. The goal here is to reject being a hippie, which in part means rejecting the urge to live entirely in a scene comprised, narcissistically, of one's own generation. "If It Be Your Will," another of Cohen's great war horses, is heard mid movie, a psalm to mourn a listener who killed himself. A cover version of "Everybody Knows," by the then current California rock band Concrete Blonde, launches the action segment, where Harry transmits from a moving jeep, evading the Federal Communications Commission and preaching a samizdat we now recognize as social media. The characters say "hallelujah" a lot.

Cohen's dank cave in the center of the world had become alternative rock's idea of a shiny stage. "Curiously enough, the generation after punk has cited me as an influence," he told writer Mark Dery in the 1980s. "There's something intransigent [in my work] that I think allows them to refer to me as someone who has stood outside [of mainstream music] – voluntarily stood outside – but with a certain longing for the inside."[10] Outside, longing for inside: *I'm Your Fan*, a tribute album named for *I'm Your Man*, released in the same 1991 weeks as *Nevermind* and *Ten*, began with Michael Stipe of R.E.M. singing "First We Take Manhattan" like he was still gliding off "Losing My Religion." The Pixies continued the *I'm Your Man* cover material – Simmons tells an amazing story of how the band, burnt out beyond reconciliation, tried to go their separate ways in Spain, but Black Francis and Kim Deal wound up booked side-by-side in a beach hotel, so the offstage Charles Thompson stayed in his room playing Cohen's album on repeat. Nick Cave bashed out "Tower of Song," making Cohen his Hank Williams in the verse: "I said to

---

[10] Mark Dery, "Leonard Cohen's Impeccable Chop," *Frets* (November 1988), accessed at Rocksbackpages.com.

Leonard Cohen, how lonely does it get?" And, dipping back an album, with consequences that would not become apparent too quickly, John Cale (Lou Reed's key collaborator in the Velvet Underground) revised and sang "Hallelujah."

If we take *Various Positions* (1984), *I'm Your Man* (1988), and *The Future* (1992) as Cohen's second key trilogy of albums, the parallels that *Pump up the Volume* and *I'm Your Fan* propose between Cohen's music and that of college radio and alternative rock become still more striking. *Positions*, refused a domestic release by Columbia initially, was the closest Cohen came to releasing an indie record, in the same year that groups like the Replacements, Hüsker Dü, Minutemen, and Meat Puppets were selling few albums but establishing enduring legacies. *I'm Your Man* emerged as major labels started signing and promoting indie bands, as grunge acts in Seattle pumped Black Sabbath into the indie mix to make the darkness louder. Cohen was an elder in a moment that saw the Berlin Wall fall and the first serious efforts to sacralize the underground lineage of noncommercial rock; for example, that forever treasured appearance in 1989, on the fringe-friendly *Night Music*, performing "Who by Fire" with Sonny Rollins. And *The Future* came out a month before Bill Clinton's election day ended twelve years of Reagan–Bush, in the aftermath of Nirvana and Pearl Jam ending hair metal. It was a wave of short-lived newness: New Democrats in office, new rock mainstream, that end of the Cold War rah-rah-rah, liberal version. As Cohen sang: "democracy is coming – to the USA."

Everybody knows what happened next: the new turned out to be the neo (liberalism, but also Keanu as Neo replacing Christian in the pop-culture *Matrix*), with arena rock returned to metal once grunge imploded. In 1994, the same year his grudging admirer Kurt Cobain killed himself, Cohen took himself out of the mix to stay Zen on Mt. Baldy for five years. *The Future?* So much for that. Cohen had always hedged his bets: "I've seen the future, baby – it is murder," his title track went. The song nodded back to the avalanche, "the blizzard of the world." Songs from *The Future* featured in the Trent Reznor–produced soundtrack to another rocking movie, *Natural Born Killers*. "Waiting for the Miracle" played to start the film, quickly replaced by L7's "Shitlist": much more rocking and badass, like Juliette Lewis.

"Anthem," including the part about cracks letting the light in, was heard during the violent prison riot sequence. "Future" came on for the closing credits of this Oliver Stone–directed film of a Quentin Tarantino film – cabaret blues as *Pulp Fiction / The Doors*. "Everybody Knows" itself in 1994 moved to a different picture, Atom Egoyan's *Exotica*. Mia Kirshner, like Cohen a McGill graduate, played the strip-club dancer who did her featured number to the song's ungroove. More than in *Pump*, the lyric about infidelity took precedence: the social realm abandoned for cracked-up male heteronormativity.

What felt at the time like an alternative route for rock, for Generation X, turned out to feed back into the main highway, with Cohen's always socially rooted disaffection (he was a pussy hound, but also a child of the Holocaust years) fodder for eternal arty white male disaffection. The avalanche in Cave's favorite hiding song came to serve as a metaphor for all the rebels through the generations, piled – bohemians, Beats, beatniks, hipsters. The parallels are easy to draw: James Joyce got to Cave's "darkness, obfuscation, concealment and secrecy" decades earlier, famously writing: "I will try to express myself in some mode of life or art as freely as I can and as wholly as I can, using for my defence the only arms I allow myself to use – silence, exile, and cunning." Cohen had a knack for making that endless lineage his subject, rather than getting nailed to a specific scene. No wonder Phoebe Bridgers pokes fun at Cohen from within a power trio of female singer-songwriters named boygenius. That's how it goes. And everybody knows.

CRACKED ANTHEMS: COHEN IN THE MADISON SQUARE GARDEN

What is Leonard Cohen's relationship to rock & roll in the 2020s, then? As many have observed, when pop culture becomes lore a kind of unpredictable freeze-framing takes place: that image of Marilyn over the air grate, that Nirvana t-shirt, and *Hamilton* meme about immigrants. In Cohen's case, the shot-glass encapsulation for the tourists is "Hallelujah." David played a secret chord, first to please the cool lords like Dylan and Cale but ultimately to soundtrack sex in a failed *Watchmen* movie and sanction modulation in televised singing competitions. Rock & roll, in the twenty-first-century pop-rock bazaar, is a mixture of old songs streamed by the billion, merch counters real and virtual grinding away the differences between a Brando and a Marley, and endless adaptations: the shriek Cohen never had in him *Transformered* into a Shrek.

But you can also read that story the other way: even in the DreamWorks version of rock & roll, holes open and Leonard Cohen gets in. His final years, of course, saw him return to touring to make money after his manager stole his funds and sold his publishing. But on the stage this time he was cheery, skipping, telling jokes as he had all along (check out the stand-up that begins the first Canadian documentary on him, *Ladies and Gentlemen, Mr. Leonard Cohen*, for verification), but cornier than ever. Evidence that he was connecting came at Glastonbury, one of those big festival gatherings which, at Monterey, Woodstock, and in Cohen's case the Isle of Wight, had first allowed rock to separate itself from rock & roll. Now, many decades later, festivals were a nostalgic claiming of a lost role, like the VMA Awards; they allowed rock to integrate itself back into a version of youth culture. Cohen sang "Hallelujah," Glastonbury sang with him, and other stadium-sized audiences followed. This time, the big gatherings included the United States – Leonard Cohen, who might have been imagined playing Carnegie Hall, like his mentor Judy Collins, now filled Madison Square Garden, the ultimate rocker validation.

There was much on the first tour document, *Live from London*, deriving from *I'm Your Man* (six tracks) and *The Future* (four); nothing from *Songs of Love and Hate*. Had the "Avalanche" protopunk version of Leonard Cohen, the 1990s alt-rock version of Leonard Cohen, become a mainstream Leonard Cohen? He loved his line about the "little Jew who wrote the Bible," got his friends drunk on a signature cocktail to play Irving Berlin's "Always" to the point of gagging. Had the nomad from Montreal with the Dylan fixation learned assimilation lessons from the immigrant from Russian pogroms who came to author "White Christmas"? Hardly. Or at least, as the former president of his college fraternity, the charmer, learned soon enough, at the end of the pop-rock era "you want it darker" was not a mandate reserved for those catering to the fringe, Warhol to grunge. It was a kind of credentialing, updating Sinatra the swinger for viewers of *The Sopranos*. "It's Not MOR. It's

Leonard Cohen." *Songs of Love and Hate* material featured on subsequent tours and live releases.

What Cohen's relationship to rock & roll became in this third act, I believe, was a combination of a stunning catalog and a no less mesmerizing set of reference points. In place of the Great American Songbook, he offered a global syllabus, telling the host of KCRW-FM's "Bookworm" show, in 2006, about his inspirations:

> I read a lot of Lorca at the time and a lot of Isaiah and apocalyptic literature appealed to me. The prayer book, the synagogue, the labor movement, collectors like Alan Lomax, singers like Pete Seeger, the *People's Songbook*, the Almanac Singers. Or the European side, singers like Amelia Rodriguez and the flamenco singers, the fado singers, the French chanteurs. Those were the influences.[11]

No mention of rock & roll here, but more than enough to take a dedicated listener into the roots of "Suzanne," which did not in 1966–67 require that its author and eventual singer go electric, like the Dylan who for an instant was trying to kill both Tin Pan Alley and folk music. "Suzanne" quickly became part of the global pop-rock songbook. Then, belatedly, "Hallelujah." Maybe now, even later still, "Anthem."

But the songs are not the full story; they mix with the life, the people that – to use language he never would, post-rock language at that – Leonard Cohen fucked with, sexually, professionally, and monastically. Fans know that the Suzanne of the song, connected to Montreal bohemia and late nights by water, was different from the Suzanne who bore his two children, different from the Marianne he sang "So Long" to, who returned from Hydra to Norway. Those of us with overly large record collections can play musical chairs: Lorca, Cohen's daughter, has a child who is mostly being raised by Rufus Wainwright, son of Loudon and Montreal's Kate McGarrigle (of the cult duo Kate and Ana McGarrigle), this modern-day family also connected via Loudon's later marriage to the Roches. Only Cohen seems not to have sung with any of them; he preferred k.d. lang's "Hallelujah" and cowrote "Everybody

---

[11] Interview with Michael Silverblattt, June 24, 2006, "Bookworm," KCRW-FM (Santa Monica, California), in Burger (ed.), *Leonard Cohen on Leonard Cohen*, 519.

Knows," "Waiting for the Miracle," and then the entirety of *Ten New Songs* with his former backing singer, Sharon Robinson, who in the same years, too, was part of the team that made the song "New Attitude" for Patti LaBelle to sing in *Beverly Hills Cop*. The sometime resident of Mt. Baldy made his most lasting home in a condo in Los Angeles proper and always found new ways to connect to the industry; yeah, Walter Yetnikoff dissed him, but it's not like he left Columbia Records over it.

Boygenius were hardly the first cool rockers to have a bit of fun with Leonard Cohen. In *Mystery Train*, Greil Marcus gleefully cited a comment that singer-songwriter Randy Newman had made from onstage about an answer song of a kind. "This isn't Leonard Cohen's 'Suzanne'," Newman said about his song about a stalker's late-night fantasies. "It's on a somewhat lower moral plane, actually."[12] Just as he was never removed from commerce (Randy Newman, with all those film soundtracks, could identify with that part), Cohen was never removed from the charge of insufferable cult-stud, no matter how many jokes he told. He couldn't rock out, but he could have sex with Janis Joplin and then tell about it with chilling dismissiveness ("I don't think of you that often") and that great line, projecting a rock-star identity he did not yet possess, "giving me head on the unmade bed while the limousines wait in the street."

But if we are to put that onto Cohen's ledger sheet, it would be remiss to not immediately cite another classic from pop rock's Tower of Song, the time Joni Mitchell made Cohen her muse for once in his philandering life and got "A Case of You," Prince's favorite of her canon, out of it. Maybe the current-day champion warhorse singer, Lana Del Rey, target of many a smirk, who along with citing "Anthem" unsarcastically has covered "Chelsea Hotel No. 2" with Cohen's son, Adam, knows best – embracing not just Cohen's cabaret but his sexist complicity.

Or maybe you hear funny voices in the tower. During Covid, Will Oldham, as Bonnie Prince Billy, and fellow indie songwriter Bill Callahan (formerly Smog), with the great Louisville punk guitarist David Grubbs accompanying, recorded "Night of Santiago," a Lorca work (the 1928 "La Casada Infiel"), given a very different treatment by

---

[12] Marcus, *Mystery Train*, 131.

Philip Glass, that Leonard and Adam worked on together at the end, with help from Spanish musicians and some Jew's harp by Beck. Adam:

> I'd heard it under construction for years, on the front lawn or while we were having coffee or dinner, and I'd always begged him to attempt to write music to it. In a weakened state, he said, "Look, I'll just recite the poem to a certain tempo and you go ahead and you write the music and try to tell the story."[13]

It is a song that, faithful to Lorca, assumes that "any man" would take the faithless woman here to the river and see what happened. Oldham, an actor alongside his own long indie-tweaking discography, raises an eyebrow as the nonmaiden takes off her dress and "We tore away the rest." But he, Callahan, and Grubbs fully apply themselves to the line Cohen added in translation, the needle he offered every balloon: his rock & roll. "You were born to judge the world/ Forgive me but I wasn't."

---

[13] https://music.apple.com/us/album/thanks-for-the-dance/1480060931.

PART III

RELIGIOUS CONTEXTS

CHAPTER 8

Judaism

At the Peripheral Center

Elliot R. Wolfson

THE PROFOUND IMPACT OF LEONARD COHEN'S JEWISH upbringing on his prose writing, poetry, songs, and painting has been well documented. Despite the restlessness of his spirit and his embrace of other spiritual and religious traditions, most notably Christianity and Zen Buddhism – indeed, the convergence of the mystical streams of these three was a central component to Cohen's worldview[1] – there is little room to question that Judaism was the Archimedean point that anchored him throughout his life as he himself has openly acknowledged.[2] His childhood home was steeped in observance of

---

[1] The concurrence of Judaism, Christianity, and Zen Buddhism is essential to my analysis in Elliot R. Wolfson, "New Jerusalem Glowing: Songs and Poems of Leonard Cohen in a Kabbalistic Key," *Kabbalah: A Journal for the Study of Jewish Mystical Texts* 15 (2006): 103–52. This orientation without proper attribution is accepted by Aubrey Glazer, *Tangle of Matter & Ghost: Leonard Cohen's Post-Secular Songbook of Mysticism(s) Jewish & Beyond* (Boston: Academic Studies Press, 2017), 181. See also Maeera Y. Schreiber, *Holy Envy: Writing in the Jewish Christian Borderzone* (New York: Fordham University Press, 2022), 137. After acknowledging that my aforementioned study recognized that Cohen drew on Zen Buddhism, Christianity, and Judaism to assemble a repertoire of symbols and tropes to name his longings, Schreiber concludes that my primary focus on the Lurianic kabbalah and presenting Cohen as a Jewish mystic "necessarily downplays the theological restlessness that informs so much of Cohen's work – as well as perhaps diminishes the profound humanity underwriting his lifelong interest in making poems." Lamentably, this misconstrual of my argument blatantly ignores my insistence that, for Cohen, the particularity of Judaism must always be measured against a universalism that is embracive of the other. As I explicitly noted, it is precisely this keen sensitivity to alterity that was the crux of his spiritual disquiet. See Wolfson, "New Jerusalem," 105–06, 125–26.

[2] For example, consider Cohen's remark in the interview with Ray Martin, May 24, 1985, reprinted in *Leonard Cohen on Leonard Cohen: Interviews and Encounters*, ed. Jeff Burger (Chicago: Chicago Review Press, 2014), 179. In response to the question whether he

Sabbath and Jewish holidays and the time spent at the synagogue left a deep impression that long influenced his poems, lyrics, and melodies. Moreover, on the personal front, he took great pride in his priestly pedigree, and in the fact that his maternal grandfather, Solomon Klonitsky-Kline, was a distinguished rabbi and Talmudic scholar, and that his paternal grandfather, Lyon Cohen, was a prominent figure in the Montreal Jewish community, serving as one of the leaders of Congregation Shaar ha-Shamayim, and helping to establish hospitals, a free loan association, and the first Anglo-Jewish newspaper in North America.[3]

To be sure, as a young adult, Cohen expressed dismay with the materialism of that community and the seeming desolation at its spiritual core. Moreover, his capacious mind made him adverse to viewing Judaism in ethnocentric or autochthonic terms. Consider, for instance, the warning that Cohen offered in the *Book of Mercy* (1984):

> Israel, and you who call yourself Israel, the Church that calls itself Israel, and the revolt that calls itself Israel, and every nation chosen to be a nation – none of these lands is yours, all of you are thieves of holiness, all of you at war with Mercy . . . Therefore, the lands belong to none of you, the borders do not hold, the Law will never serve the lawless.[4]

From Cohen's perspective, to fulfill its prophetic mission, Judaism must serve as the speculum through which to envision the universalization of the particular in the particularization of the universal. The Jew attests figurally to the fact that the general must always be measured from the standpoint of an individuality that withstands collapsing the difference between self and other in the othering of the self as the self of the other. The marker of being Jewish, consequently, is not primarily religious, cultural, or political, but it is rather the spiritual-ethical directive to uphold the dignity of the other based on a keen sensitivity to one's own destiny of being other in this world. Hence, his criticism of and wandering from the Jewish past never

---

felt Jewish, Cohen replied forthrightly, "I know that I am and I came from a good Jewish family, conservative and, yeah, I certainly feel that tradition deeply."

[3] As Cohen acknowledged in the interview with Tom Schnabel, July 13, 1988, in Burger (ed.), *Leonard Cohen*, 237.

[4] Leonard Cohen, *Book of Mercy* (Toronto: McClelland and Stewart, 1984), sec. 28.

entailed a rejection of his roots. As the poem "Last Dance at the Four Penny," addressed to Irving Layton, his Canadian friend and bard, reveals, Cohen considered the act of writing a natural continuation of the rabbinic form of creativity and mystical contemplation: "Layton, when we dance our freilich . . . the miracle rabbis of Prague and Vilna/ Resume their sawdust thrones."[5] Towards the end of his life, confronting a terminal illness, Cohen was even more overt about embracing the tradition from which he temporarily departed. In "Never Mind," he succinctly captured the sentiment of being entrenched in the very soil whence he was deracinated, "In places deep/ With roots entwined/ I live the life/ I left behind."[6]

The influence of his knowledge of Hebrew scripture, Jewish liturgy, and other ritualistic customs is well attested in his writings.[7] Consider, for instance, that his second collection of poems is called *The Spice-Box of Earth* (1961), a title that alludes to the ritual object used in the *havdalah* ceremony at the termination of Sabbath that marks the transition from the holy to the mundane. Indeed, the intent of the title is disclosed in the second poem, which is called "After the Sabbath Prayers." The inspiration of Jewish mysticism is attested by the fact that the poet invoked the image of the butterfly of the Baal Shem, the master of the name, a reference to Israel ben Eliezer, the Baal Shem Tov or founder of modern Hasidism.[8] In spite of the homage paid to this legendary figure in Jewish religious and social history, one cannot neglect to note the irony here, as several of the poems included in this anthology, which deal quite explicitly with Cohen's Jewishness, challenge the credibility of making a hard and fast distinction between the domains of the saintly and the secular. For Cohen, to scale the heights of joy and to plumb the depths of despair are one and the same gesture. In the space of the nonspace of the prayerful heart, there is no discrepancy between the sacred and the cataclysmic.

The quintessential Jewish wisdom found expression years later in "Hallelujah," arguably Cohen's most celebrated hymn: "There's a blaze

---

[5] Leonard Cohen, *The Spice-Box of Earth* (Toronto: McClelland and Stewart, 1961), 64.

[6] Leonard Cohen, *The Flame: Poems Notebooks Lyrics Drawings*, ed. Robert Faggen and Alexandra Pleshoyano (New York: Farrar, Straus, and Giroux, 2018), 137.

[7] See Harry Freedman, *Leonard Cohen: The Mystical Roots of Genius* (London: Bloomsbury Continuum, 2021).

[8] Cohen, *Spice-Box*, 2.

of light in every word;/ It doesn't matter which you heard,/ The holy, or the broken Hallelujah!"[9] In these words, we can detect a theme that is central to Hasidic lore, based on earlier kabbalistic sources, regarding the infusion of light in language; each letter (needless to say, in the Jewish texts, the point is restricted to Hebrew) is an ark that contains the spark of divine luminescence. In a manner consonant with Jewish mystics who have demonstrated the capacity to extend the boundary of tradition without breaking it, Cohen drew the logical conclusion: if the divine light is truly in every word, then there is no difference whether one exalts God with the holy or the broken utterance of praise.[10] Indeed, the latter may be the more authentic acclamation of worship. As Cohen put it in another stanza of the song, "it all went wrong," a typical articulation of Cohen's uncompromising despondency, albeit uttered without bitterness or remorse, because he will still proclaim "Hallelujah!"

In the beautifully melodic "If It Be Your Will," Cohen similarly appropriated the wisdom of kabbalah by demarcating the place of fragmentation as the fount of his song and all prayer: "From this broken hill/ All your praises they shall ring."[11] The song offered by the poet rings forth from the broken hill. In *Book of Mercy*, we encounter the same motif: "You led me to this field where I can dance with a broken knee."[12] To dance with a broken knee, an arresting metaphor to convey that poeticizing is a continual effort to speak of the unspeakable suffering. Within the matrix of that torment the possibility of supplication is born. In the chasm of the fractured soul, all that is left is the possibility to pray for the possibility to pray. Only prayer in this most destitute form, the prayer divested of prayerfulness, can mend the heart broken by the threefold brokenness of God, humanity, and the world. Cohen well captured the predicament of the pilgrim on the spiritual journey: the one who is unworthy is empowered to pray, but one who is unworthy has no power to pray. He surely would have concurred with the talmudic tradition that from the day the Temple was destroyed the gates of prayer are closed, but

---

[9] Leonard Cohen, *Stranger Music: Selected Poems and Songs* (New York: Pantheon Books, 1993), 347.

[10] See Wolfson, "New Jerusalem," 126–27. [11] Cohen, *Stranger Music*, 343.

[12] Cohen, *Book of Mercy*, sec. 10.

the gates of weeping remain open.[13] The gates of mercy mentioned in "Come Healing" (2012) are the gates of weeping, for tears are the agency that stimulates the compassion necessary in a place of rupture, the arbitrary space that seems capricious from the standpoint of the strict measure of the law but which represents the place of forgiveness where guilt is transposed into innocence. Mercy, as the kabbalists teach, holds sway betwixt divine wrath and divine love, the response apposite for one undeserving of cruelty or grace.[14] Attunement to the broken heart is the means to break the brokenness.[15]

Cohen did not ask to be released from his pain; quite the contrary, he insisted that he not be separated from his tears, for the tears are the rungs on the ladder that lead to compassion and light. "You gave my soul a beam to travel on," Cohen expressed his gratitude to God, "You gave the injury a tongue to heal itself."[16] The healing comes not in the suppression or eradication of affliction, but in the agony that trickles from its very nucleus. Repeatedly, Cohen stayed faithful to the Jewish penchant to uncover in melancholia the way to jubilation, to exhume the glimmer of hopefulness from the gloom of hopelessness, to fathom that the shadow is an inflection of, rather than an obfuscation of, light. A resonance of this theme can be heard in "Heart with No Companion" (*Various Positions*): "I greet you from the other side/ Of sorrow and despair/ With a love so vast and shattered/ It will reach you everywhere."[17] The image of the "other side of sorrow and despair" corresponds to the kabbalistic notion of the demonic force, which is called in the zoharic anthology the *sitra achara*, literally, the other side, the place of grief and misery.[18] Only by standing in darkness can one apprehend the light. Echoing Isaac Luria's teaching that the vessels were

---

[13] Babylonian Talmud, Berakhot 32b. [14] Cohen, *The Flame*, 116.

[15] See Elliot R. Wolfson, "Breaking the Brokenness and the Healing of the Poem: A Brief Meditation," in Glazer, *Tangle of Matter & Ghost*, 247–51. Compare the author's own discussion of the motif of brokenness, ibid., 150–66.

[16] Cohen, *Book of Mercy*, sec. 19.

[17] https://lyricstranslate.com/en/leonard-cohen-heart-no-companion-lyrics.html.

[18] Gershom Scholem, *Major Trends in Jewish Mysticism* (New York: Schocken Books, 1956), 177–78; Scholem, *On the Mystical Shape of the Godhead: Basic Concepts in the Kabbalah*, translated by Joachim Neugroschel, ed. and rev. Jonathan Chipman (New York: Schocken Books, 1991), 73–87; and Isaiah Tishby, *The Wisdom of the Zohar* (Oxford: Oxford University Press, 1989), 448–546.

broken on account of the abundance of light, Cohen spoke of the shattering being caused by the vastness of love. And just as Luria maintained that the sparks of light that remained attached to the shards of the broken vessels must be unshackled by the benevolent and righteous acts of humanity, so Cohen affirmed that a residual of love is found everywhere, awaiting redemption and restoration.[19] It is chiefly in this regard that I consider "mystical" an apt term to characterize Cohen's poiesis, for, in my view, the repeated emphasis on union on the part of the mystically inclined bespeaks a fervent awareness of disintegration, displacement, alienation. In the song "Anthem" on *The Future* (1992), Cohen reiterated the point in what he himself identified as a profoundly Jewish idea, "There is a crack in everything/ That's how the light gets in."[20] With this kabbalistic insight, Cohen carries forward the burden and the blessing of Jewish messianism: even though the promise count for nothing, we must keep it nonetheless. It is the brokenness, not the wholeheartedness, which must be gathered, the splinters that one carries and the cross that one leaves behind, which provide the conduit to healing of the body and to healing of the mind.[21]

Attentiveness to this wisdom holds the key to another characteristic dimension of Cohen's artistry, his signature propensity to blend the sacred and the erotic, a juxtaposition that likely was one of the factors that stimulated him to pursue the study of kabbalah and that colored his respect for masters of Eastern European Hasidic dynasties, a reverence that is evident not only in the cadence of his language, but also in the rhythm of his tunes that often strike the ear as contemporary *niggunim*.[22] We can fathom the confluence of the ostensibly clashing themes of eroticism and asceticism in Cohen's attunement to the insight that the strongest of desires may be the desire not to desire, the most seductive of pleasures the pleasure of pursuing no pleasure.[23] As he wrote in "The

---

[19] On this theme in kabbalistic and Hasidic texts, see Scholem, *Major Trends*, 269, 280, 330, 346, and Louis Jacobs, "The Uplifting of Sparks in Later Jewish Mysticism," in *Jewish Spirituality from the Sixteenth-Century Revival to the Present*, ed. Arthur Green (New York: Crossroad, 1987), 99–126.

[20] Cohen, *Stranger Music*, 373.   [21] Cohen, *The Flame*, 116.

[22] Wolfson, "New Jerusalem," 129–35. On the nexus of the sacred and the erotic, see also Marcia Pally, *From This Broken Hill I Sing to You: God, Sex, and Politics in the Work of Leonard Cohen* (London: T&T Clark, 2021), 103–27.

[23] Wolfson, "New Jerusalem," 135–47.

Night Comes On" (1984), "I needed so much to have nothing to touch/ I've always been greedy that way."[24] One endowed with spiritual vision apperceives that at the innermost door, there is nowhere to go and nothing to say, just the unconditional willingness to say goodbye and to abandon all expectation.[25] Interestingly, Cohen also found inspiration for this appetite to curb all appetite in Christian and Zen Buddhist monasticism.[26] A common thread that may account for this triangulation was Cohen's long-standing struggle with depression that helped him cultivate the consciousness to know that liberation is to be achieved through the acceptance of suffering and the nurturing of the discipline of nonattachment even to the point that one cannot even be attached to being not attached. In the final analysis, renunciation and longing complement one another and should not be seen as antinomic.[27] In a poem extolling the carnal lust to cohabit with a woman, curiously entitled "Disturbed This Morning," Cohen gave voice to a mystical state of "having nothing on my mind/ but to be inside/ the only place/ that has/ no inside,/ and no outside."[28] The breakdown of the distinction between interiority and exteriority experienced in sexual conjunction is a tangible channel to access the orienting disorientation of mystical ecstasy.

We can confidently assert that Cohen imbibed the Buddhist wisdom that to be cognizant of the Buddha is to heed the dharma of the mindfulness of no-mind, to become enlightened in the way of detachment from all form, even the form of detachment, to awaken to the fact that there is nothing to which to be awakened, to void the heart so that it can abide in voidness, an abiding that is neither abiding in abiding nor abiding in nonabiding. In the final stanza of the poem "My Mentors" from the collection *Flowers for Hitler* (1964), Cohen

---

[24] Cohen, *Stranger Music*, 345. [25] Cohen, *The Flame*, 95.
[26] Wolfson, "New Jerusalem," 106–22. On the Jewish and Christian imagery in Cohen, see Pally, *From This Broken Hill*, 93–101; and compare the brief description of Cohen's sense of Jewish identity and his interest in the New Testament and in Christian iconography in the 2001 interview with Mikal Gilmore, in Burger (ed.), *Leonard Cohen*, 503–04.
[27] Ira B. Nadel, *Various Positions: A Life of Leonard Cohen* (New York: Pantheon Books, 1996), 202.
[28] Leonard Cohen, *Book of Longing* (Toronto: McClelland and Stewart, 2006), 39.

seemed to have been hinting at this gnosis. He caught his Zen master worshiping him, "so I made him stand in a foul corner/ with my rabbi, my priest, and my doctor."[29] The young poet audaciously displayed an iconoclastic spirit, debunking four mentors, rabbi, priest, doctor, and Zen master. In his sharp wit, Cohen informed us of an archaic wisdom – no one who occupies a position of power is beyond rebuke – but, even more keenly, he has brilliantly turned the power hierarchy on its head by noting the folly of the teacher in worshiping the disciple. To avoid falling prey to this frailty, the master must lift the veil of being master. Cohen imparted this teaching as well in the verse from the song "Teachers" (*Songs of Leonard Cohen*, 1967), which deftly catalogs the poet's search for a guru, the teacher of his heart, "Follow me the wise man said/ But he walked behind."[30] The true sage leads by following, a theme that was similarly expressed in the *Tao Te Ching*, "The Sage puts his own views behind/ So ends up ahead,"[31] a text that may very well have been a source for Cohen's own musing.

Despite Cohen's serious engagement with Buddhist meditation, including spending the years 1994–99 at the Mt. Baldy Zen Center, where he was even ordained as a monk in the Rinzai tradition under the guidance of Roshi Kyozan Joshu Sasaki, he never fully relinquished the repository of theistic symbols derived principally from Judaism in his effort to depict the spiritual yearning for union, a quest that for him was not at variance with the enlightenment taught in the Zen tradition, the breaking of the bonds of conditional experience and confronting reality as it is in the suchness of its emptiness and in the emptiness of its suchness. As he put it in "Never Mind," he can't distinguish eternal truth from the mortal kind, "So never mind."[32] In recounting his decision to ascend the mountain to join the Zen community, he insisted that he was not looking for a new religion or a new series of rituals to replace

---

[29] Leonard Cohen, *Flowers for Hitler* (Toronto: McClelland and Stewart, 1964), 54.
[30] Cohen, *Stranger Music*, 97.
[31] *Tao Te Ching: The Definitive Edition*, trans. and comm. Jonathan Star (New York: Penguin Putnam, 2001), sec. 7, 20.
[32] Cohen, *The Flame*, 135.

or supplant his Judaism.[33] Perhaps the most salient example of the influence of Cohen's youthful exposure to Jewish belief and practice is his "Who by Fire" (1974), a contemporary reworking of a medieval hymn included in the traditional Jewish prayer book for Rosh Hashanah and Yom Kippur, a solemn poem in which the poet depicts the drama of the divine judge inscribing and signing the fate of each person for the upcoming year. There is nothing exceptionally mystical, let alone kabbalistic, about this song, but it clearly illustrates Cohen's deep connection to his Jewish roots, and particularly his fascination with matters pertaining to judgment and the handing-down of sentences, a theme repeated in many of the poems and songs. Needless to say, Cohen transforms the traditional theological trope by introducing a note of doubt, which is distinctive to the modern predicament, with the refrain that ends each stanza "And who shall I say is calling?"[34] The original expresses no such ambivalence; the contemporary poet is not certain, not in these times when judgment is conspicuous but the face of the judge invisible.

These doubts notwithstanding, and the devotion to Zen, did not dissuade Cohen from struggling to make sense of this basic tenet of Jewish monotheism and to disavow the heresy that there is neither judge nor judgment. In the dwindling days of his life, as he stood at the

---

[33] Thus, responding in the interview with Arthur Kurzweil to the query regarding his ability to reconcile his Jewish background with being a student of a Zen monk, Cohen opined:

> One of the patriarchs, when asked "What is the essence of Zen?," replied, "Vast emptiness and nothing special." So there's not only room for it, there's boundless space available for whatever mental constructions you happen to wish to establish. I've inherited an extremely good religion. I have no need to change it... In other words, there's something that is not negotiable about the absolute, some refusal to name qualities about the absolute that fits in with my most rigorous, deepest appetites, about matters of which I was taught or were indicated to me... Zen, or at least the lineage of this particular teacher, seems to be able to provide a landscape where Jewish practitioners can manifest their deepest appetites concerning the absolute.

The text is reprinted in Burger (ed.), *Leonard Cohen*, 375–76. In the same interview (384), Cohen acknowledged that it was his studies with the Zen monk and his experience of meditation in the zendo that opened up a path for him to reconnect to Jewish practice in what he called a "happy homecoming."

[34] Cohen, *Stranger Music*, 207.

threshold of death, Cohen found a way to preserve and to uproot his kabbalistically inflected faith. In the opening stanzas of "You Want It Darker" (2016), the poet displays the stark honesty of one confronting mortality without any guise or ruse. The opening of this song – a kind of self-avowed dirge, or what I think of as the haunting portrait of Cohen saying the mourner's prayer (*kaddish*) for himself – is striking and evocative in its candor. In facing the prospect of his imminent demise, there is no mystery left that demands decoding, no more wearing of the river's disguise,[35] no donning of the mask of a face that is not unmasked as the mask of the face. Nakedly embodied, the poet addresses God directly, utilizing the scriptural elocution *hineni* to mark his compliance to serve by accepting the fate decreed for him – if God is imagined as a dealer, then Cohen is out of the game; if God is imagined as a healer, then Cohen admits he is broken and lame; if the glory is ascribed to God, then Cohen acknowledges his portion is shame. All that remains in this dying moment is the power to acquiesce and to comply with the divine will – "You want it darker/ We kill the flame."

Years before Cohen humbly gave voice to the quietistic resolve to serve by intoning, "If it be your will/ That I speak no more."[36] The same spirit of surrender returns in "You Want It Darker," albeit at the critical existential juncture as the poet prepared to let go and to pass from the death that is life to the life that is death. God, it seems, shows no mercy at this moment: he simply wants it darker. The poet has no choice but to emulate Abraham – when called by God to sacrifice Isaac, he proclaimed *hineni*, "I am here" (Genesis 22:1), demonstrating his unequivocal readiness to obey. In an earlier song, "The Story of Isaac" (1969), Cohen utilized the narrative about the attempted sacrifice of Isaac to criticize contemporary acts of violence. The sharp sociopolitical critique is placed in the mouth of Isaac, using his own experience to admonish those who would coerce the false martyrdom of others: "You who build these altars now/ To sacrifice the children,/ You must not do it anymore."[37] Even in that context the submission of Abraham is never in question, "I've had a vision/ And you know I'm strong and holy/ I must do what I've been told."[38] In the past, Abraham's zeal to sacrifice his son issued from a vision, whereas those who

---

[35] Ibid., 354. [36] Ibid., 343. [37] Ibid., 140. [38] Ibid., 139.

wage war and commit murder in the present have only a scheme. Out of that vision came forth the alacrity to succumb. Analogously, the final darkness, the extinguishing of the light, was dependent on Cohen's claiming his own agency to sacrifice his bodily self. The demise of the physical is transformed into a path of ascesis and piety.

Cohen pivoted from self-denial to a theme well-known from his poetry and songs: the holy name crucified in the human frame. I call this incarnational motif "transconfessional," insofar as a version of it can be found in different faiths seeking to bridge the gap between the invisible and the visible, the immaterial and the material. In an earlier study, I argued that it is not possible to appreciate the kabbalistic resonances in Cohen without considering his complex fascination with the Christian doctrine of incarnation.[39] I will not rehearse my argument here, but it is noteworthy that in the intimacy of confronting death – Cohen's direct encounter with God reminiscent of Biblical figures like Abraham and Job – he invoked precisely that theme but extended it to every human being: God becoming a body is an act of kenosis and degradation of the holy name. On display here is the syncretistic impulse of Cohen, combining the opening line of the *kaddish*, whereby the name is sanctified, and the fundamental axiom of Christian faith. But even more revealing is the intent of this invocation, which is made clear in the next line: a million candles burning for the help that never came. The sadness and resignation here are palpable. Cohen elicited from the vilification and crucifixion of the holy name in the human frame the inescapable and irredeemable affliction of the human condition. The point is enunciated more adamantly in the second stanza of "You Want It Darker," where he speaks of "a lullaby for suffering."[40] This is a perfect description of Cohen's poetic offerings to the world, lullabies that celebrate tribulation as a means to a more intense commitment to love that can at times even be based on a paradox, as in the case of the story of Isaac. Scripture sanctions the suffering and the need to heed the divine voice even if the command defies the dictates of reason and the prescriptions of the heart. In the case of Jesus, too, the help never came because the savior could not be saved from the affliction he had to endure for the sake of saving others. Each person must similarly bear the cross in facing the

---

[39] Wolfson, "New Jerusalem," 106, 144–45. [40] Cohen, *The Flame*, 143.

ephemerality of one's being. "A million candles burning/ For the help that never came." Repeating this line towards the end of the song, Cohen evocatively changed "help" to "love."[41] The image is searing in its sadness. A million candles did not suffice to conjure the love necessary to topple the divine demand for darkness.

Suffering has always been foremost in Cohen's mind, his deepest and most erotic passion, as it is the passion that gives gravitas to the pursuit of all other passions. The religious promise to alleviate suffering, he once said, is cruel because it is not possible to live without suffering.[42] Wholeness is to be sought in the fissures of our being. No heart is as whole as the heart that is broken. Cohen's belief that worship and creativity both ensue from a sense of anguish or impending catastrophe has long framed his understanding of Jewish devotion, informed particularly by the wellsprings of kabbalah and Hasidism. Nevertheless, his attraction to Christianity and Zen Buddhism likewise stemmed from the discernment that hope flings from the place of hopelessness, and in an even deeper register, that hopelessness is itself an expression of hope to the extent that it is a catalyst that stimulates the craving to serve without the craving to serve. Although born in chains, Cohen evoked the Jewish myth of being taken out of Egypt, but this emancipation left him with one burden, to bless the name of the nameless that was written on his heart in burning letters. Thus, his soul unfolded in the chambers of this longing, a longing that could be lifted only through the descent of the night.[43]

Of his many gifts, Cohen was able to plumb the depths of darkness to unfetter the sparks of light trapped therein. He lived not only in the Tower of Song but from the other side of sorrow and despair. As noted above, one of the kabbalistic motifs that especially captured Cohen's fecund imagination was the Lurianic doctrine of the shattering of the vessels and the consequent dispersion of the light. The task is to uplift those sparks and restore them to the infinite, to mend the disharmony of existence and to liberate God from being exiled in the world. Following a more monistic approach, attested in some Hasidic interpretations of the Lurianic symbolism, Cohen envisioned the darkness as a form of light

---

[41] Ibid., 144. [42] The comment is cited in Wolfson, "New Jerusalem," 123.
[43] Cohen, *The Flame*, 139.

and not its antithesis. His genius and sensitivity related to positing a form of rectification based on categorically accepting the brokenness. Redemption comes not by dispelling the darkness but by transforming it into light. It was Cohen's steadfast allegiance to Judaism that imparted to him the mandate to raise a tent of shelter even though every thread is torn.[44] Precisely when the threads are torn, the need for shelter is ever more pressing.

[44] Cohen, *Stranger Music*, 337.

CHAPTER 9

Zen and the East

Leonard Cohen as Buddhist Monk and Bodhisattva Poet

Christophe Lebold

THE TITLE OF LEONARD COHEN'S FIRST BOOK — *LET US Compare Mythologies* — defined a spiritual program that was carried out throughout the poet's career. We will study here the part Eastern spiritualities played in the constitution of Cohen's poetic vision and in his reception as spiritual poet, and how Zen Buddhism provided a landscape that both enabled him to make sense of his fundamental experience of angst and alienation, and to transform the despaired existentialist troubadour of his early years into the great bringer of light of his late career.

In love with his native religion and convinced of his place in it as a *kohen*, the young Cohen was also wary of some of the dogmatic aspects of rabbinical Judaism, and therefore bound to explore alternative spiritual paths. Christian mysticism, psychedelic shamanism, Sufi, and scientology were famously among these, but in the post-Beat context an encounter with Buddhism was unavoidable. This first happened as a teenager through an anthology of Chinese poetry, but it was on Hydra, surrounded by religious seekers (like George Lialios, Steve Sanfield, or the Tibetan nun Zina Rachewski), that Cohen really encountered Eastern philosophies, practices, and books, the *I-Ching* among them.[1] In late 1971, he drove 6,500 feet up Mt. Baldy, California to the new monastery of a sixty-four-year-old Zen teacher named Roshi Kyozan Joshu Sasaki for his first *rohatsu* retreat. Although he fled in mid retreat, convinced it was "the revenge for World War

---

[1] Sarah Hampson, "He Has Tried in His Way to Be Free," *Shambhala Sun* (November 2007).

Two," the poet then started a regime of regular Zen *sesshins* that would continue at least until 1999.² From the mid 1970s on (so he told reporters), he was spending two or three months a year (including a long summer retreat and – when his touring schedule allowed – the December *rohatsu*) in Sasaki's monasteries in Mt. Baldy, Los Angeles, and New Mexico. This meant days structured by sutra-chanting, koan practice, private interviews with the master (or *sanzen*), collective work, and silent meals, not to mention four to sixteen hours of seated meditation (or *zazen*), all of it ordered by rules derived from ancient Chan monastery laws.

Sasaki Roshi was famous for his adherence to a particularly severe form of traditional Rinzai. Derived from the Chan school of "sudden enlightenment," Rinzai Zen is reportedly more eager than other schools to actively provoke experiences of awakening. Hence a more severe daily regime, the centrality of koan study, and a tradition of provocative masters practicing "crazy-wisdom," what Borup calls "freak Zen masters."³ Sasaki Roshi's specific teaching insists on the necessity to embrace opposites: self *and* no-self, life *and* death, expansion *and* contraction of the universe, and to constantly return to a fertile state of vacuity and vibrant potentiality he calls "zero."⁴ Students must locate within themselves a "center of gravity" and realize that this center – "the Buddha" – is also the center of gravity of the universe and the source of all authentic actions.⁵ Clearly perceptible in Sasaki's teaching is a typically Zen yearning for radical freedom, as well as a clearly amoral streak (at least from a Judeo-Christian perspective).⁶

---

[2] Namely, a Japanese master and his German assistant torturing American kids (Jeff Burger [ed.], *Leonard Cohen on Leonard Cohen: Interviews and Encounters* [Chicago: Chicago Review Press, 2014], 12). Known as "monk-killer," the *rohatsu sesshin* is the toughest moment in Zen's liturgical year (see Jorn Borup, *Japanese Rinzai Zen Buddhism* [Leiden & Boston: Brill, 2008], 208).

[3] Borup, *Japanese Rinzai*, 89.

[4] Joshu Sasaki, *Tathagata Zen* (Los Angeles: Rinzai-Ji Press, 2014), 35.

[5] Joshu Sasaki, *Buddha Is the Center of Gravity* (San Cristobal: Lama Foundation Press, 1974), 61 and 83.

[6] Cohen often spoke of radical freedom as the quality that attracted him to Sasaki, a freedom that the teacher apparently abused for decades as he exacted sexual favors from his female students.

By the mid 1970s, Sasaki was for Cohen a mentor and a father figure, and he often accompanied the man he later described as "my rabbi"[7] to retreats in Trappist monasteries or visits to Japan. An active member of Sasaki's *sangha* (community) and one of its major financial supporters, he famously took up residence at Mt. Baldy in 1994 for five years of intense practice, during which he was ordained as monk under the name of *Jikan*.[8] As cook and private assistant to his teacher, he travelled with Sasaki and did literally every retreat the latter conducted: "*sesshin* after *sesshin* after *sesshin*."[9] When he left the monastery in 1999, Cohen had spent close to eight and a half years in Zen centers: not exactly a tourist in Zen. The singer was originally discreet about this part of his life, but when images of him in full Buddhist garb began to circulate, Zen became part of Cohen's legend, although he was always keen to remind that he remained a Jew and never considered Zen a "religion." In its modern form, Zen is basically nontheistic and nonreverential, and therefore compatible with the life of a *kohen*.[10]

Despite a Buddhist flavor in much of Cohen's work, Zen and Eastern spiritualities were rarely thematized as such. Two songs obliquely mention Sasaki Roshi and one, "Waiting for the Miracle," is clearly a satire of monastery life. While *Book of Mercy* contains a striking portrait of Sasaki as a ruthless teacher determined to wage war against his students, it's not until *Book of Longing* in 2006 that we get a sequence of twenty-five poems (with titles like "The Lovesick Monk" or "The Collapse of Zen") that are consistently and explicitly about Zen life.[11] The tone is one of irreverent

---

[7] Burger (ed.), *Leonard Cohen*, 387. Cohen claimed several times that he "wouldn't exist" without Sasaki Roshi (see Pico Iyer, "Several Lifetimes Already," *Shambhala Sun*, [September 1998], 68) and dedicated two records and one book to his teacher.

[8] A traditional monk name which does *not* mean "silent one," but "interval of time" and, by extension, "ordinary silence" (Burger [ed.], *Leonard Cohen*, 450).

[9] Eric Lerner, *Matters of Vital Interest: A Forty-Year Friendship with Leonard Cohen* (New York: Da Capo, 2018), 188.

[10] To a great extent, the form of Rinzai that penetrated America is the epitome of the "Buddhist Modernism" described by David McMahan in *The Making of Buddhist Modernism* (Oxford: Oxford University Press, 2008, 27–59): a demythologized, undogmatic "science of the mind" that claimed compatibility with science and modern psychology.

[11] See Leonard Cohen, *Book of Mercy* (London: Jonathan Cape, 1984), 21; and Leonard Cohen, *Book of Longing* (New York: Ecco, 2006), 2–29 – referenced within the main text of this chapter as *BoL*.

satire: the roshi is a clown, a nuisance, and the source of blissful resurrections, the monks "the marines of the spiritual world" (*BoL* 26), and the speaker a comedy figure, who wavers between hope, despair, and *satori* (i.e., awakening) experiences. His Zen robe cannot conceal his "gigantic hard-on" (*BoL* 21 – so much for getting rid of desire), and his advice to novices is to kill all insects and mystics with a "petrified giant daikon radish" (*BoL* 24). The iconoclastic tone is typical of Rinzai Zen's long tradition of "laughing at the Buddhas and abusing the patriarchs," but those poems are a parenthesis in the poet's work. More important is the influence of Buddhism on Cohen's imagination and on the spiritual landscape of the songs.[12]

Buddhism is fundamentally a doctrine of individual salvation, and that would have appealed to a man who by the early 1970s had been battling with depression for at least two decades. It takes suffering seriously and locates its causes in desire and in our clinging to the illusory idea of a stable, separate self. Zen provides a technology of salvation based on direct, embodied teaching from master to student, a return to simple forms of living, and discipline of the body–mind through meditation practice. This path supposedly fosters experiences of *kensho* (seeing though one's own nature) which, repeated, will organically bring on a *satori*:[13] a concrete method bound to please someone who as early as 1969 had defined religion as "a technology for strength and for making the world hospitable."[14]

Zen's fundamental vision of reality, known as *Trilakshana* or the "three marks of existence," would also have appealed to Cohen. It holds that everything in life is impermanent (the doctrine of *anitya*), empty of essence (the doctrine of *anatman*), and incomplete and imperfect – "broken," so to speak (the doctrine of *dukkha*). The experience of the absolute is the experience of *shunyata*, the great vacuity that pervades all things.[15] Fully experiencing that vacuity (also known as "Buddha Nature") is highly

---

[12] See Conrad Hyers, *Zen and the Comic Spirit* (London: Rider & Co., 1974), 103, and passim.

[13] Ingrid Fischer-Schreiber, Kurt Friedrichs, and Franz-Karl Ehrhard, *The Encyclopedia of Eastern Philosophy and Religion* (Boston: Shambhala, 1989), 180 and 308.

[14] Michael Harris, "Leonard Cohen: The Poet as Hero: 2," *Saturday Night Review* 84, no. 6 (June 1969): 30.

[15] The doctrine of *shunyata* (*Mu* in Japanese) is famously expressed in the *Heart Sutra* (sung every day at the monastery) as "form is emptiness, emptiness form" See Fischer-Schreiber, Friedrichs, and Ehrhard, *Encyclopedia*, 128.

emancipatory and supposedly leads to the organic development of universal compassion and a sense of being fundamentally at home in the universe. In a 1995 interview, Cohen identified "emptiness" as what originally attracted him to Mt. Baldy, and he connects Zen to a "form of Judaism by emptiness."[16] One last Buddhist motif that Cohen would integrate (and eventually embody, as we shall see) is the ideal of the *bodhisattva*, the enlightened being who suspends his entry into nirvana to relieve the suffering of others, an ideal that must have struck a chord with an artist who famously wished to reconfigure the poet as saint.

With their heroic diegetic universe made of train stations, hotel rooms, and snowstorms, the singer's first trilogy of albums seems a study of the first noble truth (life is suffering) and an account of the 1,000 ways in which you can roam in *samsara* – the conditioned world of endless rebirths, governed by desire, craving, and illusion.[17] Characters are existentialist "strangers" and "travelling ladies" on a quest for salvation, looking – sometimes desperately so – for teachers, masters, or lovers.

By his own account, Cohen was himself at this stage plagued by amphetamine-fueled depression and mostly lived a peripatetic life, his vision defined by a blend of existentialism and troubadour-like idealization of women. In terms of public persona, he cut out a resolutely romantic figure: a raincoat-clad existentialist seeker, who oscillated between the calls of love and the temptation of despair, himself lost in *samsara* with "no secret chart to get you to the heart of this or any other matter" (*SM* 121).[18] This is the character that Cohen brought onto stage in concerts that seemed both a liturgy of the night and a celebration of the beautiful loser as martyr and saint. The shows were clear reminders that life is indeed *dukkha*, although a longing "to be free" was asserted at the beginning of every concert (with the hymn-like "Bird on the Wire"), while another pivotal song promised that one day "We'll come from/ The shadows" (*Songs from a Room*, 1969).[19] Even in that early work, there

---

[16] Gilles Tordjman, *Les Inrockuptibles* no. 1 (March 15, 1995): 20.

[17] See Fischer-Schreiber, Friedrichs, and Ehrhard, *Encylopedia*, 116 and 298.

[18] Leonard Cohen, *Stranger Music: Selected Poems and Songs* (New York: Pantheon Books, 1993) – referenced within the main text of this chapter as *SM*.

[19] To a great extent, Cohen transformed Ana Marly's French Resistance song into an allegory about resisting inner darkness.

were breakthroughs into worlds where pain and self are dissolved ("Suzanne" and "Sisters of Mercy" among them). Particularly in line with Cohen's future study of Buddhism is "Love Calls You by Your Name," a song whose protagonist – a slave of desire who collects "women in scrapbooks" – is summoned by Love (while his lady is – interestingly – "meditating") until he dissolves (repeating a scene from *Beautiful Losers*) into the light-beam of a cinema projector, a clear allegory of the dissolution of self.

In the early to mid 1970s, Cohen's Buddhist practice is correlated with clear shifts in his themes and fictional universes, as well as in the personae he created in songs and onstage. In accordance with Zen's satire of "ego, ignorance, and desire," there was a gradual replacement of the heroic mode with satire and irony, as the poet deconstructed his own romantic mythologies.[20] This is obvious in *The Energy of Slaves* (1972), a series of cynical anti-poems where the narrator flirts with hypermasculinist views (a symbolical killing of Cohen's troubadour persona), while the songs of *New Skin for the Old Ceremony* (1974) and *Death of a Ladies' Man* (1977) introduce a less idealistic vision of love as war. In parallel, Cohen increasingly resorts to self-deprecation. The self-portrait as a cheap radical-chic James Bond figure in "Field Commander Cohen" is an obvious example, but the singer's whole 1970s output seems an attempt to de-heroize his male protagonists. A whole cycle of his work (a record, a book, and a song) is significantly called *Death of a Lady's/Ladies' Man*, and in the 1977 song of that title (literally filled with gallows humor), a lover is able to impress his mistress only after hanging himself (*SM*, 231).

With *Recent Songs* (1979), *shunyata* – the great vacuity that lies at the heart of things – becomes a central theme. While many things were on fire on Cohen's first trilogy, objects and feelings tend to *dissolve* on that album, while the speakers in the songs begin to see the great insubstantiality of things not exclusively as a problem but also as a gateway into a perception of life where things are "Light enough/ Light enough/ To let [them] go."[21] Two texts of that period are actually rewritings of classical Zen texts. One ("The End of My Life in Art")[22] seems a fictionalized version of a *sanzen*

---

[20] Hyers, *Zen*, 118.   [21] "The Smokey Life," *Recent Songs* (1979).
[22] *Death of a Lady's Man* (Harmondsworth: Penguin, 1978), 206.

session with Sasaki, in which a "Roshi" illustrates the ego's fears of releasing his grip by "hanging from a tree with his teeth" (a classic image taken from *The Gateless Gate*, a thirteenth-century collection of koans).[23] The other, "Ballad of the Absent Mare," about a cowboy's search for his lost horse, is inspired by a twelfth-century set of poems and drawings (known in the West as *The Ten Bulls*) about a herdsman in search of a lost ox, an allegory of the Self looking for its supposedly lost "true nature" (and disappearing when he finds it).[24] In "The Smokey Life," the singer adopts the voice of a teacher of the dharma, as a narrator shows a girlfriend how to "walk on air" to the backdrop of a cool jazz tempo. A new Zen-like state of mind emerges, based on an appreciation of the beauty of the cosmic order, and some poems of the period – like "Every Pebble," with its metaphor of the "small self" as a self-absorbed pebble who "dreams of itself" – seem quasi-orthodox Zen Buddhist statements (*SM*, 406).

In the course of the 1980s, with his voice now well engaged in its journey towards absolute gravity, and with his Zen practice still intensifying, Cohen starts regularly adopting in song the persona of the spiritual teacher. The position is characterized by a warm combination of wisdom and compassion, a milder, kindhearted irony directed not just at the ego but at life in general, and the use of epigrammatic wisdom in songs meant to convey spiritual ideas. In "Heart with No Companions," Cohen greets his listeners from "the other side of sorrow and despair" and invites another array of beautiful losers escaped from a Zen parable (captains with no ships, mothers with no children) to embrace the vacuity in their lives, with the promise that they will join the *bodhisattva*-singer and his love "so vast and shattered/ It will reach you everywhere" (*Various Positions*, 1984). In "Dance Me to the End of Love," Cohen similarly uses a bouzouki-driven Greek waltz tune to invite his listeners to dance with the "end" of things and their inherent transience.

As for irony, both *Various Positions* and *I'm Your Man* are tinged with a new, kinder form, synthesizing the three types of humor central to Zen: the satire of "the folly of the desiring self," the laughter of awakening (or,

---

[23] See " Kyogen Mounts the Tree," in Paul Reps, *Zen Flesh, Zen Bones* (London: Penguin, 2000), 99.
[24] Ibid., 135–47.

as Hyer puts it, of "getting the point of the joke"), and the *bodhisattva*'s "irony of compassion," simultaneously enlightening and consoling.[25] That irony is sometimes very explicit, as in the lyrics of "First We Take Manhattan" (a clear take at the self-aggrandizing fantasies of that little inner fascist called the ego), and sometimes milder, as in the title *Various Positions* (1984), which presents the nine songs of the album as a spiritual Kama Sutra.[26] In both cases, there is an expansion of irony in which life itself is presented as a cosmic joke, while humor becomes a Buddhist exercise in detachment. "Waiting for the Miracle," for example, presents life simultaneously as tragedy *and* comedy with a stoical character who has "fallen on the highway" but claims to be "waiting for the miracle."[27] More generally, irony becomes an alchemical tool that transforms what is heavy in life into what is light, in line with the way Cohen would later define enlightenment as "lightening up ... not taking your predicament so seriously."[28] That combination of levity and gravity was also present in Cohen's public persona of the period, as the singer often facetiously *played* with the connotations of virility and spiritual authority conveyed by his voice's depth and grit. The concerts of 1988 and 1993 – essentially *mimodramas* of spiritual life where, from song to song, the singer invested successive positions and masks (lover, seeker, prophet, priest) – added a new identity to Cohen's lyrical theatre: the ironic Armani-suited Zen master, who balanced spiritual teaching, cosmic irony, and seduction.

After a five-year stay at the monastery and several stays in India, which led, as the poet explained in interviews, to the "lifting" of his depression,[29] *Ten New Songs* (2001) – Cohen's most explicitly spiritual record to date – could be seen as a phenomenological examination of enlightenment: how to get it (by releasing your grip), when to expect it (in traffic jams and marble chambers), what it feels like (good). The album features many descriptions

---

[25] See respectively Hyers, *Zen*, 119 and 153–55; and Hyers, "Humor in Zen: Comic Midwifery," *Philosophy East and West* 39 no. 3 (July 1989): 274–76.

[26] The self-deprecating irony is also explicit in the videos of the period that show Cohen either as a ghost who guides his former lover to the end of their love affair ("Dance Me to the End of Love") or as an apocalyptic prophet dancing as rain pours down on him in a hotel lobby ("The Future").

[27] Whether the miracle is to be spared or run over by a car is unclear.

[28] See Laurie Browne, "Leonard Cohen," *On the Arts* (filmed interview, CBC, 1997).

[29] Burger (ed.), *Leonard Cohen*, 466.

of *satori* experiences and can actually be construed as the fragmented narrative of a spiritual awakening. Cohen's protagonist, a bummed-out seeker "who smiles when he's angry," has finally received his "orders" to "cross the borders" of his "Secret Life."[30] This entails the ego's ritual suicide as he consents to be "wrecked" to reach the deeper life that awaits "A Thousand Kisses Deep." Feeling "forgiven" ("That Don't Make It Junk"), he is submitted to repeated experiences of dissolution into Light and Love and successively discovers his love for all the polarities of life ("Here It Is") or that "Love Itself" manifests in the flickering flecks of dust in a sunbeam. Letting go of the past ("Alexandra Leaving"), and now considering egoistic life with amused detachment ("You Have Loved Enough"), the protagonist is finally kissed by a "crown of light" ("Boogie Street") and ends the album with a universal prayer for light to "shine on the truth some day" ("Land of Plenty").[31]

Well-served by crystal-clear writing and exquisite pop tunes, the album presents a spiritual poet using all the tools of his art (epigrammatic wisdom, clever metaphors, parables, and paradoxes) to exhort the listener to let go of the ego (that comedy character), approach impermanence as what makes life poignant and precious, and, more importantly still, accept the fundamental tempo of spiritual life: you dissolve, and immediately you're back. Back on "Boogie Street" – that is, the world of duality, judgment, and self-based thinking. That is the album's central theme: that the dualistic world of separate selves (*samsara*) and the nondual world of pure awakening (*nirvana*) are just two sides of the same coin, two worlds separated (as Zen has it) by a "gateless gate."[32] Which means that anything (a sunbeam, a hug, a nervous breakdown) can serve as a gateway between them, and enlightenment waits at every turn. With Sharon Robinson's warm soul music, *Ten New Songs* is perhaps the singer's most luminous album: Cohen's *Birth of a Buddhist Cool*. Of

---

[30] The image of "crossing the border/ reaching the other shore" is a classic Zen metaphor for enlightenment. See Meido Moore, *The Rinzai Zen Way: A Guide to Practice* (Boulder, CO: Shambhala, 2018), 23 and 186.

[31] For all lyrics, see Cohen, *Book of Longing*, 72–86. In "That Don't Make It Junk," the protagonist's "diamond" might be a reference to the Lotus Sutra – which famously compares enlightenment to a diamond hidden in the lining of our coats.

[32] See Fischer-Schreiber, Friedrichs, and Ehrhard, *Encyclopedia*, 298.

course, this is not textbook Buddhism. The Jewish God is present as guest star (who tricks Leonard's protagonist into love), and the term "love" is used rather than "compassion," but love is now a vast and egoless feeling that enables the *bodhisattva* singer to greet (like Francis of Assisi) even death as a friend in a metaphysical rewrite of the Beatles' "Hello-Goodbye": "May everyone live/ May everyone die/ Hello, my love/ And my love Goodbye" (*BoL* 253).

Accompanying the record was a new, smiling Leonard Cohen, embodying wisdom and grace. Available footage of the period does indeed testify to an aura of lightness and clarity in Cohen's demeanor, as though he had indeed dropped a burden. Many signs pointed to a clear spiritual turn in the singer's public persona. The voice, now even deeper – actually seismic – connoted someone both in touch with the gravity of life and able to play with it: an artist of gravity. And there was the poet's omnipresent *komboloi* (an object with obvious religious connotations), as well as a noticeably leaner silhouette (like a sign of a fundamental commitment to a lighter life), and the now-subdued elegance, as mid-gray, double-breasted suits and subtly striped shirts became Cohen's signature-dress.[33] With the added light in the face, there was something definitely glorious about Cohen's presence, something that it is tempting to interpret as Cohen's version of the glory of the *sambhogakaya* – the Buddha's "body of delight," thought to manifest the joy of enlightenment. As though he had indeed awoken his inner *bodhisattva*, who, through a deep understanding of the delicate balance of life and death, relative and absolute self, now exuded a warm combination of wisdom (*pranya*) and universal compassion (*karuna*). Or maybe he was just a "lazy bastard living in a suit" (*TF* 160)[34] – an incognito *bodhisattva*.

Another noticeable new aspect in Cohen's persona was that, as he reached old age, the poet started to gloriously embody (in physique and voice) the three marks of existence: transience, suffering–brokenness, and insubstantiality – so much so that his body and his voice had become

---

[33] Rather than the more aggressively masculine black pinstripes of the late 1980s. For the lighter life, see Cohen, *Book of Longing*, 88.

[34] Leonard Cohen, *The Flame*, ed. Robert Faggen and Alexandra Pleshoyano (Edinburgh: Canongate Books, 2018), referenced within the main text of this chapter as *TF*.

wabi-sabi objects, objects that manifested "the beauty of things imperfect, impermanent and incomplete."[35] In his mere living presence therefore, Cohen transmitted, in an immediate and deeply affecting way, an intimation of the true nature of our inscription in this world: that we are indeed "so lightly here" (*BoL* 87). But, simultaneously, the eyes of steel, the luminous smiles, and the voice of grit and fire added power to grace and frailty, as though we were both in presence of the Buddha's glorious body recycled as rock-&-roll cool, and the frail, *wabi-sabi* body of an old master (the Buddha's finite worldly body).[36] Zen claims enlightenment brings the ability to manifest one's "Buddha nature" (*bussho*) in the smallest actions of daily life, and Cohen's warm and graceful manners did indeed seem to make every interview an act of light.

The last stretch of Cohen's career featured an even more urgent engagement with transience. In many songs, death was no longer presented as a scandalous occurrence, but rather (in Taoist fashion) as just the flipside of life. At worst, the ending of a game (the game of being), at best, the awakening from a dream (the dream of separate self) and an act of "going home," the end of our exile in the world of duality. But, throughout, Cohen insists that we are all experts in the game of dying who have "to die a little/ Between each murderous thought" (*TF*, 187). His own disappearances are staged in the self-portraits in *Book of Longing*.[37] Like the traditional portraits of Zen monks, they combine a cartoonish portrait in clear line with a signature stamp and a short commentary that usually calls the ego's bluff and mocks his heroic posturing.[38] The face, often evoked with just a few strokes, seems about to vanish into the blank of the page, as

---

[35] Leonard Koren (sic), *Wabi-Sabi for Artists, Designers, Poets and Philosophers* (Point Reyes: Imperfect Publishing, 2008), 7.

[36] In Mahayana theology, the Buddha has three bodies: the *shamgakaya* (the worldly body), the *sambhogakaya* (the glorious body which manifests enlightenment), and the *dharmakaya* or eternal body (which is vacuity itself and the totality of past, present, and future manifestation). See Fischer-Schreiber, Friedrichs, and Ehrhard, *Encylopedia*, 377–78.

[37] To a great extent, the book is the chronicle of how a lonely sixty-year-old monk on a mountain turns into a seventy-year-old Taoist traveller in love with every moment of his life.

[38] Namely, Cohen's Order-of-the-Unified-Heart symbol plus the *kanjis* of his monk-name.

though Cohen would "not be staying for the entire performance" (*BoL* 197). The echoes with the songs of mortality are striking, but there is a lightness of tone to the whole affair.

Simultaneously, Cohen went through a new streak of syncretism as he sought, after *Ten New Songs*, to integrate the insights of Zen into the theological landscape of Judaism. Interestingly, he found a shortcut between the two traditions in the modernist form of Advaita-Vedanta he studied with Ramesh Balsekar between 1999 and 2003. Advaita asserts that everything, the world, our souls, is Brahma-God-Consciousness, or a manifestation of it, and that any feeling of separation from God is therefore an illusion. Life, Balsekar insists, is "a movie written, cast, directed, and watched by God," and free will or the belief that we are the "doers" of our actions are enslaving illusions. All it takes to awaken is to understand "*in the heart* that there isn't and never was a doer or seeker" and that you can therefore "relax" with God.[39]

To someone addicted to burdens (as Cohen was), such ideas can be immensely liberating, and Balsekar's vision enabled the poet to transcend his old motif of the "slave" with the idea that we are not exactly slaves of God, but slaves who *are* God.[40] More importantly still, Advaita was a theistic tradition, and thus a way for Cohen to retrieve the idea of a God that can be experienced *personally*, and spoken to. While prayers as petition had been scarcer in the poet's work of the 1990s, Cohen was deeply attached to the tradition of Jewish prayer (which he once called a "4,000-year-old conversation with God"), and God was indeed going to make a spectacular comeback as partner in speech on the last string of albums.[41] There Cohen would also propose a new theological landscape that combined Eastern and Judeo-Christian traditions. In "Going Home," for example (on *Old Ideas*), God borrows Leonard's voice – a voice now so deep it chars – to speak about his old crony, Leonard Cohen. And quite interestingly, his message is fully compatible with Advaita or Zen: he wants "Leonard" to stop carrying the burden of Self and become who he really is, a "lazy bastard," who can "go

---

[39] All the quotations are from Ramesh Balsekar, *Your Head in the Tiger's Mouth* (Mumbai: Zen Publications, 1998), 405–09.

[40] The poet made fun of that tendency in a poem where he climbs up Mt. Baldy "with a grand piano" strapped to his back (Cohen, *Book of Longing*, 3).

[41] In Bernhard Brendan, "Angst and Aquavit," *LA Weekly* (September 28, 2001), 31.

home" (*TF* 159). With Cohen's health declining, this good-humored perspective could not be maintained on *You Want It Darker*, but the album also combined the drama of the Old Testament (on the eponymous track) with an Advaita-Buddhist vision of the blissfulness of things as they are. "Travelling Light" thus claimed that life can be crossed with the weightlessness of a light-beam, provided you chose (like the speaker) to forget the dream of separate selves and become "just a fool/ A dreamer who/ Forgot to dream/ Of the me and you" (*TF* 220).

It finally appears that Zen Buddhism was more than just another manifestation of his "favorite hobby," but a key ingredient in Leonard Cohen's art.[42] Eastern spiritualities (the dissolution of self, vacuity as a gateway to enlightenment, appreciation of the natural order) helped the poet find a path from his early explorations of angst and despair to his later celebration of light, lightness, and spiritual irony. That the Jewish prophet and priest in Cohen interacted with a humble and humorous Buddhist gentleman in an Armani suit was also clearly a factor in the global success he encountered in later life. Perhaps we could even locate Cohen's spiritual songs as a *highbrow* example of what McMahan calls a "global folk Buddhism," a contemporary form of popular lay devotion that integrates doctrinal elements of Buddhism with transnational pop culture and allows people around the world to fashion new Buddhist selves on the globalized market of identities.[43] In the case of Cohen, however, a deep love of subversiveness preserves his poetry from becoming lightweight Buddhism. Because, for all his talk about enlightenment, that particular poet knew that even though we may "travel light," a part of us – maybe also divine – still "wants it darker."

---

[42] This is how Cohen defined "religion" in Elena Comelli, "Virtueless Monk," *La Nazione* (November 25, 1998).

[43] McMahan, *Making of Buddhist Modernism*, 262–63.

CHAPTER 10

Christianity

The Little Jew Who Wrote the Bible and Much about Jesus

Marcia Pally

INTRODUCTION: COHEN IN THE PROPHETIC VOICE "GETS THE POINT" ABOUT JESUS. In the 1992 song "The Future," the "poet laureate of despair" Leonard Cohen called himself "the little Jew who wrote the Bible."[1] The Bible he's referring to is that of the prophets. He, like them, is God's servant, who has been told "To say it clear, to say it cold." The message? We've broken our bonds with God and each other and have reached the apocalypse of self-destruction. "The Future" is Cohen's answer to the Book of Revelation. We abuse sex and drugs, torture each other, destroy the planet, and do not repent our rent commitments. The future we've made for ourselves, Cohen writes, will make the killing fields of Stalin and Hitler look like picnics.

Cohen wrote vividly in the Jewish idiom from his earliest poems in the 1950s to his final song collection, *You Want It Darker* (2016). Biographers Lorraine Dorman and Clive Rawlins note, "Whatever we may make of Leonard's Judaism, he is a man seized by its traditions."[2] For much of those sixty years of writing, Cohen favored something like the prophetic voice, as he told *Rolling Stone* in a 1970 interview: "The songs are inspired. I don't pretend to be a guide. I do pretend to be an instrument for certain kinds of information at certain moments."[3]

---

[1] Simon Worrall, "Leonard Cohen: Out of the Monastery and back on the Road," *Independent* (June 15, 2008), www.independent.co.uk/arts-entertainment/music/features/leonard-cohen-out-of-the-monastery-and-back-on-the-road-845789.html.
[2] Lorraine Dorman and Clive Rawlins, *Leonard Cohen: Prophet of the Heart* (London: Omnibus Press, 1990), 91.
[3] Jiří Měsíc, "Leonard Cohen, the Priest of a Catacomb Religion," *Moravian Journal of Literature and Film* 6, no. 1 (2015): 29–47.

Cohen grew up in an observant Jewish family in Montreal (b. 1934). His great-uncle, Tzvi Hirsch Cohen, was the city's chief rabbi; his maternal grandfather, Rabbi Solomon Klonitsky-Kline, wrote commentaries on the Talmud, and his paternal grandfather, Lyon Cohen, was the founding president of the Canadian Jewish Congress and cofounded the *Canadian Jewish Times*. Leonard Cohen observed many of the Jewish rituals and was a serious student of Jewish texts.[4] His theistic beliefs were Jewish, he told Stina Dabrowski in 1997: "I was always happy with the religion I was born into and it satisfied all the religious questions."[5]

And yet Cohen speaks often about Jesus, from the outset of his career in the novel *Beautiful Losers* (1966) and "Suzanne" (*Songs of Leonard Cohen*, 1967) through fourteen collections of poetry and fourteen song collections to the final *You Want It Darker*.[6] Why? It is not the Christian church or history that nabs Cohen but Jesus – an interest that sparked both critiques and appreciations of his work.[7] While Cohen drew from Buddhist, Sufi, and Muslim imagery as well,[8] this chapter investigates Cohen's frequent evocation of the Christian son of God.

"As a Jew," the philosopher Babette Babich insightfully writes, "Cohen reminds us to feel for Christ, not to be a Christian necessarily but to get the point about Christ . . . And we're at Golgotha again."[9] In her remark

---

[4] For a rigorous study of kabbalistic imagery in Cohen, see Elliot R. Wolfson, "New Jerusalem Glowing: Songs and Poems of Leonard Cohen in a Kabbalistic Key," *Kabbalah: Journal for the Study of Jewish Mystical Texts* 15 (2006): 103–53.

[5] Jeff Burger (ed.), *Leonard Cohen on Leonard Cohen: Interviews and Encounters* (Chicago: Chicago Review Press, 2014), 414, 453.

[6] Douglas Todd, "Leonard Cohen: Jewish, Buddhist and Christian, Too," *Vancouver Sun* (November 25, 2016), https://vancouversun.com/opinion/columnists/douglas-todd-leonard-cohen-jewish-buddhist-and-christian-too.

[7] Babette Babich, "Hallelujah and Atonement," in *Leonard Cohen and Philosophy: Various Positions*, ed. Jason Holt (Chicago: Open Court, 2014), 123–36; Peter Billingham, "Crosses, Nails, and Lonely Wooden Towers: The Leitmotif of 'The Wounded Man' in Selected Songs of Leonard Cohen," in *Spirituality and Desire in Leonard Cohen's Songs and Poems: Visions from the Tower of Song*, ed. Peter Billingham (Newcastle-upon-Tyne: Cambridge Scholars Publishing, 2017), 27–42; Stina Lundberg Dabrowski, "TV Interview: Swedish National Television," in Burger (ed.), *Leonard Cohen*, 439–77.

[8] Jiří Měsíc, "The Nature of Love in the Work of Leonard Cohen," *Journal of Popular Romance Studies* (October 4, 2018), https://www.jprstudies.org/2018/10/the-nature-of-love-in-the-work-of-leonard-cohenby-jiri-mesic/; Wolfson, "New Jerusalem."

[9] Babich, "Hallelujah and Atonement," Kindle ed.

about Golgotha, Babich echoes a 1968 interview where Cohen explained that "Our natural vocabulary is Judeo-Christian. That is our bloodmyth. We have to rediscover law from inside our own heritage, and we have to rediscover the crucifixion. The crucifixion will again be understood as a universal symbol . . . It will have to be rediscovered because that's where man is at. On the cross" – indeed, at Golgotha.[10]

Cohen "got the point": Jesus – fully human, beset by the fears and temptations that riddle us all, forsaken by his people and at moments seemingly by God – abandons neither God nor people. He persists in commitment. That steadfastness impressed Cohen. It is highest among Cohen's concerns because of his ontology and theology of covenant. The world is structured as interlocking covenantal relations. Jesus sustained covenantal bonds; no one else has (save Abraham and Moses). Instead, we abuse and abandon each other, and the prophet is left to rail at humanity's covenant breaches. In order to understand Cohen on Jesus, we must first look at Cohen's covenantal worldview.

COHEN'S COVENANTAL THEOLOGY AND THEODICY. Cohen did not leave us with a pastiche of individual poems but rather with a lifelong theodicy-in-verse. We are made as covenantal creatures, dependent on relationship to survive and flourish. Yet we fail to act covenantally with God and other persons, betraying and violating each other. In short, Cohen gave us a diagnosis for our times, how we get to the loneliness, greed, abandonment, and violence around us. If these sins are rooted in breach of covenant, what precisely comprises this bond? The Jewish covenant is a *reciprocal* relationship between unique parties where each gives for the flourishing of the other. To become the unique persons we are, each person develops through networks of relations with others and our transcendent source. In contrast to the theocracies of antiquity, where the bond is between God and monarch or priest, the Biblical covenant is between *all* the people – each person – and God, whose forgiveness and grace are the standard by which human conduct,

---

[10] David Cowan, "Leonard Cohen's Life of Poetry and Song," *American Conservative* (December 16, 2016), www.theamericanconservative.com/articles/leonard-cohens-life-of-poetryand-song/.

including the monarch's, is judged.[11] Covenant, in Robert Bellah's words, is "a charter for a new kind of people, a people under God, not under a king, an idea parallel to Athenian democracy though longer lasting . . . a people ruled by divine law, not the arbitrary rule of the state, and of a people composed of responsible individuals."[12]

Contract protects interests. Covenant protects relationship. Moreover, covenant expands from a bilateral relationship – God–Adam, God–Noah, God–patriarchs – into community. Persons give to God by giving to persons in need (*hekdesh* in Hebrew). Reciprocal giving becomes a giving network, where gift from God to person (of life, sustenance) generates gift from person to neighbor and on to the next person through the giving loop, thus sustaining it.[13] Indeed, covenant is double or entwined: between God and person and *among* persons.

Who is in the covenantal loop? All the nations. The covenantal promise with Noah is with all humanity, and covenant with the Biblical patriarchs, declared thrice, stipulates that "all peoples on earth will be blessed through you" (Genesis 12:3, 26:4, 28:14). This is the basis for the Biblical requirements to care for not only the domestic poor but the stranger and enemy (Exodus 22:21; Leviticus 19:34, 23:35–39).[14] And then there are the prophets, who teach that one cannot have a bond with God without covenantal care for neighbor. Insisting on compassion over ritual, Amos writes: "I [God] hate, I despise your religious festivals; your assemblies are a stench to me . . . But let justice roll on like a river, righteousness like a never-failing stream" (Amos 5:21–24; see also Hos. 6:6, Mic. 7:2–7, and Prov. 21:3).

There are particularist readings of covenant, where the bond applies only to the Israelites. But they are not Cohen's reading. In a 1994 interview, he explained, "A confident people is not exclusive. A great religion

---

[11] Christine Hayes, *Introduction to the Bible* (New Haven: Yale University Press, 2012).
[12] Robert Bellah, *Religion in Human Evolution* (Cambridge, MA: Harvard University Press, 2011), Kindle ed.
[13] See Jacques Godbout and Alain Caillé, *The World of the Gift*, trans. Donald Winkler (Montreal: McGill-Queen's University Press, 1998).
[14] See Robert Gibbs, "Returning/Forgiving: Ethics and Theology," in *Questioning God*, ed. J. Caputo, M. Dooley, and M. Scanlon (Indianapolis: Indiana University Press, 2001), 73–91 on poor laws in rabbinic sources.

affirms other religions. A great culture affirms other cultures. A great nation affirms other nations. A great individual affirms other individuals, validates the beingness of others."[15]

What does covenant sound like in Cohen's words? In the 1984 *Book of Mercy*, Cohen's modern psalter, Cohen writes of God: "you gave my soul a beam to travel on."[16] Poem forty-five plunges into covenantal intimacy: "Not knowing how to speak, I speak to you." Thirty-two years later, Cohen still writes of living *within* his relationship with God ("If I Didn't Have Your Love," *You Want It Darker*, 2016). The world would be empty and life, barren, without God's love. From covenantal commitment to God, Cohen moves to covenantal commitment to other persons in "Don't Pass Me By" (*Live Songs*, 1973). The "I" of the song passes a blind man on the street. His makeshift sign beseeches, "Don't pass me by." Passing others by precludes seeing and seeing to them. It forecloses at/tending to our connection with them, however close or attenuated. It makes *us* blind. And no flourishing can come of that.

We are, in Cohen's worldview, made for devotion to God and others. And yet humanity fails. Cohen was, by his own account, a covenant fail-er par excellence. As Irving Layton, a poet and Cohen's mentor, remarked, Cohen is "a narcissist who hates himself" for being inconstant to God and too self-protected to stick it out with the women he loved.[17] What gets in the way of covenant? Everything human. We follow the call of Babylon and Boogie Street, two images running throughout Cohen's work to signify our pursuit of power, sexual adventure, and economic gain. We fall prey to pride. In *Book of Mercy*, Cohen writes, "When the heart grins at itself, the world is destroyed. And I am found alone with the husks and the shells. Then the dangerous moment comes: I am too great to ask for help."[18] It is not only relationship that is undone by pride but "the world itself is destroyed," because the world and humanity depend on relation.

---

[15] Burger (ed.), *Leonard Cohen*, 388.
[16] Leonard Cohen, *Book of Mercy* (Toronto: McClelland and Stewart, 2010), 19.
[17] Calev Ben-David, "Leonard Cohen: Artist, Mensch and 'kohen gadol'," November 13, 2016, https://www.jpost.com/israel-news/culture/leonard-cohen-artist-mensch-and-kohen-gadol-472432.
[18] Cohen, *Book of Mercy*, 31.

Who is responsible for our yo-yo between covenant and breach? Cohen is a religious thinker; he called himself "the poet of the two great intimacies," with God and women.[19] So the question is not only why *humanity* breaches covenant, but why *God* created us so prone to breaching it. Free-will theories didn't satisfy Cohen. Free will may be necessary in order for humanity to be *moral* agents. We'd otherwise be bots preprogrammed to do good automatically, not out of moral understanding. But why do we use our free will to commit personal and political cruelty so often? Could God not have made us less prone to its worst excesses?

We breach covenant because breaching is easy for us. And whose fault is that? If the propensity to breach covenant is human nature, it cannot be only humanity's sin. God, on Cohen's troubled reading, is the source of human evil because he is the source of humanity. Cohen doesn't let God squirm out of it. In the 1974 song "Lover Lover Lover" (*New Skin for the Old Ceremony*) Cohen confronts God: "He [God] said, 'I locked you in this body/ I meant it as a kind of trial'." God, under Cohen's pen, admits that he, as author of creation, is the author of our trials. He made us for committed love yet gave us wandering desires that betray it. What kind of rigged "trial" is that? What kind of God?

JESUS. Cohen understood that one doesn't solve the theodical problem of human wrongdoing. He rather tried to find moments of covenant sustained, one of which is the moment of Jesus. A covenantal bond between humanity and Jesus *is* the entwined covenant: with God (Jesus as divine) and among persons (Jesus as person). This is the event of the incarnation and one reason why Jesus is important in Cohen's work. For Cohen, Jesus was a figure of both the unbroken, double covenant (in his life and lessons) and of the human suffering that follows its breach (in his death). I'll discuss both aspects of Jesus in sequence.

JESUS: COVENANT SUSTAINER. Cohen grew up in what he called a "Catholic city." His nanny was Catholic and took him to church. The

---

[19] Leonard Cohen, "Commentary – My Wife and I," *Stranger Music: Selected Poems and Songs* (New York: Vintage, 1994), 230.

power of New Testament imagery and its weight in our cultural–emotional repertoire was, in Cohen's view, unavoidable, regardless of one's religious beliefs. "The figure of Jesus," he explained to Robert O'Brien, "is extremely attractive. It's difficult not to fall in love with that person."[20] Cohen explains his interest in Jesus in terms of covenantal care:

> Any guy who says blessed are the poor, blessed are the meek, has got to be a figure of unparalleled generosity and insight and madness. A man who declared himself to stand among the thieves, the prostitutes and the homeless. He was a man of inhuman generosity, a generosity that would overthrow the world if it was embraced.[21]

Exactly so. Such covenantal giving would overthrow the world as we now have it. But if Jesus were only "inhuman," only divine, humanity would have a different sort of relationship with him. God acting godlike may set aspirational goals for humanity towards which we may strive, never reaching them precisely because they are divine. But the event of the incarnation is that Jesus was also fully human and sustained covenantal commitment to both the Father and humanity in spite of the human propensity for self-absorption and through moments of ridicule and betrayal. Therein lies the lesson that captivates Cohen. The divinity of Jesus sets a model for us, and the person of Jesus exemplifies it in sustaining covenant.

Humanity, in the image of a covenanting God and following the person Jesus, has the *capacity* to act covenantally even if we ignore it. Cohen put it this way in "Avalanche," the story of God's covenantal promise and hope that humanity will return it (*Songs of Love and Hate*, 1971). In the body of Jesus – the human body – God steps into the "avalanche" of worldly life and is not embraced but abandoned. God continues to long for us nonetheless precisely because persons are endowed with the possibility of covenantal love. "God entreats us: It is your turn, beloved/ It is your flesh that I wear." In *Book of Mercy*, it is Cohen, the human person, who longs for God's love. "Avalanche" is the

---

[20] Burger (ed.), *Leonard Cohen*, 183.
[21] Alan Hustak, "Mr. Cohen, It Was a Privilege Knowing You," *Catholic Register* (November 16, 2016), www.catholicregister.org/item/23611-mr-cohen-it-was-a-privilege-knowing-you.

other side of the coin, the divine side of covenant: God longs for us. God, having gone so far as to step into human flesh to love and save us, hopes that a humanity capable of reciprocating will return covenantal love. "Into the heart of every Christian," Cohen said,

> Christ comes, and Christ goes. When, by his Grace, the landscape of the heart becomes vast and deep and limitless, then Christ makes His abode in that graceful heart, and His Will prevails. The experience is recognized as Peace. In the absence of this experience much activity arises, divisions of every sort.[22]

When the heart does not make space for God, the bond with God is broken, and because the covenants are entwined, we then breach commitment to each other and create divisions among ourselves.

"The Window" (*Recent Songs*, 1979), similarly ponders God's–Jesus' covenantal commitment to humanity in spite of our divisions, negligence, and cruelty.

> Why do you stand by the window
> Abandoned to beauty and pride
> The thorn of the night in your bosom
> The spear of the age in your side.

Why, Jesus, do you bother to stand at the window to the world, making yourself accessible to all, while humanity abandons you to beauty, pride, and to the violence of the spear and crucifixion? How is it that in your *human state* you nonetheless sustain such love? The implicit, theodical question whispers: why do we not follow?

JESUS: COVENANT SUSTAINER AND STANDARD IN COHEN'S POLITICAL WORKS. The question of following Jesus in covenant pertains not only to our personal but to our political commitments. Cohen's political writings are anchored in the idea that humanity does not betray its commitments one by one: with God, in our personal lives, and then

---

[22] Cited in Doron B. Cohen, "The Prayers of Leonard Cohen: If It Be Your Will," lecture delivered at the Leonard Cohen Event, Amsterdam, August 14, 2016, www.leonardcohenfiles.com/doron-amsterdam.pdf.

with strangers, politically. It is humanity's great talent to betray them at once, seeing to our self-protection and self-interest in all arenas. Cohen's political works rail against a trinity of covenant breaches: with God, with other persons, and in political crimes – a dark mirror to the Trinity that is to guide us to the moral life.[23]

The song "Everybody Knows" (with Sharon Robinson, *I'm Your Man*, 1988) is a template for Cohen's triune understanding of the political world. It begins with our political betrayals of the poor, moves to personal infidelities, and ends with our abandonment of Jesus on the cross. With covenant thrice trounced – in politics, love, and faith – the world is ready to blow. Indeed, what bonds remain to keep it together? Again in "Democracy" (*The Future*, 1992), Cohen understands covenant breaches as the root of our political brutalities, and he holds Jesus' lessons as a way to democracy and peace. "From the staggering account/ Of the Sermon on the Mount . . . Democracy is coming to the USA." The political covenant of democracy will emerge from the covenants preached in Jesus' Sermon, remembered in kneeling prayer, and promised in grace – if it comes at all.

Cohen is less hopeful about democracy a decade later in "Land of Plenty" (*Ten New Songs*, 2001), where he prays for "For the millions in a prison," but also for Christ "not risen" and "what's left of our religion." The Cohen catechism is reprised: the abandonment of persons and God together abound. He reminds us, as the ancient prophets reminded the Israelites, that covenant with God cannot flourish (Christ cannot be risen) if we neglect each other (the poor, the imprisoned).

"Amen" (*Old Ideas*, 2012), among Cohen's most disturbing political works, is a companion piece to "Everybody Knows" in its dark-trinity interweaving of the personal, political, and theological. While in the 1988 song, everybody knows our commitments are thrice "coming apart," in "Amen," we're thrice tuning out of the mayhem around us. The song begins with the personal: you can tell me what's going on in the places of world misery when I'm off drugs and sober. Till then, I'm too out of it to pay attention. Political blindness then moves in: tell me of the

---

[23] Marcia Pally, *From This Broken Hill I Sing to You: God, Sex, and Politics in the Work of Leonard Cohen* (London: T&T Clark, 2021), chapter 7.

political atrocities "When the victims are singing/ And the laws of remorse are restored" – when just governance has returned and the citizenry is content, so I don't have to worry about it. Religious complacency then enters in a staggering image: tell me of the world's sins "when the filth of the butcher/ Is washed in the blood of the lamb." Tell me about the suffering when our butchery is already redeemed. Until then, we don't want to be bothered.

Bothered by what? Not only by the world's butcheries but by love. Each stanza ends: "tell me that you want me," "love me," "need me *then*," after I'm sober, victims are healed, and humanity is redeemed. Don't tell me now; I don't want to deal with love now. The personal and political rejection of commitment are of a piece, joined in each stanza as it melds the two together. Who is the narrator rebuffing? Perhaps a woman whom the narrator wants to be rid of, so he makes the bar to love impossibly high: don't tell me about love till the messiah comes. But these lines are also an indictment against God, and indeed, each verse closes with "Amen." Cohen charges: You, God, don't tell me about your wanting peace and covenant with humankind while you allow us such barbarism. You can wax grandly of love in scripture after you've stopped the cruelty down here on Earth. Until then, talk of love is a hollow show piece.

Cohen did not believe God is deceiving humanity. Indeed, Cohen caught moments of covenantal giving in his life, lost it, missed it, and sought it throughout his own suffering born of the many relationships he could not sustain, with God and women.[24] God in Cohen's world is not a trickster but inscrutable in allowing us our recidivist evils. Jesus is thus all the more remarkable for resisting them. "Come Healing" (*Old Ideas*, 2012, with Patrick Leonard) understands Jesus as offering a way out of our foibles. Out of "The splinters that you carry/ The cross you left behind" comes healing. It is from the splinters of the cross, from the shards of love offered of its lesson to turn suffering to love, that humanity may heal.

JESUS AS SUFFERER WITH HUMANITY WHEN WE REND COVENANT – AND AS A WAY BACK TO IT. When we ignore those shards, we are at Golgotha, bludgeoned and abandoned again, as Cohen

---

[24] Ibid., chapter 6.

said in 1968: "The crucifixion will again be understood as a universal symbol ... It will have to be rediscovered because that's where man is at. On the cross." After Jesus' first lesson of covenant *sustained*, this is the second: when we *ignore* our covenantal relationality, the world itself is undone, because it is founded on the entwined covenants. Suffering swells in the land. For Cohen, the human condition *is* Jesus' condition on the cross, broken and suffering from humanity's own hand. But the God–man, in his brokenness, suffers with humanity and offers restoration of "the wholeness (holiness) of humankind and creation."[25] When we understand the sources of Jesus' woundedness as human self-absorption, and when we grasp Jesus' response as continuous giving, we again have the chance to learn covenantal love for God and each other. Cohen put it this way: Jesus "was nailed to a *human* predicament, summoning the heart to comprehend its own suffering by dissolving itself in a radical confession of hospitality."[26]

Suffering turned to hospitality is something that we humans, following the suffering God–man, can do. This was the kind of love and covenantal commitment that Cohen understood – and understood that he, and we, regularly fail. But through our failures and suffering, there's a chance: "There is a crack in everything/ That's how the light gets in" ("Anthem," *The Future*, 1992). Cohen called this "as close to a credo as I've come."[27] If we dare to reach for God in our cracked brokenness, so begins the possibility of receiving God's love and giving to others. Aubrey Glazer writes that "the brokenness that is incurred is meant to be a teacher," a guide to relation and redemption.[28]

On Doron Cohen's counting, "brokenness" appears in over 10 percent of Cohen's recorded lyrics, often evoking Jesus, in such songs as "Suzanne," "Hallelujah," "The Guests," and "The Window."[29] A few examples: as early as 1969, "You Know Who I Am" (*Songs from a Room*), Cohen writes us a promissory note from God, who pledges to "leave with

---

[25] Billingham, "Crosses, Nails, and Lonely Wooden Towers," 30.
[26] Cowan, "Leonard Cohen's Life of Poetry and Song," emphasis mine.
[27] Burger (ed.), *Leonard Cohen*, 366.
[28] Aubrey Glazer, *Tangle of Matter & Ghost: Leonard Cohen's Post-Secular Songbook of Mysticism(s) Jewish & Beyond* (Boston: Academic Studies Press, 2017), Kindle ed.
[29] Doron B. Cohen, "The Prayers of Leonard Cohen," 4–5.

you one broken man/ Whom I will teach you to repair." If humanity seeks ("tracks down") God, God will "surrender" in covenant and leave us a gift: one man "broken," Jesus on the cross, who will be repaired by humanity *because*, as God's gift, the broken God–man will teach us to repair the broken among us. As we do – *if* we do – we also near God. This is the entwined, reciprocal covenant incarnate. God gives us Jesus, and should humanity heal his brokenness, we would simultaneously heal both the man Jesus and covenant with God.

Fifteen years later, in "Hallelujah" (*Various Positions,* 1984), Cohen writes, "And it's not a cry that you hear at night .../ It's a cold and it's a broken Hallelujah." Our declaration of thanks and praise of God, "Hallelujah" – the recognition of our need for this bond – is not glorious or confident, but from a chilled, broken place. Also on *Various Positions,* the song "If It Be Your Will" is drawn from the Jewish Atonement Day service, where the praying ask for forgiveness. Cohen sings: "From this broken hill/ I will sing to you" near you, bind myself to you, God. The "broken hill" evokes both Sinai, where covenant is broken by the people's worship of the Golden Calf, and Golgotha, where Jesus is broken. And it evokes humanity, broken by banal isolation and heinous cruelty. It is from this desolate brokenness, bonds with God and persons rent, that Cohen seeks God.

Late in his career, in *Old Ideas* (2012, with Patrick Leonard), Cohen comes again to the "old idea" of brokenness that had been his since the 1960s. In "Come Healing," the speaker asks that we gather our "brokenness" – and bring it to him in "The fragrance of those promises/ You never dared to vow." Bring your never-made commitments here. To whom were those promises never made? God? Persons? Both? It is not-promising, not-vowing, not-committing, that is the human failing. It breaks not only the heart of the promisee but also the promiser and surely the relationship. In the next verse, Cohen writes that Jesus offers a way to heal our breached promises in giving for the sake of the other as he gave, pierced by the splinters of the cross.

JESUS AS COVENANTER AND SUFFERER: COHEN'S POETIC TECHNIQUES. "Suzanne" (*Songs of Leonard Cohen,* 1967) bridges the two aspects of Jesus, the persona of covenantal commitment and the suffering that follows from its breach. The song also showcases another doubling: Cohen's poetic technique. To lyrically represent the entwinedness of covenant, Cohen crafts images that describe each bond. Two techniques are employed: first, the interweaving of separate images (one evoking bond with God, the other, bond with persons) and second, single images that evoke both relationships at once. The second technique, for instance, is seen in the lyric, "Oh, take this longing from my tongue," understood as both prayer (intimacy with God) and sex (intimacy with a lover).

"Suzanne" contains both techniques. First, Cohen interweaves separate images. The first and third stanzas tell of a fragile, possible love with Suzanne (love among persons). The second stanza, however, interpolates a fellow named Jesus, who watches and speaks to us "drowning men" (God's offer of love and God's hope that we will reciprocate). Mostly, we don't, and both God and humanity suffer: "he himself was broken ... he sank beneath your wisdom like a stone." We are so busy with our "wisdom" that we forsake Jesus (covenant with God, trounced). And because the covenants are entwined, we also forsake Suzanne by telling her that "you have no love to give her" (commitment to persons rejected). The entwined covenant is breached twice, once with Suzanne (in the first stanza) and once with God (in the second).

In the third stanza, Cohen employs the second technique of using images that simultaneously evoke bonds with God and with the person of Suzanne. Suzanne wears "rags" as the God–man Jesus did, and she "shows you where to look amid the garbage and the flowers," amid the refuse strewn inattentively over nature, where Jesus too strode. She carries a mirror, symbol both of human lust (as in the Biblical story of Susannah and the Elders) and of salvation (as in the fourteenth-century *Speculum Humanae Salvationis, Mirror of Human Salvation*). She walks beneath "our lady of the harbour," statue of the Virgin Mary atop the mariner's church in Montreal. She wears clothes "from Salvation Army counters," a pun highlighting Susanne's salvific role. And she is the one in whom you can place your faith. You can trust her because she has touched you with her "mind," that is, with her spirit.

This melded person of verse three, part salvific, part erotic, is Suzanne as the God–man. If s/he "gets you on her wavelength," you might not forsake her/Jesus. In an ephemeral moment, you might grasp (both understand and embrace) a moment of recognition and commitment. In "Suzanne," Cohen confronts us with the almost-automaticity of our withdrawal from others (stanza one) and from God (stanza two). Yet the song ends with the possibility of being "touched" by the spirit of the rags-wearing Jesus–Suzanne.

CONCLUDING THOUGHTS. This chapter has sketched out Cohen's prime concern with things Christian: the person of Jesus as covenant sustainer and as sufferer with humanity in our recidivist breaches. Jesus' covenantal love offers a path out of the breach. In Cohen's last song collection, *You Want It Darker* (2016), half of the songs rely on Christian references. I'll close with "Treaty," which bridges Cohen's frustration with God (who allows us cruelty and indifference) and Cohen's recognition that, however inscrutable, it is God to whom we are bound in covenant. When we ignore it, we are divisive, destructive, and lost. "Treaty" begins with frustration: "I've seen you change the water into wine/ I've seen you change it back to water too." Cohen has seen God–Jesus be miraculous in turning water into wine. But he has also seen God withdraw his miracles, leaving us to our machinations. Why trust this God? Yet a few stanzas on, Cohen returns to relationship and faith. "Treaty" continues, "You were my ground, my safe and sound." For all Cohen's frustration, God grounds him. This is the same spiritual-emotional move he made in the 1967 "Suzanne": from being too self-absorbed to have any love for Suzanne or Jesus to being caught on the "wavelength" of the Jesus–Suzanne. The refrain of "Treaty" is not "I wish there was a treaty/ Between you and me," as if God and Cohen were enemies needing a cease-fire. It is rather, "I wish there was a treaty/ Between your love and mine." There is no question of the love between Cohen and God.

Throughout life, Cohen battled with falling in and out of relationship with God and persons, despite being a committed practitioner of Judaism and Buddhism and a student of other traditions. One place to which he turned frequently was Jesus, the guy "nailed to a *human* predicament."

PART IV

CULTURAL CONTEXTS

CHAPTER 11

Canadian Literature

Ian Rae

Ira Nadel's landmark biography, *Various Positions: A Life of Leonard Cohen* (1996), introduces Cohen's metamorphosis from writer into popular singer with an anecdote about an "all-day poetry party" organized by F.R. Scott in 1966.[1] This party included some of the leading male poets from the modernist movement in Canada: the literary magazine editors Scott, A. J. M. Smith, and Louis Dudek; the anthologist Ralph Gustafson; and the iconoclasts Irving Layton and Al Purdy. These poets were mostly a generation older than Cohen, and he had joined their ranks as their student or mentee. Dudek was Cohen's undergraduate English professor at McGill University who devised a subscription-based publishing series for Cohen's first book, *Let Us Compare Mythologies* (1956). Scott, the former Dean of Law at McGill, published poetry while using his legal acumen to fight the censorship of books, champion bilingualism, and invent the social democratic Co-operative Commonwealth Federation party. Into this august company, Cohen brought his Bob Dylan records and guitar. Cohen forced his elders to listen to Dylan's *Highway 61 Revisited* and encouraged them to take the songwriter seriously. Purdy left the room in disgust, and the other poets were as unimpressed by the music as they were by Cohen's declaration that "*he* would become the Canadian Dylan, a statement all dismissed."[2]

---

[1] Ira B. Nadel, *Various Positions: A Life of Leonard Cohen* (Toronto: Random House, 1996), 141.
[2] Ibid., 141.

The second-class status implied by the term "the Canadian Dylan" was not the future that these mentors had imagined for their golden boy. Cohen was the only son of a prominent Westmount family, the descendant of rabbis and industrialists, and a meteoric literary talent who had published four collections of poetry and two novels in the previous decade. At thirty-two years of age, he wanted to move to New York to become a folksinger?

The Dylan precedent identifies the scene that Cohen was trying to make in 1966, but not the music that ultimately earned Cohen acclaim. Although Cohen describes himself as one of the "workers in song" in "Chelsea Hotel No. 2," he understands song as an extension of poetic practice, in particular of the lyric technique that he honed in his early books, a fact that distinguishes him from Dylan and his peers.[3] Hence Cohen's literary executors take pains to underscore Cohen's status as a poet first and foremost in *The Flame* (2018), his final collection. Cohen's son, Adam, writes in the foreword: "My father, before he was anything else, was a poet."[4] Robert Faggen and Alexandra Pleshoyano confirm in an editorial note that the priority of poetry in Cohen's oeuvre is not just a matter of the chronology of his career: "All the lyrics for Leonard's songs begin as poems, and thus they can be appreciated as poems in their own right more than those of most songwriters."[5]

Conversely, the young poet is bursting into song throughout his early collections: "Prayer for Messiah," "Song to Make Me Still," "Morning Song." These poems renovate literary conventions to suit the needs of the time, and eventually this logic will lead Cohen to the recording studio. A "Morning Song," for example, is a colloquial way of invoking the traditional genre of the aubade. Likewise, when the protagonist in Cohen's first novel, *The Favourite Game* (1963), declares that "Canadians are desperate for a Keats,"[6] he seems to mean the kind of traditional praise poet who finds ways to approximate the music of song, especially birdsong, in words.

---

[3] Leonard Cohen, "Chelsea Hotel," *Stranger Music: Selected Poems and Songs* (Toronto: McClelland and Stewart, 1994 [1993]), 197.

[4] Adam Cohen, "Foreword," in Leonard Cohen, *The Flame*, ed. Robert Faggen and Alexandra Pleshoyano (Edinburgh: Canongate Books, 2018), nonpaginated.

[5] Robert Faggen and Alexandra Pleshoyano, "Editorial Note," in Cohen, *The Flame*, nonpaginated.

[6] Leonard Cohen, *The Favourite Game* (Toronto: McClelland and Stewart, 20 [1963]), 108.

In "Ode to a Nightingale," for example, Keats's speaker listens to a bird chant in the darkness and wishes that he, too, could pour forth his "soul abroad/ In such an ecstasy":[7]

> Thou wast not born for death, immortal Bird!
> No hungry generations tread thee down;
> The voice I hear this passing night was heard
> In ancient days by emperor and clown.[8]

Cohen, for his part, furthers this ancient tradition in "Bird on the Wire," from his second album, when he reflects on the new telephone lines near his home on the Greek island of Hydra in anapests, an ancient Greek metre that stresses every third syllable:

> Like a **bird** on the **wire**
> Like a **drunk** in a **mid**night **choir**
> I have **tried** in my **way** to be **free**.[9]

The ancient pedigree of this song tradition adds a layer of complexity to the titles of Cohen's early albums – *Songs of Leonard Cohen* (1967), *Songs from a Room* (1969), *Songs of Love and Hate* (1971) – because it diminishes the categorical divide between poetry and music. Cohen revels in the work of any artist who also blurs this distinction – whether Dylan, Keats, or medieval balladeers – but Cohen ultimately blazes his own unique musical path, in part by looking beyond song traditions in English.

Cohen's peculiar recording history also distinguishes his music from that of the other members of the "Big Four" of Canadian folk music: Gordon Lightfoot, Joni Mitchell, and Neil Young. Cohen established his signature sound with his first album in 1967. Imagine, then, a year-end radio poll in which the pollster asked the question: "Who is the romantic balladeer we should call 'Canada's Troubadour'?" The answer would not have been Young, who would release his first solo record, *Neil Young*, in

---

[7] John Keats, "Ode to a Nightingale," *The Norton Anthology of English Literature*, ed. Stephen Greenblatt et al., 8th ed. (New York: W. W. Norton, 2006), 1846. See also Lawrence Breavman's meditation on birdsong in Cohen, *The Favourite Game*, 183.
[8] Keats, "Ode to a Nightingale," 1846.
[9] Leonard Cohen, "Bird on the Wire," *Stranger Music*, 144. I have added the bold type in this quotation to illustrate the scansion.

1969. It would not be Mitchell, who in 1967 was still pitching her songs to American artists such as Tom Rush and Judy Collins. She would release her first solo album, *Song to a Seagull*, in 1968. Cohen might have earned some votes for the singularity of his sound in 1967, but, without question, the winner of the poll would have been Gordon Lightfoot, who had appeared on Canadian radio and television since boyhood and who had already released four successful albums. Even Dylan considered Lightfoot a great songwriter and inducted him into the Canadian Music Hall of Fame in 1986.[10] Although Cohen frequently experimented with the jangling, strum-and-cry sound made popular by Dylan, and by Lightfoot on "Early Morning Rain" (1966), only two of the twelve songs on *The Best of Leonard Cohen* (1975), "Lady Midnight" and "So Long, Marianne," could be said to fit this pattern. All the other songs on *The Best of Leonard Cohen* employ the hypnotic fingerpicking and the subdued, nearly spoken, vocals that came to define Cohen's sound until the synth pop of *I'm Your Man* (1988).

The year 1967 saw Canada's centennial celebration and its apotheosis, the Universal Exhibition in Montreal, "Expo 67." The anglophone nationalism of this era placed heavy emphasis on Canadian content, which is a demand that classics by Lightfoot, Mitchell, and Young fulfill, but none by Cohen. Lightfoot would make the telling of Canadian history a staple of his musical repertoire, as in the centennial commission "The Canadian Railroad Trilogy" (1967) or "The Wreck of the Edmund Fitzgerald" (1976). Young and Mitchell settled into the California music scene in the late 1960s, and they charted a different path by evoking Canada as a distant place of nostalgic yearning. Young famously pines for a formative Ontario home in the opening lines of "Helpless," a song Cohen admired. Cohen invokes the song's second verse in a 2009 interview: "The only thing a writer has to have for me is just one song that manages to hit me and I love him immediately. I remember hearing that song . . . (starting to sing) 'Blue, blue windows behind the stars/ Yellow moon on the rise . . .' He is very good."[11]

---

[10] Some of the points concerning Lightfoot's sound in this chapter derive from the extensive discussion of Lightfoot's legacy on CBC radio following Lightfoot's death on May 1, 2023.

[11] Quoted in Arun Starkey, "Leonard Cohen Once Named His Favourite Neil Young Song," *Far Out Magazine* (August 13, 2021), https://faroutmagazine.co.uk/leonard-cohen-once-named-his-favourite-neil-young-song/.

Nonetheless, although Cohen often celebrates Montreal locations in his novels and poems, nowhere in his better-known songs does he invoke a Canadian location in the explicit manner that "Helpless" does. The closest a hit Cohen song comes to invoking a Canadian setting is the cryptic comparison of the muse figure in "Suzanne" to "our lady of the harbour," a golden statue above the mariner's church, Notre-Dame-de-Bon-Secours, in Montreal's Old Port.[12] Montrealers instantly recognize the reference, but the song's setting is ethereal to most ears.

A year after the release of "Helpless," Mitchell would double down on Canadian content in "A Case of You." According to Sylvie Simmons, this love song from Mitchell's classic album *Blue* (1971) was inspired by the singer's affair with Cohen in 1968.[13] The song includes a verse and chorus that explicitly reference a map of Canada while hinting at a Canadian lover. The song's echoes of the national anthem locate an emotional home for Mitchell in a fashion that nothing in Cohen's touring repertoire, not even "Going Home" (2012), does. So why is Cohen's legacy indissociable from Montreal in both the critical and popular imaginations? Why, following Cohen's death in 2018, did giant murals of Cohen appear on buildings above Stanley Street in the Golden Square Mile and over the edgier, francophone Boulevard Saint-Laurent? One answer, perhaps, is that Cohen's family is deeply embedded in Montreal's Jewish community. Cohen's paternal and maternal lineages included rabbis and Talmudic scholars, the cofounder of Canada's second-oldest synagogue, a president of the Canadian Jewish Congress, and the founder of Canada's first Jewish newspaper, the *Jewish Times*.[14]

Neither rabbi nor cantor, but something related, the errant Cohen seemed perpetually on the verge of a religious homecoming, which he completed nineteen days before his death with the title track of *You Want It Darker*. This song includes background vocals from the choir and cantor of the family synagogue, Shaar Hashomayim, who intone an eerie but uplifting melody as a sonic backdrop to Cohen's mostly spoken

---

[12] Cohen, "Suzanne," *Stranger Music*, 96.
[13] Sylvie Simmons, *I'm Your Man: The Life of Leonard Cohen* (Toronto: McClelland and Stewart, 2012), 174.
[14] Harry Freedman, *Leonard Cohen: The Mystical Roots of Genius* (London: Bloomsbury, 2021), 2.

performance. As Moshe Halbertal observes, "Cohen had poetic perfect pitch when it came to the religious quest; he was the last of the psalmists."[15] Indeed, the devotional quality of Cohen's poetry and songs makes him unique in Canadian literature in the second half of twentieth century. Between the modernist Margaret Avison of *The Dumbfounding* (1966) and the appearance of Anne Carson's *Plainwater* and *Glass, Irony, and God* in 1995, there is no Canadian poet of international stature whom critics might describe as consistently a religious praise poet.

The trajectory of this religious quest charts a path that one can also map onto Cohen's literary evolution. Francis Mus's insightful *The Demons of Leonard Cohen* narrowly misses the mark on this point when he draws a sharp division between the artist's familial and literary obsessions with homecoming. Mus correctly notes that underlying Cohen's "inner urge to keep venturing out is an even deeper-rooted desire to come home":

> Although Cohen travelled a great deal in the early years of his literary career, in nearly every interview during this period he claimed that he had to keep going back to his hometown town to "renew his neurotic affiliations" (various interviews, as well as the back cover of *The Spice-Box of Earth*). In fact, despite his international success, he long presented himself as a local writer.[16]

Nonetheless, Mus assumes that Cohen's literary ties to Montreal wane because Toronto surpassed Montreal as Canada's most populous city in the early 1970s, and the rise of the Quebec independence movement in this period accelerated the shift of anglophone cultural and economic capital to Toronto. Even Layton, to whom Cohen dedicated *Parasites of Heaven* (1966), would move to Toronto to be closer to the major publishing houses and television studios, as well as to teach at York University from 1970 to 1978.

Yet, it must be emphasized, the cultural implications of this demographic shift are part of Cohen's neurotic affiliations with Montreal. He is

---

[15] Moshe Halbertal, "Foreword," in *From This Broken Hill I Sing to You: God, Sex, and Politics in the Work of Leonard Cohen*, Marcia Palley (London: T&T Clark, 2022), xvii.

[16] Francis Mus, *The Demons of Leonard Cohen* (Ottawa: University of Ottawa Press, 2020), 86.

deeply attached to the status of Montreal as the cultural capital of Canada, as both his novels attest. These novels depict anglophone Montreal's prestige as already under threat in the 1960s (think of Breavman lamenting the destruction of heritage architecture in the Golden Square Mile) and ripe for radical renewal (think of F.'s political activism in *Beautiful Losers*). The fact that Linda Hutcheon positions *Beautiful Losers* as the beginning of the postmodern novel in Canada only heightens Cohen's neuroses, because his experimental writing in the 1960s and 1970s marks the beginning of the end for the Montreal Moderns, even if Cohen would retreat from these experiments in the 1980s.[17] Works such as *The Energy of Slaves* (1972) challenge the modernist aims of artistic mastery and aesthetic unity cherished by Cohen's mentors. Stephen Scobie therefore claims that Cohen's writing stands "at the end(s) of modernism. 'End' is here to be understood both as 'aim' or 'purpose,' and as 'final point in a temporal sequence' – and it is always potentially plural."[18] Still, Cohen was anxious about the fact that he represented the last major poet directly connected to the Montreal Moderns, and that his touring and recording duties took time away from his literary projects. According to his son, Cohen's dying regret was that "he wished he had more completely stayed steadfast to the recognition that writing was his only solace, his truest purpose."[19]

Long after Cohen's fame had eclipsed that of his literary mentors, he went out of his way to pay homage to the Montreal Moderns and to ensure that they remained part of his story.[20] Cohen explains his debt to his mentors in Lian Lunson's 2005 documentary, *Leonard Cohen: I'm Your Man*:

> In Montreal there was a tight band of poets. The senior members were Irving Layton and Louis Dudek and other poets – Frank Scott. And they

---

[17] Linda Hutcheon, *The Canadian Postmodern: A Study of Contemporary English–Canadian Fiction* (Toronto: Oxford University Press, 1988), 26–44.

[18] Stephen Scobie, "Leonard Cohen, Phyllis Webb, and the End(s) of Modernism," in *Canadian Canons: Essays in Literary Value*, ed. Robert Lecker (Toronto: University of Toronto Press, 1991), 59.

[19] Adam Cohen, "Foreword," v–vi.

[20] For more on the Montreal Moderns, see Brian Trehearne, *The Montreal Forties: Modernist Poetry in Transition* (Toronto: University of Toronto Press, 1999).

were very, very kind to me. And we would meet regularly in an informal way with drinks, of course, and food and we ... would read each other our poems and then they would be subject to savage, word-by-word criticism. I mean, you couldn't get away with anything. We really wanted to be good writers, good poets, great poets ... We thought we was [sic] the most important thing in the world. We thought every time we met it was a summit conference. You know, we really took seriously – I think it was Shelley who said "poets are the unacknowledged legislators of the world." I mean, an incredibly naïve description of oneself, but we certainly fell for that. We thought it was terribly important, what we were doing. Maybe it was, who knows?[21]

Cohen's quip about summit conferences underscores that a Montreal poetry party in 1966 still had the feeling of a gathering of national heavyweights, in a way that only a few years later it would not, as Toronto poets (Margaret Atwood, bpNichol, Michael Ondaatje) and Vancouver poets (George Bowering and the Tish group) were in the ascendency.

Cohen's response to this decline is to transform the legacy of the Montreal Moderns into song on *Dear Heather* (2004), where he sets F. R. Scott's "Villanelle for Our Time" (1944) to music and includes a drawing of Scott by his wife, the painter Marion Scott, alongside the original poem in the liner notes. The recurring phrases in Scott's villanelle express the wartime sense of high vocation in the face of calamity that Cohen describes to Lunson in his documentary: "From bitter searching of the heart,/ We rise to play the greater part."[22] *Dear Heather* also includes an adaptation of Lord Byron's poem, "We'll Go No More A-Roving," which Cohen dedicates to the ailing Irving Layton, depicted in a drawing in the liner notes. Cohen's *Book of Longing* (2006) includes the poem "Irving and Me at the Hospital," which celebrates the poets' long-standing friendship:

> I loved to read his verses
> He loved to hear my song

---

[21] *Leonard Cohen: I'm Your Man*, dir. Lian Lunson (Christal Films and Lionsgate Films, 2005).

[22] F. R. Scott, "Villanelle for Our Time," *Poetry: A Magazine of Verse* (March 1944): 317.

> We never had much interest
> In who was right or wrong[23]

Despite differences of age, temperament, and style, Cohen saw himself in dialogue with the Montreal group to the end. Layton's poetry is more combative than Cohen's best-known verses, but the bombastic voice in Cohen's *Beautiful Losers* and *Death of a Lady's Man* owes a debt to Layton, who combined the rage of the Jewish prophets with the surprising tenderness of a lyricist and a fine eye for female beauty and natural phenomena.

Cohen's song "To a Teacher" on *Dear Heather* emphasizes the long duration of another Montreal influence, but this time the teacher is a literary role model, not a personal friend or professor. The song is dedicated to the poet A. M. Klein, and the song lyrics derive from the poem "To a Teacher" in Cohen's *The Spice-Box of Earth* (1961). Klein was a multilingual Montreal lawyer and editor of the *Canadian Jewish Chronicle* (1938–55) whose true passion was poetry. Raised in an Orthodox Jewish household, Klein led the transition of Montreal Jewish writing from Yiddish to English, and he approached his literary tasks with a kind of messianic zeal for reconciling the English, French, and Jewish communities. As M. W. Steinberg argues, Klein aimed "to inform the non-Jewish world of the Jewish condition – its achievements and its plight – but even more important, to convey to the young Jewish North American–born generation some knowledge of their cultural heritage."[24] Klein sought an international audience through his experimental novel, *The Second Scroll* (1951), about the reestablishment of Israel and differing perspectives on the diasporic experience.[25] Klein constructs a narrative based on contemporary events as interpreted through the Torah (the first five books of the Bible), while retaining much of the lyricism of his poetry. Klein's rhapsodic prose and genre-blending narrative set important precedents

---

[23] Leonard Cohen, "Irving and Me at the Hospital," *Book of Longing* (Toronto: McClelland and Stewart, 2006), 205.

[24] M. W. Steinberg, "A. M. Klein," in *Canadian Writers, 1920–1959*, ed. W. H. New (Detroit: Gale, 1988), 197. Accessed in the online *Dictionary of Literary Biography*, vol. LVIII.

[25] A. M. Klein, *The Second Scroll* (Toronto: McClelland and Stewart, 1994 [1951]).

for future Canadian poet–novelists, including Cohen and Michael Ondaatje, who published his first book of criticism on Cohen in 1970.[26]

This multifaceted legacy helps to explain why Cohen imagines himself as A. M. Klein's "honoured son" in "To a Teacher."[27] Cohen willingly enters under the dark roof of his "father's house," which seems to be an asylum.[28] This detail points to Klein's dire end. After a burst of creativity and public activism in the early 1950s, Klein suffered a mental breakdown, attempted suicide in 1954, and subsequently maintained a near-total silence until his death in 1972. To assume the title of Klein's honorary son is therefore a perilous act of homage, a fact that Cohen compounds through allusions to the Biblical myth of the sacrifice of Isaac:

> Who could stand beside you so close to Eden,
> when you glinted in every eye the held-high razor,
> shivering every ram and son?[29]

Klein's path carries the risk of burnout and public execution, as Cohen's allusion to the burnt offering of Isaac in "To a Teacher" makes clear. Hence both Ira Nadel and Winfried Siemerling cite a controversial 1964 speech that Cohen delivered at the Jewish Public Library of Montreal as evidence that "Cohen interpreted Klein's breakdown as the result of being exiled by his community."[30] The lawyerly mien of Klein, which Cohen wreathes in flame in *Dear Heather*, obscures the social and physical risks he took by translating Hebrew and Yiddish traditions into English in *Hath Not a Jew* (1940), openly mocking Hitler at the height of the despot's powers in the *Hitleriad* (1944), and working to bridge communities scarred by histories of racism and mutual suspicion in the French Canadian portraits of *The Rocking Chair and Other Poems* (1948).[31]

---

[26] Michael Ondaatje, *Leonard Cohen* (Toronto: McClelland and Stewart, 1970). For more on Klein's influence on Canadian poet–novelists, see Ian Rae, *From Cohen to Carson: The Poet's Novel in Canada* (Montreal: McGill-Queen's University Press, 2008).

[27] Leonard Cohen, "To a Teacher," in his *The Spice-Box of Earth* (Toronto: McClelland and Stewart, 1961), 22.

[28] Ibid.   [29] Ibid.   [30] Nadel, *Various Positions*, 67.

[31] A. M. Klein, *Hath Not a Jew* (New York: Behrman's Jewish Bookhouse, 1940); *The Hitleriad* (New York: New Directions, 1944); *The Rocking Chair and Other Poems* (Toronto: Ryerson, 1948).

The final great danger that Klein identified for Cohen was the broad-based indifference to poetry in Canadian society, which Klein dissects in one of his finest poems, "Portrait of the Poet as Landscape." In this 1948 poem, the titular poet has nearly disappeared from a milieu dominated by radio, cinema, and commercial interests. The poet is not dead but ignored and forgotten, unremarkable as landscape in a technology-obsessed society: "No actress squeezes a glycerine tear for him./ The radio broadcast lets his passing pass."[32] Klein's resigned bard therefore:

> makes of his status as zero a rich garland,
> a halo of his anonymity,
> and lives alone, and in his secret shines
> like phosphorus. At the bottom of the sea.[33]

Less flatteringly, Cohen depicts Klein as a "weary psalmist" in "Song for Abraham Klein" (1961), one who takes up his lute (Klein taught courses on Renaissance literature at McGill) to no effect beyond his own self-improvement:

> He sang and nothing changed
> Though many heard the song.
> But soon his face was beautiful
> And soon his limbs were strong.[34]

To avoid this isolated fate, Cohen learned to get people's attention, to get on the radio, to make audiences shed tears. He learned from Layton, who made regular appearances on Canadian talk shows, to construct a persona that was difficult for stakeholders to ignore. He became a savvy manipulator of electronic media, frequently engaging in radio and television interviewers, obsessively taking and disseminating self-portraits, hijacking a National Film Board documentary about a tour of Canadian poets and converting it into a film about him: *Ladies and Gentlemen, Mr. Leonard Cohen* (1965). In a country saturated in the ideas

---

[32] A. M. Klein, "Portrait of the Poet as Landscape," *Selected Poems*, ed. Zailig Pollock, Seymour Mayne, and Usher Caplan (Toronto: University of Toronto Press, 1997), 99.
[33] Ibid., 104.   [34] Cohen, "Song for Abraham Klein," in Cohen, *Spice-Box*, 74.

of Canadian media theorist Marshall McLuhan, Cohen understood that the crisis of modern poetry demanded a shift in medium.

In retrospect, Cohen's announcement of a career change at the poetry party in 1966 is less a symbolic rejection of the "small pond of Canadian letters,"[35] or a wedge driven between generations, and more like the formal boast of an epic hero in the mead hall of an imperilled kingdom. The young champion of noble birth wanted his elders to know that he was about to go on a long journey (to New York, London, Hydra, Jerusalem, Paris, Los Angeles, Mumbai); he would do battle with a powerful force that his elders would have considered a monster (American popular culture); he would enter into alliances and affairs with a variety of women from different cultures who would prove crucial to his success (Judy Collins, Buffy Sainte-Marie, Marianne Ihlen, Jennifer Warnes, Dominique Issermann, Sharon Robinson); he would suffer terrible losses (of lovers, friends, and money) but also break hearts and sin; he would pass into the metaphorical underworld (of drugs, revolutionary groups, and countercultures); he would explore the razor's edge of his own mortality ("Dress Rehearsal Rag," *Death of a Ladies' Man*); he would ironize and satirize every one of these epic conventions while also remaining perfectly serious about his quest; and he would return rich and famous, but also battle-scarred and with a burning need for his mentors to confirm the truth of his boast and the fulfillment of his quest.

So, what was the object of this quest? To raise the word into song, but also, by a clever inversion, to harness the power of song and the machinery of celebrity culture to refocus public attention on the word. Cohen would make Jewish scripture and Western poetry, including Canadian poetry, the object of mass attention. He would do so by following Klein's example and reaching beyond the culture of his parents and the language of his school. Cohen sang in English but developed his sound beyond the anglosphere, claiming to have found his voice as a poet by reading, in translation, the work of the Spaniard Federico García Lorca: "It is not that I copied his voice; I would not dare. But he gave me permission to find a voice, to locate a voice; that is, to locate a self that

---

[35] Matti Friedman, *Who by Fire: War, Atonement, and the Resurrection of Leonard Cohen* (Toronto: Signal, 2022), 25.

is not fixed, a self that struggles for its own existence."[36] This literary precedent also inspired him to learn his fingerpicking guitar technique from a Spanish flamenco artist he met in a park behind his mother's house: "It was those six chords – it was that guitar pattern that has been the basis of all my songs and all my music."[37] The arrangements of his end-of-career tours also make prominent use of the Spanish bandurria and Greek laud. Cohen's vocal technique, in turn, frequently mimics the combination of singing and the spoken word by the French *chansonnier*. Like Scott, Smith, and Klein, but unlike Layton, Cohen embraced the politics and cultural productions of Québécois and French artists. For this interest, he was rewarded with his first hit, about the charismatic dancer Suzanne Verdal, as well as one of his fans' favourites, "The Partisan" (1969), an "adaptation of a French Resistance song from the Second World War" which, in Cohen's version, became "the unofficial anthem of the Solidarity movement" in Poland that eventually overthrew the communist regime.[38] Cohen discovered that cultivating a broadly international and multicultural audience was a more powerful and resilient strategy than simply chasing stardom in the American market, where his stock soared and plummeted.

Thus, one of the pleasures of witnessing Cohen's triumphant return to the stage in Montreal in 2008 was the sense of *rassemblement* in the sold-out concert hall, a momentary mingling of Montreal's many cultural factions. Cohen's former professor at McGill, Hugh MacLennan, coined the term *Two Solitudes* in his 1945 novel to describe rival anglophone and francophone factions in Montreal. MacLennan hoped that the solitudes would reconcile, but his title became synonymous with division. Michael Greenstein's book on Jewish Montreal writers, *Third Solitudes*, expanded the cohort of solitudes, and critics have multiplied the count ever since.[39] Yet the Cohen show I attended – one of three Cohen concerts which preceded a multi-artist performance of Cohen covers to open the Festival

---

[36] Leonard Cohen, "Acceptance Address for the Prince of Asturias Prize," in Cohen, *The Flame*, 267.
[37] Ibid., 269.
[38] Colin Irwin, *Leonard Cohen: Still the Man* (London: Flame Tree Publishing, 2015), 79.
[39] Michael Greenstein, *Third Solitudes: Tradition and Discontinuity in Jewish–Canadian Literature* (Montreal: McGill-Queen's University Press, 1989).

international de jazz de Montréal – is the only concert I have ever witnessed that garnered standing ovations from teenagers and septuagenarians, anarchists and Hasidic Jews, and where an English Canadian artist won more rapturous praise from the francophone press than from the *Gazette*.[40] Alain Brunet enthuses in *La Presse*:

> Permettons-nous d'insister: ce à quoi nous avons eu droit (hier et lundi) à la salle Wilfrid-Pelletier tient du rêve, de l'échange idéal entre un public fidèle et un grand artiste revenu dans sa ville natale dont il incarne si bien le brassage des cultures. La réception survoltée de ses fans n'était-elle pas en soi une pièce d'anthologie? Aurait-on battu des records d'ovations? ... L'accueil a été délirant dès son apparition sur scène, l'émotion n'a cessé de fréquenter des paroxysmes pendant ces trois heures de récital. À maintes reprises, on a vu un Cohen sincèrement touché par son public issu des "solitudes" montréalaises (anglo, franco, juive, etc.) telles qu'il les a vécues en grandissant dans cette île. [*See endnote for translation.*][41]

To appreciate this homecoming, and by extension Cohen's questing in poetry, prose, and song, one must appreciate the multiple layers of local investment in the religious, literary, and musical elements of Cohen's career as it developed in Montreal, which he describes as "one of the sacred cities of the mind."[42]

---

[40] Bernard Perusse, "Home at Last," *Gazette* [Montreal] (June 25, 2008).

[41] Alain Brunet, "Leonard Cohen à la PdA: Notre Leonard," *La Presse* (June 25, 2008). Translation by Aurian Haller:

> Allow us to insist: what we were privy to (yesterday and Monday) at La Salle Wilfrid-Pelletier was something out of a dream, an ideal exchange between a loyal public and a great artist returned to the city of his birth, whose mix of cultures he incarnates so well. Wasn't the fans' adulation itself worthy of anthologizing? Did we not beat the record for the number of standing ovations? ... The reception was delirious from the moment Cohen stepped onto the stage, and the fans' paroxysms of emotion lasted the entirety of the show's three hours. On a number of occasions, Cohen was sincerely, visibly touched by a public issuing from Montreal's "solitudes" (English, French, Jewish, etc.), those he knew well growing up on this island.

[42] Quoted in Irwin, *Leonard Cohen*, 29.

CHAPTER 12

World Literature

Francis Mus

IN 1998, AT A TIME WHEN LEONARD COHEN THOUGHT HE WAS IN the final throes of his career, he had these words recorded on Mt. Baldy, far away from the rest of the world: "The kind of thing I like is that you write a song, and it slips into the world, and they forget who wrote it. And it moves and it changes, and you hear it again three hundred years later, some women washing their clothes in a stream, and one of them is humming this tune."[1] The statement Cohen made in *tempore non suspecto* sounds both modest (about his artistic position) and ambitious (about the distribution of the work). Judging from the success of his best-known song, "Hallelujah," his wish seems to have been fulfilled. Everyone knows this song, even though it is often attributed either to the wrong artist (e.g. Jeff Buckley, John Cale, Rufus Wainwright) or to no one at all.[2] Still, it is doubtful that Cohen sought to remain altogether anonymous. He never shied away from self-representation in his poems and songs, where one finds a ubiquitous lyrical self, occasionally made explicit through the direct reference to his own name ("Leonard Cohen") in his poems (for instance, "The Cuckold's Song") and songs (for instance, "Famous Blue Raincoat" and "Going Home"), and in a romanticized image of the poet encountered in the countless interviews he gave for radio, newspapers, and television. What he shared about his ambitions in terms of the distribution of his work proves much more convincing. For example, he expressed on several occasions that the start of his musical

---

[1] Quoted in Pico Iyer, "Leonard Cohen Unplugged," *Buzz* (April 1998), www.leonardcohenfiles.com/buzz.html.

[2] For a comprehensive overview, see Alan Light, *The Holy or the Broken: Leonard Cohen, Jeff Buckley, and the Unlikely Ascent of "Hallelujah"* (New York: Atria, 2013).

career was partly motivated by the desire to reach a wider audience. For Cohen, popular music differed from poetry in precisely this respect: "somehow, the nature of a popular song is that it moves swiftly from lip to lip and from heart to heart."[3]

Whatever Cohen's intentions, his body of musical creations – much more so than his literary oeuvre – did indeed go a long way to ensuring the international circulation of his work and the eventual translation of several of his novels and poetry collections. When his first album, *Songs of Leonard Cohen*, was released in 1967, none of his literary works – consisting, at the time, of two novels and four books of poetry – had been published in translated form yet. As a result, the general international public got to know Leonard Cohen first as a singer and only subsequently as a writer. In September 1971, for example, the leading French literary magazine, *La Quinzaine littéraire*, featured the French translation of Cohen's debut novel, *The Favourite Game* (1963) – "Le chanteur est aussi un romancier" [The singer is also a novelist]. The success of the first three albums and their respective concert tours greatly increased Cohen's international fame. Within just four years, his popularity in Europe surged, and for the rest of his career, he would find an audience and a market there that were at least as substantial as those in Canada and the United States. Today, a number of Cohen's novels and poetry collections have been translated into a range of other languages; in some of them, such as Spanish, his *entire* literary oeuvre has been translated. Very often, it was individual mediators, including journalists, translators, biographers, and musicians, who played pivotal roles in the distribution of Cohen's work. They did so, for instance, by producing cover versions – often in translation (for example, Graeme Allwright in France, Maciej Zembaty in Poland, Francesco de Gregori and Fabrizio de André in Italy) – of Cohen's material or by producing biographies of the artist or translations of his writings. These projects came about through direct, often amicable, interactions with Cohen himself (for example, Alberto Manzano in Spain, Tomislav Sakic in Croatia, Michel Garneau in Quebec). The fact that existing institutions in the target culture were already well disposed to Cohen's artistic style further strengthened the

---

[3] In Marco Adria, "Leonard Cohen: Icon of Popular Music," *Aurora Online*, 1990.

reception of his work. In France, for example, the music of Cohen's early albums, which had been created in North American folk communities, found an ideal sounding board in the magazine *Rock et folk*.

It is therefore hardly surprising that, today, Cohen's oeuvre is read within not only the framework of Canadian literature but also the context of "world literature," which David Damrosch described in 2003 (in the wake of Goethe's now well-established notion of *Weltliteratur*) as a collective term for "all literary works that circulate beyond their culture of origin, either in translation or in their original language."[4] Damrosch elaborates: "[A] work only has an effective life as world literature whenever, and wherever, it is actively present within a literary system beyond that of its original culture."[5] Whether Cohen's work should be classified as literature or as music is not only a matter of critical or popular opinion or, indeed, of representational strategies initiated by Cohen himself (who saw the two practices as inseparable).[6] The classification of Cohen's artistic output is also shaped by deliberate editorial choices. Publication strategies that have been used since Cohen's death certainly suggest an interest in ensuring that he is recognized as not only a musical artist but also a literary creator. In the preface to *The Flame* (2018), for example, Cohen's son, Adam, emphasizes that his father was a poet "before he was anything else."[7] Similarly, the release of *A Ballet of Lepers* (2022), which contains a novella and a number of short stories (many of them never published before), is evidence of the attention the Cohen estate was paying to the literary dimension of his oeuvre. The line that divides Cohen's music from his literature has always been porous. For example, many of his texts exist as both poems and songs. We also see that, from quite early on, his poetry and song lyrics appear side by side in his anthologies, *Selected Poems: 1956–1968* (1968), *Stranger Music: Selected*

---

[4] David Damrosch, *What Is World Literature?* (Princeton; Oxford: Princeton University Press, 2003), 4.

[5] Ibid.

[6] For example, he regularly spoke of an "invisible guitar" always hidden behind his poetry (see e.g. Adria, "Leonard Cohen").

[7] Adam Cohen, "Foreword," in Leonard Cohen, *The Flame: Poems and Selections from Notebooks*, ed. Robert Faggen and Alexandra Pleshoyano (Toronto: McClelland and Stewart, 2018), v.

Poems and Songs (1993), and *The Flame: Poems Notebooks Lyrics Drawings* (2018). Furthermore, during his concerts, he would regularly recite verses from his poetic work. It is therefore appropriate to study the reception of Cohen's oeuvre using a "transliterate" approach, in which different versions of a given work are studied alongside one another, precisely because they are mutually influential in terms of how each version is received.[8]

While Cohen's musical career had initially helped him in the international dissemination of his literary work, his success in popular culture subsequently hindered domestic – that is, Canadian – appreciation of his writing.[9] Consequently, many compendiums of Canadian literature focus primarily on Cohen's early writings, including his first collections of poetry and his two novels, *The Favourite Game* (1963) and *Beautiful Losers* (1966), for which he received multiple awards, including the Quebec Literary Competition Prize (1964) and the Governor General's Literary Award (1968). Thematically and poetically, these early works reflect a clear affinity with the "Montreal group,"[10] as well as with Canadian modernism[11] and postmodernism.[12] More recent publications, however, have increasingly emphasized the intra- and intercultural dimensions in Cohen's writing. Consider, for instance, Cohen's contacts with French-speaking Québécois artists – writers such as Sylvain and Michel Garneau, painters from the Automatistes group, and filmmakers from the Canadian Nouvelle Vague. Sometimes, these meetings also led to concrete collaborations, such as when Cohen provided the English subtitles

---

[8] See e.g. my analysis of "Suzanne" in *Canadian Review of Comparative Literature* 48, no. 3 (2021): 368–84.

[9] Linda Hutcheon, "Leonard Cohen," in *Canadian Writers and Their Works*, ed. Robert Lecker et al. (Toronto: ECW Press, 1992 [1980]), 32; and Brian Trehearne, "Foreword," in *The Demons of Leonard Cohen*, Francis Mus (Ottawa: University of Ottawa Press, 2020), xviii.

[10] Sandra Djwa, "Leonard Cohen Black Romantic," *Canadian Literature* 34 (1967): 32–42.

[11] Stephen Scobie, "Leonard Cohen, Phyllis Webb, and the End(s) of Modernism," in *Canadian Canons: Essays in Literary Value*, ed. Robert Lecker (Toronto: University of Toronto Press 1991), 70.

[12] See Linda Hutcheon, *The Canadian Postmodern: A Study of Contemporary English–Canadian Fiction* (Toronto: Oxford University Press, 1988); and Clint Burnham, "How Postmodern Is Cohen's Poetry?," *Canadian Poetry: Studies, Documents, Reviews* 33 (fall/winter 1993): 65.

for Claude Jutra's *À tout prendre* (1963), the English version of which appeared in 1964 as *Take It All*.[13] Further evidence that Cohen operated at the intersection of different cultures is seen in the *Histoire de la littérature québécoise* (2010), where he is compared to Mordecai Richler, another English-speaking Jewish writer from Montreal. Whereas Richler explores an urban geography in his work that is "étroitement liée à la vie de la communauté juive montréalaise"[14] [closely connected to the life of the Montreal Jewish community], Cohen turns his gaze outwards. In his own words, he was strongly influenced by A. M. Klein in this respect: "Klein came out of the Jewish community of Montreal, but [he] had a perspective on it and on the country, and on the province. He made a step outside the community. He was no longer protected by it."[15] Cohen's similar outsider position is already discernible in his first collection, *Let Us Compare Mythologies*, where, in poems like "For Wilf and His House," he contrasts Westmount's Jewish and Christian communities and thus begins, according to Ian Rae, "to address the complexities of writing in multicultural space, where traditions overlap and cultural ciphers bear multiple connotations."[16] Although many critics consider it thoroughly Canadian, such multiculturalism, multilingualism, and polyethnicity are also prominent features of *Beautiful Losers*, which might suggest that the novel should be understood as one that seeks to attract an international audience or address universal themes.[17]

Although the multicultural nature of a writer's work environment says nothing about their own ideological position, Cohen's writings show

---

[13] See Jorge Díaz-Cintas and Francis Mus, "Recontextualizing Nouvelle Vague Cinema in Québec: Leonard Cohen, Subtitler of Claude Jutra's *À tout prendre*," *Babel* 70, nos. 1–2 (2024): 277–303.

[14] Michel Biron, François Dumont, and Élisabeth Nardout-Lafarge, *Histoire de la littérature québécoise* (Montreal: Boréal, 2010 [2007]), 478.

[15] Michael Benazon, "Leonard Cohen of Montreal," *Matrix* 23 (fall 1986): 45.

[16] Ian Rae, *From Cohen to Carson: The Poet's Novel in Canada* (Montreal: McGill-Queen's University Press, 2008), 52.

[17] See Margaret Atwood, *Survival: A Thematic Guide to Canadian Literature* (Toronto: McClelland and Stewart, 1972); Peter Wilkins, "'Nightmares of Identity': Nationalism and Loss in *Beautiful Losers*," in *Intricate Preparations: Writing Leonard Cohen*, ed. Stephen Scobie (Toronto: ECW Press, 2000), 24–50; Ira B. Nadel, "Leonard Cohen," in *Encyclopedia of Literature in Canada*, ed. William Herbert New (Toronto: Toronto University Press, 2002), 218.

a clear awareness of identitarian questions. This sensitivity is also reflected in Cohen's self-representation in and around his work, which crystallizes in a tension between rootedness and alienation. In an unpublished article from 1963, he stated: "I think it is dangerous for a writer to cut himself off from his origins. Mine are in Montreal. I love the city. I love what is happening there. It will always be the scene of my personal mythology, and it will always nourish me."[18] Some twenty-five years later, his views had not changed. On Norwegian television, he confessed: "I really feel a Montrealer. I don't even know if it's Montreal; it's a certain street in Montreal where I have a little house, that's what I guess I call 'home.'" On the other hand, in texts and paratexts, he also embraced the ethos of the "stranger" and the theme of being constantly on the road. *Stranger Music* is not just the title of a collection of works: the two words are carved into Cohen's guitar case like a calling card – name and line of work. The figure of the stranger provided him with a suitable narrative for both telling his life story and positioning himself within the work, a narrative in which the nomadic life is a recurring theme. More specifically, Cohen's personae in poetry and music often locate themselves on the edges of communities, cultures, languages, traditions. When these personae are not on the move, they reside in (or close to) liminal spaces, such as hotels, bars, ports, windows, and balconies. In the documentary *The Song of Leonard Cohen* (1980), Cohen gives an interview on the balcony of his apartment near Montreal's Boulevard Saint-Laurent. Seated at an outdoor table, Cohen plays a tape with a recording of his interpretation of "Un Canadien errant," which had been released the previous year. The balcony epitomizes the Montreal urban landscape and symbolizes the dual mediating role that Cohen fulfills here. On the one hand, he translates the song into English on the spot for the filmmaker and his audience, while simultaneously commenting on the text; on the other hand, the viewer sees footage of the urban life unfolding on the street below, alternating with Cohen's watchful gaze, hidden behind flashy sunglasses.

For many writers whose work circulates transnationally, the tension between rootedness and alienation in their writings also carries over into the work's reception. For example, Malcolm Reid, in his *The Shouting*

---

[18] University of Toronto, Cohen papers, 10a–34.

Signpainters: A Literary and Political Account of Quebec Revolutionary Nationalism (1972), reproached Cohen for his house being "nowhere-in-particular" and being more interested in "America, Europe, talking to My Generation, joining the Robert Graveses and the Lawrence Durrells in their sunny, non-national Parnassi."[19] Michael Ondaatje made similarly critical remarks about *Let Us Compare Mythologies*, claiming that it was steeped in "a rhetoric that [did] not really fit."[20] However, publishers have sometimes cleverly exploited this "cosmopolitan Cohen" to introduce him to a new readership. The French translation of *Book of Longing*, for example, highlights the international dimension of Cohen's oeuvre, the back cover reading: "The Anglophone Québécois from Montreal is first and foremost a universal poet."[21] He is also described as the author of a number of "succès planétaires" (global successes), while the theme of *Le livre du désir* is summarized as "traces des voyages" (travel impressions) and "explorations spirituelles" (spiritual explorations). Because of the universal themes and socially committed topics of his songs (which would not, however, be labelled as protest songs), the receiving cultures where his work was translated or where he went to perform sometimes expected him to identify – if only partially – with the target audience. When Cohen sang "The Partisan" in Poland in 1985, controversy broke out in the audience because he did not speak out in support of the Polish Solidarity movement, of which "The Partisan" had become the unofficial anthem. Instead, he reiterated what he had regularly explained in previous years: his work was independent of ideology, party, or flag and derived its power precisely from that independence. A similar tone can

---

[19] Quoted in Sherry Simon, *Translating Montreal: Episodes in the Life of a Divided City* (Montreal: McGill-Queen's University Press, 2006), 38. Note that in 2003 Reid wrote a book (in French) on Leonard Cohen in which he highlights, in a laudatory way, how his youth was impregnated by the poetry of Leonard Cohen (*Deep Café* [Quebec: Presses de l'Université Laval, 2010]).

[20] Michael Ondaatje, *Leonard Cohen* (Toronto: McClelland and Stewart, 1970), 7. However, Ondaatje's dismissal of the first collection was too quick, as Stephen Scobie notes: "For a young Jew in a Christian country, comparative mythology is not an academic exercise but an immediate fact of repression and prejudice" (quoted in Rae, *From Cohen to Carson*, 52).

[21] Leonard Cohen, *Le livre du désir*, trans. Jacques Vassal and Jean-Dominique Brierre (Paris: Le Cherche Midi, 2008). My translation.

be detected in the short preface Cohen wrote for the Chinese translation of *Beautiful Losers*, in which he situates himself "at the outskirts of your tradition"[22] and instead expresses his admiration for the Chinese poetic tradition of which, because of his origins, he simply *cannot* be a part.

In many debates about world literature, the central question is whether – and to what extent – an international or universal aspiration can, or indeed should, go hand in hand with the local situatedness of content, style, intertextual frames of reference, and so on. The examples cited above show that the reception of Cohen's work reflects how this central question repeatedly resurfaces. But how harmonious or conflicted did Cohen himself consider the relationship between the local and the universal to be? And how did he depict this relationship in his texts? "Your most particular answer will be your most universal one," he disclosed to Jennifer Warnes in the 1990s.[23] "I live within that polarity," he had said in an interview a few years earlier.[24] In what follows, I will examine how this relationship is expressed in Cohen's texts, homing in on two issues: the decreasing presence of culture-specific references in poems and songs; and the prominence of intertextual references in translations and adaptations made by Cohen himself, specifically as they relate to Federico García Lorca.

As I have argued in *The Demons of Leonard Cohen*, while specific references to Quebec and Canada are fairly common throughout Cohen's literary work, they disappear in his later music.[25] This shift over time becomes clear when we compare texts that have appeared in a number of different versions. The process is always the same: the culture-specific items that appear in the initial text are removed or replaced by a more general formulation in the subsequent text. In the song "Light as the Breeze," for example, place-names are eventually discarded: while the lyric booklet still says "St. Lawrence River is starting to freeze," in the actual song, Cohen sticks to "The river is starting to freeze." The same happened in "Take This Longing": in Cohen's version, which was released in 1974,

---

[22] Leonard Cohen, "A Note to the Reader (foreword in the Chinese edition of *Beautiful Losers*, 2000)," www.leonardcohenfiles.com/bl-chinese.html.

[23] Quoted in Jeff Burger (ed.), *Leonard Cohen on Leonard Cohen: Interviews and Encounters* (Chicago: Chicago Review Press, 2014), 264.

[24] Benazon, "Leonard Cohen of Montreal," 50.

[25] Mus, *The Demons of Leonard Cohen*, 94–95.

the singer's plea to his beloved evokes universal heartache. Three years earlier, however, Buffy Sainte-Marie released "Bells," a version whose references are much more specific. Sainte-Marie outlines the song's rationale in the very first line ("I'm writing you to say goodbye"; this is a farewell letter) and a little later, the location is mentioned by name too ("in the midst of New York City"). In short, the specific vocabulary and tone found in Cohen's literary work were made more abstract in his music. More extensive research is needed to understand how Cohen's writing process evolved over time, how consistently he replaced local references with more general concepts that might have had greater appeal for an international audience, and whether or not his musical compositions, in particular, could be defined as "born translated" (Rebecca Walkowitz), which would mean that Cohen's writing had been shaped from the outset by its anticipated international circulation. Genetic criticism can be useful in conceptualizing the evolution in and of the oeuvre. For now, in-depth academic research of this kind will need to wait for until Leonard Cohen's archives open.

What existing scholarship makes abundantly clear is that Cohen's texts are characterized by a high degree of intertextuality. Next to the transnational circulation of his texts and the cosmopolitan topoi that he mobilizes in poems, songs and his self-representations, such intertextuality is another connection between Leonard Cohen and world literature. In the framework of this chapter, I am interested in a broadly defined understanding of intertextuality, as the integration of one text into another by means of quotations, reminiscences, allusions, and so on. The intertextual references are varied in nature, and more often than not (as will be discussed), Cohen makes this integration explicit for his readers. As a poet, Cohen was not only shaped by the work of Canadian colleagues. When he studied briefly at Columbia University, he encountered the Beat movement, which influenced him in a number of ways, despite having little impact on his poetic form. In the 1960s, researcher Sandra Djwa associated him with "black romanticism,"[26] in the wake of poets like Baudelaire, Rimbaud, and Genet, who had a major impact on collections like *Flowers for Hitler*

---

[26] Djwa, "Leonard Cohen Black Romantic."

(whose title alone is a clear reference to Baudelaire's *Fleurs du mal*). European readers and listeners, in particular, see a European dimension to Cohen's work, which is further evidenced by Cohen's admiration for Lorca or his affinity with the French tradition of *auteurs-compositeurs-interprètes* (singer-songwriters). In songs such as "The Guests," "Anthem," or "You Want it Darker," Persian and Islamic influences of authors such as Rumi and Hafiz are evident. And since Cohen's fame as a musician has outstripped his recognition as a writer, North American pop-culture references have been eagerly picked up by the media: "Kanye West Is Not Picasso" was thus the most quoted poem from *The Flame*.

As early as in 1980, Linda Hutcheon highlighted the importance of intertextuality in Cohen's oeuvre, at a time when research on intertextuality was still in its infancy. For her, it was clear that "Cohen's particular twist in most of his work ... is to force the reader to invert, to ironize the intertexts."[27] Some obvious examples in his music are "The Partisan,"[28] "Ballad of the Absent Mare,"[29] and "Un Canadien errant." In Cohen's version of this third example – the original being an absolute Canadian classic – the text remains the same, but the musical arrangement makes for a new interpretation. Or at least that was Cohen's intention, as he enlisted a Mexican mariachi band for the accompaniment: "I thought the resonances that were developed through that kind of treatment were quite interesting, and humorous, because you have a Jew singing a French-Canadian song with a Mexican band, so it really does become a statement of exile."[30] The song appeared on the album *Recent Songs* (1979), which Roscoe Beck (who collaborated on the album and on Cohen's world tours starting in 2008) labelled "world music" *avant la lettre*, and which featured American, Canadian, Russian, and Armenian musicians.[31]

---

[27] Hutcheon, "Leonard Cohen," 35.

[28] Marshall Yarbrough, "Translation as Erasure in Leonard Cohen's *Songs from a Room*," *The Brooklyn Rail* (February 2012), https://brooklynrail.org/2012/02/music/translation-as-erasure-in-leonard-cohens-songs-from-a-room.

[29] Francis Mus, "'There's Nothing to Follow, There's Nowhere to Go': Errance et arrêt dans l'œuvre de Leonard Cohen," in *Les révolutions de Leonard Cohen*, ed. Chantal Ringuet (Montreal: Presses de l'Université du Québec, 2016), 55–74.

[30] Quoted in Brian O'Riordan and Bruce Meyer, "Working for the World to Come: An Interview with Leonard Cohen," *Descant* 37 (1982): 118.

[31] Quoted in Mus, *The Demons of Leonard Cohen*, 109.

One of the best-known and most frequent intertexts in Cohen's oeuvre is the work of Federico García Lorca. In the last section of this chapter, I will use this particular case to briefly illustrate how, in his own writings, Cohen does not appropriate Lorca or aim to render his poetry in all its complexities, but considers the Spanish poet as a privileged interlocutor with whom he enters into a creative dialogue in poems, translations, and adaptations.

One thing is certain: Lorca is a prominent figure in Cohen's work – with two songs ("Take This Waltz," "The Night of Santiago") and as many poems ("The Faithless Wife," "Lorca Lives," both from *Book of Longing*) – as well as in Cohen's life (he named his daughter Lorca). Cohen was far being from the only North American writer influenced by the "Poet in New York," who has had a huge impact on an entire generation of poets, from Robert Duncan and Allen Ginsberg to Robert Creeley and Jerome Rothenberg. According to Jonathan Mayhew, however, Lorca's (American-) English translations caused him to be portrayed not so much as a Spanish poet but as an American one, a writer who had "adapted to American cultural and ideological desiderata."[32] What about Cohen? When performing "Take this Waltz" live, he would often share with the audience the memory of discovering Lorca's verses ("Under the Arch of Elvira") as a teenager in Montreal and being immediately enchanted by a world that was different but in which he nonetheless immediately felt at home. Thus, Cohen's discovery of Lorca did not stem from eventual encounters with the Beat poets; instead, it happened rather accidentally, even perhaps unavoidably, since Lorca enjoyed an iconic status in North American culture in the 1950s.

In his lesser-known poem "Lorca Lives," Cohen speaks about the Spanish poet's topicality, particularly in North America.[33] Where the title would lead readers to expect the subsequent lines to be a paean to the presence of Lorca's work in contemporary literatures, Cohen counters this expectation in a poem consisting of three stanzas. One way in which he accomplishes this is by attributing to the verb "lives" an all but symbolic meaning: Lorca's presence is apparently intended to be taken

---

[32] Jonathan Mayhew, *Apocryphal Lorca* (Chicago: University of Chicago Press, 2009).
[33] Leonard Cohen, *Book of Longing* (New York: HarperCollins, 2006), 90.

literally: "he's back in town again." In addition, he is stripped of his canonical, iconic character; through the use of familiar language and the allusion to biographical details (for instance, his stays in America and Cuba; his gruesome death), Lorca is presented in as ordinary and normal a way as possible (stanza 1), and the themes with which critics and specialists invariably associated him are no longer of interest (stanza 2):

> Lorca lives in New York City
> He never went back to Spain
> He went to Cuba for a while
> But he's back in town again
> He's tired of the gypsies
> And he's tired of the sea
> He hates to play his old guitar
> It only has one key

While most of the verses illustrate how Lorca lives today, the last line of the third stanza shows how he feels about it all:

> He heard that he was shot and killed
> He never was, you know
> He lives in New York City
> He doesn't like it though

If this poem is meant to be more than frivolous, then it is possible to read in this last verse a condemnation of the way American culture has appropriated Lorca. This hypothesis is further supported by the statements Cohen made in his acceptance speech for the Spanish Prince of Asturias Award in 2011 (subsequently printed in *The Flame*). There he reiterated his indebtedness to, and admiration for, Lorca, while at the same time indicating that he did not want to appropriate the Spanish poet:

> a voice seemed to say to me [Leonard Cohen]: "you're an old man and you have not said 'thank you'; *you have not brought your gratitude back to the soil where this fragrance [from his old guitar] arose. And so I come here tonight, to thank the soil and the soul of this people, that has given me so much* . . . Now, you know of my deep association and conformity with the poet Federico García Lorca.

I could say that when I was a young man, an adolescent, and I hungered for a voice, I studied the English poets, and I knew their work well, and I copied their styles, but I could not find a voice. It was only when I read, even in translation, the works of Lorca, that I understood that there was a voice. *It is not that I had copied his voice – I would not dare – but he gave me permission to find a voice*, to locate a voice, that is to locate a self, a self that is not fixed, a self, that struggles for its own existence.[34]

Clearly, these statements by no means express a desire for domestication or Americanization; on the other hand, a song like "Take this Waltz" or a poem like "The Faithless Wife" (later released as a song under the title "The Night of Santiago" on *Thanks for the Dance*) cannot really be seen as "faithful" translation projects; rather, they serve as starting points and sources of inspiration for Cohen's own oeuvre. In the liner notes of Cohen's music albums or in his compilations or poetry collections, the word "translation" never appears alongside these Lorca lyrics; instead, looser descriptions, such as "after Lorca," are used. The translation of the title "Take This Waltz" ("Pequeño vals Vienés") alone illustrates this relationship with Lorca's work. The reference to Vienna disappears, and the title becomes a direct address, a technique Cohen often employs to involve his audiences as much as possible in his own songs or poems. Doesn't "Take This Longing" seem to echo "Take This Waltz"? In fact, one of the main themes of the poem itself differs from the original: the translation of (the recurring) "te quiero" as "I want you." The Spanish verb *querer* expresses a general longing, while the English translation is exclusively focused on lust, at the expense of that of love. Similar shifts are noticeable in the translation of "La casada infiel" (The Faithless Wife). The translation of the title, in the version published in *Book of Longing*, corresponds well to the Spanish original. In the poem itself, as in "Take This Waltz," Cohen again avails himself of direct speech, while the original text is written in the third person. "The Night of Santiago," finally, deviates even more from the original than the version in *Book of Longing*. In "The Night of Santiago," a clichéd Spanish atmosphere is evoked (in the explicit reference to the Spanish city of Santiago in the

---

[34] Cohen, *The Flame*, 267; our italics.

title, through the sound of the guitar and rhythmic handclapping, etc.), and the general mood – as in "Take This Waltz," and in a much more explicit way than in the original – is lustful, as partly illustrated by the addition of the italicized fragment in the following: "I took her to the river/ *As any man would do.*"

Occupying a hybrid position (as a literary author and a singer-songwriter) may have complicated Cohen's literary consecration, even though it was precisely his musical success that allowed his literary work to circulate transnationally, and thus become de facto part of world literature, "works that circulate beyond their culture of origin." At the same time, many questions remain unanswered. How has Cohen's work been read abroad, in translation or otherwise? To what extent did his musical career favor specific reading or translation strategies? One thing is certain: Cohen himself was anything but insensitive to the reception of his songs and poems. Textual genetic criticism illustrates how his writing evolved as he began to garner an increasingly international audience. Translation studies and intertextual analysis, then, can demonstrate how he incorporated other authors, texts, and styles into his own work. Finally, these new perspectives can help us discover new layers of meaning in this fascinating body of work and thus shed light on why Cohen managed to sing and find a devoted worldwide audience for half a century, "even though" – as he sang in 2014 – "the world is gone."

CHAPTER 13

Cohen's Cinematic Appeal

Laura Cameron and Jim Shedden

SPEAKING ABOUT HIS 2020 FILM *DEATH OF A LADIES' MAN*, director Matt Bissonnette proposed that the seven Leonard Cohen songs featured on the soundtrack are themselves "actually a character."[1] That sensibility is in keeping with a five-decade tradition in which the legendary Canadian singer-songwriter's work has operated like mini-narratives nested within the larger narrative of a film – intertexts that have their own independent existence, and that change or are changed by the images on the screen. This was certainly the case when Robert Altman's *McCabe & Mrs. Miller* became the first in a series of art films made in the 1970s to use Cohen's to establish atmosphere, worldview, theme, and character. Altman had been such a fan of Cohen's first album, *Songs of Leonard Cohen*, that he later professed to have worn out two copies after its release in 1967. As recounted by *Rolling Stone*, the director reached back to it over three years later, during postproduction on *McCabe* in 1971.[2] He was struck immediately by the way the songs' mood and lyrics – particularly "The Stranger Song," played in its entirety during the opening sequence – matched the scenes so perfectly. It was, Altman said, as if the songs and script were written

---

[1] Brad Wheeler, "Matthew Bissonnette on His Love for Leonard Cohen's Music, and Its Role in His New Film *Death of a Ladies' Man*," *Globe and Mail* (March 11, 2021), theglobeandmail.com/arts/film/reviews/article-matthew-bissonnette-on-his-love-for-leonard-cohens-music-and-its-role/.

[2] Tim Grierson, "How Leonard Cohen's Music Turned *McCabe & Mrs. Miller* into a Masterpiece," *Rolling Stone* (November 14, 2016), www.rollingstone.com/tv-movies/tv-movie-news/how-leonard-cohens-music-turned-mccabe-mrs-miller-into-a-masterpiece-107637/.

together. "Shit, that's my movie! ... I think the reason they worked was that those songs were etched in my subconscious."

While Cohen himself is nowhere to be seen on screen, his persona – dark, mysterious, rebellious, poetic – merges with that of the eponymous John McCabe's to create a composite character forged by music and cinema. Far from being an afterthought, the music is the heart of the film. *McCabe & Mrs. Miller* opens with a lone traveller on horseback winding his way slowly up a hill in the wilderness. He arrives at a small settlement – a crude clearing among the trees and rocks, some low shacks, a rustic church. People stare as he dismounts. He mutters a few words to himself but otherwise does not speak. Instead, "The Stranger Song" wafts coolly across the landscape. The tension between Cohen's insistent fingerpicking on the guitar and his crooning, pensive voice establishes the character's state of mind – caught somewhere between urgency and melancholy, between hope and cynicism – and the lyrics operate almost like a voiceover to set up the drama that will follow. "He was just some Joseph looking for a manger," Cohen repeats, as the lone figure, McCabe (Warren Beatty), plods into town and makes his way to the ramshackle hotel. "He wants to trade the game he knows for shelter."

Rainer Werner Fassbinder, Werner Herzog, and Bruce Elder, among others, would subsequently draw from the Canadian singer-songwriter's oeuvre with similar enthusiasm. Foregrounding popular music in film without showing the singer on screen was, at the time, a recent innovation that originated with Mike Nichols's use of widely recognizable Simon & Garfunkel songs in *The Graduate* (1967). Previous filmmakers had used orchestral scores to varying effects in the background but incorporated popular music only when the musician was part of the scene – one might think of Elvis Presley singing in *Love Me Tender* (dir. Robert D. Webb, 1956), for example, or Ricky Nelson and Dean Martin in *Rio Bravo* (dir. Howard Hawks, 1959). When Nichols featured Simon & Garfunkel songs like "The Sound of Silence" in *The Graduate*, the band was nowhere in sight, but the songs were meant to be noticed. Although this approach is familiar to us today, it represented an important shift in filmmaking in the late 1960s.

Leonard Cohen combined the earnest charm of Simon & Garfunkel and the political urgency of Bob Dylan with a unique blend of personae all his own – the countercultural rebel, the Jewish philosopher, the spiritual seeker, the unapologetic seducer. In 1971, when *McCabe* was released, the thirty-six-year-old Cohen was still relatively new to the music scene, though his first volume of poetry had come out more than a decade earlier, and he had published four other collections and two novels in the meantime. But the charismatic "son of Montreal" fast outgrew the burgeoning and yet still provincial poetry scene in Canada. When the National Film Board of Canada set out in 1964 to make a documentary about four poets – Earle Birney, Irving Layton, Phyllis Gotlieb, and Leonard Cohen – Cohen so outshone the others that they ended up making the film all about him, and it became the now-classic *Ladies and Gentlemen, Mr. Leonard Cohen* (1965). It features clips from a reading tour, and intimate but staged scenes from Cohen's "life" (long before reality TV): in one sequence, he takes a bath in his Montreal hotel room and then orders a sandwich; in another, he fools around on the harmonica as a late-night party comes to an end. When, a few years later, Cohen won a Governor General's Award for his *Selected Poems: 1956–1968*, he turned it down because, as he wrote in a charmingly elusive telegram from Europe, "The poems themselves forbid it absolutely."[3] As opportunities in the music world multiplied, Cohen was beginning to forge the celebrity persona for which he would become known. He chased contradiction and relentlessly pursued enigma. Cohen was a cool intellectual, a bourgeois gentleman, an intimate exhibitionist, a popular outsider.

When filmmakers use his music in their movies, they import those personae, to varying degrees, along with the melodies and lyrics. This chapter only scratches the surface of the broad corpus of films that feature Cohen's songs, but our goal is to draw out a few commonalities among them in order to offer some sense of the role that his music plays in cinema – the qualities that make it "cinematic." We move chronologically through the decades from those early experimental works to the blockbuster Hollywood productions that incorporate Cohen songs today, such as the TV series *True Detective* (2014–19) and, perhaps best known of all, the movie *Shrek* (dir. Andrew Adamson and Vicky Jenson,

---

[3] Quoted in Michael Posner, *Leonard Cohen, Untold Stories: The Early Years* (Toronto: Simon & Schuster, 2020), vol. I, 415.

2001). Just as Cohen himself moved from the fringes of popular culture to the mainstream from the 1970s up until his death in 2016, so too did his music. But while the genres of film might have changed and Cohen's own cocktail of personae has shifted and reconstituted over the years, the effect of his music in films has remained relatively stable. Whether the lyrics support the narrative by serving as a kind of voiceover, as in *McCabe & Mrs. Miller*, or whether the music offers an aural counterpoint to poetic imagery, Cohen's songs tend to work against the linear medium of film, creating meditative pockets of time, mood, and emotion even as the "moving picture" itself runs on.

THE 1970S: ARTHOUSE ENTHUSIASM

No one incorporated more Cohen songs into his films than the German filmmaker Rainer Werner Fassbinder. In *Beware of a Holy Whore* (1971), a self-referential film about filmmaking, six Cohen songs play on a jukebox, along with selections by Elvis Presley, Ray Charles, and Spooky Tooth. The jukebox is situated in the lobby of a seaside hotel in Spain, where the cast and crew of a film are milling about, waiting for their production money to come through, and obsessing over the power dynamics that define their relationships in the meantime. *Beware of a Holy Whore* is all about biding time, and about the anxious and claustrophobic inertia that can be involved in the artistic process – both the mundane stuck-ness of waiting for people and money, and the grander, more enigmatic stasis of waiting for inspiration. Cohen's music, meanwhile, creates a different kind of stillness that heightens the tension through contrast. While the film crew is exiled in the hotel lobby, their progress hampered by acrimonious infighting and the vagaries of the film industry, the songs offer a contemplative stillness, a "seeking" that feels pure rather than petty. The cacophony of the scene drives the juxtaposition home on a visceral level; there is a fruitful disjunction between, as Margaret Barton-Fumo puts it, the impetuous yells of the film's high-strung producer (played by Fassbinder himself) and Cohen's "undulating baritone."[4] Not only that,

---

[4] Margaret Barton-Fumo, "Deep Cuts: Leonard Cohen," *Film Comment* (February 6, 2017), filmcomment.com/blog/deep-cuts-leonard-cohen/.

but Fassbinder's audiences in Europe, where Cohen was already wildly popular in 1971 (though his fame had not yet skyrocketed in America), would have associated his voice with dark intellectualism and spiritual searching – that is, with the complex persona he was cultivating. The expansive stillness of the lyric mode works against the anxious stasis that Fassbinder portrays on screen.

Fassbinder used Cohen's music to the same kind of ironic effect in several other works throughout his career, often introducing the songs as moments of refuge or escape for the characters on screen. In *Fear of Fear* (1975), it represents the space into which the protagonist retreats from her marriage, her children, and her middle-class life. Such an emotional shift is impossible to render visually, and so Fassbinder renders it aurally, through the qualities of the songs – the minor chords, the exquisitely understated guitar, the sonorous vocals, the pensive lyrics. He makes a similar move in his epic miniseries *Berlin Alexanderplatz* (1980), which features a relentless soundtrack playing behind equally relentless dialogue, with music ranging from classical to popular German music from the 1920s and 1930s to contemporary songs by artists such as the Velvet Underground and Kraftwerk. In one episode, Fassbinder superimposes Cohen's "Chelsea Hotel No. 2" over a hellish sequence in which the protagonist, Franz Biberkopf, experiences several powerful but illusory visions while staying in an asylum. The ironic juxtaposition of the romantic song with the confused and lonely scene ratchets up the tension; Cohen's music represents an idea, a space in the mind far away from the character's physical reality.

If for Fassbinder, Cohen's songs offer refuge from the inexorable demands of narrative logic while still allowing the story to develop, Werner Herzog's juxtaposition of music and imagery in *Fata Morgana* (1971) purposefully defies meaning. Cohen's "Suzanne" and then "So Long, Marianne" play one after the other as the camera tracks fluidly from left to right across the Sahara. Mesmerizing footage of mirages, small roads, fences, huts, and warehouses runs on, almost like a series of still images, and over it all Cohen sings of longing and love. The barren imagery, understood in the context of Herzog's own comment that this was a film about colonialism, evokes both an ending and a beginning – a place in ruins, one that has been emptied out, and a new place, empty and waiting to be filled. And even for viewers who do not understand the English lyrics (the voiceover narration, done by Herzog himself, is in German), the music itself, the sweeping crescendos of the choruses, creates an impression of rolling hills, an aural plane that contrasts with the flat desert landscape. Similarly, the continuous panning shots operate horizontally, while the expression of the individual lyric voice operates vertically, capturing a single feeling in all its multiple dimensions. The scenery is desolate, the camera work monotonous; and yet the songs are so full, their rhythms and swells pulsing with life, that they demand our attention. There might be a thematic relationship between these visual and aural landscapes, or they might simply create a contemplative counterpoint of image and sound, two tracks running in parallel, the closest that cinema can take us to a daydream.

The Canadian filmmaker and scholar Bruce Elder incorporated Cohen's "Teachers" to similar effect in *The Art of Worldly Wisdom* (1979), an autobiographical film from the start of his *Book of All the Dead* cycle. Elder splintered Herzog's contrapuntal technique, running multiple soundtracks and image tracks in competition with one another to create a visually and aurally polyphonic effect. And yet here, the lyrics are definitely harmonious with the theme of the film: both are about seeking at a moment of personal crisis – recalling, explicitly in the film's case, Dante at the beginning of *The Divine Comedy*. Cohen's "Teachers," also from *Songs of Leonard Cohen*, focuses on a young artist's coming to voice. The singer faces two paths and worries that they cannot coexist: either he embraces the ascetic life of the artist, or he embraces life's pleasures – food and women – and sacrifices the purity of his art. Elder and Cohen were both in their early thirties when they made these works, and their similar expression of crisis and confusion might reflect a certain stage of adulthood. The polyphony of the film, which forces the viewer to engage with it at a macromorphological level, taking in the whole thing rather than understanding each of its constituent parts, in some ways embodies the overwhelming experience of anxiety or depression; Cohen's lyrics, too, evoke the claustrophobia of trying to choose the right path. Both works express or at least meditate on the paralysis of creative crisis.

THE 1980S: AN EXPERIMENTAL INTERLUDE

In the late 1970s and early 1980s, Leonard Cohen himself was experiencing something of a creative crisis. He felt that poetry had abandoned him – that, as he wrote in *The Energy of Slaves* (1972), the "poems [did] not love [him] anymore" – and after the hedonistic production of his 1977 album *Death of a Ladies' Man* with Phil Spector, he retreated even from the world of music-making. "I felt I had been gagged and silenced for a long, long time, a number of years," Cohen has said of that period: "I was silenced in all areas ... I could pick up my guitar and sing, but I couldn't locate my voice."[5] He would eventually reemerge in 1984 with the album *Various Positions* and the collection of prose poems *Book of Mercy*, both of which reflect a significant shift in his method and vision in comparison to the gritty and often disillusioned works of the late 1970s. During the otherwise barren years in between, however, Cohen cowrote and starred in *I Am a Hotel* (1983), a Canadian television production based around his music.

With its episodic structure, *I Am a Hotel* is neither "video art" – the sort of highbrow art piece that would be exhibited in a museum – nor a "music video" as we now understand that form, but something in between, what we might call a "video musical." It was initially commissioned by the short-lived C Channel, a subscription television channel specializing in Canadian culture, and then taken over by Moses Znaimer of City TV – though ironically, it was also Znaimer's affiliated station MuchMusic that promoted the fast-paced, manic montage music video culture that would promptly render *I Am a Hotel* obsolete. Shot in the iconic King Edward Hotel in Toronto and featuring several stars of the Canadian theatre and dance world, including Anne Ditchburn and Celia Franca, as well as Cohen himself, the twenty-eight-minute video was inspired by several songs from Cohen's recent albums, in particular "The Guests" from *Recent Songs* (1979).

I Am a Hotel is unique among filmic engagements with Cohen's music because of how closely the songs correlate with the action – that is, it is

---

[5] First quotation is from Sylvie Simmons, *I'm Your Man: The Life of Leonard Cohen* (Toronto: McClelland and Stewart, 2012), 330; second quotation is from "Leonard Cohen: A Sad Poet Gets Happy," *The Toronto Star* (June 30, 1973), 31.

not a two-track experience where the music creates an alternative space running alongside the visual narrative, as we saw in several of the films from the 1970s, but rather a visual representation of that emotional or meditative space itself – the space of the songs. "One by one the guests arrive,/ The guests are coming through," sings Cohen in "The Guests," as, on screen, the hotel guests enter the lobby and are shown to their rooms. Like the song, the film dwells on the characters' romantic entanglements – the interactions, in the liminal space of the hotel, of "the open-hearted many,/ The broken-hearted few." In one section, the bellboy pursues the chambermaid from the laundry room to the ballroom while, in Cohen's "Memories" (from *Death of a Ladies' Man*), the singer pleads to see his beloved's "naked body." In another, Ditchburn's character dances on a table as Cohen sings, in "The Gypsy's Wife" (from *Recent Songs*), "A ghost climbs on the table in bridal negligee,/ She says, 'My body is the light, my body is the way'." *I Am a Hotel* suggests that an album can be like a hotel – or perhaps that a hotel can be like an album, a group of individual consciousnesses held together in physical space or artistic form. If other filmmakers use Cohen's songs to render emotional space, in *I Am a Hotel* the lyrics are not merely thematically harmonious with the film, but they actually propel the narrative.

Several years after this somewhat awkward mainstream avant-garde mashup, Bruce Elder returned to Cohen's music in *Consolations (Love Is an Art of Time)* (1988), a fourteen-hour experimental film and part of his even longer film cycle, *The Book of All the Dead*. Like *The Art of Worldly Wisdom*, *Consolations* weaves together a vast array of images, texts, and sounds: experimental footage of bodies and landscapes; digital graphics; and readings of poetry by Ezra Pound, Charles Olson, and Robert Duncan, and of philosophical works by Spinoza, Heidegger, and Simone Weil. Similar to both Weil and Cohen, Elder's film explores, as Bart Testa puts it, "what a modern saint might be, in the aftermath of the death of religion. For Weil," Testa continues,

> the principal virtue is "attention," and *Consolations* works with a grave rigor ... to find an equivalent in cinema for that virtue. Understanding "attention" to be a work of sensibility, not an act of the will, Elder seeks to

induce a meditative quiet in the viewer so that the labor of the film ... can become a letting go.[6]

Both Elder and Cohen draw from the gnostic tradition in viewing this meditative condition or attentive perceptiveness as a pathway or mode of connection to the divine. Both artists, too, were committed to drawing on multiple theological and philosophical traditions in order to explore the meaning of "the divine" in a post-Auschwitz and post-Hiroshima world. For Cohen, adopting a humble, attentive stance and surrendering to the "will" of another also became essential to the creative process.

Elder featured three Cohen songs in *Consolations*: "If It Be Your Will," "Heart with No Companion," and "The Captain." We will focus here on the first of these, "If It Be Your Will," which straightforwardly articulates both artists' vision of the radical acceptance that is fundamental to creativity. The song comes at the end of the film's Part 1 (Reel 7), following a montage of receipts related to the film's production and overlaid with an angry rant by Elder about having been rejected by an arts council jury. Elder's diatribe, whether real or fictional, expresses the perpetual despair of an artist trying to create in a world that is so often at odds with the poetic. The song begins as the credits roll, signaling an abrupt and welcome departure from the cyclical and overwhelming angst of the preceding montage. The music is sweet, remote, and tentative, and the lyrics invite a release of ego, fear, and resentment: "If it be your will/ That I speak no more ... I shall abide until/ I am spoken for." The singer suggests that he will stop desiring or lusting after things; "instead he will wait – 'abide' – until *he* is claimed, or 'spoken for,' by the will of another."[7] He adopts a prayerful stance in this song, where "prayer" implies listening, paying attention; as W. H. Auden wrote: "Whenever a man so concentrates his attention – be it on a landscape, or a poem or a geometrical problem or an idol [...] – that he completely forgets his own ego and desires in listening to what the other has to say to him, he is praying."[8] In Elder's film, "If It Be Your Will" creates space for attentive

---

[6] Bart Testa, in *The Book of All the Dead*, dir. Bruce Elder (Anthology Film Archives, 1988).
[7] Laura Cameron, "'A Strange Gestation': Periods of Poetic Silence in Modern Canadian Creative Careers," unpublished PhD thesis, McGill University, 2015, 242–43.
[8] Quoted ibid., 232.

stillness amid visual and aural chaos, not only through its lyrics, but through the whisper of Cohen's voice and the close range of the melody.

In 1988, the same year that Elder released his fourteen-hour experimental epic, Jean-Luc Godard created *Puissance de la parole*, a twenty-five-minute experimental short film that draws on techniques similar to those in *Consolations* but engages with Cohen's music to very different effect. The soundtrack in Godard's film, a collage of moments of dialogue between couples, is interwoven with music and other overlapping sounds, and it runs in tension with the image track, a montage of rapid cuts and slow takes. "Take This Waltz," from Cohen's 1988 album *I'm Your Man*, is cut into this mélange, along with excerpts from classical composers such as Ravel, Bach, and Beethoven, and from contemporary and popular musicians such as John Cage and Bob Dylan. The image track is equally heterogeneous, and includes references to such artists as Francis Bacon, Max Ernst, and Vincent Van Gogh, and to filmmakers, including Godard himself. By deconstructing other artistic works and reassembling them into something new, Godard evokes the continuity of human dialogue. Notably, Cohen's song does not disrupt that continuity; it does not provide refuge or create a parallel space for feeling or story, and neither does it operate in ironic counterpoint to the visual narrative or effects. Instead, the song is simply part of the frenzied cultural mashup that makes up the film as a whole. Cohen's inclusion in this group, the situation of his music on an equal footing with the works of Bob Dylan and Beethoven, anticipates a development that would become much clearer by the end of the next decade: Cohen was on the verge, if not already over the precipice, of attaining the status of a popular culture icon.

THE 1990S AND BEYOND: COHEN'S NEW COOL

While Cohen's reputation arguably slumped in the early 1980s – his album *Various Positions* was largely dismissed when it was released in 1984 – several songs from his 1992 album *The Future* feature in Oliver Stone's 1994 film *Natural Born Killers*, part of a super-cool soundtrack assembled by Trent Reznor (of Nine Inch Nails) that reinforced Cohen's continuing relevance in the 1990s. Unlike Herzog, Stone self-consciously engages Cohen's music to convey the message of the film. The protagonists, Mickey and Mallory Knox (Woody Harrelson and Juliette Lewis), are criminals engaged in a ruthless killing spree. After they commit their final murder, Stone runs a sequence of real television news clips depicting violent events from the era, offering a bitter comment on the way in which the media glorifies horrific violence. Then the credits roll, with Cohen's "The Future" playing over a montage of earlier scenes from the movie, as well as images of Mickey and Mallory's "happily ever after" life, apparently free at last from crime. The lyrics of "The Future" are some of Cohen's most explicitly political, concluding with "I've seen the future, brother/ It is murder." By playing this song about the inevitability of murder over "happily ever after" images, by playing a song about the "future" over scenes from the "past," Stone creates an ironic trap that closes the film in on itself – insisting, as the song does, that history repeats itself, that our ending is in our beginning. As in the Altman, Fassbinder, and Herzog films, in *Natural Born Killers* Cohen's music stops linear progress, though it does so not by adding a "vertical" emotional dimension to "horizontal" narrative time but by simply denying the possibility of ending (or of ending violence) – a denial that the lyrics and the movie both endorse.

Cohen's lyrics also ironically support the narrative in Lars von Trier's *Breaking the Waves* (1996), though in this case the music indicates not a conclusion but a startling and tragic emotional turning point. Von Trier's film tells the story of a devoutly religious Scottish woman, Bess McNeil (Emily Watson), who marries a Norwegian oil rigger, Jan Nyman (Stellan Skarsgard). When Jan becomes paralyzed in an accident and is unable to perform sexually, he asks Bess to have sex with other men – for his sake. Reluctantly, she seeks out several encounters, but finds herself repeatedly in humiliating, violent, and dangerous situations. The soundtrack features songs by many popular artists, including David Bowie, Jethro Tull, and Deep Purple. In the film's fifth chapter, which is entitled "Doubt," Cohen's "Suzanne" plays over a meandering shot of a house in ruins on the foggy Isle of Skye. Just before this interlude, Bess has refused to do Jan's bidding and find a new lover; just after, however, she will finally acquiesce. Cohen's smoky, meditative vocals create a melancholic moment of reflection before the emotional and physical chaos that will follow. The lyrics, meanwhile, are bittersweet. "Suzanne" is a song about faith and doubt: about how romantic trust may be easier to cultivate than religious faith. The singer "want[s] to travel blind" with Suzanne, and he knows that she, in turn, "will trust [him]/ For [he's] touched her perfect body with [his] mind." At the same time, he longs for religious faith: in the middle verse, he observes that Jesus, who was "broken," forsook himself, but "sank beneath" the speaker's "wisdom" – that is, his doubt, or his conscious thought as opposed to his intuition – "like a stone." Though the singer "*think[s]* maybe [he'll] trust" Jesus, he remains uncertain, whereas he "*know[s]* that [he] can trust" Suzanne. In *Breaking the Waves*, the pious Bess must sever her faith in a higher ideal in order to "travel blind" on the quest that her husband has set her.

Music signals a similar sort of turning point in what might be the best-known example of a Cohen song in cinema: John Cale's cover of "Hallelujah" in the 2001 DreamWorks production *Shrek*. As in *McCabe & Mrs. Miller*, the song offers a kind of voiceover in *Shrek*, running on top of the visual imagery to express the character's innermost feelings; and as in *Beware of a Holy Whore* and *Fata Morgana*, the music works against the linear progress of the narrative and imagery, slowing the story to insist on self-reflection. Near the end of the film, a misunderstanding provokes Shrek to renounce both Princess Fiona and his best friend, Donkey. "Hallelujah" plays as Shrek returns home to the solitude of his swamp and Fiona prepares to marry the odious Lord Farquhar. Both Shrek and Fiona are lonely and regretful, and some of the lyrics quite unambiguously express Shrek's feelings in the moment: "I used to live alone before I knew you" – indeed. Crucially, the song intervenes when the conflict has reached a fever pitch and the narrative cannot progress any further without a spiritual or emotional reckoning. In this way, the song, almost like a *deus ex machina* – the Greek theatrical device that magically resolves the drama before the play's conclusion – does what the dialogue, action, and mise-en-scène of film cannot: it makes space for feeling and holds us there with the characters. As Alan Light writes, the song's "sorrowful but unsentimental tone fit the sophistication of [the cartoon]."[9] *Shrek*, like

[9] Alan Light, *The Holy or the Broken: Leonard Cohen, Jeff Buckley, and the Unlikely Ascent of "Hallelujah"* (New York: Atria, 2012), 100.

"Hallelujah" and like Cohen, embodies contradictions – the kindly ogre, the monastic "ladies' man"; the sophisticated cartoon, the unsentimental sorrow.

In *The Holy or the Broken: Leonard Cohen, Jeff Buckley, and the Unlikely Ascent of "Hallelujah,"* Light acknowledges the central role of *Shrek* in the song's meteoric success, but notes that the song actually made its film debut in Julian Schnabel's 1996 biopic *Basquiat*. *Basquiat* incorporates music aggressively, with cuts from thirty different artists, ranging from the Pogues to Bush Tetras, Charlie Parker, and Henryk Gorecki. John Cale's version of "Hallelujah" plays at the close of the film, indicating – like "The Future" in *Natural Born Killers* – a moment of emotional summation: a "Big Emotional Moment," as Nick Murray has put it.[10] Indeed, since its origins in *Basquiat*, "Hallelujah" come to operate as shorthand for emotional reckoning to listeners and viewers across the world. In a 2002 episode of *The West Wing*, for example, released just one year after *Shrek*, Jeff Buckley's cover of "Hallelujah" plays over an intricately and poignantly edited sequence depicting a character's unexpected death.[11] In the first season of *The OC*, the same version of the song is used first diegetically, on a CD mix gifted from one character to another, and then as the soundtrack to the season-ending montage, which shows all of the characters moving on to their next chapters; in the third season, Imogen Heap's cover overlays a fatal car accident. If in the experimental films of the 1970s and 1980s Cohen's music was often called upon to create ironic distance from chaotic or cacophonous moments on screen, by the 1990s and early 2000s, "Hallelujah" had developed a well-defined role as the sound of reverence, reckoning, and self-reflection.

Beyond just "Hallelujah," the presence of Cohen's songs in cinema increased exponentially after *Shrek*, which was the top-grossing film of 2001, and which catapulted Cohen's music (if not Cohen himself) to

---

[10] Nick Murray, "How Pop Culture Wore out Leonard Cohen's 'Hallelujah'," *New York Times* (September 19, 2016): www.nytimes.com/2016/09/20/arts/music/leonard-cohen-emmys-hallelujah.html.

[11] Other creative and well-known uses of "Hallelujah" include: *Lord of War*, dir. Andrew Niccol, 2005; *ER* (season 3 finale), 2007; *Watchmen*, dir. Zack Snyder, 2009; *Saturday Night Live*, November 13, 2016, sketch featuring Kate McKinnon as Hilary Clinton; and *Supergirl* (season 3, episode 4), 2017.

fame in the eyes of a new generation. In Sarah Polley's *Take This Waltz* (2011), Feist's cover of "Closing Time" plays over a warm and erotically charged party scene. In the second season of *True Detective* (2015), the more recent song "Nevermind" is layered over the visually arresting opening credits, cut so that different parts of the song and different lyrics are featured in each episode. In the final episode of the first season of *The L Word*, the sexy and rebellious "I'm Your Man" plays over a scene in a parking lot as Ivan (Kelly Lynch) vamps around his car, lip-syncing along with Cohen and using the lyrics to make Kit (Pam Grier) an offer she cannot refuse: "If you want a driver, climb inside/ Or if you want to take me for a ride/ You know you can,/ I'm your man."

The films we have discussed here diverge wildly in subject matter and approach, taking us from the barren Sahara of *Fata Morgana* to the animated swamp of *Shrek*. Yet, in all cases, Cohen's songs create an emotional or contemplative space, a kind of refuge (or trap, in *Natural Born Killers*) for filmmaker and viewer alike from the linear time and narrative logic of the film. His distinctive voice, once reedy, by the end faded to a gravelly whisper, can stand in for a filmmaker's consciousness or a character's inner thoughts. The cinematic appeal of Cohen's music might lie in the atmosphere of its rhythms, jaunty or plodding or smooth, or in the emotional expressiveness of the songs' lyrics. It might lie in the characters they create – Suzanne, Marianne – or in the character of Cohen himself, which shifted shapes so many times over his long career – Jewish Montrealer, poet, folk crooner, pop star, saint, "a sportsman and a shepherd,/ ... a lazy bastard living in a suit" – and continues to metamorphose today, even as his death recedes into the past.

CHAPTER 14

Neurotic Affiliations

Montreal and Belonging

Erin MacLeod

WHEN I MOVED TO MONTREAL IN 1995, IT WAS IN THE DIRECT run-up to Quebec's second referendum on sovereignty – the first, in 1980, had 60 percent voting against the plan, but this time around the contest was much closer. And I was also much closer to the action, having left my home in southern Ontario to enter McGill University as an English literature major. "Oui" (sovereigntist) and "Non" (federalist) signs were everywhere in the city, and I was told it was possible to tell the linguistic majority in any given neighborhood – more yes means probably French; more no, English. The university residence where I lived was right next to the metro station named for the famed Quebec nationalist – and infamous anti-Semite – conservative Catholic priest Lionel Groulx, even though multiple petitions[1] have asked for it to be changed to jazz pianist Oscar Peterson, reflecting the neighborhood and culture of Little Burgundy, the historically Black anglophone area in which the station is located and where Peterson grew up.

One morning as I left to make the short commute to downtown, the exterior wall of the student hall had been spraypainted with "Anglos go home" in huge letters. Though standard identifiers in Quebec, the terms "anglophone" and "francophone" are not commonly used, and the term "allophone" for literally everyone else seems archaic and, frankly, reductive.[2]

---

[1] One in 2008 and another in 2020. See Taylor Noakes, "On Naming Montreal Places after Oscar Peterson," *Cult Mtl* (September 22, 2021), https://cultmtl.com/2021/09/on-naming-montreal-places-after-oscar-peterson-mcgill-college-plaza-lionel-groulx-metro/.

[2] Toula Drimonis, in her 2022 book *We, the Others: Allophones, Immigrants, and Belonging in Canada* (Montreal: Linda Leith Publishing), explains that "to be an allophone is to

I found this graffiti message a curious novelty more than any kind of threat. I had just moved away from home in Ontario to Montreal, and I hadn't yet thought about feeling at home, or even welcomed, in this new place. Though Quebec didn't move further towards independence on the day of the referendum, it was a nail-biter to the end, with just over 1 percentage point separating the winning federalist "non" side from the sovereigntist affirmatives.

Through that whole first year in Montreal I spent time every day practicing how to ask for cigarettes at the *dépanneur*[3] and order beer (and McDo – the Quebec term for McDonald's) in as perfect Québécois French as I could muster. It was at this very time someone told me, quite confidently, that to become a real Montrealer, you had to have run into Leonard Cohen on the street. My familiarity with Cohen at the time was limited: he was the cigarette-inflected, gravel-voice behind "Everybody Knows," which I personally knew because it had been featured in 1990s teen hit *Pump up the Volume,* and "Hallelujah," because I, like many young people back then, was obsessed with Jeff Buckley's 1994 version.[4] I was aware of this singer-songwriter's fame and Canadianness, specifically the fact that he grew up in Montreal. But here he was described to me as a mystical Anglo individual with the power to transform people from mere mortals into citizens of a magical island city by virtue of his presence, regardless of language and/or attitude towards separation. It wasn't enough to live here for a long while and weather the long, cold winters. The so-called "two solitudes" of English and French were apparently transcended by this erstwhile poet-cum-lyricist and pop star.[5] A brush with his suit-sporting and fedora-wearing self was the only way

have a mother tongue that is *allos* (other): a language other than French or English" (4).

[3] The particularly Québécois word for "corner store," the direct translation meaning "troubleshooter" or "repairer," i.e. the store offers what can help put yourself back in order.

[4] Released in 1990, it was written and directed by Allan Moyle, whose first wife was Cohen's sound engineer. Moyle is both a former Montrealer and my cousin.

[5] So called after Anglo novelist Hugh McLennan's famed 1945 novel *Two Solitudes* (Toronto: McClelland and Stewart), a book about a character trying to sort out his English and French affiliations.

that I might be able to manage to feel like this place was my home, rather than being told to go back to a home that was clearly somewhere else.

Shortly after the announcement of Cohen's death in 2016, there was an impromptu gathering at Parc du Portugal, the tiny park that faces the incredibly nondescript gray house that he owned. People brought flowers and candles that ended up taking residence for weeks at a time – until the city announced months later that they would have to be removed. Kathy Kennedy, a local musician and choral director, led the crowd in song – "So Long, Marianne" and, of course, "Hallelujah." The event marked more than two decades of my life in Montreal. Never in any of those years where there could have been even a slight possibility of crossing paths with this so-called "secular saint of Montreal" did he grace my presence.[6] But during that time, Cohen's reputation and relationship to Montreal has grown in the mind of Montrealers. How has Leonard Cohen come to represent the ultimate Montrealer – one with the perceived power to induct others into the city's club? Is it possible (or even necessary or desirable) to ask what Montreal meant to Leonard Cohen, or is the question rather what Leonard Cohen means to Montreal?

I have written about how what hip hop superstar Drake means to Toronto reflects what Cohen means to Montreal – this is not only the surface reality of each being artistic ambassadors of a sort, providing a connection recognized internationally, even to people who know little or nothing about their respective cities.[7] After I published my article, for the Canadian Broadcasting Corporation (CBC) no less, comment sections and social media were chock-full of people reacting violently to the idea that a pop phenom like Drake be compared to the near saintly Cohen. There's no denying that Drake has drawn attention to the city he calls the "6ix," deeming Toronto cool. Cohen, however, had a decades-long jump on him in terms of communicating to the world

---

[6] Dan Bilefsky, "Is Leonard Cohen the New Secular Saint of Montreal?" *New York Times* (March 6, 2018), www.nytimes.com/2018/03/06/arts/music/leonard-cohen-montreal.html.

[7] Erin MacLeod, "The Uncanny Parallels between Drake and Leonard Cohen: How Toronto's 6ix God Mirrors Montreal's Secular Saint," *CBC Music*, November 29, 2019, www.cbc.ca/music/the-uncanny-parallels-between-drake-and-leonard-cohen-1.5377002.

that Montreal has a certain *je ne sais quoi*. I was drawn to the comparison because I also found it ironic that these two iconic superstars could be seen as outsiders to the cities that have embraced them as representatives. Drake grew up outside of Toronto proper, as did Cohen, who actually grew up not in Montreal but in Westmount, which is a borough that is adjunct to Montreal.

Montreal is a place where over 70 percent[8] of the population claim French as their first language – in Westmount, where Cohen was born and raised, almost the same amount indicate English as their mother tongue.[9] One of the richest neighborhoods in the country, Westmount has always stubbornly resisted being subsumed into Montreal, demerging only two years after the city became "une île, une ville" (one island, one city).[10] Cohen attended McGill, the also very English Montreal university that ranks among the best in Canada year after year. It was at McGill where Cohen began writing poetry and, as legend has it, originally dreamt of getting out of Dodge and moving away to eventually become a pop star. There is even a comic book detailing this trajectory, written by Quebec cartoonist Philippe Girard.[11]

In addition to having hailed not quite from Montreal, Cohen's outsider status, like that of many other Montreal writers to emerge out of the mid 20th century, is cemented by his Jewishness.[12] His family was very much part of the Jewish community in Montreal – Cohen's bar mitzvah group celebrated their seventieth anniversary in 2017. Rabbi Aubrey Glazer, author of *Tangle of Matter & Ghost: Leonard Cohen's Post-Secular Songbook of Mysticism(s) Jewish & Beyond*, therefore speaks of Cohen as representative of a Canadian Jewish mystical tradition, engaged in writing of home from exile. Cohen represents an outsider identity: as an

---

[8] Distribution of People Living in Montreal, Quebec in Canada in 2021, by First Official Language Spoken and Gender, www.statista.com/statistics/1339075/population-mo ntreal-canada-official-language-spoken-gender/.

[9] The amount is 68 percent, as reported in the 2021 Canadian Census (www12.statcan .gc.ca/census-recensement/index-eng.cfm).

[10] "Demerger Vote Will Change Map of Quebec," CBC News, June 21, 2004, www.cbc .ca/news/canada/montreal/demerger-vote-will-change-map-of-quebec-1.472893.

[11] The book is called *Leonard Cohen: On a Wire*, translated from French by Helge Dascher and Karen Houle (Montreal: Drawn and Quarterly, 2021).

[12] It should be noted that Drake's Jewishness is yet another similarity between the two!

anglophone Jew, he holds membership in what has been called the "third solitude" in Quebec. These groups of layered identities, for Glazer, can be seen as informing Cohen's artistic creation. Glazer sees Cohen as a mystic with the ability to "subvert categories and to create these hybrids."[13] Drawing on inherited tradition and history and subverting it is, for Glazer, "the process the mystics look at as their calling as a way to be able to immerse themselves in the source of all being and to also be able to repair the brokenness; that's what they're constantly yearning for."[14] Yes, Cohen is unique, a beloved singer internationally, challenging listeners, engaging with different sounds and cultures, but occupying an outside position in Montreal. It's therefore ironic that he appears to have changed the world's perspectives on his hometown, and perhaps changed the way that Montreal sees itself.

To find Cohen's engagement with Montreal in his work requires looking back to his earliest writings. He found success within the Canadian cultural landscape as a student – Cohen's first work, the 1956 *Let Us Compare Mythologies* contained poems written while a teenager. A move to the United States was, for Cohen, ostensibly to attend graduate school after finding a poetic home in the artistic community of McGill, but in reality the goal was to move away from the limited literary circles of Montreal and Canada as a whole, going to New York, then London, then Hydra, Greece.[15] In the very promotional documentary *Ladies and Gentlemen, Mr. Leonard Cohen*, there is a scene when the young poet is reciting in the large Leacock 132 lecture theatre of McGill University. As a student, I watched that film in Leacock 132 and felt strangely connected to this individual who seemed to make the place I had moved to profoundly cool. But Cohen didn't see Montreal as particularly desirable in terms of nurturing his writing, hence the travelling that fueled what would eventually become his musical output in the late 1960s. It's also worth noting that the pre-"Suzanne" Cohen wasn't solely focused on

---

[13] Interview by the author with Rabbi Aubrey Glazer, November 16, 2019. All interviews quoted in this chapter were originally conducted for MacCleod, "The Uncanny Parallels."

[14] Ibid.

[15] Sylvie Simmonds, *I'm Your Man: The Life of Leonard Cohen* (Toronto: McClelland and Stewart, 2021).

poetry in Montreal, initially trying his luck with country, singing in a band called the Buckskin Boys.

Brian Trehearne, who has taught Leonard Cohen to generations of undergraduates at my and Cohen's alma mater, has also written that although the legend that is Leonard Cohen may have started in Montreal, Quebec, Canada, his fame moved him from this space. As Cohen's music was released (initially in 1967 with *Songs of Leonard Cohen*) to international acclaim, his literary output all but ceased for years. The Montreal references in Cohen's songs are few and far between. The "Our Lady of the Harbour" statue, located in the Vieux Port, is mentioned in "Suzanne." I once read that "Hallelujah" is supposed to be an allegory for Montreal's fraught relationship with religion, but that might be seriously wishful thinking.[16] His two early novels, *The Favourite Game* (1963) and *Beautiful Losers* (1966), as well as his pre-songwriting poetic output, make explicit Montreal references, but as his reputation for music grew, so too did the distance between Cohen and Canada. As Trehearne has put it, "Canadians found they were no longer in command or even familiar with the terms of Cohen's global cognition ... by the mid-1970s ... Cohen was an acquired taste at best among Canadians."[17]

This has not changed. Trehearne reports that reading *Beautiful Losers* is shocking for students in his Cohen-focused class at McGill. In one instance, Trehearne recalls that he "had a sense that we were all gathered to do a ritual shaming"[18] – perhaps by people more familiar with the "Hallelujah" Cohen than the one whose novels take place in Montreal. In addition to graphic scenes of sexual violence, the book has characters that include a folklorist engaged in the study of an invented "A— tribe" and provides multiple explicit scenes with now-canonized Saint Kateri (Catherine in the novel) Tekakwitha – fiction-writing moves that would be more than frowned on (and for good reason) now. It's an

---

[16] Alanna Moore, "How to Experience the Montreal That Leonard Cohen Immortalized in Poetry & Song," *MTL Blog*, November 7, 2019, available at Wayback Machine: web.archive.org/web/20230201033718/www.mtlblog.com/montreal/experiencing-leonard-cohens-montreal-through-his-songs-and-poems.

[17] Brian Trehearne, "Foreword," in *The Demons of Leonard Cohen*, Francis Mus (Ottawa: University of Ottawa Press, 2020), xvii.

[18] Interview by the author with Brian Trehearne, October 25, 2019.

uncomfortable book, and one that most likely wouldn't be published today.[19] But if one is reckoning with Cohen and Montreal, it's 272 pages that can't be avoided.

The works that root Cohen in Montreal are his least known and, arguably, his least enjoyable – and perhaps his least good.[20] As Trehearne says:

> We'd rather imagine Cohen without *Beautiful Losers*. But I would rather, because I think human beings are really messy things, grapple with and struggle with the problem *Beautiful Losers* gives me next to the stunning beauty of something like "Anthem." That to me is a human being, right? And be the first to say it. We are terrifically over-reverencing, sanctifying him in the process, we are hollowing him out and making him far less interesting. Of all the pictures to go up on the building, why did we do that saintly wise old man? That's what we seem to want now.[21]

Trehearne is right – there is messiness and uncomfortableness that is papered over. His statement is also a reference to how Cohen literally looks over the city in the form of a 10,000 sq ft, 21-story-high mural painted on the side of a downtown apartment building. The "saintly wise old man" Trehearne speaks of is depicted in sepia tones, like a benevolent ancestor, gazing at those who look up, sporting his iconic fedora and suit. There's also another mural that's half the size, but still rather large, on a street off Saint Lawrence Boulevard (Boulevard Saint-Laurent), allowing Cohen's somber face, this time bathed in cool tones of mauve, to look over his old neighborhood. For Trehearne, "representing all that is Montreal is not a phrase I would ever use about Leonard Cohen; he represents something Montreal wants to think about itself. I guess whether Cohen in his writings, in his songs, really embodied something is essentially moot."[22] Perhaps it's Montreal and Montrealers who imbued Cohen with his magical powers. It's not that Cohen's songs

---

[19] Myra Bloom, "The Darker Side of Leonard Cohen," *The Walrus* (April 9, 2018), https://thewalrus.ca/the-darker-side-of-leonard-cohen/.
[20] I, personally, struggled to complete *Beautiful Losers*.
[21] Interview by the author with Brian Trehearne, October 25, 2019.   [22] Ibid.

are about or set in Montreal, but rather his relationship to the city seems paramount, as does the city's relationship to him.

Having Cohen represent Montreal has been a boon to the city. Montreal offers up a place of pilgrimage for fans; there are countless articles and blog posts that detail "must-visits," including everything from Cohen's favorite bagel shop (apparently St. Viateur) to his grave.[23] There's no doubt that tourism based on the man who sang "Suzanne" is more than evident throughout the city. From *New York Times* travel pieces mapping important sites – including where Cohen had coffee (Bagels Etc.) and purchased Foamtreads slippers (J. Schreter),[24] to audio walking-tours of key Cohen sites,[25] to the art show initially presented at the Musée d'Art Contemporain de Montréal, only to then tour America and Europe, Leonard Cohen is a selling point.[26] Rabbi Glazer recognizes that commodity culture is not a stranger to Cohen: "the need to be able to monetize is endless. So, there's a kind of cult of personality that ultimately will continue to generate things that are worthwhile and things that are kitschy, you know, or that are just really schlocky."[27]

Cohen (according to his son, Adam), though not living in the city, was devoted to his hometown, and "very suspicious of anyone who didn't love Montreal."[28] But these outward declarations of allegiance may not connect with Cohen's actual lived experience, given that he did live most of his life away from the island. This is where the constant quoting of Cohen's famous statement of loyalty comes in – that he had to keep

---

[23] Richard Burnett, "The Montréal of Leonard Cohen," *MTL.org*, October 12, 2023, www.mtl.org/en/experience/montreal-leonard-cohen.

[24] Rose Maura Lorre, "Exploring the Montreal That Leonard Cohen Loved," *New York Times* (February 10, 2017), www.nytimes.com/2017/02/10/travel/leonard-cohen-musician-montreal-canada.html.

[25] CBC Arts, "A Mobile, Location-Aware Audio Walking Tour of Leonard Cohen's Montreal," CBC, November 22, 2017, www.cbc.ca/arts/a-mobile-location-aware-audio-walking-tour-of-leonard-cohen-s-montreal-1.4413659.

[26] Musée d'Art Contemporain de Montréal, "The MAC Announces the International Tour of the Leonard Cohen Exhibition," November 13, 2018, https://macm.org/en/news/the-mac-announces-the-international-tour-of-the-leonard-cohen-exhibition/.

[27] Interview by the author with Rabbi Aubrey Glazer, November 16, 2019.

[28] "Émouvant hommage à Leonard Cohen," *Le Droit* (November 6, 2017), www.ledroit.com/2017/11/07/emouvant-hommage-a-leonard-cohen-4a5d60b0e75ed8a454f1d09c1ef58c29/. My translation.

"coming back to Montreal to renew my neurotic affiliations."[29] Not only is this taken from the dust jacket of *The Spice-Box of Earth*, a book written in 1961, but it also omits the lines that come immediately before: "I shouldn't be in Canada at all. Winter is all wrong for me. I belong beside the Mediterranean. My ancestors made a terrible mistake."[30] This attitude reflects Cohen's response when asked for his feelings about Quebec separatism: "I'm not interested in political separation, I'm interested in geographical separation. I think everyone should lean the same way at the same time and actually break off from Canada and move down to the coast of Florida. It would improve the climate."[31] But all this matters little to those banking on tourist dollars and international brand prestige.

I don't mean to deny that Cohen felt connected to his birthplace, or that he did not feel "chez moi." But his life took him to many other places, and his creative output required this movement. Perhaps what stems from looking at the disjuncture between how Cohen has enabled Montreal to represent itself on the world stage in terms of tourism and branding and the reality of Cohen's life enables a critical perspective that can help avoid reducing multifaceted urban spaces to easy, safe images. And this has the potential to complicate Cohen as well and to demonstrate some of that human messiness of which Trehearne speaks.

This more complicated, messy Cohen is important, given that Montreal has embraced, especially after his death, images, celebrations, and concerts that have allowed it to play the role of international multicultural city rather than the reality of the city being a Francophone space – as dictated by law. Two years after Cohen's death, the Coalition Avenir Québec swept to power with a majority government able to pass legislation to fight what they see as the decline of French, which will require the use of Canada's "notwithstanding clause" to avoid any challenges to these laws on the basis of human rights.[32] It's perhaps easier to

---

[29] Lorre, "Exploring the Montreal That Leonard Cohen Loved."
[30] Leonard Cohen, *The Spice-Box of Earth* (Toronto: McClelland and Stewart, 1961).
[31] "Leonard Cohen: Poet-Singer Urges a Move South," *Star-News* (Wilmington NC) (August 6, 1995).
[32] Philippe Authier, "Legault Doubles down on Decline of French as Bill 96 is Signed into Law," *Montreal Gazette* (June 1, 2022), https://montrealgazette.com/news/quebec/bill-96-gets-royal-assent-minister-responsible-for-french-gets-a-new-title.

celebrate Cohen as a great uniter than deal with the legacy of both English and French colonialism. Rabbi Glazer usefully reminds us of how, in spite of "the virulent anti-Semitism that is still very much rooted in the history of Québécois culture," it is still a culture that could produce someone like Leonard Cohen: "It makes you wonder whether through that oppositional force sometimes, you know, that friction can also produce remarkable art. I don't think that there's been enough of a reckoning in terms of that history … It makes a big impression even if it hasn't been fully resolved."[33] The Lionel-Groulx metro station still exists.

That Cohen could escape anglo–franco arguments and end up mentioned as a great Québécois chanteur, celebrated by the government on June 24, Quebec's National Day – St. Jean Baptiste, is testament to his ability to get outside of the province's linguistic politics. Commemorating St. Jean in 2021, Premier François Legault listed "our singers" and included Leonard Cohen alongside Félix Leclerc and Céline Dion.[34] This is especially ironic, given that the festivities don't allow English-language music.[35] Musician, producer, and erstwhile Montrealer Aisha C. Vertus's 2017 *cri de coeur* regarding the role of language in the music industry in Montreal described "the reality of making bilingual, multicultural art in a Francophone province."[36] She interviewed a range of artists, anglo and franco, and expressed frustration with the necessity to "contain 70% French content" to be classified as a Québécois artist and gain access to the opportunity of being "subsidized by the majority of granting institutions," not to mention the reality that 65 percent of radio play must be in

---

[33] Interview by the author with Rabbi Aubrey Glazer, November 16, 2019.

[34] "On a des artistes qui nous rendent fiers. Je pense notamment à nos chanteurs, nos Félix Leclerc, nos Céline Dion, nos Leonard Cohen qui nous font vibrer" (We have artists who make us proud. I'm thinking in particular of our singers, our Félix Leclercs, our Céline Dions, and our Leonard Cohens, who thrill us), François Legault, Facebook post, June 12, 2001.

[35] Brendan Kelly, "Montreal's Fête Nationale Show Open to Everyone, but en français s'il vous plait," *Montreal Gazette* (June 21, 2022), https://montrealgazette.com/news/local-news/montreals-fete-nationale-show-open-to-everyone-but-en-francais-sil-vous-plait.

[36] Aisha C. Vertus, "Why Québec's Music Industry Is Still Divided over Language," *Fader* (January 12, 2017), www.thefader.com/2017/01/12/english-bilingual-music-quebec.

French.[37] Cohen did speak French, and did perform a handful of songs in the language – but the majority of his work is in English, and he is an anglophone. He appears to be a special exception to the requirements.

Cohen's position as secular saint and established hagiography seem to demonstrate a desire on behalf of Montreal to see its urban island space in a particular way. It allows the city to transcend language issues, because even though Cohen was bilingual, he was not francophone. It's an idea that he can kind of represent all of Montreal when in fact he really is only representing a very, very specific element of it. As Rabbi Glazer puts it,

> saying you could argue that the raising to iconic status of the Jew is a way for Montreal to evade and displace its linguistic tensions. And of course, Cohen also embodies that nicely because anybody who reads a biography knows that in those heady revolutionary days, he nevertheless had close friends among francophone artists of the time. He was that, as Jews are often asked to be, kind of bridging figure between communities because he's neither one nor the other.[38]

A quotation often cited when journalists want to connect Cohen to Montreal is, "I feel at home when I'm in Montreal – in a way that I don't feel anywhere else ... I don't know what it is, but the feeling gets stronger as I get older." I can't find a citation for it, as there appears to be no source. It's been quoted by the *Globe and Mail*, the *New York Times*, and Montreal's own website, attributed to an interviewer in 2006, but even when I asked the very journalists who used the line, they can't name the source. What I have found, however, is how many people wanted to assure me that Cohen always adored Montreal – that he was always connected to this space. Beyond not being able to track the source down, what's interesting to me about the quotation is what it doesn't say. It's a statement not of love, but of feeling at home "in a way" that is not explained. I mean, Cohen grew up in Montreal and therefore would have the same sort of understanding and familiarity with the space as anyone has regarding where they spent formative years. And as Cohen aged, he did fulfill this quotation, whether or not he actually said it. Though he was ordained as a Zen Buddhist monk in Mt. Baldy,

---

[37] Ibid. [38] Interview by the author with Rabbi Aubrey Glazer, November 16, 2019.

California in 1996, his final album engaged directly with Jewish spirituality, and featured the cantor and men's choir from his Westmount synagogue (even though he recorded his own vocals in Los Angeles).[39] He is also buried in Montreal.

I must admit a level of sadness that I never ran into the man, but I also must admit, even though it would have made a good story to recount here, I don't think it would have been the transformative experience that was described to me. Yes, I'm an anglophone, but the anglophone community in Montreal is a very particular thing, and it seems to require generations of membership in the same way that the concept of interculturalism underlines the importance of an historic, French culture. The concept "takes for granted the centrality of francophone culture. From there it works to integrate other minorities into a common public culture, all while respecting their diversity."[40] The problem with this model is that it suggests that there is some core culture existent in Quebec, rather than all cultures engaged in a negotiation of Québécois identity. The idea of integration was pushed more forcefully during and after[41] the 2022 election, when the then immigration minister stated that "80% of immigrants go to Montreal, don't work, don't speak French."[42] Not to mention that although maps call this island Montreal, it's Tiohtià:ke in Kanien'kéha, and Mooniyang in Anishinaabemowin – two additional cultures and languages that existed in this space long before the

---

[39] Elysha Enos, "The Westmount Synagogue behind Leonard Cohen's Grammy-Winning *You Want It Darker*," CBC News, January 28, 2018, www.cbc.ca/news/canada/montreal/cohen-wins-grammy-1.4508038.

[40] J. Montpetit, "Quebec Group Pushes 'Interculturalism' in Place of Multiculturalism," *Globe and Mail* (March 7, 2011), www.theglobeandmail.com/news/politics/quebec-group-pushes-interculturalism-in-place-of-multiculturalism/article569581/.

[41] A member of parliament, Saul Polo, originally from Colombia and Spanish-speaking, reacted to Premier François Legault's statements bemoaning a decline of French spoken at home: "Based on the premier's vision, I should be leaving my identity at the airport as soon as I get off the plane"; see Verity Stevenson, "As New Language Law Takes Effect, Legault Comment on Speaking French at Home Sparks Heated Debate," CBC News, June 1, 2022, www.cbc.ca/news/canada/montreal/bill-96-debate-saul-polo-1.6474330.

[42] Daniel J. Rowe, "'80 Percent of Immigrants Go to Montreal, Don't Work, Don't speak French': CAQ Immigration Minister," CTV News Montreal, September 29, 2022; www.theglobeandmail.com/news/politics/quebec-group-pushes-interculturalism-in-place-of-multiculturalism/article569581.

solitudes showed up and started stealing land. Cohen seemed to acknowledge this in his first novel, *The Favourite Game*, when the main character says, "Some say that no one ever leaves Montreal, for that city, like Canada itself, is designed to preserve the past, a past that happened somewhere else."[43] In effect, there are "no Canadians [and] no Montrealers."[44]

When on a recent flight back to Montreal from the United Kingdom, I decided to watch the documentary *Hallelujah: Leonard Cohen, a Journey, a Song*,[45] which, among many other things, talked about how the song's appearance in the animated film *Shrek* led to its present ubiquity. The other thing it talked about, however, was Cohen's need to return to touring late in life to make up for the theft of his money by a manager. The film suggests that Cohen offered up himself onstage because there was little else to do, given the circumstances. It tracked his constant touring near the end of his life, and then it featured footage from a tribute concert held on the first anniversary of his death at the Bell Centre in Montreal. I attended this concert with a friend, another anglo Montrealer, though with roots in the city deeper than mine. The concert featured a wide range of different artists covering Cohen's extensive catalog, but the film featured "Hallelujah," as performed by k.d. lang. I wasn't expecting this, though I probably should have, given the film.

I cried on the plane just as I did when I experienced it the first time. Maybe it was the plane, but I think it might also have to do with my struggle to both write this chapter as well as belong in Montreal.[46] At that moment, with tears running down my cheeks faster than I could wipe them, I felt like I was the only person in the world who really understood the meaning of the song. I felt like I was on my way home to a space that I am growing to feel at home in, even though, as phrased in that mystery Cohen quotation, "I don't know what it is." There, in an airplane, hundreds of miles from Montreal, while watching lang, someone who hails from Edmonton, Alberta, halfway across Canada, singing Cohen's most famous song, I felt like I understood the man's transcendental power to

---

[43] Leonard Cohen, *The Favourite Game* (Toronto: McClelland and Stewart, 1970), 117.
[44] Ibid.   [45] Dir. Dayna Goldfine and Dan Geller (Sony Pictures Classics, 2022).
[46] Christian Jarrett, "Why Do I Always Cry When I Watch Films on a Plane?," BBC Science Focus, 2023, www.sciencefocus.com/the-human-body/why-do-i-always-cry-when-i-watch-films-on-a-plane/.

make a Montrealer out of me. It's not about some kind of intrinsic power that is gained while walking in Little Portugal, where Cohen lived, nor is it about some type of transcendence accessible through Cohen; it's perhaps what I think can be learned from him about occupying the in-between. Anyone who lives in Montreal knows that it's a literal and figurative island – and the 2022 election underlined this – as a huge majority of the city's population voted differently from the rest of the province.

Cohen completes his version of "Hallelujah," one that is heard much less often, with a statement: "I've done my best, I know it wasn't much; I couldn't feel, so I tried to touch." It seems to me that this instruction to try one's best provides enough support for someone like me to stay in Montreal, even though I find the language politics frustrating: the idea that two colonial cultures fight over a space neither owns, each side acting like the one who has been wronged. Perhaps this is what both Cohen and Montreal do very well. They both deal with this reality and teach us that there's really nothing else to do but to do one's best with this reality of being in-between.

CHAPTER 15

Boudoir Poet

A Thousand Kisses Deep with Leonard Cohen

David Yaffe

LEONARD NORMAN COHEN SHAMELESSLY SANG THESE UNGALlant words: "Don't go home with your hard-on/ It will only drive you insane." Allen Ginsberg and Bob Dylan were in the background, and Phil Spector was, when not shoving a semi-automatic pistol against Cohen's neck, producing. *Death of a Ladies' Man* (1977) was not an environment for tenderness or introspection. It was not even released with Cohen's permission: Spector stole the tapes, and that was the least of it. If the muse is summoned at gunpoint, and then the goods are hijacked, you don't always get reliable information. It's no secret that Leonard was a very naughty boy, but while coitus was half of his grand theme – the other half was pursuit of the unreliable narrator known as God, or G-d – it was not usually in the spirit of "Don't Go Home with Your Hard-On." It was about the thing that haunts you when you don't meditate, or ponder the abyss, or seduce, or fail to seduce, or still feel the hunger when the body inevitably fails.

Fucking is officially about reproduction, but it's really about the force of life itself, making love when it's love, what Leonard called the only engine of survival. There is a poem in your past, your projection, your dirty secrets, and your sweetest self; you are inspired, you have expired, you seek succor when the desire is exhausted. Your relationships are plagiarisms of previous relationships, and the more they proliferate, the less you know what you are doing. You are long past deluding yourself that you will ever get it right, but you appreciate what you have when you have it. You toast and offer a sacrament, a wild, little bouquet. Leonard has commemorated all of this and more in song, and in this respect, he is the most sex-besotted great anglophone songwriter, though Marvin Gaye and Prince loomed large in this arena, too. Bob Dylan, the one who first inspired Cohen to turn his poems into songs, avoided the subject of sex almost entirely. He left that space for Leonard, who ran with it on every album. If you were to listen to Cohen's complete oeuvre and play a drinking game, taking a shot every time sex comes up, you'd need your stomach pumped.

Exhibit A: "Suzanne." I was fortunate enough to have dinner with Leonard in January 2015, under much more humane conditions than the Phil Spector sessions. We met at a Pizzeria Uno off Wilshire. I asked him if "Dress Rehearsal Rag" was a song about *not* committing suicide. He said, "Yes." Then I asked if "Suzanne" was a song about *not* seducing a beautiful woman. He said, "Yes." And there was so much seducing in that *not seducing*. That *not seducing* is Auden writing of "Eros, builder of cities." It is Stevens writing of being "too dumbly in my being pent." Eros is not just desire, but wanting what you don't or can't have. It is waiting for the miracle. It is the stirrings still near the end. Judy Collins covered it, then brought Leonard to her Town Hall show, where he panicked and ran backstage, then was coaxed back by Collins, who held his hand to get him through it, and it was deemed a triumph. It began the pattern he would follow for most of his performing life: he had to be accompanied by women, and they looked as lovely as they sang. Part of it was that he lacked confidence in his voice, which they cushioned. Part of it was the continual need for female beauty. "Wasn't it a long way down?" he asked. On his way there, the ladies took the edge off. As "Recitation" has it, "Our perfect porn aristocrat/ So elegant and cheap/ I'm old but I'm still into that."

First the "perfect porn aristocrat," then the kneeling. First the experience, then the poem. There was another Suzanne, his long-term lover and mother of his two children, but that was not the Suzanne of "Suzanne." The Suzanne of "Suzanne" was the wife of his friend, the sculptor Armand Vaillancourt. Did the experience inspire the song or was it the other way around? Leonard's life was a poem, a parable. Was it too on the nose that his name was a near-homophone for koan? Listen, read, take it all in. Among English-language songwriters – especially with so many lyrics that qualified as raunchy poetry – was there anyone else so preoccupied with desire, and all he could desire, while also elevating the profane to the sacred, the booty calls to high poetry? His grandfather had the Torah memorized. He learned to read so that his grandson could write. When he was recording poetry as a young man, he told the engineer that there were no dirty words. The dirty words were about experiences that could also be exalted, as we hear in "Hallelujah": "And I remember when I moved in you/ And the holy dove she was moving too/ And every single breath we drew was Hallelujah."

The unedited "Hallelujah" is legendary, said to be around 150 verses, maybe 180. If you were to narrow down the theme of those verses, it would be failure. But what a failure. The Hebrew Bible is there, and so are all the women, the ones he could seduce and those he could not. He failed to sleep with Nico, and he never forgave Lou Reed for succeeding at this. "I cannot sleep with Jews anymore," she told him, but she made an exception for another landsman. Reed inducted Cohen into the Rock & Roll Hall of Fame, and, completely out of character, waxed rhapsodic about his lyrics. From where Leonard was sitting, it seemed shambolic, and he stoically endured the ceremony. (Back in the Chelsea days, Reed was honored to meet the author of *Beautiful Losers*.) Nico died bloated and addicted in 1988, Reed left us after a failed liver transplant in 2013, and when I met Leonard in 2015, he could still not let go of it. Nico haunts Leonard's notebooks. She was more than the one that got away. She was a muse, a trope, an everlasting no. The unfulfilled act was as inspiring as not sleeping with the first Suzanne. Except that she rejected him. She was the wound that never healed.

Joni Mitchell and Leonard Cohen were lovers, briefly and not exclusively, when their careers were beginning in 1967. As the years went by and a friendship with Leonard became harder to sustain – "What do you say to an old lover?" he once asked her, frostily, over dinner – she, who had called herself a "stone cold Cohenite," became increasingly dismissive. She called him, sneeringly, a "boudoir poet" and liked to say, "He owns the phrase 'naked body' ... it appears in every one of his songs." I checked, and he used it just once, in "Memories."

> I said, "Won't you let me see?"
> I said, "Won't you let me see your naked body?"

But I can see why Joni Mitchell thought that he owned the phrase and put it everywhere. It is used once, the way "friend-o" is used just once in *No Country for Old Men*. Their singular use feels ubiquitous. Naked bodies are everywhere in Cohen's oeuvre. There are dresses waiting to be tortured, flags to be placed on the marble arch. There is part of Cohen that is compelled to be gallant. He's a boudoir poet, but how dirty does he talk? From "Democracy": "We'll be going down so deep/ The river's going to weep/ And the mountain's going to shout Amen!"

It is typical for a songwriter to write of desire, but when Bob Dylan wrote "I Want You" it stopped there – at wanting and wordplay. When John Lennon called a song "I Want You," it was a hymn of praise and fear that this feeling was so strong, he compared it to drowning; the passion was deep, the lyrics were minimal. When Elvis Costello called a song "I Want You," it was about sexual jealousy, about being tormented by the wanting. There is no Leonard Cohen song called "I Want You," but the wanting is everywhere, and it becomes more specific. Desire is where a poem begins. A man who says that the sex will make the river weep and the mountain shout "Amen" is not exactly writing from a place of modesty. But then this is a poem. Leonard told me that he enjoyed the fact that much of his association with Joni Mitchell was not deep. I was surprised:

"But the songs you wrote for each other are deep."
"That's what I'm saying. The songs were better than we were."[1]

The songs were better than we were. Even in the lyrics from "Democracy," it's a promise, not a report. "I sang my songs, I told my lies/ To lie between your matchless thighs." "Matchless thighs": as if he had a ranking and these thighs outmatched them all. Does he say that to all the girls? Yes, he does. He said it to all of us; he put it on an album, one called *New Skin for the Old Ceremony* (1974), which delivers what it promises. "You were K-Y Jelly/ I was Vaseline."

Before the writing happens, he told me, there is an appetite to write, and you don't know what you're doing. The appetite, the wanting, turns into voice – or it is taken over by voice – and suddenly

---

[1] Leonard Cohen, interview by David Yaffe, January 2015.

Suzanne is taking you down. Sex is everywhere, even when it isn't anywhere. Vaseline rhymes with Mr. Clean; Leonard, like Iggy Pop, wants to be your dog. It is Nico, always turning you down, it is the unconsummated Suzanne of the song and the Suzanne in real life, the one who became his gypsy wife. Leonard gets jealous? He gets everything. He's been everywhere. "And where, where is my gypsy wife tonight?" Dear Reader, Leonard and Suzanne Elrod were never married. She was a gypsy girlfriend, a common law, a partner, a plus one, an arm candy. She was also mother to Adam and Lorca. She was, in his bohemian way, a family, but in this world of swollen appetites and not going home with one's hard-on, becoming a gypsy wife was inevitable. Sex happens to someone else; you get frustrated and write a song, say, "One of Us Cannot Be Wrong": "But you stand there so nice in your blizzard of ice/ Oh please, let me come into the storm." This is the final line of the song. He does not get into the storm. He's right where he was, a five-foot-six Jew at the Chelsea – the Little Jew Who Wrote the Bible – going home with his hard-on. Nico's refusal to have sex with Leonard was a poetry grant that kept giving, worth a stack of Guggenheims.

But many women fell for whatever he gave them, and here's where the trouble really begins. They did not all look like Joni or Nico. It is well known – a little too well known – that "Chelsea Hotel No. 2" is about Janis Joplin, and he regretted kissing and telling, though he kept performing it as long as he strode the stage. "Giving me head on the unmade bed/ While the limousines wait in the street." This is not Leonard's usual style. There is nothing exalted in the head on the unmade bed or anything else, just totems of status at a bohemian hostel that was once his home. At the end of the song, he is still unsentimental. "I remember you well in the Chelsea Hotel/ That's all, I don't even think of you that often." Ouch, not that she was around to hear it – that was the point. If we believe the song, Janis wasn't very nice to him. She was looking for Kris Kristofferson, she said she preferred handsome men, but for him she'd make an exception. She was not a beauty – no Suzanne Elrod, no Nico. Head in an unmade bed, not a big deal. The only thing that carries weight in the song is that she's dead, but even this gets a shrug. He refuses to be haunted by her.

Before Joni, before either of the Suzannes, there was Marianne Ihlen, the Norwegian muse of "So Long, Marianne," along with "Hey, That's No Way to Say Goodbye" and "Bird on the Wire." (Joni told me she thought "Bird on the Wire" was about a painting she had made of herself as a bird hanging upside down.) She was a conquest before the fame, even before the songs. She was as much of a blonde bombshell as Nico, except that she said yes. They had a little family in Hydra, and he was a father figure to her son, Axel. She would have devoted her life to him, but he was who he was. The women panting after him nearly made her kill herself, she said. But the women panting after him was the whole point. She brought him out of crippling depression to write "Bird on the Wire," but it was going to take a lot more than that. The relationship lasted eight years until it fell apart "like falling ashes," as Leonard put it. Still, she is known to many of us when her image appeared on the back of his second album, *Songs from a Room* (1969). She was wearing only a towel.

> But let's not talk of love or chains and things we can't untie
> Your eyes are soft with sorrow
> Hey, that's no way to say goodbye

How beautiful, and how cold. Deep and warm kisses, the sleepy golden storm of her waking up. It's all so lovely except that misery is a bad look. What did he expect? She was already contemplating suicide from the panting women. How is one supposed to say goodbye when one is devastated? Yet as a poem, it needs no apology. The beauty of the "eyes soft with sorrow" speaks for itself. The love and the chains are the cause, and now they are digging in. "Now so long, Marianne, it's time that we began/ To laugh and cry and cry and laugh about it all again." Has anyone ever dumped so eloquently? It sounds like so much fun, it could inspire nostalgia for the experience of catharsis. Laughter! Tears! The idea of laughing and crying about it all again might be the most romantic thing he ever wrote. We are already at the other side of this entanglement. What hysterics we were! What terrible things we said to each other, things we actually meant at the time! And now – how sad, how hilarious! Our hearts will break, they will heal, they will break again, and so it will go. Will it end on laughter or misery in the end? If one is Leonard, one would need to exhaust all the antidepressants, then meditate on Mt. Baldy to truly get perspective. The hunger is still there until illness and actuarial odds lay you low, and even then, it is on the page. "What a brute he had been! At it again?" asks James Joyce when Leopold Bloom is jerking off to Gerty MacDowell in *Ulysses*. *At it again?*

Leonard Cohen has seduced, has acquired, has shaken out all that Eros and Thanatos could deliver. And on a Greek island, no less. "So Long, Marianne" is evidence that our Leonard is at it again. The speed of the track makes it sound too celebratory, but maybe the Godfather of Gloom needed a little variation. (Listen to the slower, lumbering version at the Isle of Wight, and you can hear why he went for the faster tempo in the studio.) It might have felt like celebration to him, but it would have been a dirge for Marianne; even if she could move on, it was definitely harder for her to let go. He has much to move on to, and he will move on from whatever that is, too. Attachments would last longer in older age – Rebecca de Mornay, Anjani – but he will move on from those, too. He will move on from us in public. His only loyalty is to the muse. Through extreme pain and advanced age and illness, the verse persisted till last call. As the song advances, the heaving gets heavier. And while the chorus and title have Leonard announcing "So long," the song tells us that it is Marianne who has had enough. All those panting women, plus the need to move on from Hydra to the Chelsea. What happened? "For now I need your hidden love/ I'm cold as a new razor blade." "Hidden love"? That's the hottest thing he's said so far. There was something to hide? Something too intimate for this song? The imperfect, wrote Wallace Stevens, is so hot in us. Even Leonard. He was curious to go after those panting ladies. But he needed Judy Collins to hold his hand at Town Hall. If he was really as cold as a new razor blade, there would be no song. They are both laughing and crying about it all over again. But does one need surgical precision to make a move, to remove oneself from an entity of two?

Of course, Marianne looks hotter in retrospect. Why do you think he put that picture of her in a towel on the back of *Songs from a Room*? "So long" is also a form of being haunted. He now sounds like a stalker, and the song makes it sound like it was he who was left, when we know that's not the whole story. Sure, she moved on and got married at the appointed hour. She would now be wearing a towel for someone else.

Leonard did not climb a mountainside. He moved to the Chelsea and tried and failed with Nico, then succeeded with Joni, then kept moving. "There's a concert hall in Vienna/ Where your mouth had a thousand reviews." These lines, from "Take This Waltz," were adapted from a Lorca poem, though Leonard is fully responsible for "Where your mouth had a thousand reviews." Leonard went back to his beloved Lorca, to return a couple of decades after Marianne imaging a lover getting a reputation, even more extravagantly than the Gypsy Wife. So many writers are afraid to write about sex. They are afraid it will sound too purple, or too pornographic. It just makes them uncomfortable. But Leonard is up to the challenge. He could not be who he is without it. Take notes and the pain goes away, said Virginia Woolf. If you're Leonard, write lines and the misery lifts. At least enough to keep writing. Irony helps. It's what makes the mouth getting a thousand reviews land. Leonard looks for competition everywhere, someone who could finish the job that he couldn't start. Given the odds, he probably had lovers who faked their orgasms; if so, imagine the disappointment. He was even threatened by the competition of masturbation: "And she will learn to touch herself so well/ As all the sails burn down like paper." Unthinkable! One day a woman would write a bestselling book called *Are Men Necessary?* He would make a case, even if it were to appeal to someone to take the pain away. In his case, could they make an exception?

Leonard went to Mt. Baldy because Sasaki Roshi was laughing all the time, and he wanted to learn how to be that way. He got out of his head, but he never got out of bodies. "I ache in the places where I used to play," he announced, and yet he kept playing. *At it again?* Leonard sang "So Long, Marianne" every night on the tour he had between 2008 and 2012, when he finally became financially solvent, even after a former manager robbed him blind while he was getting ordained at Mt. Baldy. The audience loved the song. He appeared to be a survivor, and the crushing disappointment for all the carnal verses of "Hallelujah" spoke to an enormous audience. Everyone could identify with it. And the people who filled those stadiums cheered along with him, saying so long to the Nordic blonde from the back of the record jacket.

Many lifetimes later, when Leonard was informed that Marianne did not have long to live, he summoned an email that was really a postscript to his song, an acknowledgment that we always love the ones we made love to, that "so long" is not forever:

> Well Marianne, it's come to this time when we are really so old and our bodies are falling apart, and I think I will follow you very soon. Know that I am so close behind you that if you stretch out your hand, I think you can reach mine. And you know that I've always loved you for your beauty and your wisdom, but I don't need to say anything more about that because you know all about that. But now, I just want to wish you a very good journey. Goodbye old friend. Endless love, see you down the road.[2]

This went viral in a cultural moment when things went viral – 2016, a year Cohen did not complete. Sure, they were surrounded by panting women, but she was a panting woman that got a song that was a staple of his final years of performing. As Leonard entered deep old age, the Eros was still in the songs, even if it couldn't be anywhere else.

Love's the only engine of survival, he told us in "The Future." But we are not here to merely talk about love. We are here to talk about desire, about having and not having, about a hunger that is satiated, but not for long. If Lord Byron could have been this explicit, he would have. Leonard opened the decadent *Dear Heather* (2004) with Lord Byron's "Go No More a-Roving."

> Though the night was made for loving
> And the day returns too soon
> Yet we'll go no more a-roving
> By the light of the moon

What's not to like here? The night is made for loving, so of course that's the time the roving stops. Compared with Leonard's work, it's chaste. Lord Byron was, of course, explicit in his life, a much more scandalous one than Leonard's. Leonard, who spent the Sabbath with his children every Saturday, had quite a reputation, but no real scandals. When Lord Byron was in the midst of one of his scandals – he had

---

[2] Leonard Cohen, email to Marianne Ihlen, quoted in "Leonard Cohen Makes It Darker," David Remnick, *New Yorker* (October 10, 2016), www.newyorker.com/magazine/2016/10/17/leonard-cohen-makes-it-darker.

accidentally impregnated Mary Shelley's stepsister – he wrote about the condition of being a poet caught doing something that is a long way from "She Walks in Beauty":

> I never loved her nor pretended to love her, but a man is a man, and if a girl of eighteen comes prancing to you at all hours of the night, there is but one way, the suite of all this is that she was with child, and returned to England to assist in peopling that desolate island. This comes of "putting it about" (as Jackson calls it) and be damned to it, and thus people come into the world.[3]

Indeed, they do. Lord Byron did not go home with his hard-on.

Sex could be exalted, sex could be a power move ("Are your lessons done?" asks the Professor of Desire in "Teachers"). But it could also be the thing that haunts you, when you want more, or wish you wanted more, or wish that you could want more. In "I'm Your Man," he is a confident fifty-four-year-old specimen. Look no further. He could give as much or as little as his lover could want. It's funny, because he's not really that confident. If you really knew him, you'd detect the irony. But his priorities are real. The song could be played at a strip club. The strippers supply the visual. He provides the language. "If you want a lover/ I'll do anything you ask me to." This bravado is not just in spite of being fifty-four. There are actuarial benefits. He has been around long enough to be grateful. He is aware of the man–woman dynamic going on. He is older and has, by 1988, a kind of alt-rock star charisma, and he is, in his way, a gentleman. "Ah, the moon's too bright/ The chain's too tight/ The beast won't go to sleep."

The strippers continue. The garments come off. $20 bills are placed in halter tops. A waitress comes by and asks you, "What brings you here?" You say, "Desperation." Leonard would understand. Not every night is a success. The song swaggers, but, really, failure is his brand. He's your man in the sense that the Grocer of Despair is available. When he is appreciated, he accepts it with great ceremony, but that can depend on the grace of the moment. Sometimes the beast won't go to sleep. He may

---

[3] Lord Byron, *The Project Gutenberg Ebook of the Works of Lord Byron: Letters and Journals*, vol. I, ed. Roland E. Prothero, Posting Date: February 22, 2015 [Ebook #8901].

be your man, but that may not be enough. It is never enough. That's the nature of desire and all its gradations. The hunger is exhausted, until the hunger is lessened and diminished, and one writes songs of nostalgia for it. On the same album, he sang that he ached in the places where he used to play.

Sometimes, it all piles up, the detritus of all those conquests, and all the static that broke them apart. You forget the details about the arguments, but you remember the feeling. What was that all about? Leonard called an album *Songs of Love and Hate*. He saw it coming, but what good was that? "My reputation as a ladies' man was a joke that caused me to laugh bitterly through the ten thousand nights I spent alone." He said something like this to me when he was speaking of Nico's rejection. I said, "That doesn't sound like your game." He said that he wished he understood his game. Here I am, still trying to understand it. But then he knew that there is a divine mystery to it all. He wasn't a heartless operator. He lived and loved as a poet. He wanted the bodies to follow the muse. Bodies are exalted until they fail, they age, they decline, and even then, they deserve a chance. His note to Marianne at the end acknowledged that, while still praising her beauty until they could somehow follow each other to the Tower of Song. The experience comes and goes. The words remain. As long as people want, they will have a guide who was committed to the dance, as he explained in "Hallelujah": "I did my best, it wasn't much/ I couldn't feel, so I tried to touch/ I've told the truth, I didn't come to fool ya."

Leonard Cohen would not have called himself a "ladies' man," but he did write *Death of a Ladies' Man*. It is a quieter moment in the Spector sessions, and the song sounds less like the Wagner of the Girl Groups and more like Pink Floyd. But the theme was far from mellow. It brimmed with frustration, disappointment. His longtime relationship was ending, and the ancillary ones did not provide succor. He needed someone to dance him through the panic, but not yet. "So the great affair is over but whoever would have guessed/ It would leave us all so vacant and so deeply unimpressed." Allen Ginsberg wrote an Ode to Failure. Leonard wrote many of them. If lust is a muse, that lust, in the bodies of mere mortals, is bound to disappoint. He wrote about his own failings, his own quest, his own unquenchable appetites that led him to his final destination.

2016: a year that took Bowie and Prince and elected Trump also took Leonard. His passing was devastating, but he had suffered enough. When he was confined to the barracks of a medical chair where he recorded his final album completed with his permission – *You Want It Darker* – while he was using his Buddhist discipline to block out pain so excruciating even the opiates failed. They are always broken hallelujahs. And the memories of the flesh kept haunting him. On June 24, 2016, a few months before he left us, he remembers when he thought he knew what pain was. "It ain't pretty, it ain't subtle/ What happens to the Heart" (*Thanks for the Dance*, 2019)." Looking at her was trouble from the start. Why get into trouble? This is what happens to the heart. *Happens to the Heart* was what he wanted to call his final volume. But when you make plans, especially when one is a boudoir poet, G-d says ha. He saw it coming the whole time. He touched your perfect body with his mind. That couldn't last forever. *Wasn't it a long way down?* It was, but it was also glorious, including the failures. We're present, we're gone. Leonard was more present than most. He lived his life as if it's real. Yet he went the way of all flesh. What was that all about? "We are so lightly here," he told us in "Boogie Street," "It is in love that we are made. In love we disappear."

CHAPTER 16

For the Matriarchy

Women and the Music

Heather S. Arnet

IN HER FOREWORD TO *LEONARD COHEN ON LEONARD COHEN*, Suzanne Vega tells of running into Cohen, in 1993, at a Los Angeles hotel. They met poolside, and he had his guitar and extemporaneously began to play a tune. As Cohen strummed the guitar and sang, first one beautiful girl, and then another, appeared. By the end of the song, as Vega tells it, there were nine girls surrounding Cohen at the pool. Vega shares how as a teenager she listened to Cohen "fervently, every day after school" with an intensity that felt like intimate friendship, though, as her poolside story illustrates, as she grew older she would come to realize that she would need to share him with a vast sisterhood of Leonard Cohen fans.[1]

Vega's tale positions Cohen as some sort of modern-day Pied Piper, though to characterize it so would be to underestimate both the musician and his audience. While Cohen's significant and dedicated female fan base has widely been acknowledged, an explanation for the phenomenon has been lacking. Some might attempt to explain fan interest in Cohen in relationship to physical attraction, though Cohen was known for his self-effacing assertions that he was not traditionally handsome. As he writes in his first novel, *The Favourite Game*, of his autobiographical protagonist Breavman, "He could not help thinking that . . . he wasn't tall enough . . . that people didn't turn to look at him in streetcars, that he didn't command the glory of the flesh."[2] And then again in "Chelsea

---

[1] Suzanne Vega, "Foreword," in *Leonard Cohen on Leonard Cohen: Interviews and Encounters*, ed. Jeff Burger (Chicago: Chicago Review Press, 2014), xiv.

[2] Leonard Cohen, *The Favourite Game & Beautiful Losers* (Toronto: McClelland and Stewart, 2009), 239.

Hotel No. 2," the protagonist tells him she "preferred handsome men" but would make an exception for him. Cohen's notorious stage fright also meant that, as a performer, he did not attract his fan base with gyrating stage performances of the likes of James Brown, Elvis, Jim Morrison, or Mick Jagger. Yet he most certainly developed a reputation for being a "ladies' man," as he acknowledged in titles (*Death of a Ladies' Man*), and through a lifetime of romantic poetry and song lyrics.

By exploring the qualities of Cohen's music that particularly resonated with and inspired female listeners, we can better understand what differentiated the songs, and the artist, from other songwriters of his time and which continue to attract multiple generations of fans. In what follows, I will explore several core aspects of Cohen's music: the rhythm and orchestration, his lyrics (with emphasis on narrative structure and character development), and Cohen's baritone voice, considering how each element appeals to audience members and how these components work collectively as a whole.

In 1968, early in his career, Cohen said, "I wish the women would hurry up and take over. Then we can finally recognize that women really are the minds and the force that holds everything together; and men really are gossips and artists. Then we could get about our childish work and they could keep the world going. I really am for the matriarchy."[3] Cohen recognized the emotional depth and understanding that women found in his music and acknowledged their role in his artistic journey and career. In an interview with the *Guardian* in 2001, Cohen shared, "Women seem to be able to hear my work deeper than men. Women seem to be able to enter it more easily, and I think they have a better time in it."[4] In conversation with Terry Gross in 1986, Gross remarked that some at the time referred to Cohen's songs as "gloomy and despairing."[5] Cohen responded that "On the contrary, I don't get a lot of mail, but most [conveys], that song got me through the night, or your songs got me through the night." Cohen added,

---

[3] Leonard Cohen, interview by William Kloman, "Interview with Leonard Cohen," *New York Times* (January 28, 1968), in Burger (ed.), *Leonard Cohen*, 16.

[4] Leonard Cohen, interview by Nick Paton Walsh, "I Never Discuss My Mistresses or My Tailors: An Interview with Leonard Cohen," *Guardian* (October 13, 2001), www.theguardian.com/theobserver/2001/oct/14/features.magazine37.

[5] Leonard Cohen, interview by Terry Gross, "The 'Serious' Sounds of Leonard Cohen," *Fresh Air, NPR* (April 29, 1986).

"I prefer the word 'serious' to sad, or melancholy, I think seriousness is a voluptuous kind of enjoyment that we don't find too often."[6]

Cohen's music is known for its complex lyrics and emotive vocal delivery, while his artistic style incorporated various rhythmic and melodic elements. His music reflected several diverse influences, including the cadence of Jewish prayer services, the pulse of klezmer, the tempo of waltz, and Spanish flamenco.[7] He combined all of these to create his signature sound, often utilizing a 3/4 time signature. As a result, his compositions have a meditative quality reminiscent of a steady pulse, the consistent beat of a heart. Cohen's use of 3/4 time, in "Suzanne," "Hallelujah," "Bird on the Wire," "Famous Blue Raincoat," and "Dance Me to the End of Love," contributed to the distinctive atmosphere and mood of his songs. This time signature provides a contemplative nature to his music and lends itself well to supporting a wide range of emotions, particularly those associated with introspection, longing, and romance. The gentle, flowing rhythm also enhances the lyrical content of his songs.

In *Where the Girls Are*, Susan J. Douglas explores the impact of American popular culture and mass media of the 1950s through the 1990s on the female body and mind. Her chapter on "Why the Shirelles Mattered" explores the impact of the girl groups of the 1950s and 1960s. As Douglas argues of the Shirelles' Number 1 hit, "Will You Love Me Tomorrow," written by Carole King, that the song's strong appeal to young women at the time can partly be explained by the song's musical arrangement. Douglas explains that while the main subject of the song was sex, it did not "rely on the musical instrument so frequently used to connote sex in male rockers' songs." Douglas continues, "saxes were banished, as were electric guitars, instead, an entire string orchestra provided the counterpoint to Shirley Owen's haunting, earthy, and provocative lead vocals ... along with a pulsing rhythm."[8]

---

[6] Ibid.

[7] Cohen spoke often of each of these influences. In regard to flamenco, he did so passionately in his acceptance speech on October 21, 2011, for the Prince of Asturias Award, in Oviedo, Spain, https://speakola.com/arts/leonard-cohen-prince-of-asturias-awards-2011.

[8] Susan J. Douglas, *Where the Girls Are: Growing up Female with the Mass Media* (New York: Random House, 1994), 84–85.

Those who first heard "Will You Love Me Tomorrow" as teens would have been in their early twenties when Leonard Cohen released "Suzanne" less than a decade later. Scholars and critics often discuss Cohen and his body of work in relationship to the likes of Bob Dylan and James Taylor, but what if we considered his work in relationship to the Shirelles and Carole King? Perhaps women appreciated the sound of Cohen's music because in it they heard familiar musical techniques that aroused and empowered them combined with lyrics acknowledging their sexual agency, just as they had in the music of the Shirelles. Cohen remarked on his interest in attempting to reproduce this kind of sound later on in his interview with Jian Gomeshi on *Q*:

> I never thought I was really one of the big guys so the work that was in front of me was ... to do something with self-investigation without self-indulgence ... I was very influenced by women's background voices ... Yes, I liked those songs that had that feel. Those are the songs of the fifties. So those were the sounds I wanted to try to reproduce. Also, my own voice sounded so disagreeable to me when I listened to it that I really needed the sweetening of women's voices behind me.[9]

In fact, it was the strong sweet voice of a woman that propelled Cohen onto the world stage as a performer for the first time. Judy Collins recorded Cohen's "Suzanne" in 1966 on *In My Life*. A year later, after the album went gold in 1967, she and Cohen were backstage at a SANE Against Vietnam War Concert at New York City Town Hall. As the crowd cheered, Collins encouraged Cohen to go onstage, for the first time in front of a live audience, to perform his song himself. Up until that point, Cohen was known as a poet, a novelist, and – just recently – a songwriter, but it took Collins's encouragement to get Cohen to embrace the idea of singing his own songs onstage. In her 1989 autobiography, *Trust Your Heart* (and in several interviews since), Collins shared the story of a nervous Cohen walking with shaking legs onto the stage and quietly beginning the first few lines, then running offstage, only to be coaxed

---

[9] Leonard Cohen, interview by Jian Gomeshi, "Leonard Cohen Interview," *Q with Jian Ghomeshi*, QTV (Quebec), CBC Radio One (Canada), April 16, 2009, in Burger (ed.), *Leonard Cohen*, 553–54.

back by Collins to the warm embrace of a delighted audience. Collins reflected on the impact of Cohen's songs on her, as a performer: "His songs carried me through dark years like mantras or stones that you hold in your hand while the sun rises or the fire burns. They kept me centered as I stood in front of thousands of people, my eyes closed, my hands around the neck of a guitar, my voice singing his ethereal lyrics."[10]

For Cohen, one of the origins for his deep admiration and connection to women began with his mother. Leonard said that his mother taught him never to be cruel to women.[11] "What he also learned from his mother," remarks Sylvie Simmons in her book *I'm Your Man*, "was to count on the devotion, support, and nurturing of women."[12] It was in his mother's kitchen, Jennifer Warnes says, that Cohen first heard the notes of klezmer music.[13]

Warnes, in an interview just after Cohen's death in November 2016, explains that since Cohen's mother was the daughter of a Talmud scholar, it was also from her that he first learned the art of storytelling.[14] Warnes is one of several of Cohen's lifelong friends who transitioned from backup singer to colleague and musical collaborator. Sharon Robinson's musical career was entwined with Cohen's for nearly four decades. Initially introduced to Cohen as a backup singer, Robinson credits Cohen with "giving me the sense that I could step out of my lane as backup singer and ask him if he wanted to hear a melody," thus propelling Robinson's journey to become one of Cohen's most significant and trusted creative collaborators.[15] They share writing credits on several songs including, "Everybody Knows," "My

---

[10] Judy Collins, *Trust Your Heart: An Autobiography* (Boston: Houghton Mifflin, 1987), 145–47.

[11] Leonard Cohen, quoted in Sylvie Simmons, *I'm Your Man: The Life of Leonard Cohen* (New York: HarperCollins, 2012), 47.

[12] Ibid.

[13] Jennifer Warnes, quoted in interview by Randall Roberts, "'Born to Be His Conduit': Jennifer Warnes Remembers Her Friend and Collaborator Leonard Cohen," *Los Angeles Times* (November 14, 2016), www.latimes.com/entertainment/music/la-et-ms-jennifer-warnes-leonard-cohen-20161111-story.html.

[14] Ibid.

[15] Nathalie Atkinson, "Sharon Robinson Shares Memories of Leonard Cohen Ahead of New AGO Exhibit, 'Everybody Knows,'" *Everything Zoomer* (December 8, 2022), www.everythingzoomer.com/arts-entertainment/2022/12/08/sharon-robinson-shares-memories-of-leonard-cohen-ahead-of-the-opening-of-new-ago-exhibit-everybody-knows/.

Secret Life," "Waiting for the Miracle," "Alexandra Leaving," and "Boogie Street."[16]

Cohen's lyrics contain rich imagery, profound metaphors, and captivating narratives. He had a remarkable talent for crafting evocative and thought-provoking verses that paint vivid pictures and that convey deep emotions. Other singers and songwriters working at the time – Carole King, Judy Collins, Nina Simone, Joni Mitchell, Joan Baez, Aretha Franklin, and Etta James (just to name a few) – were producing dozens of important songs and presenting perspectives of multidimensional women. Female listeners embraced these songs, identifying with the main characters in the stories. Cohen's portrayal of women in his music was influenced by these songwriters, and several, including Simone, Baez, and Collins, performed Cohen's songs to great effect.

While he was not writing from a woman's perspective in the first person, Cohen often focused his musical tales around the woman in the story and her agency, her will, her desire and actions, creating a whole character. "Cohen's music and poetry resonated with women because he allowed them to see themselves in his work," jazz composer Lisa Hilton wrote shortly after Cohen's death; "he captured their desires, their vulnerabilities, their strength, and their longing for connection."[17]

Cohen had a gift for writing lyrics which depicted female-identifying characters as individuals with their own desires and vulnerabilities, and centering their stories. Women in Leonard Cohen songs had names: Suzanne, Marianne, Heather, Alexandra. Their names would be just the beginning of the listener's introduction to full and vivid personae. Instead of presenting women solely as objects of desire or heartbreak, Cohen explored their inner lives, struggles, and aspirations. His songs acknowledged the complexities of women's experiences and provided a more nuanced portrayal of female identity. The women in Cohen songs did not exist solely as someone or something that happened to the songwriter. He was a moment in their story. The sense is that their story is much larger than him. One is reminded of the artist Lee Krasner's statement that she "painted before Pollock, during Pollock, and after

---

[16] Ibid.   [17] Lisa Hilton, *Lisa Hilton Music*, www.lisahiltonmusic.com/blog.

Pollock."[18] As one listens to a Leonard Cohen song, one has a sense that the women in the stories existed before, during, and after Cohen.

This is especially true in the song which introduced Cohen to audiences, that day he shared the stage with Judy Collins in 1967, "Suzanne." Cohen referred to the writing of "Suzanne" as journalism, telling Paul Zollo, "It was a matter of reportage, of really just being as accurate as I could about what she did."[19] He tells Zollo of how Suzanne, the wife of a friend, "took me down to a place near the river."[20] Asked whether she fed him tea and oranges, Cohen responded, as he often did in interviews, that "the tea was Constant Comment, which has small pieces of orange rind in it, which gave birth to the image."[21]

The real-life muse for the song, Suzanne Verdal, confirmed these details in a radio interview in 1998, saying:

> He was drinking me in more than I even recognized, if you know what I mean . . . I just would speak and I would move and I would encourage and he would just kind of like sit back and grin while soaking it all up . . . I felt his presence really being with me . . . We'd almost hear each other thinking. It was very unique . . . I would always light a candle and serve tea and it would be quiet for several minutes, then we would speak, and I would speak about life and poetry and we'd share ideas.[22]

Cohen's attention to detail brings Suzanne to life in the song. Describing Nina Simone's 1969 electrifying performance of "Suzanne," Jack Whatley said that she "takes the Canadian's ethereal lead protagonist and every mystical moment and purely embodies her."[23] Whatley rightly points out how Simone clearly chose not to play the passive role of the male observer in her interpretation of the song. Through the savvy

---

[18] David Bourdon, "Lee Krasner: I'm Embracing the Past," *Village Voice* (March 7, 1977), 57.
[19] Leonard Cohen, interview with Paul Zollo, "Leonard Cohen: Inside the Tower of Song," *SongTalk* (April 1993), in Burger (ed.), *Leonard Cohen*, 286.
[20] Ibid. [21] Ibid.
[22] Kat Saunders, interview with Suzanne Verdal McCallister, June 1998, BBC Radio 4 FM, https://www.leonardcohenfiles.com/verdal.html.
[23] Jack Whatley, "Revisit Nina Simone's Soaring Cover of Leonard Cohen Song 'Suzanne'," *Far Out Magazine* (December 10, 2021), https://faroutmagazine.co.uk/nina-simone-cover-leonard-cohen-song-suzanne-cover/.

transference of pronouns during the final stanzas of the song, Simone instead embodies the part of Suzanne. "By making the character even more real, she does the impressive balancing act of adding grandeur to her iconography and weight to her ideals, all the while adding humor at the expense of her adorer."[24] For many a female fan, even those who have not seen Simone's transcendent performance, this so beautifully captures the experience of listening to a Leonard Cohen song. We hear the story of this complex female protagonist, her free-spirit style, her dancer moves, her philosophical imaginings, her warm bohemian hostess ways, her ambivalence towards the visitor and his longing. We can imagine her, and we can imagine being her.

In this way, Cohen's lyrics differed dramatically from many of the other male artists of his time. Bob Dylan and James Taylor, singer-songwriters working in a similar genre and time as Cohen, enjoyed long careers which have appealed to gender-diverse audiences, though most would agree that their audience bases skew male. Dylan and Taylor wrote confessional, philosophical songs reflecting on personal heartache with political conviction. Their songs include women, refer to women, and delve into experiences and relationships with women, but rarely do the songs center the experiences, feelings, or agency of the women. An interesting linguistic exercise is to look at the lyrics of Cohen's "Suzanne" and Taylor's "Fire and Rain." Both begin by introducing the listener to a main character, Suzanne, who was at one time in the songwriter's life, but is now no longer. From there they diverge. In "Fire and Rain" the words "I" and "me" are used thirty-three times. The word Suzanne is said once, and the word "you" (when used as the pronoun referring to Suzanne) is used six times. In contrast, in Cohen's song, Suzanne's name is said three times, and the pronouns referring to her (she/her) are used nineteen times. The words me and/or I do not appear at all in this song. Suzanne's name is also, notably, the title of the song. By the conclusion of Taylor's "Fire and Rain" the listener has a profound sense of the songwriter's grief, anger, loss, and sadness, but an extremely vague sense of the Suzanne mentioned at the start of the song.

---

[24] Ibid.

This is not to say that one of these songs tells a better or more important story, and they are different stories, to be sure. Rather, in considering why Cohen's music was preferred by women, it is useful to consider how each of these singer-songwriters was distinct from the other. The thirty-three uses of "I" and "me" make it clear who the central character of Taylor's song is. The focus in Cohen's song on the female character, through several mentions of her name, and the centralizing of her actions in the story, center her agency for the listener.

This centering of female agency was unusual for a male singer-songwriter at the time, though Cohen's music and lyrics challenged societal gender norms and expectations placed on men in other ways as well. He explored unconventional love and desire, addressed taboo subjects such as adultery and oral sex, delved into complexities of relationships, positioned himself as the vulnerable party, the object of short-term sexual use and desire, the broken-hearted, the one left behind. In "Chelsea Hotel No. 2," it is the woman in the story who is the more famous of the two, who tells him that "she preferred handsome men, but for me, you would make an exception." Cohen's nuanced approach to gender dynamics appealed to female fans who found his music liberating and empowering and to the women who covered his songs, especially in live performance.

In 1995, Tori Amos began to perform Cohen's "Famous Blue Raincoat" on her live tour sets. Her recorded version of the song was included in *Tower of Song*, a Leonard Cohen tribute album. "To say Amos covers Leonard Cohen's pensive epistle from a cuckolded man to his betrayer would be inaccurate; she uncovers it," wrote Joe Vallese for *PopMatters*.[25] In fact, Amos's live performances of "Famous Blue Raincoat" are so powerful, the song has remained a cornerstone of her tour set list since the 1990s. Vallese points out that through "Famous Blue Raincoat" Amos was able to begin to explore an early blueprint for her 2001 persona-shifting cover album, *Strange Little Girls*. From her earliest performances of Cohen's song, Amos ignited the tale with depths of emotion, pathos, and passion. As her performances evolved, she began to sing from the perspective of Jane, the

---

[25] Joe Vallese, "The Top Tori Amos Covers," *Pop Matters* (October 1, 2012), www.popmatters.com/163784-the-top-tori-amos-covers-2495810930.html.

woman at the center of the love triangle, "and manages to create a new vantage point entirely without changing a single lyric."[26]

In addition to "Famous Blue Raincoat" Amos has performed covers of Cohen's "Suzanne" and "Hallelujah" in her repertoire for decades, and all of these took on additional warmth and poignancy after Cohen's passing. Yet she has rarely spoken about what is clearly a deep connection to Cohen and his music. When she released her *Strange Little Girls* concept album, an opportunity presented itself to glean a greater sense of Amos's relationship to these songs and her process. The twelve tracks on *Strange Little Girls* are all covers of songs written and originally performed by men. On the album Amos reinterprets each song from a female point of view. Reflecting on the album twenty years after its release, Annie Zaleski described it this way, "What if some very famous songs by very famous men were instead centered on and about women?"[27] This quote in many ways summarized Amos's performative interpretation of Cohen. Or perhaps it is what attracted her to his music in the first place. "This is not just about songs that meant something to me when they came out," Tori Amos said, referring to her process in creating the album. "This is about how men say things and how a woman hears."[28] As Jeanette Leech pointed out, "it is through her voice, intonation, arrangements, and emotion" that the women take shape; some as they were "intended by their male creators, while others almost as newly formed Amos inventions."[29]

Cohen's songs, like "Suzanne," "Famous Blue Raincoat," and "Chelsea Hotel No. 2," follow a narrative structure, unfolding like short stories or vignettes. His songs begin with an opening line that instantly draws you in, then so often introduce romantic characters, build tension, and deliver poignant conclusions. If Leonard Cohen's songs were books, they would be novels written by Austen, Patchett, Erdrich, or Allende.

---

[26] Ibid.

[27] Annie Zaleski, "Tori Amos' 'Strange Little Girls' Is a Quietly Triumphant Covers Collection That Endures 20 years On," *Salon* (September 19, 2021), www.salon.com/2021/09/19/tori-amos-strange-little-girls-20th-anniversary/.

[28] Jeanette Leech, "'Strange Little Girls': Understanding Tori Amos' Bold Covers Album," *Dig!* (September 18, 2023), www.thisisdig.com/feature/strange-little-girls-tori-amos-album-story/.

[29] Ibid.

Like these novelists, Cohen weaves stories, transports us, and takes time to paint pictures of places and complex characters we want to know, and be, and love. His songs speak of longing and heartbreak, of women who cast spells, who serve you tea with oranges, who tie you to kitchen chairs, and who haunt your dreams.

While women read more books (of all types) annually than men, several studies in the United States, Canada, and the United Kingdom consistently quantify a dramatic gender gap in readership of literary fiction. Women account for 80 percent of the fiction market (with men only accounting for 20 percent). These market trends have held true for several decades with little change.[30] While conducting research for a book, Helen Taylor surveyed more than 400 female readers asking how and why they related so passionately to reading fiction.[31] Inspired by Taylor, Johanna Thomas-Corr, reviewing the book for the *Guardian*, asked the magazine's staff to answer similar questions. One of the published staff responses, from Marie-Claire Chappet, echoes Cohen's reflection on why he thought women were attracted to his music: "Women are more curious [than men], that's probably why fiction appeals. I guess we've got more to escape from, haven't we? And we've got more access to other kinds of perspectives, because we're othered by society."[32] In considering the impact of Cohen's lyrics on his fans, Judy Collins said, "The audience responded to his writing, the songs were like water to a person dying of thirst. They were songs for the spirit when our spirits were strained to the breaking point."[33]

Finally, no exploration of Leonard Cohen would be complete if one did not comment on or at least consider the role of the sound of his "golden voice" (as he referred to it in "Tower of Song"). Leonard Cohen's vocal register was a crucial component of his artistry. It contributed to the timeless quality of his music, played a significant role in the emotional impact of his

---

[30] Johanna Thomas-Corr, review of *Why Women Read Fiction: The Stories of Our Lives* by Helen Taylor, "Without Women the Novel Would Die: Discuss," *Guardian* (December 7, 2019), www.theguardian.com/books/2019/dec/07/why-women-love-literature-read-fiction-helen-taylor#:~:text=Women%20are%20not%20only%20keener,literary%20societies%20and%20evening%20classes.

[31] Helen Taylor, *Why Women Read Fiction: The Stories of Our Lives* (Oxford: Oxford University Press, 2019).

[32] Johanna Thomas-Corr, Review of *Why Women Read Fiction*.

[33] Collins, *Trust Your Heart*, 145–47.

songs, and in so many ways only became deeper with more layers of complexity with age. While in his younger years Cohen disliked the sound of his own voice, it irrefutably contributed significantly to the unique and emotive quality of his music. In his 1992 interview Paul Zollo asked Cohen about his deepening voice. Cohen responded, "My voice really started to change around 1982. It started to deepen, and I started to cop to the fact that it was deepening." "I thought it was because of fifty thousand cigarettes and several swimming pools of whiskey that my voice has gotten so low. But I gave up smoking a couple of years ago and it's still getting deeper."[34]

A voice that debuted onstage with Judy Collins in 1967, raspy, a bit nasal with awkward edges, had by 2009, at seventy-three years old, developed the honey of age, resplendent in charm, grace, authenticity, and wisdom. Cohen's voice had the ability to convey a wide spectrum of emotions, from introspection and vulnerability to strength and intensity. This emotional range made his performances and recordings deeply engaging to his audience. As his voice deepened it developed a velvety timbre, which added to the sensual and melancholic atmosphere of his songs. This timbre helped create a distinct and recognizable sound that became an integral part of Cohen's musical identity.

In this regard, research on memory and cognition provides some intriguing theories. In two experiments, a group of UK neuroscientists were able to demonstrate a quantifiable difference in memory recall by women subjects related to the sound of male voice pitch.[35] In both experiments, women demonstrated a strong preference for the low-pitched male voice and remembered objects more accurately when they had been introduced by a deep male voice.[36] An earlier study by Sarah A. Collins investigated the relationship between male human vocal characteristics and female judgments about the speaker. Men with lower-pitched voices were judged as being "more attractive, older, more likely to have a muscular body type and have a hairy chest," although there was no relationship between any vocal characteristics of the men and the

---

[34] Cohen, interview by Paul Zollo, in Burger (ed.), *Leonard Cohen*, 280.

[35] D. Smith et al., "A Modulatory Effect of Male Voice Pitch on Long-Term Memory in Women: Evidence of Adaptation for Mate Choice?," *Memory & Cognition* 40 (2012): 135–44, https://rdcu.be/dBxok.

[36] Ibid.

described body characteristics being attributed to them by the listening subjects. With these research findings in mind, it is amusing to consider that there might be a scientific argument to be made as to why female listeners prefer Cohen's music and can so easily recall his lyrics.

Cohen's singing style sometimes bordered on a kind of rhythmic speaking, which emphasized the poetic nature of his lyrics and was no doubt connected to his roots as a poet. As a result, his music had a conversational quality that drew listeners into his storytelling. This is perhaps most notable in one of his last songs recorded, "You Want It Darker." For Cohen, this delivery style traced back to early memories of being a child listening to the *kohenim* leading prayer services in temple in Montreal. This Cohen grew up to lead us in a very different meditative prayer, though holy and unbroken in its own way. Cohen's voice, combined with his 3/4 time signature, produces a powerful meditative result in "You Want It Darker." The song's rhythm and spoken-word style are not the only prayer references, as here the songwriter explicitly includes and calls out the Hebrew word *hineni*, a central word from one of the earliest prayers in the Jewish Bible.

In September 2016, a couple of months before he passed away, Leonard Cohen received a piece of fan mail, via a Facebook post, from a young woman in Melbourne, Australia. In her message, Anita Lester wrote to Leonard that she had been ten years old when her father passed away, and she was introduced to the novels and music of Leonard Cohen through her father's library and record collection. Her post included a video recording of Lester, now in her twenties, sitting on a rooftop with a guitar singing Cohen's then newest release, "You Want It Darker."[37]

Cohen told those around him at the time that he wanted to write back to her, as in her message "he recognized an artist singing from the same primal wound."[38]

In 2020, Lester organized a *Ladies Who Sing Leonard* tribute to Cohen for the Festival of Jewish Arts and Music. The lineup included sixteen artists, including Kylie Auldist, Kate Ceberano, Deborah Conway, Emily

---

[37] Michael Dwyer, "Sure, Men Liked Leonard Cohen, But, for Women, It Was Something Else," *Sydney Morning Herald* (October 30, 2020), www.smh.com.au/culture/music/sure-men-liked-leonard-cohen-but-for-women-it-was-something-else-20201026-p568m4.html.

[38] Leonard Cohen, quoted ibid.

Lubitz, Katie Noonan, Melody Pool, and Israeli singer Ninet Tayeb. While promoting the festival, in an interview with the *Sydney Morning Herald* Lester reflected on when she first heard "You Want It Darker" and what prompted her to write that fan letter to Leonard back in 2016:

> I went on a trip to Paris with my mum for the Jewish holiday of Yom Kippur. We went into the synagogue where my grandparents were married, broke the fast there, and they do this prayer, which is called the Mourner's Kaddish. It was the most spiritual musical experience I'd ever had to that point. And then the next week, Leonard released that album, and I realized that the song "You Want It Darker" is that prayer, essentially. It's the same message, the same kind of language. "Hinene, hinene," Cohen intones, echoing Abraham's surrender when God asks him to sacrifice his son, Isaac, in the book of Genesis, "Here I am, I'm ready" . . . And that started this whole little journey . . . He's definitely my mentor; my invisible mentor. I read him, I listen to him, and I also understand his foundation, which is a deep study of spiritual texts and poetry. There's a world underneath him.[39]

It feels most fitting to end this chapter with Lester, a young woman who sent a piece of fan mail to Leonard Cohen, perhaps one of the last ones he received, and Leonard watching Lester performing his song on that rooftop, strumming her guitar and singing his song, just as Suzanne Vega had sat and watched Cohen all those decades ago. As he listens to his songs performed by Madeleine Peyroux, k.d. lang, Tori Amos, Anohni, Batsheva Capek, Anna Calvi, Lana Del Rey, Johanna and Klara Söderberg, and more to come, from a hundred floors above us in the Tower of Song.

---

[39] Dwyer, "Sure, Men Liked Leonard Cohen."

CHAPTER 17

The Counterculture

Sarah Hill

"DON'T TRUST ANYONE OVER THIRTY" RAN A POPULAR 1960s slogan.[1] As pure a statement of generational shift as imaginable, it was one of the key phrases that solidified a sense in the popular imagination that the counterculture – an amorphous group of activists, artists, and dropouts – was a dangerous new youth movement. Generations are not always clear markers of belonging, however, and the idea of "the" singular "counterculture" is difficult to sustain, as is the suggestion that the people aligned with countercultural ideals were uniformly younger than thirty. Leonard Cohen is such a person. Well into his thirties by the time he released his debut album in 1967, Cohen was an unlikely pop star by most metrics of the decade. In this chapter I will track Cohen's association with the counterculture through contemporary accounts of his creative process and his reflections on the 1960s across the span of his career.

The term *counterculture* was first coined by Theodore Roszak in 1968:

> What is special about the generational transition we are in is the scale on which it is taking place and the depth of antagonism it reveals. Indeed, it

---

[1] According to an uncredited article in the *Berkeley Daily Planet* (April 6, 2000), Free Speech Movement figure Jack Weinberg uttered the phrase while being interviewed in November 1964 "primarily to get rid of a reporter who was bothering him" and to counter the suggestion that the Communist Party was somehow the driving force behind the rise in student activism. The phrase was repeated by Ralph Gleason, jazz critic for the *San Francisco Chronicle*, and invoked in variation by activists throughout the 1960s to embed more deeply the idea of a generation gap. See www.berkeleydailyplanet.com/issue/2000-04-06/article/759.

would hardly seem an exaggeration to call what we see arising among the young a "counter culture." Meaning: a culture so radically disaffiliated from the mainstream assumptions of our society that it scarcely looks to many as a culture at all, but takes on the alarming appearance of a barbaric intrusion.[2]

By the time Roszak published *The Making of a Counter Culture*, "hippies" had entered mainstream North American consciousness: they were long-haired creatures, living communally, espousing drug use and free love, rejecting the social norms of monogamy and capitalism. The hippies did not emerge from the soil fully formed, however: their ideological predecessors were the beatniks, a generation of iconoclasts driven by a love of jazz, sexual depravity, and amphetamines, whose manifestos included Allen Ginsberg's *Howl* (1956) and Jack Kerouac's *On the Road* (1957). At the same time, Aldous Huxley's *The Doors of Perception* (1954) and Alan Watts's *The Way of Zen* (1958) signaled a shift towards a new psychedelic consciousness fueled by the use of hallucinogenic drugs such as peyote, mescaline, psilocybin, and LSD-25. The ultimate countercultural text, however, was *The Psychedelic Experience* (1964), written by Timothy Leary, Ralph Metzner, and Richard Alpert, a guide to the process of ego loss and spiritual rebirth associated with an acid trip. Although for many people acid consumption was simply recreational, for many others it was the first step on a quest for higher consciousness. The desire for experiences outside of the strictures of postwar conservative society was no longer merely a subcultural concern: for the 1960s and beyond, the radical shifts in creative and personal expression, in politics, and in lifestyle ultimately became mainstream.

It is impossible, therefore, to insist that people aged out of membership in either the beatnik or hippie movement, or that they were ever too old to join. And given the status of some key figures of the counterculture – in the 1960s, Ralph Metzner and Richard Alpert were in their thirties; Allen Ginsberg and Timothy Leary were in their forties – clearly, age was just a number. That warning against "trusting" people over thirty did not reckon with the wisdom accrued in "older age." Into this mix I would

---

[2] Theodore Roszak, *The Making of a Counter Culture: Reflections on the Technocratic Society and Its Youthful Opposition* (Garden City, NY: Anchor Books, 1969), 42.

like to add Leonard Cohen. Born into the same generation as Ralph Metzner and Richard Alpert, working the literary seam between beatniks and hippies, and ultimately releasing his debut album at the ripe old age of thirty-three, Leonard Cohen defies any suggestion of countercultural belonging. As I aim to show in this chapter, however, he remained in bemused orbit around the myth of the 1960s for the duration of his long career. As he told a reporter in 1988 who asked him what the 1960s "meant" to him, Leonard Cohen replied:

> There are very few singers who have survived even at my modest level who've had to bear so completely a tag of being connected to a certain decade or movement. I was never part of that movement or any other. This was not an intention, but I feel my work reveals a radical independence from most of the things that were going on. If I wasn't such a thick-skinned chap I might have gotten depressed after reading a few hundred reviews that said I was obsolete, that my sensibility was flower-power.[3]

BEFORE "THE 60S": BEATNIKS AND BOHEMIANS

Leonard Cohen made his first trip to the Greek island of Hydra in the spring of 1960. There he fell immediately into the community of expatriates centered around Australian writers Charmian Clift and George Johnston. Hydra in the 1960s was the same kind of bohemian enclave that later gelled in San Francisco in the mid 1960s: a community of like-minded people, living simply and cheaply on the outer edges of the "real world."

> Hydra in the early 60s was ... a golden age of artists. We weren't beatniks, and the hippies hadn't been invented yet, and we thought of ourselves as kind of international bohemians or travellers, because people came from all over the world with an artistic intent. There was an atmosphere there that was very exciting and I think touched everyone who was there. There were revolutions going on in literature, and there was the sexual revolution which we thought we'd won and we probably lost, and

---

[3] Mat Snow, "Leonard Cohen: A Mercy Mission with ... the Man with a Golden Voice," *Sounds* (February 20, 1988).

a number of us ... began to examine different spiritual paths like Tibetan Buddhism and the I Ching.[4]

The reference to a "revolution in literature" suggests a universal shift in style and approach. Although the work of Kerouac and Ginsberg were formative influences on a new generation of poets and musicians, this did not necessarily translate to a universal shift away from formal structures. Cohen was already a published poet with a well-established voice in his native Montreal, though decidedly not on the cutting-edge as he felt the beatniks perceived themselves to be:[5]

> I was writing very rhymed, polished verses and they were in open revolt against that kind of form, which they associated with the oppressive literary establishment ... I felt that our little group in Montreal was wilder and freer and that we were on the right track, and we, in our provincial self-righteousness, felt that they were not on the right track and that they ... weren't honouring the tradition as we felt we were.[6]

There is more than a little self-deprecation at work in this memory, and a clear and abiding respect for the poets whose work he refers to here, but Leonard Cohen, in that 1960s moment and in the later act of retrospection, seemed always to find himself floating on the outside of artistic movements and trends. This has little to do with a generational detachment – Cohen was only eight years younger than Allen Ginsberg – and more to do with a deeper attachment to tradition and precedent. Leonard Cohen and Allen Ginsberg did become friends, and Ginsberg introduced Cohen to the Beat poet Gregory Corso; but Cohen's own spheres of influence remained closer to his Montreal roots.[7]

---

[4] Steve Sanfield, quoted in Sylvie Simmons, *I'm Your Man: The Life of Leonard Cohen* (London: Vintage, 2013), 83–84.

[5] For a full account, see Simon Warner, *Text and Drugs and Rock 'n' Roll: The Beats and Rock Culture* (New York; London: Bloomsbury, 2014); and Simon Warner and Jim Sampas (eds.), *Kerouac on Record: A Literary Soundtrack* (New York; London: Bloomsbury, 2018).

[6] Leonard Cohen, quoted in Simmons, *I'm Your Man*, 57.

[7] Leonard Cohen also saw Jack Kerouac give a reading at a jazz club in New York in 1956, before the publication of his *On the Road*. At the after-party at Allen Ginsberg's apartment, Cohen remembers Kerouac "lying beneath the dining room table 'pretending to listen to jazz'." See Harvey Kubernik, *Leonard Cohen: Everybody Knows* (London: Omnibus Press, 2017), 22.

For all of its distance from the beatnik nuclei of Greenwich Village and San Francisco, Montreal was nonetheless a multicultural city. Hydra in the 1960s, by contrast, was a five-hour boat ride from Athens. Once docked, Cohen found himself on an island without electricity, indoor plumbing, or telephones: the perfect conditions for creative exploration. As Sylvie Simmons notes, Cohen:

> thrived in the Mediterranean climate. Every morning he would rise with the sun, just as the local workmen did, and start his work. After a few hours writing he would walk down the narrow, winding streets, a towel flung over one shoulder, to swim in the sea. While the sun dried his hair, he walked to the market to buy fresh fruit and vegetables, and climbed back up the hill. It was cool inside the old house. He would sit writing at the Johnstons' wooden table until it was too dark to see by the kerosene lamps and candles. At night he walked back again to the port, where there was always someone to talk to.
>
> The ritual, routine and sparsity of this life satisfied him immensely. It felt monastic somehow, except that this was monk-with-benefits; the Hydra arts colony had beaten the hippies to free love by half a decade.[8]

The description of Cohen's life on Hydra echoes the descriptions of hippie life in the Haight-Ashbury later in the decade: sparse, unaffected by the world of international commerce, surrounded by nature, and it prefigures the simplicity that Cohen later embraced at the Mt. Baldy Zen Center, at once a holdover from the countercultural quest for spiritual enlightenment and the simple desire to live with a lightness of being.

The work that Cohen produced while on Hydra is significant for two reasons: first, as the creative result of a countercultural lifestyle, and second, in its misalignment with the radical artistic trends of the period. Cohen's second novel, *Beautiful Losers*, presents a particularly interesting example.[9] Eschewing any traditional sense of storyline, narrative voice, or structural coherence, in *Beautiful Losers* Cohen explores many of the themes that later emerged in his songwriting – love, ecstasy, spiritual connection – landing on the ultimate message that "suffering is madness, but it is also the sacred ground where Man encounters God."[10]

---

[8] Simmons, *I'm Your Man*, 81. [9] First published by Viking Press in 1966.
[10] Richard Goldstein, "Leonard Cohen: Beautiful Creep," *Village Voice* (December 28, 1967).

It was an experimentation in form and style, written in two intensive periods with the aid of amphetamines.[11] Amphetamine use is generally associated more readily with the beatnik subculture than with the hippie counterculture, and *Beautiful Losers* is perhaps more aligned with an earlier moment of experimentation typified by William Burroughs's *Naked Lunch* (1959) than with later postmodern works such as Richard Brautigan's *Trout Fishing in America* (1967) or Thomas Pynchon's *Gravity's Rainbow* (1973). And although the catalog of people, artists or otherwise, overindulging in recreational drug use in the 1960s was already fairly lengthy by midway through the decade, Cohen's own recollections of the experience of writing *Beautiful Losers* are telling:

> I wrote *Beautiful Losers* on Hydra, when I'd thought of myself as a loser, financially, morally, as a lover, and a man. I was wiped out; I didn't like my life. I vowed I would just fill the pages with black or kill myself. After the book was over, I fasted for ten days and flipped out completely. It was my wildest trip. I hallucinated for a week. They took me to a hospital in Hydra. One afternoon, the whole sky was black with storks. They alighted on all the churches and left in the morning ... and I was better. Then, I decided to go to Nashville and become a song writer.[12]

"Flipping out," hallucinating, enduring a "wild" trip: whether Cohen's intention in writing *Beautiful Losers* was to experience the visceral force of liberated creative energy or to purge himself of psychic negativity, his pharmaceutical adventures were entirely typical of the 1960s, as was his desire to float from one artistic pursuit to another. As for songwriting, Cohen did eventually go to Nashville, but his musical career had actually already begun in his "provincial" home of Montreal.

OF THE 1960S: SONGS AND SURVIVAL

The first of Leonard Cohen's songs to reach a wider audience was "Suzanne," in the version recorded by Judy Collins in 1966;[13] the following year Cohen recorded it for his debut album, *Songs of Leonard*

---

[11] See Simmons, *I'm Your Man*, 102.   [12] Goldstein, "Beautiful Creep."
[13] Released on the album *In My Life* (Elektra, 1966).

Cohen (1967). Inspired by the young dancer Suzanne Verdal, the lyrics traverse the spaces between stillness and desire ("And just when you mean to tell her that you have no love to give her"), mind and body ("Then she gets you on her wavelength/ And she lets the river answer that you've always been her lover"). Suzanne emerges in the lyrics as an idealized flower child, "wearing rags and feathers," seeking beauty "among the garbage and the flowers," reflecting a vision of love to all who see her. These are images that could only have been conjured up in the 1960s. But Leonard Cohen was still remote, geographically and chronologically, from the hippie strongholds of North America, just as the narrative voice in the song remains aloof, observing Suzanne's grace.

The other tracks on *Songs of Leonard Cohen* are similarly observational, their lyrics often couched in metaphor or addressing an unnamed "you." Keeping company with Suzanne and Marianne and the Sisters of Mercy are soldiers and teachers and masters, situated somewhere between the real world and a more heavenly place. These are not unusual themes for a singer-songwriter operating in the 1960s, but Cohen did not have the kind of voice that blended in well with the pervading sound of 1967. As Harvey Kubernik recalls, the first time he heard Cohen's voice over the airwaves of an underground radio station in southern California, it was a "peculiar" voice, "sort of scary, a dirge-like grumble sequenced between the blue-sky harmonies of *Magical Mystery Tour* and the Byrds' *Younger than Yesterday*."[14]

It would be a mistake to assume that all music released in the latter half of the 1960s was uniformly saturated with the acid experience or driven by anti-war protest. There was still a market for acoustic ballads, and *Songs of Leonard Cohen* somehow found its niche:[15]

> Its songs sounded both fresh and ancient, sung with the authority of a man used to being listened to, which he was. Their images and themes – war and betrayal, longing and despair, sexual and spiritual yearning, familiar to readers of his poetry – were in keeping with the rock-music zeitgeist, but the words in which they were expressed were dense, serious and enigmatic.

---

[14] Kubernik, *Everybody Knows*, 9.

[15] This did not necessarily extend to record sales and royalties, however. *Songs of Leonard Cohen* peaked at #83 on the US Billboard 200 and #13 on the UK albums chart.

> There is an hypnotic quality to the album – the cumulative effect of the pace and inflection, the circular guitar, Leonard's unhurried, authoritative voice – through which the songs are absorbed and trusted as much as understood.[16]

Contemporary reviews seemed untroubled by either Cohen's age or his high-minded poetic sensibilities, one reviewer going so far as to call Cohen "one of the most exciting songwriter-performers of today. A sensitive, ruggedly handsome and unapologetically tough-tender young man of our time, Leonard explores and gently teaches ideology of love in his lyrical and universally poignant songs."[17] Here Cohen is a "young man" who nonetheless has enough world experience and wisdom to "gently" teach "ideology of love" to his listeners. His metaphorical lyrics are "universally poignant" rather than opaque or pretentious. For another reviewer, Leonard Cohen was unlike "any other phenomenon": "Cohen is a rarity, if not a scarcity. And though he will always be rare in the true sense of the word, he will be listened to, sung, and read by an ever-increasing entourage, those of the new awareness, those seeking artists of sensitivity."[18]

One of Cohen's "rare" qualities was surely his age. He looked every minute of his thirty-three years in the cover image for *Songs of Leonard Cohen*. More particularly, his lyrics reflected a set of life experiences appropriate to a man of his age. For all the "growing-up" that songwriters like Bob Dylan and Paul Simon might have displayed in their writing across the 1960s, for all of their world travels and international acclaim, Dylan and Simon were still seven years younger than Cohen: "Generational proximity aside, the Zeit does not fuse Cohen and Dylan into a single Geist."[19] This is not to suggest that there was a universal musical taste that determined stylistic "rightness" for the hippie palate; on the contrary, although the era of heavy psychedelic "trip" music was peaking in 1967, there were plenty of people whose

---

[16] Simmons, *I'm Your Man*, 183–84.
[17] Uncredited writer, "New Stars on the Horizon: The Devil's Anvil, the 5th Dimension, Leonard Cohen," *Hit Parader* (September 1967).
[18] Ellen Sander, "Leonard Cohen ... the Man," *Sing Out!* (August 1967).
[19] Todd Gitlin, "Grizzled Minstrels of Angst: Leonard Cohen and Bob Dylan, Forever Old," *The American Scholar* 71, no. 2 (spring 2002): 95–100 at 97.

preferred soundtrack to an acid trip was acoustic folk or classical music, or no music at all. This was not a matter of generational trend, but rather of subjective taste.

The impact of the 1960s is not just measured out by tabs of acid:

> There is in the rising generation at large a new and growing interest in the life of the spirit. At first, no doubt, that interest was the result of the "surprising conversions" produced by drug experience, but by now it is clear that drugs have been only a temporary impetus toward a more abiding concern. The hippie insistence on self-awareness and on the transcendental experience has restored vitality in the mid-twentieth century to those ideas of feeling and the sublime which many of us thought had glimmered out at the end of the Victorian era.[20]

Leonard Cohen's 1960s creative and personal life certainly reflect "the life of the spirit." Although his drug experiences in the 1960s were not entirely in sync with the pervading quest for expanded consciousness, and although his work did not conform stylistically to psychedelic aesthetic, it explored the "transcendental experience" in all its possible manifestations.

OUT OF "THE 60S": REMINISCENCE AND RETROSPECTION

Cohen later asserted, "I don't think the sixties ever began. I think the whole sixties lasted maybe fifteen or twenty minutes in somebody's mind. I saw it move very, very quickly into the marketplace. I don't think there were any sixties."[21] *Songs of Leonard Cohen* was released at a transitional time for the counterculture: in October 1967 the hippies of the Haight-Ashbury held a ceremonial "Death of Hippie," an acknowledgment that the co-opting of the countercultural lifestyle by the mainstream culture had rendered it just another fashion trend absent all signification.[22] The

---

[20] Leonard Wolf, *Voices from the Love Generation* (Boston: Little, Brown, 1968), 271–72.
[21] Leonard Cohen, speaking in 1992, quoted in Kubernik, *Everybody Knows*, 80.
[22] I cover the end of the hippie dream and its after-effects in *San Francisco and the Long 60s* (New York: Bloomsbury, 2016). For more on the co-optation of "hip," see Thomas Frank, *The Conquest of Cool: Business Culture, Counterculture, and the Rise of Hip Consumerism* (Chicago: University of Chicago Press, 1997).

political turmoil of 1968 was followed in 1969 by the Woodstock Festival, long mythologized as the ultimate celebration of the Aquarian Age, and then by the Altamont Festival, the free concert punctuated by a violence that represented the symbolic "end" of the 1960s.[23] But there were two residual "hippie" events in 1970 that tied Leonard Cohen to the counterculture. First was his performance at the Isle of Wight Festival in August; second was the death of Janis Joplin in October.

The 1970 Isle of Wight Festival was the third and largest iteration of the event, and also the most politically and socially fractious. Although it was a commercial disaster – the open-air site was vulnerable to gate-crashers, and following destructive pressure by many thousands who felt that music should be "free," the promoters allowed everybody in, with or without a ticket – the weekend did feature many indelible performances, from folk to rock and everywhere in between.[24] And as with Woodstock before it, some of those indelible performances happened in the middle of the night.

Leonard Cohen was the penultimate act of the festival weekend, taking the stage after Jethro Tull, Jimi Hendrix, and Joan Baez, and just before Richie Havens, whose set greeted the dawn. It is difficult to understand the programming logic behind this particular run of acts, and more difficult to imagine the focus required of a crowd of 600,000 people to hear Leonard Cohen across that sea of humanity.[25] One reporter suggested that "he seems such a private singer, his music speaking to its listeners on such personal terms that it's best heard in comparative seclusion."[26] For Cohen himself, performing at the Isle of Wight

---

[23] For more detail, see the documentary films *Woodstock* (dir. Michael Wadleigh, 1970) and *Gimme Shelter* (dir. Albert Maysles, David Maysles, and Charlotte Zwerin, 1970).

[24] See Joni Mitchell dealing with audience disruption and hecklers during her set, and offering twenty-first-century analysis of the event, in the documentary *Both Sides Now: Live at the Isle of Wight Festival 1970* (dir. Murray Lerner, 2018), and on the opposite end of the genre spectrum, the Who's set, *Live at the Isle of Wight Festival 1970* (dir. Murray Lerner, 1998).

[25] His full performance was captured on *Leonard Cohen: Live at the Isle of Wight 1970* (dir. Murray Lerner, 2009).

[26] Mark Plummer, Michael Watts, Chris Welch, and Richard Williams, "The Isle of Wight Festival: Five Days That Rocked Britain," *Melody Maker* (September 5, 1970).

Festival had been a strange prospect, and he admitted to feeling "a little nervous" about it:

> There are so many people on, and so many that I want to see. I'm not a top rank star you know ... This is something that has been on my mind for a long time recently. I have thought much about it. You know what the greatest thing would be? It would be to play a concert in front of 50,000 middle-aged people. God, that would be so great. ... God these older people really do know what they are talking about. They have wisdom. Young ideas could be mixed with them. Older people could add mature things. Oh yes, if we could get together. We must you know, we really must.[27]

Cohen moves seamlessly here from imposter syndrome to age denial. If the life expectancy of a North American male in 1970 was roughly seventy-one years, then Leonard Cohen, aged thirty-six, was already middle-aged. His song lyrics imparted a certain wisdom accrued through his upbringing, social status, and life experience. By playing at the Isle of Wight Festival Leonard Cohen was "mixing" his ideas with "young ideas," and adding "mature things," and subconsciously preparing for the moment in 2008 when, as an even older man, he took to the Pyramid Stage at the "countercultural" Glastonbury Festival. But one year after the Isle of Wight Festival, Cohen remarked: "[The guy who ran that Isle of Wight Festival in 1970] was complaining about me, not about my playing but about me. I read somewhere that he called me a 'boring old drone.' Well, that's an honest reaction."[28]

Cohen's singular approach to the delivery of melody may have struck some ears as drone-like, but that belied the emotional and sensual charge of his lyrics. His first two albums recount relationships of varying sorts with various women – Marianne, Suzanne, Sisters of Mercy, Lady Midnight, Nancy – who remained suspended in their 1960s incarnations.[29] But one song from his 1974 album *New Skin for the*

---

[27] Roy Hollingworth, "Leonard Cohen: 'The Greatest Thing Would Be to Play a Concert in front of Fifty Thousand Middle-Aged People'," *Melody Maker* (September 5, 1970).

[28] Roy Hollingworth, "Leonard Cohen: The Cohen Songs You'll Never Hear," *Melody Maker* (March 4, 1972).

[29] This has presented problems for at least one male critic, who mused: "It's strange to consider that many of the women who populate his earlier songs, whose names still

Old Ceremony offers an additional, possibly more significant, backward glance at the 1960s.

Janis Joplin (1943–70) was one of the original hippie superstars. Launched onto the national stage in 1967 with Big Brother and the Holding Company at the Monterey Pop Festival, she became a metonym for the San Franciscan counterculture itself: deeply committed to the Haight community, sexually emancipated, musically and sensually voracious. Cohen met Joplin in the spring of 1968 and immortalized their assignation in the song "Chelsea Hotel No. 2." Although she was an anonymous "you" in the lyric, she was "famous," her "heart was a legend," and though she and Cohen were "ugly" they still "have the music"; it would not have been difficult for a contemporary listener to conjure a face out of the imagery. Once Cohen wrapped Joplin's name into his onstage banter, however, their brief encounter became just another tale in the debauched annals of the Chelsea Hotel.

Cohen and Joplin were operating in different wings of the same business, so were bound to have crossed paths at some point. The lyrics of "Chelsea Hotel No. 2" have as much to do with the trappings of the music industry ("we were running for the money and the flesh") as they do regret at the extinction of one bright flame ("you got away, didn't you babe?").[30] Though the opening couplet paints an enduring image of Joplin servicing Cohen, the final couplet is a blunt dismissal of their encounter: "I remember you well in the Chelsea Hotel/ That's all, I don't even think of you that often." But what is less well-circulated than the lyrics of "Chelsea Hotel No. 2" is Janis Joplin's own abiding memory of that particular night:

> Sometimes you're with someone and you're convinced that they have something to tell you . . . And then all of a sudden about four o'clock in the morning you realize that, flat ass, this motherfucker's just lying there.

---

evoke a fancy-free youth, are now middle-aged mothers." It was not, apparently, strange to consider that Leonard Cohen was still singing about these women in his fifties. See Steve Turner, "Leonard Cohen: The Profits of Doom," *Q* (April 1988).

[30] For more on the various changes to the lyrics and the attendant representation of Janis Joplin in "Chelsea Hotel No. 2," see Stephen Scobie, "Racing the Midnight Train: Leonard Cohen in Performance," *Canadian Literature* 152–53 (spring/summer 1997): 52–68.

> He's not balling me. I mean, that really happened to me. Really heavy, like slam-in-the-face it happened. Twice. Jim Morrison and Leonard Cohen. And it's strange, 'cause they were the only two that I can think of, like prominent people, that I tried to ... without really liking them up front, just because I knew who they were and wanted to know them. And then they both gave me nothing. I don't know what that means. Maybe it just means they were on a bummer.[31]

Cohen did not need Janis Joplin to provide him with countercultural validation, but she essentially does so here. In the 1970s Cohen often prefaced this song with a story about Joplin "mistaking" him for Kris Kristofferson during the fateful elevator ride from the Chelsea lobby that ended on Cohen's "unmade bed"; but according to Joplin, Cohen was a target and an ultimately disappointing conquest.

When asked to reflect on the 1960s during a press junket for the release of *New Skin for Old Ceremony*, Leonard Cohen again acknowledged his chronological distance from the counterculture:

> LEONARD COHEN: I think that people are interested in the phenomenon of survival, and one has, in a sense, become an old-timer on that scene, and one has survived.
>
> DANNY FIELDS: Do you feel guilty about having survived?
>
> LC: Not at all. I was already into my middle thirties when I came into this scene.
>
> DF: And you were never victimized by it like, let's say, Janis was?
>
> LC: She was just a girl. She was in her twenties when she died.
>
> DF: Twenty-seven.
>
> LC: So it really happened to her when she was twenty-five, maybe even earlier, when she became able to command huge audiences. That's quite young. I believe that between twenty-five and thirty-five, an enormous chunk of undigested experience tends to filter out. I mean, anything can happen to any of us to crush the spirit and make us destroy ourselves, but just the scene itself – I always did

---

[31] Janis Joplin, speaking in 1969, in Richard Avedon and Doon Arbus, *The Sixties* (New York: Random House, 1999), quoted in Holly George-Warren, *Janis: Her Life and Music* (New York: Simon and Schuster, 2020), 239–40.

have the impression that there was a sense of overdramatization and all the people involved: the artists, the journalists, the critics, taking this thing a bit too seriously.[32]

Perhaps Cohen's ability not to take the 1960s "too seriously" is what truly separated him from the counterculture. But his desire to understand deeper truths chimed exactly with the general turn towards Eastern spiritual traditions and practices that resulted from the acid "awakening." Indeed, from the 1970s to his death, Cohen balanced his traditional Jewish faith with a devotion to Zen practice, driven by a deep and abiding spiritual friendship with his master, Roshi Kyozan Joshu Sasaki. In his own way, Cohen embodied the larger messages of the counterculture – "advancing the struggle for human liberation" – in his lyrics and in his life, well into the twenty-first century.[33]

---

[32] Danny Fields, "Leonard Cohen Interviewed," *SoHo Weekly News* (December 5, 1974).
[33] Michael P. Lerner, *Counterculture & Revolution* (New York: Random House, 1972), xvi.

CHAPTER 18

Politics

Insincerely L. Cohen

David Boucher

LATER IN HIS LIFE LEONARD COHEN LOOSELY TRANSLATED Lorca's "The Faithless Wife"[1] and published it in *Book of Longing*, adding "After a poem by Lorca."[2] For dramatic effect the title changes to "The Night in Santiago," and appears in a much-shortened version on the posthumous album *Thanks for the Dance* (2019). In both versions we find the lines, which are not in Lorca, and which may serve as a fitting epitaph: "You were born to judge the world. Forgive me but I wasn't." In his public persona, and to a considerable degree with his friends and lovers, Cohen refused to express strong political opinions, or he would equivocate to the extent that it wasn't clear which side he was on. His main priority was gratification, both carnal and spiritual. He said, for example, after seeing Nico, Velvet Underground's lead singer, at Warhol's club "La Dom," he forgot about the "good society" and followed her obsessively all around New York.[3]

It is almost a cliché to contend that Leonard Cohen is a man of many contradictions. He was a misogynist who loved women; an intensely religious man obsessed with the profane; and an anarchic hedonist and strict disciplinarian. His friend Irvin Layton described him as a self-loathing narcissist.[4] This self-loathing is forcefully proclaimed on his *Live Songs*

---

[1] Federico García Lorca, *Selected Poems*, trans. J. L. Gill and Stephen Spender (London: Hogarth Press, 1947), 25–26.
[2] Leonard Cohen, *Book of Longing* (New York: HarperCollins, 2006), 147–48.
[3] Leonard Cohen, quoted in Jim Devlin (ed.), *In His Own Words, Leonard Cohen* (London: Omnibus Press, 1998), 84.
[4] An oral history taken from interviews with over 400 of Cohen's friends and acquaintances has been compiled in three volumes by Michael Posner, *Leonard Cohen, Untold Stories: The Early Years* (Toronto: Simon and Schuster, 2020), vol. I; *Leonard Cohen,*

(1973). In "Please Don't Pass Me By (A Disgrace)," recorded in London in 1970, Cohen exhorts the audience to return home transformed. He tells them, don't be the person who came: "I'm not going to be. I can't stand him! I can't stand who I am."

Like Jean-Jacques Rousseau in *The Confessions*, filled with remorse and self-loathing, Cohen looks for redemption.[5] In the case of Rousseau, it was by writing *The Social Contract*, encouraging society to transform itself by formulating and following the General Will.[6] In Cohen's case it was by retreating to a Buddhist monastery and losing himself completely in contemplation, and the landscape of the inner self. Songwriting for Cohen is not merely the exorcising of demons, but also the calming of the spirit. It is certainly cathartic, serving to purge inner thoughts and feelings. The effect, however, is a severe withdrawal into himself, wounded, flesh torn, with his personality under attack. The completion of each creative phase or projection is also the disintegration of the self, which each time has to be painfully and laboriously rebuilt. The process invoked is whatever works – Prozac, Deseryl, the synagogue, yoga, or the Buddhist monastery.

In this exploration of Leonard Cohen's political beliefs and expressions, I want first to examine his actions during, and attitudes towards, selected political events and crises, suggesting that far from exhibiting a social or political conscience, he was an extreme individualist, at times delusionally narcissistic, equivocal, and ambivalent. From his early days at McGill University a girlfriend, Freda Gutman, complained that he was a career-driven opportunist who didn't share her social concerns.[7] In the recently published novel and essays, dating from 1956 to 1961, politics are conspicuously absent, except for a contemptuous reference to a "doomed socialist brotherhood."[8]

Untold Stories: From This Broken Hill (Toronto: Simon and Schuster, 2021), vol. II; and *Leonard Cohen, Untold Stories: That's How the Light Gets In* (Toronto: Simon and Schuster, 2022), vol. III. See ibid., vol. I, 49.

[5] Jean-Jacques Rousseau, *The Confessions*, trans. J. M. Cohen (Harmondsworth: Penguin, 1973).

[6] Jean-Jacques Rousseau, *The Social Contract and Other Essays*, trans. Maurice Cranston (Harmondsworth: Penguin, 2012).

[7] See Posner, *Leonard Cohen, Untold Stories*, vol. I, 113.

[8] Leonard Cohen, *A Ballet of Lepers: A Novel and Other Stories* (London: Canongate, 2022), 208.

Many of Cohen's friends believed that he deliberately disguised his political beliefs in order to avoid alienating his audience. The success of the popular song required appealing to as wide a demographic as possible. Barrie Wexler, a Canadian broadcaster, writer, and friend of fifty years, maintained that deep down there were few positions to which Cohen was wedded. He sometimes argued persuasively, as a way of amusing himself, but deep down he didn't really care about having a position.[9] Cohen himself confirmed this in a 1988 interview with John Wilde in *Blitz* magazine: "I've never been very attached to my opinions. I'm not flippant about them but, whenever I hear myself say something, I recognize my own unwillingness to stand behind it."[10]

Cohen knew that the vast majority of his audience was inclined towards the left in politics and would automatically assume that he was too. He certainly didn't want to alienate them, even to the extent of keeping his pride in being a long-standing member of the National Rifle Association (NRA) a closely guarded secret.[11] Willie Aron, an American cantor and friend, claimed Cohen showed his membership card to him and Mordecai Finley a few times. He was undoubtedly a proud NRA member.[12] In fact, he had a fascination with guns for most of his life. In his *Tennessee Notebook* (1968), for example, he included a photograph of a row of guns from an army surplus store. He wrote: "My heart jumped up when I beheld the glass counter with the magic row of revolvers."[13]

If he did or said something that might commit him to a particular side, he quickly qualified it in order to obfuscate where he stood. Even on one of the most unsettling catastrophes to befall New York, 9/11, he is

---

[9] Posner, *Leonard Cohen, Untold Stories*, vol. II, 177.

[10] *Blitz*, www.webheights.net/speakcohen/blitz88.htm. Cf. *Rolling Stone* (November 8, 2001), 7.

[11] Albert Insinger, a Dutch singer and friend, claimed that Cohen loved Ronald Reagan. He reports Cohen telling him that he was "right of right." He says that he was very much a Republican and "completely against gun control." Posner, *Leonard Cohen, Untold Stories,* vol. II, 309.

[12] Ibid., vol. III, 398.

[13] Reproduced in Julian Cox and Jim Shedden (eds.), *Leonard Cohen: Everybody Knows: Inside His Archive* (New York: AGO, 2023), 47. The book was published to coincide with the exhibition "Leonard Cohen: Everybody Knows," organized by the Art Gallery of Ontario (AGO) from December 10, 2022 to April 10, 2023.

noncommittal, expressing opinions that others may think, but, having nothing to say himself, responding by saying: "I wouldn't know/ I'm just holding the fort" ("On That Day," *Dear Heather*, 2004). When he appears to be making a strong political statement, he suddenly makes light of it by flippantly undermining it with something highly personal, but trivial in comparison, such as equating torture and killing with all his bad reviews ("Almost Like the Blues," *Popular Problems*, 2014). Or, when talking of the "The Future" (*The Future*, 1992), he said that he had been warning of such a catastrophe for fifteen or twenty years. As far as he was concerned, the catastrophe had already happened. No one could be in any doubt that we are in the flood: the lights have gone out and there's something deeply wrong with society. Making light of the seriousness of his remarks, when asked what inspired the song he answered: "I left my antidepressant pills at home." The redeeming features of the song are that it "is set to a hot little dance track. It's an apocalyptic dance, but nonetheless, you can move to it."[14]

In 1978 Cohen had been promised that his photograph would grace an edition of *Maclean's* magazine in Canada. Instead, the cover featured a photograph of Israeli Prime Minister Menachem Begin and Egypt's Anwar Sadat, at the time of the peace negotiations at Camp David, which were to result in the Peace Accords. A friend of Cohen's, Sandra Anderson, a Montreal psychologist, said that she had never seen him so angry. She was surprised that he thought a photograph of him took precedence over the prospect of peace in the Middle East: "He just didn't get it at all. It was the first time I perceived the massive ego behind the self-effacing, oh-so humble public persona."[15]

The traditional labels of right and left in politics are inadequate and inappropriate to define Cohen. He took no clear ideological stance on any of the major political issues that punctuated his long career, nor was he one for participating in demonstrations, or for overtly condemning political acts. Cohen's friend David Solway commented that "Leonard wasn't really left, he wasn't really right, and he wasn't really center. I found his politics tepid."[16] He said himself in the song "Democracy" (*The Future*, 1992), "I'm

---

[14] Jim Slotek, "Cohen's Future Is Now," *Toronto Sun* (November 19, 1992).
[15] Posner, *Leonard Cohen, Untold Stories,* vol. II, 255.   [16] Ibid., vol. III, 291.

neither left nor right/ I'm just staying home tonight." In fact, he claimed that he was appalled when reviewers starting identifying "Democracy" with the victory of Bill Clinton in the presidential election. It was not that he had something against Clinton, but that his songs should be compared to the longevity of a Volvo, about thirty years. He added, "I just don't like to be identified with transitory events."[17]

Cohen was not someone like Pete Seeger, Tom Paxton, Phil Ochs, Joan Baez, or the early Bob Dylan who was passionately collectivist. Unlike many in the folk scene in Greenwich Village in the early 1960s who were self-congratulatory about their fingerpointing political protest songs and who vociferously supported the downtrodden, Cohen made no strong political stand on civil rights, Vietnam, the nuclear bomb, or on anything else. He occasionally made uncharacteristic outbursts. Interviewed by Danny Fields, Cohen suddenly went into a rant, arguing that his peers who were opposed to the Vietnam War had been brainwashed and poisoned by the communists. To believe in the particular vison they peddle is a failure of imagination, spiritually and psychically. We all know, he maintained, "that with that particular vision there comes a certain kind of harshness ... intolerance ... They put you in jail for smoking grass in America for a little bit of time, but in Cuba they put you in for good."[18]

Cohen exhibited no deeply held social convictions. Instead, he gravitated towards the Beats, who were radically individualist, harboring a thinly veiled admiration for their anti-establishment bohemian anarchistic individualism.[19] They were not a political movement, in that they had no manifesto for change, but they were utopian in believing that the citizen-artists would become the leaders in a new society.

Cohen initially unsuccessfully sought out the Beats when he first lived in New York in 1957, establishing only a tangential acquaintance with them. He prided himself on being the Beat of Belmont Avenue. He had met Dylan Thomas at McGill in 1952, the poet who Lawrence Ferlinghetti

[17] Slotek, "Cohen's Future Is Now."
[18] Posner, *Leonard Cohen, Untold Stories*, vol. II, 147.
[19] Many of them, such as Ginsberg and Kerouac, like Cohen, were curious about exotic religions and spiritualities, eventually finding a home in Buddhism. Elizabeth Jones, "The Beats and Eastern Religion," *Peace Review* 7, no. 1 (1995) 61–65, https://doi.org/10.1080/10402659508425853.

credits with being the progenitor of San Francisco performance poetry.[20] Cohen was awestruck by Thomas.[21] Cohen's alter ego, Breavman, in *The Favourite Game*, is described as "a kind of mild Dylan Thomas, talent and behavior modified for Canadian tastes."[22] Cohen himself described Thomas's attraction for his generation: "Dylan Thomas was the great voice of poetry when I was at college. We (all the young poets) were all intrigued with his fame, his genius, his drinking, his unconditional sense of social irresponsibility."[23] Subsequently Cohen's view of the Beat glamorization of drugs was that it was a dangerous experiment that had disastrous consequences, but that for some it may have served a purpose, and that for a few it had led to some revelations.

CUBA, THE YOM KIPPUR WAR, AND GREECE UNDER THE COLONELS

Cohen's visit to Cuba for political reasons and his involvement in the Arab–Israeli War were aberrations from what was otherwise a life of political self-denial, an unwillingness to become involved in things overtly political. The Cuban Revolution of 1959 was romanticized by the growing counterculture that threatened the Cold War politics that dominated the West in the 1950s. Che Guevara and Fidel Castro were the great revolutionary heroes who overthrew the US puppet regime of Fulgencio Batista on the Caribbean island. The socialist, anti-imperialist government established by Castro had the allure of revolution and social justice in the face of capitalist exploitation. In 1961 Castro's government was just two years old, and very much under threat of a counterrevolution that the United States was covertly trying to foment. Cohen was curious to experience Castro's Cuba, yet his motives for travelling there are far from clear. The Spanish poet García Lorca, Cohen's poetic hero, had visited

---

[20] Lawrence Ferlinghetti and Nancy J. Peters, *Literary San Francisco* (New York: HarperCollins, 1980), 166.

[21] Email from Marianne Macdonald, a fellow student with Cohen, to Jeff Towns of "Dylan's Books," Swansea, Friday June 13, 2008. In the possession of the recipient.

[22] Leonard Cohen, *The Favorite Game* (Toronto: McClelland and Stewart, 1994 [1963]), 108.

[23] Email to the author dated September 20, 2004.

Cuba for three months in 1930. Restless and disillusioned with the Canadian poetry scene in comparison with that of America, which he had experienced briefly at Columbia University in 1957, Cohen sought adventure. Cuba held out the prospect of experiencing danger and excitement. It was, he claimed, alluding to Lorca's death at the hands of the fascists, his Spanish Civil War.[24]

In 1964 he claimed that "I was very interested in what it really meant for men to carry arms and kill other men ... The real truth is that I wanted to kill or be killed."[25] Havana was decaying, but many of the decadent bars and entertainments had re-emerged in order to reverse the economic decay. The semi-nocturnal existence Cohen had lived in Montreal continued in Cuba. He fraternized with petty criminals, gamblers, pimps, and prostitutes. He also socialized with artists and writers who complained of political oppression and the regulation of artistic freedom. He was by no stretch of the imagination a communist sympathizer when he went to Havana. By the time he left he was passionately anti-communist.[26]

In Montreal, he had been fascinated with the communists because of their paranoia and absolute conviction. In a poem, many years later, he says, "I admired the Communists/ For their pig-headed devotion/ To something absolutely wrong."[27] They found him a privileged, pretentious *poseur*. The American communists that Cohen met in Havana were, to his mind, quite obnoxious. They thought him disingenuous, insincere, and a "bourgeois individualist." For them he was a symbol of the decadence and decline of capitalism. He could never quite affect the style of a revolutionary, and his family did, after all, own a clothing factory.[28]

Cohen's position in Havana became less and less comfortable. Tensions were mounting over the prospect of an American invasion. The fears were

---

[24] Posner, *Leonard Cohen, Untold Stories*, vol. I, 182.
[25] Devlin (ed.), *In His Own Words*, 23.
[26] Tom Chaffin, "Conversations from a Room," *Canadian Forum* (August–September 1983), 10.
[27] Leonard Cohen, "The Party Was Over Then Too," *Book of Longing*, 26.
[28] Richard Goldstein, "Leonard Cohen: Beautiful Creep," *Village Voice* (December 28, 1967), 20. Reprinted in *Leonard Cohen: The Artist and His Critics*, ed. Michael Gnarowski (Toronto: McGraw-Hill, 1967), 43.

justified. On April 17, 1961, there was an American-supported invasion at the Bay of Pigs in an attempt to overthrow Castro.[29] It was an operation that went disastrously wrong. Understandably, Cuban troops were vigilant, and they were suspicious of anyone with an American-sounding accent. Cohen "escaped" from Cuba on April 26 after being detained at the airport. It is not surprising that he was detained. He had grown a Che Guevara–style beard and wore paramilitary clothing, which in the circumstances immediately drew attention to him.

His motives for going to Cuba were ambivalent, but his conclusions about the society and regime were not. During the Cuban Missile Crisis of 1963, Cohen was accused of being pro-Castro and anti-American. He defended himself by claiming that he had gone to Cuba to see a socialist revolution at first hand, and not blindly to support it. In fact, what he found was an oppressive and repugnant regime. It was obsessed with control by censorship and suppression of individualism in favor of collectivist policies. The regime wanted to suppress "bourgeois intellectuals," among whom Cohen was aptly categorized. He reveled in the excitement and energy of revolution, but recoiled from the loud, obtrusive anthems and overbearing propaganda posters. In 1976 he acknowledged that much of what he saw in Cuba was great, but for him personally "everything was too public and up-front. You had to participate all the time and I'm just a bourgeois individualist."[30] Cuba stood against everything that Cohen was, an individualistic bourgeois and an aesthete. Capitalism, he observed in 1993, with all its faults, had a more benign grip on people than any other system yet invented.[31]

He repeated his experiment in danger again in early October 1973 when he flew, at the age of thrity-nine, to Tel Aviv from Athens to join the Israeli army a day after Yom Kippur, the Day of Atonement, which was October 6. There was little sense outside of Palestine, at this time, of a Palestinian people. They were simply Jordanians to the west, and the idea of a two-state solution had not arisen. Israel was under attack from Syria and Egypt, with a coalition of individual sympathizers across the Middle East, against which Cohen believed that Jews must stick together.[32] The Israelis should

---

[29] Ira B. Nadel, *Various Positions: A Life of Leonard Cohen* (London: Bloomsbury, 1996), 94.
[30] Devlin (ed.), *In His Own Words*, 23.   [31] Ibid., 60.
[32] Posner, *Leonard Cohen, Untold Stories*, vol. II, 109.

have anticipated the attack. The Egyptians had been mobilizing troops for days, and King Hussein of Jordan secretly alerted Prime Minister Golda Meir to the prospect of an imminent assault.

Initially, it seems, Cohen wanted to enlist in the Israeli army, and with characteristic bravado he claimed that he wanted to stop Egypt's bullets. He did not take his guitar to Israel and had toyed with the idea of helping out by working on a kibbutz in order to free up some younger men to fight.[33] Instead, he was recruited in a Tel Aviv bar to join an entertainment troupe that would travel the front line and play for the soldiers. He was there for nearly three months, playing a borrowed guitar and giving anything up to eight short, impromptu concerts a day.[34] In Ismailia, Cohen shared cognac with the Israeli general and future prime minister Ariel Sharon. Cohen's friend, Barry Wexler, claimed that Cohen had fantasized about become a general himself, and of taking Sharon's job. He thought of exchanging his pen for the role of the Lion of the Desert.[35] Cohen refers to the meeting in his notes written during the war suggesting that he silently demanded "how dare you" of Sharon, who didn't repent.[36]

There is no reason to doubt his commitment to the survival of Israel as a separate state, nor his desire to stand with its people in a crisis. He lived through World War Two and was fourteen in 1948 when the Jewish State was created. In the 1967 Arab–Israeli War both Cohen and his close friend and mentor Irvin Layton had contacted the Israeli embassy in Toronto to enquire how to enlist. Both were told their services were not required. According to Layton's wife, Aviva, this was before her husband and Cohen had any political stance on Israel one way or another.[37] After the Six-Day War of 1967, he supported Arab demands for Israel to return the captured territories.

Cohen seemed to be excited by the danger of war, romanticizing it, but the sight of wounded Egyptians disturbed him and caused him to become less enthusiastic. Of the Yom Kippur War, Cohen wrote to his sister from

---

[33] Matti Friedman, *Who by Fire: Leonard Cohen in the Sinai* (New York: Spiegel and Grau, 2022), 58.
[34] Liel Leibovitz, *A Broken Hallelujah: Leonard Cohen's Secret Chord* (Dingwall, Scotland: Sandstone Press, 2014), 128.
[35] Posner, *Leonard Cohen, Untold Stories*, vol. II, 109. This is what Sharon was known as.
[36] Friedman, *Who by Fire*, 143.   [37] Friedman, *Who by Fire*, 38.

Israel in 1973, describing it as "Tragic human madness."[38] At the beginning of the adventure Cohen wrote a draft of "Lover, Lover, Lover," and performed it. Its early iteration is decidedly partisan, writing "I went down to the desert/ To help my brothers fight." He later replaced "my brothers" with "the children" before discarding the verse altogether.[39] Those soldiers who heard him sing the song in Israel were proud that Cohen explicitly identified with them. The commitment to the Israelis is missing in the recorded version, and after the war he avoided the question of partisanship altogether. Onstage he would acknowledge where he had written the song, but added that he wrote it for soldiers on both sides of the conflict.[40] The war was something he preferred to forget. He rarely spoke of it, perhaps because in victory Israel came under more scrutiny from the international community, which became less sympathetic to its predicament.

After the war Cohen flew back to the Greek island of Hydra, where he had been living with his lover, Suzanne Elrod, and their son, Adam. Cohen wrote an account of this time in an unfinished manuscript that has only recently been unearthed in the archives of his publisher, McClelland and Stewart.[41] Again his motives for going were ambivalent and highly personalized.[42] Writing of his predicament on Hydra through a thinly veiled character in the story, and revealing a very unpleasant side rarely seen in public, Cohen wrote in various passages of how much he felt trapped; of how intensely he hated his "wife"; of how stopping Egyptian bullets, and the excitement of war, were preferable to being on Hydra with Suzanne and Adam. He wrote: "I was listening to the war between the Arabs and Jews. I wanted to go fight and die because she was so ugly to live with."[43] In *Death of a Lady's Man* Cohen is vicious in his attack on his "wife" Suzanne. In "This Marriage" he writes: "Fuck you, I said. You shit. Stop screaming. I can't stand it."[44] His immediate reason

---

[38] Postcard reproduced in Cox and Shedden (eds.), *Leonard Cohen Everybody Knows*, 59.
[39] Friedman, *Who by Fire*, 79. [40] Ibid., 138.
[41] Ibid., 6. The archive is housed in McMaster University, Hamilton. Parts of the manuscript are published by Friedman, *Who by Fire*, for the first time. See 29–36 and 43–49.
[42] Sylvie Simmons, *I'm Your Man: The Life of Leonard Cohen* (London: Jonathan Cape, 2012), 261.
[43] Cohen in Friedman, *Who by Fire*, 32.
[44] Leonard Cohen, *Death of a Lady's Man* (London: Black Spring Press, 1995), 54. First published in 1978.

for going to the war, then, was to escape from the situation he was in on Hydra, and not because he was committed to the cause. Witnessing war, however, seemed to have momentarily spurred him to a firmer commitment to his relationship with Elrod: "seeing what happens to people in war, I thought I'd try to make a go of it, of this situation."[45]

Given his close association with Greece from 1960, owning a house on Hydra, during particularly turbulent political times, including the right-wing Coup of the Colonels, one might have expected him to take a public stand against the brutal dictatorship of which some of his acquaintances on Hydra were victims. In 1967 a dictatorship led by Georgios Papadopoulos overthrew the democratically elected Georgios Papandreou, who fled the country and exiled himself in Canada, where he had a great deal of support from left-wing intellectuals. Papadopoulos established a military junta and assumed dictatorial powers. His regime was authoritarian, anti-communist, and ultranationalist. It replaced the monarchy with a republic, elevating Papandreou to the position of president. Greeks were subjected to the right-wing dictatorship of the colonels from 1967 to 1974. Cohen was later criticized for having enjoyed the so-called fruits of democracy under Papandreou and for not taking a stand against the colonels who overthrew him.

From the time of the coup, and unlike many of his Canadian compatriots who publicly supported and fundraised for Papandreou the deposed prime minister, Cohen did not speak out against the military regime; nor did he publicly support it. He was criticized in 1969 for continuing to live in Greece, despite the repressive rule of the colonels. Cohen gave the impression that he had moved out of his house in Greece, after the coup, in protest against the regime. This was not the case. He continued to visit regularly, and Suzanne Elrod lived in their house there. Again, he personalized the issue, defending himself by saying that it was no big deal to vacation in a country ruled by fascists. He had a house and friends there and didn't consider it collaboration with the regime.[46]

---

[45] Friedman, *Who by Fire*, 171. Quoting an unpublished conversation between Sylvie Simmons and Cohen decades later.

[46] Nadel, *Various Positions*, 176.

His public explanation was that there was something in the country and in himself that changed, and he rarely went to Greece after that. The implication was that he took a stand against the military seizure of power. That was not entirely true. He returned to Hydra almost every year when the colonels were still in power.[47]

Privately, as early as 1961, from a purely self-interested point of view, Cohen complained to his sister Esther that everywhere was going communist and stamping out corruption and poverty. The West was too expensive, and anyway it was rigid and hysterical. What chance was there for a fun-loving literary parasite in this world.[48] Again in 1963 he was expressing concerns. He was worried about the political situation in Greece under Papandreou. He already sensed that the political situation was leaning towards the right. Greece was becoming a more dangerous place to live, because the opposition was being driven to desperate measures. Demonstrations were brutally suppressed, and Cohen was afraid that bohemians like himself would not be tolerated for long. In a letter to Esther, Cohen quotes a poem on tyranny by the Hungarian poet Gyula Illyés, written in 1956, which Cohen thinks indicative of the regime in Greece. He did not, however, advocate any political stance. Again, his attitude is highly personalized. He was currently living well and would continue to do so until the axe fell. What else could be done?[49]

POLITICS IN THE SONG

Although proud of his early songs, such as "Suzanne" and "So Long, Marianne," Cohen did not wish his most successful compositions to date to define him as a sentimental singer. He insisted that his "songs are political, with a small p."[50] He contended that "if you were going to talk

---

[47] Posner, *Leonard Cohen, Untold Stories*, vol. I, 441–42. [48] Nadal, *Various Positions*, 103.
[49] Leonard Cohen to Esther, June 8, 1963. Leonard Cohen Papers, Box 11, file 12. Thomas Fisher Library, University of Toronto.
[50] Posner, *Leonard Cohen, Untold Stories*, vol. II, 26. Andy Greene, "How Lost Leonard Cohen Doc *Bird on a Wire* Finally Made It to Theaters," *Rolling Stone* (January 19, 2017), www.rollingstone.com/movies/movie-features/how-lost-leonard-cohen-doc-bird-on-a-wire-finally-made-it-to-theaters-123707/. A poor re-edited version was released and had a one-night screening in London in 1973, but Cohen hated it.

about the political aspect of my music I would say that it is the music of personal resistance."[51] While he did not wish to establish a link between his songs and specific events, except for those which he described as *reportage*,[52] such as "Suzanne" (*Songs of Leonard Cohen*, 1967) and "Chelsea Hotel No. 2" (*New Skin for the Old Ceremony*, 1974), many are political in that they portray a dystopian, disturbing, sinister, and dark world, almost Kafkaesque. The power of the imagery, when it works, has a profound and unsettling effect. There is often self-mockery and overstatement, sometimes to the extent of voicing an extreme opinion more for effect than substance. The type of lyric poetry he consciously tries to emulate is what some of his poetic heroes, Rimbaud, Lorca, and Dylan Thomas, strived to achieve. Rimbaud reveled in the derangement of the senses to rupture appearances and attain a deeper reality. Lorca describes it as the poetry of inspiration, which delves into the darkest recesses of humanity and surges through one's veins like ground glass or lacerates the flesh with vicious thorns.[53] Thomas, the self-proclaimed "Rimbaud of Cwmdonkin Drive," expressed the terrifying reality of facing one's own demons. Thomas confessed: "Very much of my poetry is, I know, an enquiry and a terror of fearful expectation, a discovery and facing of fear. I hold a beast, an angel, and a madman in me, and my enquiry is as to their working, and my problem is their subjugation and victory, downthrow and upheaval, and my effort is their self-expression."[54] This is what Cohen alludes to in an interview in 1995, while still at the Zen monastery on Mt. Baldy. He maintained that any impressive piece of work has a subversive element, and it only becomes uncomfortable or disturbing when political and social activity results from it. Subversiveness is one of the most desirable characteristics of a piece of art, because of that feeling of groundlessness you experience in hearing, seeing, or reading it.[55]

---

[51] Harry Rasky, *The Song of Leonard Cohen: Portrait of a Poet, a Friend and a Film* (Oakville, Ontario: Mosaic Press, 2001), 118.

[52] Adrian Deevoy, "All Good Things," *Q Magazine* (February, 20017), 91.

[53] David Boucher and Lucy J. Boucher, *Bob Dylan and Leonard Cohen: Deaths and Entrances* (New York: Bloomsbury, 2021), 247–52 and 274–5.

[54] Dylan Thomas, *The Collected Letters*, new ed., ed. Paul Ferris (London: Dent, 2000), 343–44.

[55] Radio interview with Cindy Buissaillon, August 26, 1995, "Definitely Not Opera," CBC.

There are overt political themes in his work, such as the anti-totalitarian "A Singer Must Die," a song full of bitter irony condemning artistic repression by the state. Cohen adopts the persona of a wearied and worn-down artist whose spirit is broken and who, like the suspect in a criminal interrogation after hours of mental torture, breaks down and confesses not because of guilt, but to experience the relief at the process ending. It is in the context of fear that the singer is resigned to nonresistance – the manner of detention, one's own reflection in the reflector-coated sunglasses, the knee in the balls, the fist in the face. The singer ironically confesses in court that the totalitarian state's vision represents the truth, and his a lie. He apologizes for contaminating the purity of the air with the words of his song and contemptuously, as if to wash his hands of politics altogether, declares, may the state live forever by whoever institutes it.

Cohen often projects an all-enveloping darkness, an edginess with disorienting images that fracture the latest received wisdom, with an unrelenting and menacing despair, through which glimmers of refracted light sometimes appear. "Teachers," for example, is a Kafkaesque nightmare, with an unhinged unreality, stripping the subject of all anchorage and certainty: "In some lost place I had to find/ Follow me the wise man said/ But he walked behind" (*Songs of Leonard Cohen*). "Bird on the Wire" gives us this expression of despair in a song that has become definitive of him: "Like a beast with his horn/ I have torn everyone who reached out for me" (*Songs from a Room*).

In an early 1970s interview, Cohen announced that: "I want to take over the unconditional leadership of the world, I want to lead the world to a new sensibility, and there has to be a leader, a figure to do it."[56] The notorious Glaswegian Beat writer Alexander Trocchi exhibited similar delusions of grandeur, induced by narcotic psychopathy, when his main political focus throughout the 1960s was Project Sigma, which he envisaged would result in an international worldwide organization of intellectuals, poets, and writers, equipped to bring about a revolutionary transformation of society.[57] In

---

[56] Susan Lumsden, "Leonard Cohen Wants the Unconditional Leadership of the World"; see www.linkedin.com/pulse/number-leadership-lessons-from-leonard-cohen-josip-bala%C5%BEevi%C4%87.

[57] Allan Campbell and Tim Niel, *A Life in Pieces: Reflections on Alexander Trocchi* (Edinburgh: Rebel, 1997), 21.

more threatening and sinister tones, Cohen declares that he is intent on revenge. He resents the sentence of twenty years of boredom handed down to him for trying to fight back against the system from within. He warns: "I'm coming to reward them. First we take Manhattan, then we take Berlin" (*I'm Your Man*, 1988). When it came to the crunch, Cohen, like Trocchi, backed off – Trocchi because of a lack of courage, and Cohen because he was a self-proclaimed anarchist incapable of throwing the bomb.[58]

That same menace permeates *The Future* (1992), which is one of Cohen's most politically outward-facing albums. He began writing the title track when the political unrest in Eastern Europe was being taken for a "democratic resurrection," but he was extremely skeptical. Cohen claimed that he felt the fall of the Wall would cause catastrophic disequilibrium: "That's why I say, 'Give me back the Berlin Wall/ Give me Stalin and St. Paul,' because this is not the beginning of a period of liberation ... That's what I felt when the Wall came down, freedom to murder."[59] He saw the world on the edge of a precipice. The consumption of millions of Prozac pills a week by society indicated to him there must be some kind of collective nervous breakdown. He said that the whole album was expressive of an "interior catastrophe," and that he had warned about it for a long time.[60]

One reviewer remarked that never had Cohen's outlook been so grim. Cohen responded by indicating that we would all settle for the Berlin Wall in comparison with what is to come. You'll settle for crack cocaine; social unrest; the Los Angeles riots: "This is kindergarten stuff compared to the homicidal impulse that is developing in every breast!"[61] The flood has come, and asking what is the appropriate thing to do transcends the ideological posturing of conservatism or liberalism, "given the gravity of the situation."[62] Cohen contended that the social contract had become unraveled and dissolved, precipitating a return to tribalism. He proclaimed that "the voices of the extreme have taken the glamour and the allure, and the center can no longer defend itself, can't mount a rhetoric

---

[58] Ibid., 22. Cohen, interview with Jacoba Atlas, *The Beat* (March 9, 1968).
[59] Posner, *Leonard Cohen, Untold Stories*, vol. III, 50.
[60] *Ottowa Sun* (November 20, 1992).   [61] *New York Times* (November 29, 1992).
[62] *Independent* (November 22, 1992).

that is inspiring."[63] In an ominously dark tone, Cohen predicts that the predators from all levels of society – from Wall Street to the streets – are poised to take over: "And they are laughing at our laws."[64]

Insofar as there is a political message to be gleaned from *The Future*, it is relatively direct and simple. You think the present is bad. Be careful what you wish for! There is no recognizable ideological position as such. It is more like the Old Testament warnings of Armageddon. The solutions he offers for redemption are surprisingly authoritarian and reactionary: an increase of police presence on the streets; a censoring of violence on the television; and the systematic application of force.[65] His psychological attachment to discipline is not frivolous. Indeed, his solution to the problem of social dysfunction and violence in Los Angeles was distinctly unimaginative: the authorities "should put boys and girls into uniform. There should be universal North American conscription again. It's us against drugs. If you don't understand that you're gonna lose."[66] In response to the drug problem in the United States he was equally reactionary. He believed that the supplying of drugs constitutes an attack on America, just as serious as a conventional attack. He suggested that: "I think this is a real attack and I think that it should be met with real force … with the full force of the American armed community. So, I would really go in and bomb the countries that are supplying drugs to America."[67]

After the tour to promote *The Future* concluded in 1993, Cohen retreated to Mt. Baldy, where he lived the sporadically disciplined life of a Buddhist, eventually becoming an ordained monk. When he re-emerged in 1999, the apocalyptic and prophetic demeanor of *The Future* dissipated. The suppression of the ego and the waning of his clinical depression had partially worked. The starkness of dystopian imagery remained, and the darkness became gradually and increasingly all-enveloping, but there were no more prophesies or warnings. After the

---

[63] Interview with David Fanning, "The D-Files: Leonard Cohen," www.webheights.net/speakingcohen/fanning.html.
[64] *Sunday Times Magazine* (December 12, 1993). [65] Ibid.
[66] Cited in John Walsh, "Research. You Understand … Leonard Cohen," *Mojo* (September 1994), 56.
[67] Canadian Broadcasting Corporation documentary, "Leonard Cohen: A Portrait in the First Person," first broadcast 1988.

terrorist attacks of 9/11 he was asked by a reporter how he felt. He replied that in Judaism "one is cautioned against trying to comfort the comfortless in the midst of their bereavement."[68]

After years of searching for his elusive inner self for a certainty amid the comic and the tragic, he concluded that there is no fixed point to excavate.[69] He could not trust his inner feelings; "inner feelings come and go" ("That Don't Make It Junk," *Ten New Songs*, 2001). It was his capacity to characterize the disturbing, to portray uneasiness, and to disorient by portraying the grotesque in familiar situations that are the hallmark of many of Cohen's more deeply emotional and powerful songs. He complained that he had been used by others to illustrate how love had become a cultural phenomenon. On the contrary, for him, far from society manifesting love, it was on the precipice of violence – if not physical, then psychic. He claimed that he had no special gift or insight to share with the world. Right from the beginning in the "Stranger Song" he made it clear: "Please understand I never had a secret chart to get me to the heart of this or any other matter" (*Songs of Leonard Cohen*, 1967). Almost fifty years later Cohen reaffirmed the inconsequential nature of the message in his art: "Listen to the mind of God/ Don't listen to me."[70]

He claimed that he had no political program and no political identity, and that in fact he hardly had any personal identity at all.[71] There is a fatalism in the later recordings and poems that is perhaps more disturbing than the fractured and chilling emotional landscapes of his earlier years. There was always a glimmer of optimism, a way for the light and happiness to break through in the belief that there was something there to find, something the poet could express. The journey for inner truth for which he searched in the holy books of exotic religions far and wide ultimately resulted in the realization that the only thing that is certain is

---

[68] Cited in Leibovitz, *A Broken Hallelujah*, 163.
[69] Alan Franks, "Love's Hard Man," *The Times Magazine* (October 13, 2001), 16.
[70] Leonard Cohen, "Listen to the Hummingbird," in *The Flame: Poems Notebooks Lyrics Drawings*, ed. Robert Faggen and Alexandra Pleshoyano (New York: Farrar, Straus, and Giroux, 2018), 65. It also appears on the posthumously released album *Thanks for the Dance*, 2019.
[71] Michael Harris, "Leonard Cohen: The Poet as Hero: 2," *Saturday Night Review* 84, no. 6 (June 1969). Reprinted in Gnarowski, *Leonard Cohen*, 7.

uncertainty itself. Whatever plan may be unfolding, it is beyond our comprehension: "We don't write the play, we don't produce it, we don't direct it and we're not even actors in it."[72] Having been dragged to the depths by depression and having finally, in old age, broken the chains that tethered him to despair, a new type of clarity and resignation broke through. The darkness of death is no longer as terrifying: it is there to be confronted, an unwelcome guest we are forced to entertain, and even embrace.

The post–Mt. Baldy iteration of Cohen, post–*The Future*, is more deeply cynical, disengaged, and infused with an unrelenting intensity. He becomes even more obsessed with the mystery of darkness. The consequence is a greater degree of skepticism and a stubborn reluctance to accept the new versions of reality constantly sold to us. It is not a politics of indifference, but a more passive-aggressive resistance. Discovering he had no aptitude for spiritual matters,[73] he was resigned to fate and the inevitability of the fading light: "life is a drug that stops working."[74] He surrenders to "the pull of the moon and the thrust of the sun" ("Different Sides," *Old Ideas*, 2012). Darkness "is inkier, vaster/ More profound/ And eerily refrigerated/ Filled with caves/ And blinding tunnels."[75] The darkness is a mysterious, all-pervasive force that drains the life out of the future, present, and past ("Darkness," *Old Ideas*, 2012). For Cohen, there is "Only darkness now" ("Born in Chains," *Popular Problems*, 2014), and just as you thought it couldn't get any darker, he waits for the "love that never came/ You want it darker/ We kill the flame" ("You Want It Darker," *You Want It Darker*, 2016). As his demise got closer, he prayed for courage "To see death coming/ As a friend."[76]

CONCLUSION

I have shown in this chapter that Leonard Cohen rarely wanted to express any firm political opinions, and when he did he would often obfuscate for

---

[72] Quoted in Doug Saunders, "State of Grace," *Globe and Mail* (Saturday, September 1, 2001).
[73] "Leaving Mount Baldy," Cohen, *Book of Longing*, 22.   [74] Ibid., 154.
[75] "Better," ibid., 11.
[76] Leonard Cohen, *The Flame: Poems Notebooks Lyrics Drawings*, ed. Robert Faggen and Alexandra Pleshoyano (New York: Farrar, Straus, and Giroux, 2018), 87 and 108.

fear of alienating his fan base, which he thought was predominantly left-wing. His own views were highly personalized, reflecting on how an event or political situation impacted upon him. Unlike most of his contemporaries, he did not engage in public protests against, for example, the Vietnam War, or against nuclear war, or in favour of civil rights. He always declined invitations to perform at fundraising concerts for particular political causes. When he does express political views, they do not neatly fall into the right–left spectrum and may more fruitfully be explored through the prism of the collectivism-versus-libertarian divide. In relation to specific issues such as the revolution in Cuba, the dictatorship of the colonels in Greece, and the Yom Kippur War, he was guarded and often disingenuous in his responses.

I have suggested that some of the poems and songs betray an apocalyptic and menacing tendency in which he emulates Lorca's poetry of inspiration in its dark, destabilizing undertones. The despair that drove him to his last extended withdrawal to Mt. Baldy and the discipline of Buddhism ended in failure and the realization that there is no fixed and final truth, no inner self, to discover, and that we have to resign ourselves to fate and the enveloping darkness that accompanies it. This is a theme that we see Cohen develop with increasing intensity in the studio albums of the new millennium. Its political import is that of passive-aggressive resistance. A refusal to buy the new version of reality that ideologues and politicians try to sell us. It is a politics of disengagement, and heavily skeptical.

PART V

RECEPTION AND LEGACY

CHAPTER 19

"You Know Who I Am"

From Writer to Rock Star

Loren Glass

O N DECEMBER 28, 1956, LEONARD COHEN WROTE TO PAUL Engle, Director of the Iowa Writers' Workshop. "I would like to apply for a fellowship or assistantship in creative writing," he begins,

> and work towards an M.A. or Ph.D. at Iowa. I am 22 years old, a graduate of McGill University in Montreal, and at present I am doing graduate work in English at Columbia University. But I find that what really interests me is the production of poetry and I want to present a creative thesis rather than an academic one.[1]

Six months later, having received no reply, Cohen wrote again, asking, "Did you receive my tedious letter about the Admissions Office and the poet and the scholar in the university? You are driving me into the Clothing Industry."[2] If Cohen had come to Iowa City, he would have joined an illustrious cohort of young American poets studying under Donald Justice, including Robert Bly, Philip Levine, and Mark Strand. Iowa was entering the reputational arc that would place it at the pinnacle of creative-writing programs, and Cohen could well have become one of its more celebrated graduates. It isn't hard to picture him as a dashing and distinguished Program Era professor of poetry with a light teaching load and a large youthful following on the campus reading circuit. He had the talent, the discipline, and the looks. But Engle never answered,

---

[1] Leonard Cohen to Paul Engle, 12–28–56. Papers of Paul Engle. University of Iowa Special Collections Library, MsC 514. Box 7.
[2] Leonard Cohen to Paul Engle, 5–4–57. Papers of Paul Engle. University of Iowa Special Collections Library, MsC 514. Box 7.

and Cohen would return to Montreal, confident in his talent but uncertain of his future.

When Cohen wrote to Engle he had just published his auspicious debut, *Let Us Compare Mythologies* (1956), as the inaugural title in the McGill Poetry Series, and after returning to Montreal he would publish two more well-received collections of poetry, *The Spice Box of Earth* (1961) and *Flowers for Hitler* (1964), with the prestigious Canadian publisher, McClelland and Stewart, and a well-received novel, *The Favourite Game* (1963). He became a literary celebrity, but only in Canada, which, as his recent biographer Sylvie Simmons confirms, "is a dot on the cultural map barely visible to the naked eye" in New York.[3] Cohen was well aware of his marginality to the US literary marketplace, and the ironic contrast between his renown in Canada and his obscurity in the United States would shape his career as a representative figure in what Joel Deshaye calls the "era of celebrity in Canadian Poetry."[4]

Cohen's arrival as a Canadian literary celebrity was prominently recognized in a documentary devoted to his life and career produced by the National Film Board of Canada in 1965. Entitled *Ladies and Gentleman, Mr. Leonard Cohen,* the film was initially intended as a promotional group portrait of four poets published by McClelland and Stewart on a reading tour of Canadian universities, but Cohen's performances so outshined the other three that a new project was conceived focusing exclusively on him. The resulting forty-five-minute film profiles Cohen on the brink of his transition from marginal Canadian writer to major international rock star, in the process both revealing and constructing the celebrity persona that would facilitate the shift. Opening with a voiceover of the title followed by applause as Cohen walks onstage for a reading at McGill, the film immediately makes it clear that this is a young writer quite comfortable with the stage. Smooth and suave, dapperly dressed in a formal shirt and tie with a leather jacket, he looks very much like the photo on the cover of *The Best of Leonard Cohen,* the 1975 album that

---

[3] Sylvie Simmons, *I'm Your Man: The Life of Leonard Cohen* (New York: HarperCollins, 2012), 58.

[4] Deshaye demarcates the era as spanning 1955–80 and sees the peak of the period as being defined by Cohen's career. See Joel Deshaye, *The Metaphor of Celebrity: Canadian Poetry and the Public, 1955–1980* (Toronto: University of Toronto Press, 2013).

would mark the initial culmination of his celebrity as a singer-songwriter. Cohen opens not with a poem but with a comic monologue about visiting a friend in a mental hospital and being mistaken for a patient. The scene features multiple audience reaction shots, focusing prominently on young women and emphasizing his impeccable timing and easy rapport. This is a poet who is comfortable performing in public, and whose sex appeal is palpable. Clips from this opening scene, along with other readings, are then interspersed across the rest of the film, reinforcing Cohen's charismatic aura and performative aplomb.[5]

The scene then shifts to Cohen walking the streets of Montreal, with the voiceover announcing, "out of the crowds of Montreal has come an exceptional talent with four books under his belt. Not primarily a stand-up comic, he's a novelist, poet, and a very confident young man." Then Cohen's voice enters in, over a cool jazz soundtrack and a series of clips of him chatting with his friend and mentor Irving Layton and the rest of their entourage. Cohen had been experimenting with reading his poems to live jazz accompaniment, enhancing his popularity across Eastern Canada, and these scenes trope on this innovation, adding a Beat undercurrent to his gentlemanly charm. "I'm beyond the common pack of poets," Cohen proclaims, cockily enacting the confidence the film so comfortably conveys.

The film documents Cohen's Jewish family background and childhood of wealth and privilege, featuring clips from his father's home movies with voiceovers by Cohen from *The Favourite Game*, which had just been published when the film was being produced. And it features numerous shots of and scenes in postwar Montreal, characterizing Cohen as both a local flaneur and a former BMOC (Big Man on Campus) at McGill, from which he had graduated in 1956, and where he had flourished under the mentorship of Professor Louis Dudek, a major Canadian literary tastemaker who had been instrumental in getting Cohen's first book published. It also features him recording an album of his poetry and appearing on a television talk show, revealing his comfort and facility with the modern media of the era. It documents his more recent life on the Greek island of

---

[5] *Ladies and Gentlemen ... Mr. Leonard Cohen*, dir. Donald Brittain and Don Owen (National Film Board of Canada, 1965).

Hydra, including his soon-to-be celebrated affair with Marianne Ihlen. And it presents multiple scenes in his current residence, a three-dollar-a-night hotel room in Montreal which he calls his "sanctuary." The hotel is in a French-speaking neighborhood, a fact the film makes clear by including scenes of Cohen speaking fluent French to the concierge by way of an intercom above the door. These scenes are intimate, featuring Cohen in his underwear, shaving, and washing his face. And writing, which he does five hours a day, with the radio on. Mirrors are prominent, and the entire mise-en-scène anticipates the degree to which Cohen's career would be framed, both aesthetically and thematically, by mirrors in sparsely furnished hotel rooms.

The film concludes in a screening room, with Cohen sitting beside co-director Don Brittain watching a scene of himself pretending to sleep in the hotel bed, and then taking a bath. "A man has invited a group of strangers to watch him cleaning his body," Cohen says. And then, as we watch alongside him, he writes on the bathroom wall in soap above the bathtub: "CAVEAT EMPTOR." Asked by Brittain to explain what he means he answers that he's acting as a "double agent for the filmmakers and the public ... This is not entirely devoid of the con." This sly combination of intimacy and misdirection, of "confidence" in its multiple meanings, crystallizes Cohen's emerging sense of his public persona as a complex confluence of sincerity, sexuality, and sleight of hand. The entire scene feels like a dress rehearsal for celebrity, a testing of his public image as private poet from the safety of the screening room, a dry run for the image he will soon present to the world at large. As Simmons confirms, "*Ladies and Gentlemen* ... appears in retrospect less a portrait of a serious literary figure than of a pop/rock celebrity in training."[6] The film had a limited release, but it was widely watched by the press corps that covered Cohen in the 1960s and 70s and would become the basis of his initial public image as a singer-songwriter. It is not surprising that watching it convinced John Hammond to sign Cohen to Columbia Records.

Famous as he was in Canada, Cohen's books sold poorly, and he was having difficulty making a living, so he returned to the United States, this time in search of a career as a songwriter. He was headed for Nashville but

---

[6] Simmons, *I'm Your Man*, 137.

got waylaid in New York, where Judy Collins jumpstarted his folk-rock reputation by recording what would become his first signature song, "Suzanne," on her 1966 album, *In My Life*. Cohen stayed in New York, signed with Columbia, and promptly followed with *Songs of Leonard Cohen* in December 1967, his somber debut. He entered the record industry at an auspicious moment for an artist like him. In the wake of the meteoric success of Bob Dylan and the Beatles, rock albums were beginning to be treated as high art, and the lyrics of popular music were beginning to be appreciated as poetry; his literary songwriting style fit in well. And, correlatively, as David R. Shumway affirms, the media was beginning to accept "rock stars as representative of their generation and its role in what was perceived to be the remaking of America."[7] Cohen's career and credentials as a published poet and novelist popular with the younger generation were prominent components of his early profiles in the music press, as was his residence in the Chelsea Hotel, where *Village Voice* critic Richard Goldstein visited him on the eve of his first album's release. "He will soon make his debut as a pop star," Goldstein proclaims, adding that "a year ago that would have given even me pause, but not today, when Leonard Bernstein picks the hits and the *Partisan Review* talks about 'Learning from the Beatles'."[8] William Kloman, writing a month later for the *New York Times*, also foregrounded Cohen's literary credentials, proclaiming that "Leonard Cohen, at 33, is a man-child of our time. A poet-novelist-composer-singer … Cohen has a solid reputation among the young people of his native Canada, where his poems are used by lovers. In America, until recently, he was strictly an underground celebrity."[9]

Cohen's age, in both articles, is prominently noted. On the one hand, in a youthful counterculture suspicious of anyone over thirty, he seemed too old to be a rock star. On the other hand, as he explains to Goldstein, "Around 30 or 35 is the traditional age for the suicide of the poet …

---

[7] David R. Shumway, *Rock Star: The Making of Musical Icons from Elvis to Springsteen* (Baltimore: Johns Hopkins University Press, 2014), xiii.

[8] Richard Goldstein, "Leonard Cohen: Beautiful Creep," *Village Voice* (December 28, 1967), 18.

[9] William Kloman, "'I've Been on the Outlaw Scene since 15': Leonard Cohen," *New York Times* (January 28, 1968), D21.

That's the age when you finally understand that the universe does not succumb to your command." And in case the theological implications of this patently Romantic trope aren't clear, he continues, "I had a very Messianic childhood. I was told I was a descendent of Aaron, the high priest. My parents actually thought we were Cohenim – the real thing. I was expected to grow into manhood leading other men."[10] He also waxes christological with Kloman, explaining in more general terms,

> Our natural vocabulary is Judeo-Christian. That is our blood myth. We have to rediscover law from inside our own heritage, and we have to rediscover the crucifixion. The crucifixion will again be understood as a universal symbol, not as just an experiment in sadism or masochism or arrogance. It will have to be rediscovered because that's where man is at. On the cross.[11]

That he became a rock star at the same age that Christ was crucified was clearly convenient for his semi-suicidal self-image, and the press was happy to promote this melancholy messianic message, which conveniently situated his stardom in the apocalyptic context of the late 1960s.

Comparisons with Dylan, who was simultaneously cementing his image as a reluctant messiah, were inevitable. Cohen had in fact predicted that he would become the Canadian Dylan, but the contrasts between the two are more informative than their similarities. First of all, unlike Dylan, Cohen was in fact a published poet. Many of his songs began as poems, and, unlike Dylan, he included his lyrics in his liner notes, sometimes in a separate printed insert that resembled a chapbook or broadsheet, affirming their poetic autonomy. And his literary credentials were central to Columbia's marketing scheme. Thus, their full-page ad in *Rolling Stone* for *Songs of Leonard Cohen* features the tag line, in large block letters surrounded by ample white space: "James Joyce Is Not Dead." Then, toward the bottom of the page in smaller type above a picture of the album cover: "He lives in Montreal under the name of Leonard Cohen." Dylan's lyrics were literary, but he was a college dropout with no publications; Cohen, by contrast, was an English major and a published writer whose "volumes of poetry and novels," according to

---

[10] Goldstein, "Beautiful Creep," 20.   [11] Kloman, "Outlaw Scene," D20.

the ad, "have won him astounding acclaim."[12] And the sales of his poetry, never substantial prior to his arrival as a singer-songwriter, were enhanced by his musical celebrity. *Selected Poems: 1956–68*, his first collection to be published in the United States, sold over 200,000 copies.

He was also far more accessible, to both his audience and the press, than Dylan. He embraced and identified with his fans, and his performances were veritable lovefests, frequently concluding with the audience rushing the stage to be with their hero. As Dylan withdrew into mystery and opacity, Cohen put his body on the line, reveling in his vulnerability and relatability. In the full-page ad for his second album, *Songs from a Room*, the tag line asks: "Is Your Name Leonard Cohen?" The copy that follows answers:

> From time to time you get the feeling that you want to disengage yourself from your life. Because you're no different from anyone else. And because your life is filled with the same love and the same hate and the same beauty and the same ugliness as everyone else's. You want to withdraw into some kind of solitary contemplation – a locked room or a quiet corner of your mind – just to think about everything for a while. You. Her. It. That. Them.[13]

The paratactic progression from "you" to "them" by way of "her" and "it" pithily distils the pronominal logic and paradoxically public intimacy of many of Cohen's songs and poems, which frequently figure a "you" that hovers between poet and reader, singer and listener, lover and beloved, musician and muse. Cohen embodied the private poet as public figure, and Columbia exploited and extended this powerful image, which Cohen in turn was happy to inhabit. As he claimed in a 1969 interview, "deep in myself I know that I'm the same as everyone and what I really want to do is tune in on my *sameness*, rather than on my differences."[14]

But there was a doubleness to this appeal, which was facilitated by the pronominal ambiguity in his lyrics and poetry, and symptomatized by Cohen's own ambivalence about his position relative to his audience. He

---

[12] Columbia Records ad for *Songs of Leonard Cohen, Rolling Stone* (February 24, 1968), 3.
[13] Columbia Records ad for *Songs from a Room, Rolling Stone* (May 17, 1969), 13.
[14] Jack Batten, "Leonard Cohen: The Poet as Hero," *Saturday Night* (June 1969), 30.

seemed both leader and follower, celebrity and fan; his rock-star image became a kind of pop-cultural extension of the theological self-understanding he'd been developing as a poet. As his biographer Ira B. Nadel notes, "Cohen attempts to collapse the divide between prophet and priest and to join them throughout his work – or at least give them equal time. The prophet, Cohen notes, is the visionary; the priest, his disciple."[15] Dylan was always the prophet, never the priest, which partly explains his mercurial refusal to ever stick with a style, to stabilize his appeal. Cohen, on the other hand, could and did alternate between being founder and acolyte of his own cult, and he found submission as attractive as domination. When he sings "You Know Who I Am" he can be either the "You" or the "I," or both. His lyrics, and by association his public image, leverage the logic of the shifter, whereby first- and second-person pronouns can refer differently depending on the context. Psychologically speaking, the pattern is narcissistic, a diagnosis Cohen enacted by practicing, and occasionally even recording, while watching himself in a mirror. This sense of almost overweening self-regard, qualified by a carefully calculated humility, is reflected by most of the early album covers, which frontally feature his increasingly iconic face, culminating in the famous mirror shot on the cover of *The Best of Leonard Cohen.*

There was also a martial element to Cohen's persona that provided an undercurrent of violence and war befitting the apocalyptic tenor of the times. His poetry and lyrics frequently feature sacrificial violence – the story of Abraham and Isaac is a recurrent trope, as is the figure of the martyr Joan of Arc – and generals and warriors jostle against prophets and priests in the many names dropped from history and myth, both classical and modern. In 1961, he went to Cuba "to kill or be killed," he claimed only semi-facetiously, and in the late 1960s and early 70s he came to resemble romantic revolutionaries such as Fidel and Che, as he grew his hair out and let his face get stubbly.[16] He called his supporting musicians "the Army" and fashioned himself as "Field Commander Cohen," appellations that the press was happy to amplify.

---

[15] Ira B. Nadel, *Various Positions: A Life of Leonard Cohen* (Austin: University of Texas Press, 1996), 67.

[16] *Ladies and Gentlemen* ...

In one interview he called touring "a reconnaissance. You know, I consider myself, like in a military operation."[17]

As a Jew, he was preoccupied by Israel and its military engagements. And, unlike Dylan, he embraced his Jewish identity, enhancing his aura of authenticity but arguably also limiting the scope of his celebrity. Dylan never denied his Jewishness, but he clearly subordinated it by changing his last name, in a tradition going back to Al Jolson, and denying that his Jewish past had any significance for his prophetic present. As Shumway affirms, Dylan was "a star defined by his changes rather than the consistency of his persona."[18] Dylan continuously reinvented himself, but Cohen was happy to attribute his stable identity to his ancestry. As Simmons confirms, "Leonard has never denied being born on the right side of the tracks, has never renounced his upbringing, rejected his family, changed his name or pretended to be anything other than who he is."[19] Cohen's lyrics could be complex or obscure, but he was never cryptic about his identity, and was happy to attribute much of his image and style to his privileged Jewish upbringing in Catholic Montreal.

A Canadian Jew by birth more famous in Europe than in the United States, Cohen manifested an idiosyncratic international status. Rock stardom was of course a transnational anglophone phenomenon, featuring figures from across the American empire and the British Commonwealth who became famous around the world, but the United States was the key market, and touring or living there was the consensus sign of success. Cohen did both, but he toured mostly in Europe during these years, where he had a cult following, and his US record sales were always modest; indeed, modesty became part of his image, in distinct contrast to megalomaniacs such as Mick Jagger or Jim Morrison. Cohen was a gentleman in the old style, genteel, polite, and clean-cut. Montreal, his city of birth, was predominantly francophone and resolutely cosmopolitan, more European than North American. As one of his recent biographers notes, "Montreal was in fact a kind of

---

[17] Jack Hafferkamp, "Ladies and Gents, Leonard Cohen" *Rolling Stone* (February 4, 1971), 26.

[18] David R. Shumway, "Dylan: Stardom and Fandom," in *The World of Bob Dylan*, ed. Sean Latham (Cambridge: Cambridge University Press, 2021), 313.

[19] Simmons, *I'm Your Man*, 5.

multinational interzone."[20] A Canadian Jew fluent in French with a house on a Greek island, he embodied a kind of itinerant exilic identity which kept him always slightly outside the mainstream of American popular music and cultural mythology.

Like most rock stars, Cohen was a sex symbol, but of a particularly potent variety. He was more conventionally handsome than his younger peers, most of whom were nerdy misfits who joined bands to get girls. And with Cohen sexuality was powerfully intertwined with spirituality. He already had a patently Byronic image as a poet when he entered the music industry, and both his poetry and his song lyrics blend the erotic with the theological; he worships women and loves God in the same language and, frequently, in the same song or poem. And his lovers and muses were also famous. Suzanne Verdal and Marianne Ihlen became minor stars in their own rights, opening up an unusual space for women in Cohen's celebrity orbit. From the beginning he sang with female accompaniment, figuratively giving voice to both his muses and his female fans and deepening the ambiguities of pronominal reference and identification in the lyrics. As Goldstein somewhat crassly puts it when introducing the lyrics of "Suzanne" in his collection of *The Poetry of Rock*: "No longer are women mere objects of worship or desire in rock. Most put out, and few regret it. And their souls won't fit into any text of societal norms."[21] In a sense, Cohen brought his groupies into his group, modelling a kind of charismatic community as travelling troupe. Cohen's women were sexualized and sanctified, but they were also granted agency as co-creators of his image, style, and sound, especially Marianne, who helped him navigate his initial celebrity and chose the poems that appear in *Selected Poems*.

The back cover of *Selected Poems* bills Cohen as "poet-novelist-songwriter-singer" across the top and then proliferates other appellations underneath this paratactic title, including "a sister of mercy," "a beautiful creep," "a secret all over the block," "a love object," "a psalmist," "a hallucinating acolyte," and "a hero in the seaweed." And by the time of this collection's

---

[20] Anthony Reynolds, *Leonard Cohen: A Remarkable Life* (London: Omnibus Press, 2010), 19.

[21] Richard Goldstein, *The Poetry of Rock* (New York: Bantam, 1969), 81.

publication, Cohen was beginning to process his celebrity in his poetry. In the "New Poems" that conclude it we find him "restless as an empire," "a shadow" longing "for the boundaries of my wandering," in a city "everybody calls New York." The poems are elegiac, as in "you know I am a god/ Who needs to use your body ... to sing about beauty" or in "It has been some time," which concludes with "knowing ... we would never be lovers/ Thinking much more about suicide and money."[22] And suicide would be the throughline of *The Energy of Slaves* (1972), in which most of the poems are headed by an icon of a razor blade instead of a title. Deshaye sees slavery as a masochistic metaphor for celebrity in this collection, a kind of cultural life sentence which mimics martyrdom and for which suicide is the only effective solution, but the book also surveys some other extensions of Cohen's stardom.[23] It opens with "Welcome to These Lines," which tells us, "There is a war on/ But I'll try to make you comfortable," and includes such poems as "Overheard on Every Corner," which claims "I have been chosen/ To perfect all men," and that "I was meant to be/ The seed of your new society ... the courtless invisible king." It also features the cavalier lyric, "the 15-year-old girls/ I wanted when I was fifteen/ I have them now ... I advise you all/ To become rich and famous," as well as the pugilistic challenge to his fellow literary celebrity, "Dear Mailer/ Don't ever fuck with me ... I will k – l you/ And your entire family."[24] The poems make it clear that celebrity has been at best a mixed blessing, complicating instead of resolving Cohen's spiritual and sexual conflicts.

The complex dynamics of Cohen's celebrity in the early 1970s are well-documented in *Bird on a Wire*, Tony Palmer's ill-fated film about Cohen's chaotic 1972 European tour which, appropriately, concluded in Jerusalem, making it into something of a pilgrimage. The film, which had only limited release until recently, bills itself as an "impression" of the tour and provides an intimate portrait of "the Army," Cohen's touring group, and informative insight into his intense emotional appeal to his audience and their reciprocal appeal to him. It opens with Cohen

---

[22] Leonard Cohen, *Selected Poems: 1956–1968* (Toronto: McCelland and Stewart, 1968), 221, 222, 224, 233.
[23] See Deshaye, *The Metaphor of Celebrity*, 109–36.
[24] Leonard Cohen, *The Energy of Slaves* (Toronto: McClelland and Stewart, 1972), 1, 14, 87, 93.

reciting "Any System You Contrive without Us," a poem from *The Energy of Slaves*, and his characteristically Canadian diphthongs immediately make it clear that this is not a US or UK speaker of English.[25] This prologue of sorts is followed by scenes from his show in Tel Aviv, such that the film both begins and ends in Israel. The Tel Aviv show was violently interrupted by Israeli security guards in orange jumpsuits (they look ironically like American prisoners). To quell the chaos the band launches into "Passing Through," which becomes something of a thematic throughline for the entire film and tour, but they have to stop in order to deal with the fighting on the floor before them. Over the sounds of fisticuffs and body blows Cohen deadpans: "no point in starting a war right now." The band leaves the stage, and the opening credits start to roll.

The film amply documents the standard symptoms of rock stardom. Cohen signs books and posters and album covers; he submits to multiple interviews; he is swarmed by crowds and propositioned by female fans. Throughout it all he is unfailingly polite and accessible, including onstage, from which he addresses his audience with sincere authenticity, including simply leaving the stage when he feels unable to perform up to the standard he assumes they expect from him. The mutual love is palpable. And for the performance scenes Les Young's cinematography creatively fades in and out between close-ups of Cohen and of the two women, Donna Washburn and Jennifer Warnes, with whom he sings, passing through superimpositions which blend them into one surrealistic image, visually representing the haunting harmonies of his famous hits. At one point, Cohen comments on the significance of these classics, and his difficulty in performing them repeatedly, noting, "I wrote these songs to myself and to women several years ago," and now he feels "like a parrot chained to his song night after night." At times he parodies himself, in one performance announcing, "Leonard Cohen is going to sing his song of anguish and despairrrrr." The film beautifully documents his struggles

---

[25] Tony Palmer, *Bird on a Wire* (July 1975; restored version released 2010). Cohen reportedly cried throughout his viewing of Palmer's rough cut but then, a week later, rejected it as "too confrontational." The film was then re-edited and premiered in London on July 5, 1974, after which it disappeared. The original edit was discovered in 2009 and the restored edition released on DVD in 2010. See Simmons, *I'm Your Man*, 269–70.

to maintain authenticity through all this endless repetition, to keep these songs, which have been worshipfully memorized by his fans, fresh for each performance, to somehow be himself without repeating himself.

The film concludes in Jerusalem, confirming and contemplating Cohen's Jewish identity. When asked if he is a practicing Jew he cleverly answers, "I'm always practicing." The concert at first appears to be a failure, with Cohen, tripping on acid, walking out in the middle, claiming he can't get off the ground, and quoting the kabbalah to illustrate his crisis. But then, after a backstage shave, he goes back out to perform "Hey, That's No Way to Say Goodbye," over which Palmer plays clips from Cohen's father's home movies, and then "So Long, Marianne," over which Palmer plays a montage of stills of Marianne Ihlen, while the audience sings along. The audience, both of the live performance and its cinematic representation, know Cohen intimately, Palmer seems to be saying. Afterwards, Cohen and the rest of the band weep openly backstage.

Cohen was clearly in crisis and struggling to maintain his creativity, so Columbia greenlighted a retrospective collection to capitalize on the continuing cache of his classic songs. He was given complete artistic control over *The Best of Leonard Cohen*, selecting the songs and images, including the lyrics on a separate insert, and penning liner notes reflecting on the composition of each song. The album complexly crossfertilizes the literary and the musical, the theological and the psychological, into a kind of *kunstleralbum*, a portrait of the singer-songwriter as a "ladies' man" of middle age. Mirrors multiply metaphorically, starting with the iconic cover image which, as the notes confirm, "was taken in a mirror of a hotel room in Milan." Cohen stands full frontal, but his gaze is slightly off center and unfocused. The photograph on the inner sleeve, presumably taken at the same time and place, tropes on this image. Here Cohen is seated on a bed, facing the camera; he has just blown one of his famous smoke rings, which is suspended in front of him, mimicking the circular mirror on the cover. On the other side of the sleeve is a sketch by Cohen, dated December 28, 1969, of a male figure, presumably Cohen, prostrated before a standing female figure, presumably his wife, Suzanne Elrod, naked and gazing into a mirror which she holds in her right hand. Below this image is a cryptic script, probably kabbalistic, yet to be translated by Cohen scholars, assuming it means anything at all. It has the effect of maintaining a space of privacy and opacity at the core of Cohen's public authenticity, a kernel of difference at the center of his sameness.

These visual tropes of mirrored gazes and cryptic codes refract off the anecdotal reflections of the liner notes, which reminisce on the origins of each song, starting with "Suzanne." Each note specifies the location(s) where the song was written, providing an international itinerary that ranges from Montreal to New York to Greece to London to Ethiopia. Many if not most of the songs were composed in hotel rooms, from the Chelsea to the Henry Hudson to Penn Terminal. In addition to confirming the iconicity of his muses, Suzanne and Marianne, other names are selectively dropped, including Kris Kristofferson, Ron Cornelius, Buffy Sainte-Marie, and Nico; Janis Joplin is obliquely referred to as "an American singer who died a while ago." Though the record sold poorly at the time, it would eventually stand as the distillation of this first decade of Cohen's musical career.

With the exceptions of "The Partisan" and "Who by Fire," Cohen selected songs about women and love, foregrounding his image as a sex symbol. With his next album and poetry collection he would symbolically kill this image, effectively ending this first iteration of his career as a literary singer-songwriter. Whatever one thinks of *Death of a Ladies' Man* – Paul Nelson, writing for *Rolling Stone*, called it "either greatly flawed ... or great *and* flawed" – it certainly stands as an endpoint of sorts, a ritual suicide of the celebrity persona with which Cohen was exhausted.[26] The songs express this exhaustion both verbally and musically. Thus, after two sides saturated with sexual excess and despair, the title song concludes, "So the great affair is over/ But whoever would have guessed/ It would leave us all so vacant/ And so deeply unimpressed," clearly indicating that the end of this album also marks the end of an era in Cohen's career. This thematic throughline is reinforced by Spector's characteristically heavy-handed production, which submerges Cohen's singing beneath a sea of sound, drowning his voice in a chaotic cacophony of orchestration. And, since Spector ran off with the master tapes

---

[26] Paul Nelson, "Leonard Cohen's Doo Wop Nightmare," *Rolling Stone* (February 9, 1978), 93.

before Cohen could record his final vocal tracks, the listener is left with his thin initial takes. This subordination of singer to song is reinforced by Spector's insistence that all the tracks be credited to both of them equally. There is a certain poetic justice to one of the industry's most notorious abusers of women ritually murdering one of its most celebrated lovers.

If *Death of a Ladies' Man* killed Cohen as a rock star, *Death of a Lady's Man*, the collection of poems that followed, announced the death of his more privatized poetic persona, the one who worships a single woman (or at least one at a time). If the album says goodbye to promiscuity, the book stages a complex farewell to monogamy and marriage, leaving only celibacy, to which Cohen would retreat, temporarily as it turned out, on Mt. Baldy under the mentorship of Roshi Kyozan Joshu Sasaki. Deshaye sees the book as a kind of sadomasochist symbolic suicide, marking not only the end of Cohen's public persona as a celebrity poet, but a "closing bookend to the era of celebrity in Canadian poetry."[27] More broadly, both productions, the book and the album, can be seen to mark the end of the singer-songwriter era of which Cohen was a signal avatar. Carole King had retreated to the mountains of Idaho; Dylan was about to enter his born-again period; Joni Mitchell was shifting over to jazz. Cohen would, of course, return to both poetry and song, but his period of monastic retreat would mark a watershed in his career and in the history of popular music, after which he and his cohort would re-emerge as legends of classic rock.

[27] Deshaye, *The Metaphor of Celebrity*, 135.

CHAPTER 20

Documentary (Re)presentations

"You Know Who I Am"

Robert de Young

THIS CHAPTER ATTEMPTS TO MAP SOME OF THE WAYS IN which Leonard Cohen has been represented, and has intervened in the process of his own representation, in documentary films.[1] From the release of his first volume of poetry, *Let Us Compare Mythologies,* in 1956 Cohen always exercised a high level of control over all aspects of his published work, including cover designs, artwork, and type fonts, album covers, booklets, and tour books. I have analyzed elsewhere Cohen's almost obsessive redrafting of such poems as "Thousand Kisses Deep" or the song "Hallelujah," which will be noted later.[2] This chapter will argue that, similarly, Leonard has consistently stage-managed his filmic representation in documentaries examining his life and work. He has knowingly exercised almost as much control over his representation in nonfiction films as he has over his literary publications, recordings, and performances.[3] There are several explanations as to why Cohen might

---

[1] Of course, since the early 1960s, Leonard granted innumerable radio, press, and television interviews, but many of these were brief and occasional, and have largely disappeared from public view, although some continue to appear on YouTube. While these interviews are very revealing with respect to the control Leonard has exercised over his cult status and the representation of his life and art, this material is beyond the scope of this chapter – the focus here is on the most significant "intentional" documentary films.

[2] See Robert de Young, "Leonard Cohen's Archival Mountain and the Volcanic Eruptions of 'Thousand Kisses Deep'," in *Imperfect Itineraries: Literature and Literary Research in the Archives,* ed. Michael Paduano (Nancy: Éditions de l'Université de Lorraine, 2025 [forthcoming]).

[3] See Bill Nichols, *Representing Reality: Issues and Concepts in Documentary* (Indianapolis: Indiana University Press, 1991); Bill Nichols, *Blurred Boundaries: Questions of Meaning in Contemporary Culture* (Indianapolis: Indiana University Press, 1994); and Trinh T. Minh

have done this. As an international celebrity, Cohen, one might argue, needed to preserve his privacy to maintain some personal order and stability. It has also been useful in creating an aura of mystery around his persona and his work as an artist.

Part of Cohen's public persona has been that he continually struggles with creativity, and in the 1972 volume *The Energy of Slaves*, he adopts what Stephen Scobie has called the stance of the "anti-poet":[4] "I have no talent left/ I can't write a poem anymore."[5] Cohen's representation of this "struggle" in both his life and his art, and its perpetuation in documentary films have proven to be enormously attractive both to readers and audiences. Onstage, Cohen has always striven to be transparently "authentic," but arguably the representation of himself on the screen has involved other less spontaneous and more guarded strategies.

Ira B. Nadel's biography, *Various Positions*, makes it clear that Cohen's decision to become a singer-songwriter and performer was influenced in part by his enthusiasm and admiration for Bob Dylan. Cohen's friend Professor Bob Faggen, who commenced the digitization of Cohen's notebooks while he was still alive, made the astute observation at the recent Leonard Cohen Symposium that "Leonard tends to think in verse."[6] Cohen's interest in music was long-standing, and there is clearly a continuum between his verse and song. For instance, we do see him singing one of his poems, "Twelve O'clock Chant" from *The Spice-Box of Earth* (1961), and accompanying himself on guitar in the National Film Board of Canada documentary *Ladies and Gentlemen, Mr. Leonard Cohen* (dir. Donald Brittain and Don Owen, 1965).[7] According to Nadel, early in 1966 Cohen attended a poetry party where he raved about Dylan's albums *Bringing It All Back Home* and *Highway 61 Revisited*, "solemnly announcing that *he* would become the Canadian Dylan, a statement all

---

Ha's chapter, "The Totalizing Quest of Meaning," in *Theorizing Documentary*, ed. Michael Renov (London: Routledge, 1993).

[4] Stephen Scobie, *Leonard Cohen* (Vancouver: Douglas & McIntyre, 1978), 157–63.
[5] Leonard Cohen, *The Energy of Slaves* (New York: Viking, 1972), 112.
[6] Bob Faggen's presentation at "In My Secret Life: The Leonard Cohen Symposium," held at the Art Gallery of Ontario (AGO), March 25, 2023.
[7] *Ladies and Gentlemen, Mr. Leonard Cohen*, dir. Donald Brittain and Don Owen (National Film Board of Canada, 1965).

dismissed." At the intermission for Dylan's February 20, 1965 concert in Montreal, Cohen's friend and fellow poet Irving Layton announced that Cohen was going to start singing.[8] Indeed, as early as 1965, Cohen's ambition to become an international performer was already beginning to take shape.

Ladies and Gentlemen, Mr. Leonard Cohen for the National Film Board of Canada was in part a publicity initiative on the part of Cohen's Canadian publishers, McClelland and Stewart, originally intended to profile four poets on a reading tour of Canadian universities. Some five years after the event, in a 1969 interview with Michael Harris, Cohen explained the sequence of events:

> Well, for one thing, I was surprised that the Film Board was treating me at all. The thing had happened in an unusual way. It had originally started off as a film on a tour of poets and I was one of those four poets. The others were Irving Layton, Earl Birney and Phyllis Gotlieb. It was a kind of promotion by McClelland and Stewart. For some technical reason only the parts of the film that dealt with me seemed to have been good so that they were stuck with a problem. They had invested a lot of bread in it and they had to make a film, so they decided to make one and it was a kind of a salvage job, so it took all the pressure off the production in a way because it was a salvage job. But he's a very good man, Don Brittain ... I've always had a fantasy that some director will find me sitting at a drug store counter, like Hedy Lamarr or whoever it was ... I[t] would take all the work away from it. I thought I would not have to create myself as an image.[9]

Cohen seems to have liked the idea that he'd be "discovered" and recognized as a "very particular" artist and that this might save him the work of creating and crafting an image designed to appeal to the public eye.

Brittain's film was undertaken at something of a turning point in Leonard Cohen's career. Cohen had already published three volumes of poetry – *Let Us Compare Mythologies* (1956), *The Spice-Box of Earth* (1961), and *Flowers for Hitler* (1964) – and his first novel, *The Favourite Game,* in

---

[8] Ira B. Nadel, *Various Positions: A Life of Leonard Cohen* (London: Bloomsbury, 1996), 141–42.

[9] Michael Harris, "An Interview with Leonard Cohen," *Duel* 1 (winter 1969): 99–100.

1963. At the time of the documentary, Cohen was simply a successful Canadian published poet with one novel to his credit, and largely unknown outside of his native Canada. Cohen's better-known novel, *Beautiful Losers* (1966), was still twelve months away, and it would be two years before the release of his first album for Columbia records, *Songs of Leonard Cohen*, in December 1967. The film both documents and celebrates a young poet and novelist with a growing sense of his achievements and the direction of his career, but it also sheds light on Cohen's abiding interest in the relationship between his life and art, and the creation of an "image" for himself.

The narrator tells us that Cohen obsessively keeps his correspondence, drafts, and photographs because he is convinced that these things will be of interest in the future. The last four minutes of Brittain's documentary – which sees Cohen in a screening room with the director "viewing" what purports to be the completed film to date – provides perhaps the earliest extensive insight into Cohen's interest in the process of the (re)presentation of his public and private selves. The sequence begins with Cohen watching an earlier section of the documentary where he was filmed sleeping in a hotel room. He declares,

> it's a very privileged thing to be able to see yourself sleeping. I think it's an experience very few people have. But of course the fraud is that I'm not really sleeping ... That's a privilege of a higher and more esoteric order, because there are some people who are very very interested to know how they look when they're pretending.

Cohen also provides a commentary on the next sequence of shots which he and the viewers are watching being screened. In this sequence (and these scenes have hitherto not been seen in the body of the documentary preceding), Cohen is sitting in his hotel bathtub, and, sitting next to him in the screening room, quips to Brittain:

> This is a situation which, for whatever the reason, a man has allowed a number of strangers into his bathroom. Now it's true we're making a film about my life, and the film purports to examine my life closely, and the bath is part of my life, but still regardless of the reason, here in 1964, a man has invited a group of strangers to observe him cleaning his body ...

I find it very interesting. I find it [*pause*] I find it sinister, and of course I find it flattering because there's a point where every man shares the Aga Khan's delight at selling his bathwater [*At this point of Cohen's voiced-over commentary, we watch him writing* CAVEAT EMPTOR *on the wall for the benefit of the camera*] ... so it's hateful ... Yes, caveat emptor, "let the buyer beware." I think, I think that I had to, for a moment, act as a double agent, for both the filmmakers and the public. I had to warn the public that – it's like that little beep that goes through certain recorded phone messages that you hear on the radio – I thought I would make this little beep and let the man watching me know that this is not entirely devoid of the con.

Of course, in turn, Cohen is declaring all this for the benefit of the camera, simultaneously acting as an agent for the filmmaker's "realistic" and naturalistic documentary enterprise, but also exposing it as a work that is as constructed as a work of fiction. Finally, this screening-room sequence returns to an earlier section of the documentary shot in the bedroom of the hotel where Cohen stands in his underwear looking out of the window at the snow.

> LEONARD COHEN: I look much more like a man than I thought. In fact, I think I've had a very very mistaken conception about what style of man I was. I think the whole thing is changing now.
> DON BRITTAIN: You mean just looking at this movie?
> LC: Yeah. I think I'm of a different style than I thought I was.
> DB: This may affect your whole life.
> LC: I hope it affects my whole life.

Notwithstanding the presence of the camera and the performative aspect of this screening-room sequence, Cohen seems genuinely fascinated in viewing his (re)presentation on-screen in the documentary. Some five years later, in an interview for the magazine *Duel*, Michael Harris questioned Cohen about the entire screening-room sequence: "Did you know you were being filmed at that point?" Cohen, acknowledging the "con," replies, "I knew I was being filmed. It was a very clever device of Don Brittain, the director."[10]

---

[10] Ibid., 99.

Cohen is simultaneously both the subject of the documentary and yet able, through this final sequence, to comment on its (re)presentation of him and his work as an "outsider" and the subject of the camera's gaze. The film, like much of Cohen's own work both before and especially after this period, sets up a dialogue among the man, the public celebrity, and his work. As literary critic Linda Hutcheon has observed, "From his songs to his books, all of Cohen's work revolves around his own personality as artist, his 'life in art'."[11] In the spirit of one of Cohen's aptly titled later albums, *Various Positions*,[12] Brittain's 1965 documentary sets the stage for Cohen's skillful and playful management of his textualized life. While we discover some personal details during the course of the documentary – for example, the narrator tells us something of Cohen's life with Marianne Ihlen on the Greek island of Hydra – in this final sequence of the film Cohen makes it very clear that, like most publicity initiatives, this one is "not entirely devoid of the con," and Cohen is already, very early in his career, exercising a complex agency in the service of an equally complex persona.

In 1972 Cohen was again the willing subject of a feature-length documentary. For Cohen, the stakes were very high indeed.[13] His third album, *Songs of Love and Hate*, released on March 19, 1971, had failed to attract much critical and popular attention outside his fan base in Europe, and both Cohen and his then manager Marty Machat became aware that during the fall of 1971 Columbia was seriously considering dropping him as one of their artists. As noted in Michael Posner's second volume of *Leonard Cohen: Untold Stories*, Cohen was sufficiently anxious about this that he contacted Montreal brothers Dan and Jack Lazare at Aquarius Records in case Columbia dropped him. As close friend Barrie Wexler notes: "Cohen knew he was skating

---

[11] Linda Hutcheon, "Leonard Cohen and His Works," in *Canadian Writers and Their Works*, ed. Robert Lecker et al., Fiction Series, vol. X (Toronto: ECW Press, 1989), 25.

[12] The *Various Positions* album was released in Canada on December 11, 1984, and finally in the US and Europe in February 1985. *Various Positions* was the name given to Cohen's 1985 tour of Australia and elsewhere, and is also the name of Nadel's 1996 biography, as cited above in note 7.

[13] Robert de Young, personal conversation with Tony Palmer in London, March 27, 2023.

on thin ice with Columbia ... he was fighting depression and the sense that the whole fledgling enterprise might collapse. He said he didn't care, but he absolutely did."[14] Determined to support his client, Marty Machat decided that a tour should be mounted to increase Cohen's profile and his sales, and that the tour should be filmed and recorded. While Cohen trusted Machat's financial and strategic acumen, the prospect of having the tour documented on film simply compounded his anxiety in the lead-up to the tour.

Cohen's personal life was also creating its own pressures throughout 1971. He was moving around a great deal, spending some time in his isolated cabin in Tennessee, but also travelling to Hydra, New York, Montreal, Toronto, London, Switzerland, and California. Posner's interviewees suggest that Cohen was using a lot of drugs while he was on Hydra that summer as well.[15] The long-standing relationship with Marianne effectively was over. On the 1972 tour "So Long, Marianne" continued to be popular with audiences, but Cohen would also add some new, more poignant, if not bitter, lyrics this time around:

> Your eyes, you know I'm goin' to forget your eyes,
> Your body's at home in every sea, little one
> How come you gave away your news to everyone?
> I thought you said it was a secret just for me[16]

While Cohen continued a string of casual relationships during the 1972 tour, he was starting to feel trapped by the more conventional domestic life that his then partner Suzanne Elrod clearly wanted. In December 1971 they took a brief holiday in Acapulco, and the two photos taken by Suzanne in a bathroom – one of which was used for the cover of the *Live Songs* 1973 album – portray a very thin Cohen, with a shaved head and looking unusually dark and moody for someone on a holiday. Compounding Cohen's fears about the future, Suzanne became pregnant, and Cohen openly told friends he'd been "tricked."[17]

---

[14] See Michael Posner, *Leonard Cohen, Untold Stories: From This Broken Hill* (Toronto: Simon and Schuster, 2021), vol. II, 25.

[15] Ibid.

[16] From the unreleased Amsterdam performance of "So Long, Marianne" on April 15, 1972.

[17] Posner, *Leonard Cohen, Untold Stories*, vol. II, 53.

It is not surprising then, that, as Ira B. Nadel makes clear, Cohen wanted to exercise even more control this time:

> Bob Johnston [Cohen's record producer] had suggested making a film of the upcoming tour and Tony Palmer, who had made a movie about Tom Jones, was hired to direct. Cohen's lawyer Marty Machat produced. Titled *Bird on the* [sic] *Wire*, it premiered in London at the Rainbow Theatre in 1974 and shows Cohen performing, clowning with his musicians, and trying to pick up women. Cohen was initially unhappy with the arty look of the film and wanted a stronger, documentary texture. He spent nearly six months editing the work, shifting its focus away from the visual clichés to the deeper realities of his music. Control was crucial for him, as it was in the production of his first book of poems and his first album. What Cohen wanted was a film that showed the live context of his music and his rapport with his audiences. *Bird on the Wire* did that, but it also showed Cohen emotionally wasted. He felt exposed in the film and thought that his vulnerability was inappropriate for public viewing.[18]

According to Jim Devlin, the "filming technique used on *Bird on a Wire* draws on D. A. Pennebaker's celebrated *Don't Look Back*."[19] Cohen was unwilling to allow himself to be portrayed in this way, and he came to London to supervise a new version. But the second version did not satisfy the director, Tony Palmer, who said that he would be appalled at the release of the second version, as it was "a bowdlerization of some wonderful material" and "did not represent the best" of what he and Leonard had done.[20] Both Palmer's original and Cohen's cut of the documentary film have effectively disappeared from public view. Tony Palmer released an unauthorized DVD of a "reconstructed" cut of *Bird on a Wire* in 2010,[21] with a deluxe edition in 2016 containing a second disc of Cohen's home

---

[18] Nadel, *Various Positions*, 184–85.

[19] This refers to the Bob Dylan documentary *Don't Look Back*, dir. D. A. Pennebaker (Pennebaker Associates Inc. and Ashes and Sand Inc., 1967). Given how frequently the two artists are compared, it's noteworthy that both Leonard and Bob were the subjects of their first major documentary film treatment within a twelve-month period of each other.

[20] Jim Devlin, *Leonard Cohen: In Every Style of Passion* (London: Omnibus, 1996), 56–57.

[21] Tony Palmer, *Bird on a Wire*, dir. and ed. Tony Palmer. Voiceprint, 2010.

movies, some extracts of which had been included in the 1965 National Film Board of Canada documentary.

While, in the absence of an extant version of Palmer's original cut of *Bird on a Wire*, it is difficult to draw conclusions about the exact nature and extent of Cohen's changes for public release, the 2010 version does perpetuate the image of Cohen the reluctant performer – an image that he seems to have fostered on many other occasions. Palmer also spends a large amount of screen time in the 2010 re-versioning focused on the sound problems and audience disgruntlement, and the misunderstanding in Tel Aviv is presented as some sort of public insurrection fueled by Cohen. The reality is that Cohen simply didn't understand that the resurfacing of the sports stadium had just been completed, which is why the audience was relegated to the bleachers around the perimeter. In the final section of Palmer's 2010 film, the camera finds Cohen backstage before the final concert of the European tour in Jerusalem, having taken acid. Cohen has to be actively encouraged to go onstage and, once there, breaks down in the middle of a song and tells the audience he can't go on (this echoes Cohen's first public performance in New York in 1967). After some clowning around and a shave backstage, Cohen and the band return to the stage, but the documentary focus is on what happens at the conclusion of the concert – overpowered by emotion, everyone, including Cohen, is weeping. Bob Johnston commences a rather self-conscious version of the signature tune, "Bird on the Wire," and our final glimpse of Cohen at the conclusion of the Jerusalem performance sees him smiling on the tour bus with an expression that again suggests both a discomfort with the emotional exposure and a simultaneous appreciation of his success at concealing his true self.

The material in Cohen's archives paints a very different image of the 1972 tour from that presented in Palmer's 2010 film – as shambolic, drug-fueled, and characterized by restless and unhappy audiences. Cohen may have had trepidations about touring, but the newly mixed and reviewed tapes of eleven concerts, the twenty-two hours of unseen footage, and the published and unpublished writing from 1972 reveal his artistry, camaraderie with his band, and union with the audience. What can be garnered from Palmer's reconstructed 2010 film does not jive with what we know now – from the actual recordings and recollections of the participants

Jennifer Warnes, Peter Marshall, and David O'Connor, who are interviewed for a new film.[22] With Cohen's back apparently against the wall, the 1972 tour is an astounding triumph of his ability to forge a relationship with his fellow musicians, and most importantly with his audiences. The eleven complete concerts discovered in the Cohen archives are witness to his ability to perform masterful versions of many of the best loved songs from the first three albums alongside rousing covers of popular "protest" songs like "We Shall Not Be Moved."

Some sixteen years later, in 1988, Cohen was the subject of a documentary by the prestigious BBC Omnibus team, *Songs from the Life of Leonard Cohen*.[23] Large parts of this documentary consist of performances from the 1988 *I'm Your Man* tour, but there is a core interview with Cohen which is very measured and controlled. Cohen relates many stories and anecdotes that would become very familiar in many of his later interviews, and he repeats some of the stories told to Harry Rasky in the earlier 1980 concert-based television documentary *The Song of Leonard Cohen*,[24] broadcast on the CBC. However, in terms of Cohen's control over the narrative of his career, there is an interesting comment in the BBC interview in which Cohen distances himself from the influence of Dylan:

> In hindsight it seems like a mad decision that I was going to rectify my economic situation by becoming a singer. But I had been very interested in country music for a long time, and I'd been writing songs for a long time, I thought I'd go down to Nashville and cut a country and western record

---

[22] Steve Berkowitz (who has produced all of the *Bob Dylan Bootleg Series* box sets) and Robert de Young are completing production on the first retrospective Leonard Cohen box set, which will include two curated discs of the best performances from the eleven complete concerts of the 1972 tour in the archives, two bonus discs of the final concert in Jerusalem, and a new film, directed by Robert de Young, drawn from the twenty-two hours of unseen footage of the tour. Unfortunately, there is no definite release date at this time.

[23] *Songs from the Life of Leonard Cohen*, dir. Bob Portway, BBC Omnibus, July 1988.

[24] *The Song of Leonard Cohen*, dir. Harry Rasky, CBC Television, 1980. Harry Rasky also published a book, based on the documentary, *The Song of Leonard Cohen* (Toronto: Mosaic Press, 2001). This performance-based documentary features material from the Field Commander Cohen tour which resulted in the live album *Field Commander Cohen: Tour of 1979*, released February 20, 2001. The Leonard Cohen archives contain a large number of tapes from the Brighton and Hammersmith Odeon concerts in the UK, 1979, that this album draws on.

and that would take care of everything. And on the way down to Nashville, I'd been in Greece for about six years and I wasn't really aware of what was going on, I was totally unaware of the so-called "folk song renaissance," it wasn't folk music at all, but they call it that. I didn't know who Dylan was, or Joan Baez or Judy Collins, and on the way down to Nashville I got ambushed in New York by this whole phenomenon.

While the 1990s saw some authorized (Cohen preferred the word "tolerated") documentaries, the most notable being Armelle Brusq's *Leonard Cohen: Spring 1996* which profiled his life in the Zen monastery at Mt. Baldy, it is worth mentioning in this context Nick Broomfield's recent 2019 documentary, *Marianne & Leonard: Words of Love*. In keeping with Broomfield's usual strategies in his films, the filmmaker inserts himself into the narrative, and several sections of the film detail Broomfield's own relationship with Marianne in the years following the end of the relationship with Cohen. But the film draws a rather long bow in light of a lot of archival evidence in suggesting that Marianne was the love of Cohen's life and largely perpetuates the romanticized image of an idyllic relationship that stayed with him throughout his life. At one point we see Marianne in the audience during one of Cohen's World Tour (2008–13) concerts in Oslo – the reality is that no one, including Marianne, was permitted backstage before or after the show. Cohen was making regular trips back to Montreal while he was living on Hydra and spent a period of residence in London, and this romanticized account of leading a life of complete isolation in Greece – and the romanticizing of the relationship with Marianne on Hydra – doesn't fit very well with either Ira B. Nadel's or Sylvie Simmons's accounts and analyses.[25]

In late 2014 Cohen approved the production of the most recent and commercially successful documentary to date, *Leonard Cohen: Hallelujah, a Journey, a Song*.[26] The filmmakers optioned Alan Light's work *The Holy or the Broken: Leonard Cohen, Jeff Buckley, and the Unlikely Ascent of "Hallelujah."*[27]

---

[25] See Sylvie Simmons, *I'm Your Man: The Life of Leonard Cohen* (New York: HarperCollins, 2012), 96–145.

[26] *Hallelujah: Leonard Cohen, a Journey, a Song*, dir. Dayna Goldfine and Dan Geller (Sony Pictures Classics, 2022).

[27] Alan Light, *The Holy or the Broken: Leonard Cohen, Jeff Buckley, and the Unlikely Ascent of "Hallelujah"* (New York: Atria, 2012).

The film was made over eight years, and while Cohen did not contribute a new interview for the film, this feature-length documentary includes some insightful interviews with people close to Cohen: *Various Positions* producer John Lissauer, Dominique Issermann, Larry "Ratso" Sloman, and Judy Collins, among others. While the film, like Light's study, was originally conceived as mapping the unlikely success of the song "Hallelujah," following Cohen's death in November 2016 the filmmakers' ambition shifted to producing a more in-depth analysis of his entire recording career, and necessarily some parts of Cohen's life and career are skated over. Cohen's children and romantic partners Suzanne Elrod, Rebecca De Mornay, and Anjani Thomas, and other close personal friends, are missing from the film, but there is strong use of archival material. We see some of the eighty-odd rejected verses from the song "Hallelujah" sourced from three of Cohen's notebooks, and the archival material and interviews provided by Larry Sloman with Cohen are particularly captivating. The film notes that the first cover version of the song was done by Bob Dylan during his 1988 tours (appropriately at the Montreal concert on July 8), and there is the wonderful account given by Cohen from the late 1980s in various interviews about his famed meeting with Dylan in Paris, when Cohen, embarrassed about how many years he'd worked on writing the song, misrepresented the length of time to Dylan. After Cohen praised his recent song "I and I," much to Cohen's amusement Dylan said it took him about fifteen minutes to write.

This documentary also includes some of the excellent recording studio footage and interviews with Cohen from the 1985 ZDF television documentary *Leonard Cohen – Hallelujah in Moll*.[28] This German television documentary crew had access to Cohen, producer John Lissauer, and the *Various Positions* musicians (including a young Anjani Thomas on keyboards), and this footage is well used in Geller and Goldfine's film as a contemporary record of Cohen during the recording of the *Various Positions* album. While according to Cohen's mid 1980s romantic partner, Dominique Issermann, and producer Lissauer, he was very happy with the album when it was completed, it's ironic in the context of the success of the song "Hallelujah" that Columbia executive Walter

---

[28] *Leonard Cohen – Hallelujah in Moll*, dir. Georg Stefan Troller (ZDF TV, 1985).

Yetnikov refused to release the *Various Positions* album in the United States. But, in keeping with Cohen's self-effacing comments in interviews and onstage throughout his career, both the ZDF documentary and this most recent one conclude with an endearingly philosophical Cohen declaring: "You look around and you see a world that is impenetrable, that cannot be made sense of. You either raise your fist, or you say 'Hallelujah.' I try to do both."

Documentary profiles of an artist can only ever provide one version of the subject, and the completed film depends on a multitude of factors, including the availability and willingness of interviewees, the availability of and access to archival material, and of course budget. What is impressive about a survey of documentary films about Cohen – and there are some not mentioned here, owing to considerations of space – is that, from the first, Cohen had a quiet confidence about the importance of his work as a writer and performer, in the face of hostile reviewers and music journalists, indifferent record companies, and limited sales figures. The present volume is a testament to that confidence and his place in the Tower of Song, where he's still speaking to us sweetly.

CHAPTER 21

"I'll Wear a Mask for You"

Lucy J. Boucher

LEONARD COHEN HAS BEEN ACCUSED OF WEARING HIS HEART on his sleeve, or, according to Gary Shapiro, "some less clothed part of his body."[1] A harbinger of the 1970s singer-songwriter scene, Cohen's lyrics were often rooted in his own experiences, but never entirely confessional. He has been both praised and chastised for his signature use of the first-person singular, allowing audiences and critics alike to assume that his work is entirely autobiographical. While he has not been associated with the outright theatricality of such artists as David Bowie and Bob Dylan, who created characters and costumes to embody each new album, I argue that Cohen also created several different public representations of himself. The public figure "L. Cohen" was never static, but continually evolving, corresponding to Cohen's rejection of the idea of a fixed sense of "self," claiming that "everybody's continually moving into all different kinds of characters and roles."[2] The three personae that most define the eras of Cohen's career are his early emergence as "The Poet of Rock & Roll" in the 1960s, the "Ladies' Man" or "Depressive Lothario" that defined the struggles Cohen faced in achieving critical and commercial success, and the "High Priest of the Heart" who emerged as part of a late-career resurgence when he returned from his years atop Mt. Baldy as a Buddhist monk.[3]

---

[1] Gary Shapiro, "The End of the World and Other Times in *The Future*," in *Leonard Cohen and Philosophy: Various Positions*, ed. Jason Holt (Chicago: Open Court, 2014), 90.
[2] "Leonard Cohen – Kulturen Interview Sweden 1988," 0:0.35–47, www.youtube.com/watch?v=X_FvUHENqsQ&t=55s&ab_channel=ScottishTeeVee.
[3] Christophe Lebold termed Cohen's final incarnation as the "High Priest of the Heart" in his article "The Traitor and the Stowaway: Persona Construction and the Quest for

FUNCTIONS OF MASKS

The mask is a ubiquitous symbol throughout history and culture. It is associated with ancient tribal rites, Greek and Roman theater, and the more modern tradition of absurdist playwrights such as Jean Genet and Bertolt Brecht, who sought to alienate and distance their audience through the barrier of the mask. The mask serves three essential functions for performers. The first is concealment and disguise. Cohen was adept at using masks and personae to protect his private self from the scrutiny of hostile media and audiences. The second function is revelation and truth-telling. As Oscar Wilde once quipped, "Man is least himself when he talks in his own person. Give him a mask, and he will tell you the truth."[4] The mask, or personae, of "Leonard Cohen" allowed the artist to explore universal truths through a personal lens, without fear of his true self facing criticism or condemnation. The mask's final function, and the focus of this chapter, is transformation.

The English word "mask" comes from the Arabic *maskhahra*, which means "to transform" or "falsify." Adopting a mask or persona allows the wearer to both represent and become something or someone else. Anthropologist Donald Pollock notes that in tribal contexts the mask is used in ritual practice as a "technique for transforming identity ... through the temporary – and representational – extinction of identity."[5] Given Cohen's fascination with Zen Buddhism and its ultimate objective of self-negation and transcendence, this is a particularly salient point to consider, as I will explore later.

THE POET OF ROCK & ROLL

Throughout his career, Cohen used masks to both enhance his art and attract audiences. The masks also served as a self-defense mechanism,

---

Cultural Anonymity and Cultural Relevance in the Trajectories of Bob Dylan and Leonard Cohen," *Journal of the International Association for the Study of Popular Music* 1, no. 2 (2011): https://doi.org/10.5429/322 .

[4] Oscar Wilde, "The Critic as Artist," in *Oscar Wilde: The Complete Collection*, ed. M. Mataev (Brazil: Di Lernia Publishers, 2013), Ebook.

[5] Donald Pollock, "Masks and Semiotics of Identity," *Journal of the Royal Anthropological Institute* 1, no. 3 (September 1995), 582.

protecting him from public scrutiny and criticism behind the cloak of his stage persona. The young Leonard Cohen began his ascent to literary stardom in his native Canada at the tender age of twenty-two with the publication of his first poetry collection, *Let Us Compare Mythologies*, in 1956. Though the young poet's work never sold in large numbers, he achieved a level of literary celebrity that was previously unprecedented in his homeland. He adopted the mask of, as Michael Ondaatje termed, the "pop saint," which was an exaggeration of his own personality, especially his fascination with both sex and religion reflected in the interweaving of the sacred and profane in his writing.[6] Leveraging this persona, Cohen became a frequent pundit on the Canadian Broadcasting Corporation (CBC), promoting both his work and himself.[7]

Cohen achieved acclaim for his writing but found that even after the publication of his well-reviewed sophomore novel *Beautiful Losers* in 1966 he "couldn't even pay the rent." He admitted that, in hindsight, "it seems like the height of folly – I'll take care of my financial problems by becoming a singer."[8] Cohen was not avaricious, but he was ambitious. He admired the success of artists such as Bob Dylan. At a party of eminent Canadian poets in 1966, Cohen played a Dylan record to an unimpressed audience. Cohen recalled that they asked, "Do you want to be that?"[9] Cohen demurred on this accusation. While he may not have deliberately mimicked Dylan's poetic troubadour image, he was certainly inspired by it.

When he turned to songwriting in the 1960s, his literary success did not translate into immediate acceptance in the music industry. As late as 1975, Cohen lamented the resistance he faced when attempting to break into the "rock world": "I seem to be caught in the critical establishment between two critical houses ... the literary people are very resentful ...

---

[6] Michael Ondaatje, *Leonard Cohen* (Toronto: McClelland and Stewart, 1970), 61.

[7] See "Leonard Cohen: Playing the Favorite Game," CBC, www.cbc.ca/player/play/17 36797763; and Adrienne Clarkson, "Beautiful Losers Praised and Condemned," CBC, www.cbc.ca/player/play/1736790494.

[8] Tom Schnabel, radio interview with Leonard Cohen, July 13, 1988, "Morning Becomes Eclectic," KCRW-FM, in *Leonard Cohen on Leonard Cohen: Interviews and Encounters*, ed. Jeff Burger (Chicago: Chicago Review Press, 2014), 238.

[9] Brian D. Johnson, "Leonard Cohen Wore Earplugs to a Dylan Show?," *Maclean's* (June 8, 2008), https://macleans.ca/news/canada/cohen-wore-earplugs-to-a-dylan-show/.

[and] a lot of people in the rock establishment ... suggest I don't know anything about music."[10]

To gain cultural relevance in the fickle pop-music marketplace, and to redefine himself as a songwriter, Cohen created a new character that, ironically, played upon his previous persona as the golden boy "pop poet."[11] He fashioned himself as "The Poet of Rock & Roll," playing upon his literary credentials. This persona was seized upon by the PR engine of his record label which – in a campaign mocked by *Rolling Stone* – announced in "hushed tones of reverence" that Leonard Cohen was a brilliant poet.[12] Biographer Sylvie Simmons notes that his public image mirrored the publicity around him. The cover for his first album, *Songs of Leonard Cohen*, was a sepia-tinged portrait of Cohen taken in a New York subway photo booth. Simmons comments that the "solemn man in a dark jacket and white shirt ... might as well have been the photo of a dead Spanish poet."[13] The persona of the "Poet of Rock & Roll" was intended to establish Cohen within the rock industry, but for many critics it led to intense scrutiny and questioning of his credentials. The 1968 *Rolling Stone* review of his debut album took offence at Cohen's poetic language, claiming that Cohen often prided his "poetic bag of tricks" over "meaning."[14] The writer's main gripe with Cohen's transition from poetry to songwriting was that he did not come to it "naturally" – a concern that was impossible to escape when his entire persona played upon his transition from literary *enfant terrible* to rock star.[15] Ironically, when Cohen appeared on the CBC in 1966 to discuss his novel *The Favourite Game*, he declared that American reviewers, who were not aware that this was his "debut" novel or of his standing in Canada, treated the book far

---

[10] Paul Williams, "Leonard Cohen: The Romantic in a Ragpicker's Trade," *Crawdaddy!* (March 1975), reprinted in Burger (ed.), *Leonard Cohen*, 90.

[11] Cohen was often referred to as the "golden boy" when he was a rising poet in Montreal, and Cohen sometimes used the appellation self-mockingly: "Where are you golden boy? Where's your famous golden touch?," "Dress Rehearsal Rag," on the album *Songs of Love and Hate* (1971).

[12] Arthur Schmidt, "Songs of Leonard Cohen," *Rolling Stone* (March 1968).

[13] Sylvie Simmons, *I'm Your Man: The Life of Leonard Cohen* (London: Vintage, 2017), 228.

[14] Schmidt, "Songs of Leonard Cohen."   [15] Ibid.

more "objectively" than the "patronizing" Canadian critics.[16] It is interesting then that, while Cohen appreciated his work being taken on its own terms without the burden of his previous associations or personae, when he chose to become a songwriter he would choose a persona that would do exactly that.

While Cohen presented the coherent persona of the "Poet of Rock & Roll" to his audiences, his PR engine, which had initially seized upon the image in their marketing campaigns, showed their own reservations. The US record label's advertisement for *Songs of Leonard Cohen* pulled a quote from the *Boston Globe* comparing the poet to James Joyce, switching it for the more provocative Cohen quip from a *Playboy* article, "I've been an outlaw on the scene since I was fifteen." It featured an unshaven but smiling Cohen lounging in striped pajamas before the photograph of his somber album cover. Sylvie Simmons calls the juxtaposition "incongruous," which perhaps perfectly sums up the difficulty that audiences, critics, and even advertising executives had when trying to assimilate a coherent sense of Cohen's self-identity.[17] The outlaw branding seemed more in keeping with the Dylanesque wild troubadour images beloved by audiences, but Cohen's more academic background was at odds with this "free-wheeling" image.

The representation of Cohen as a poet may have been designed to compensate for what was thought to be the weakness of the singing voice that delivered his powerful words. Cohen admitted, "I have a terrible voice,"[18] and music critic Arthur Schmidt agreed, asking why, in Cohen's novel *The Favourite Game*, the character based on himself was always being asked to sing.[19]

The "Poet of Rock & Roll" persona was an attempt to translate Cohen's literary acclaim into musical success, but it was also a mask for the surprisingly shy Canadian to hide behind. Cohen admitted to feeling insecure as a performer in his early years – even going so far as to commission his friend the artist Morton Rosengarten to create a plaster-cast "death mask"

---

[16] "Playing the Favourite Game: CBC Youth Special with Paddy Springate and Stuart Smith (1963)," CBC, https://youtu.be/3YpgBaIW1rc?si=JFRcKpo_9PuLl0um.
[17] Simmons, *I'm Your Man*, 197.
[18] Quoted in Ira Mothner, "Songs Sacred and Profane," *Look* (June 10, 1969).
[19] Schmidt, "Songs of Leonard Cohen."

of his own "expressionless" face to wear – or to hide behind – onstage.[20] The mask was made, but the idea of wearing it onstage was ultimately abandoned. Instead, Cohen embraced showmanship, using the mask of his stage persona both to enhance his art by adopting the character of the romantic poet and to hide his own private fears. At the Aix-en-Provence Music Festival in France, August 1970, he appeared onstage riding a white horse like a "knight in some old-fashioned book" ("Bird on the Wire," *Songs from a Room*). Simmons has claimed that, despite the boos and jeers from the crowd of "Maoists" who favored authenticity over theatricality, "At that moment, Leonard was the consummate showman, appearing to be in full control of both the spontaneity and the artifice of his performance."[21]

Personae were an important protection for Cohen's private self throughout his career, as he feared that his work would suffer from public scrutiny of his private life. Indeed, in his 1972 poetry book, *The Energy of Slaves*, he equated celebrity with slavery. The poem "89" reveals the tension between sharing his art with the public and protecting his private self, as he claims "His absolute privacy violates itself before our eyes/ His absolute privacy forbids the violation."[22] Cohen's personae were more than just a means to protect his private life, however. The "Poet of Rock & Roll" persona was also a means to enhance his art through the transformation of personal experience into universal truths, which is what any great writer does. In a 1963 interview, Cohen countered claims that his novel *The Favourite Game* was autobiographical by declaring that "the emotion is autobiographical because the only person's emotions I know about are my own. The incidents are not autobiographical ... I made it up out of my little head."[23]

Audiences received songs such as "Sisters of Mercy" (*Songs of Leonard Cohen*) through the fictional lens of Cohen's poetic persona. Rather than the mundane anecdote of allowing two stranded sisters to sleep in his hotel room's double bed while he took the armchair during a snowstorm, it became the quasi-religious tale of a wandering troubadour given shelter and succor.[24] The religious overtones of the

---

[20] Simmons, *I'm Your Man*, 217.   [21] Ibid., 234.
[22] Leonard Cohen, "89," *The Energy of Slaves* (London: Jonathan Cape, 1972), 99.
[23] "Playing the Favourite Game."
[24] Paul Zollo, "Inside the Tower of Song," *SongTalk* (April 1993), in Burger (ed.), *Leonard Cohen*, 284.

song, and Cohen's own chivalric character, imply finding refuge in the sanctity of a convent, the two sisters offering "comfort" to "you who've been travelling so long."

THE DEPRESSIVE LOTHARIO

The persona of the "Poet of Rock & Roll" masterminded by Cohen and seized upon by his record label's marketing drive failed to capture the imagination of a large enough audience. While the transformative mask of the "Poet of Rock & Roll" created an interesting interplay between Cohen's stage persona as the chivalrous poet and his songs of longing, it did little to boost record sales, especially in the United States. In the face of declining sales and poor critical reception, Cohen "de-poeticized his stage persona" to make himself more palatable to rock audiences.[25] He donned the transformative mask of the "Ladies' Man" – a roving lothario in a leather jacket – an echo of the outlaw image his record company had previously tried to promote.

Simon Frith has argued that in the 1960s and 1970s, music journalists were the de facto gatekeepers of popular culture. Their opinions could define a performer's persona for their public, and, unfortunately for Cohen, the critics were quick to define him as depressing and an abject artist. Allen Evans, in a damning review of the 1971 album *Songs of Love and Hate* remarked, "what a depressing guy this Cohen is!" Alec Dubro wrote in *Rolling Stone* in 1969 that he was a "sensitive person who is depressed and depressing."[26] Donald Henahan summed up his feelings in his 1968 *New York Times* review of *Songs of Leonard Cohen* by drawing an unflattering, if humorous, comparison between Cohen and Bob Dylan. "Mr. Dylan is alienated from society and mad about it. Mr. Cohen is alienated and merely sad about it."[27]

Cohen hoped to transform this image through adopting the persona of the "Ladies' Man." But the "depressive" persona projected upon him

---

[25] Lebold, "The Traitor and the Stowaway," 10.
[26] Alec Dubro, review of *Songs from a Room* by Leonard Cohen, *Rolling Stone* (May 17, 1969). www.rollingstone.com/music/music-album-reviews/songs-from-a-room-98486/.
[27] Donald Henahan, "Alienated Young Man Creates Some Sad Music," *New York Times* (January 29, 1968).

by hostile music media, combined with the depressive aspects of his self-image, transformed him into the uneasy figure of the "Depressive Lothario." This demonstrates that while Cohen may have sought to control his image through masks and personae, it was not always easy to control the image that the mask projected to his audiences and critics. His personae were intended to both attract and deflect media attention. His work was considered "confessional," but in interviews he was wary of giving too much away. This led to music journalists propagating the perception that he was morose and laconic. In a *Billboard* magazine interview in 1970, Nancy Elrich wrote, "he works hard to achieve that bloodless vocal, that dull, humorless quality of voice speaking after death."[28] Cohen's delivery often made it difficult to tell whether he was being sincere or sarcastic, and acted as a mask which allowed him to speak freely. Elrich, however, projected her own misconceptions about the man onto the mask and broadcast them to a worldwide audience. While there was always a depressive element to Cohen's persona, and indeed his own personality, as he struggled with severe depression, he felt this characterization of him was unfair. "My person," he told the *New York Times*, "has been satirized as being suicidal, melancholy, and self-indulgent."[29]

Christophe Lebold argues that Cohen's rejection of the "poetic" persona occurred around 1974, but it is interesting to note that Columbia Records continued to refer to him as "the poet of rock" both on posters and ticket stubs for his subsequent European tour.[30] In the poster, Cohen appears in a shirt and tie and stares wistfully at the camera, far more in keeping with his "Poet of Rock & Roll" image than the louche "ladies' man" he wished to be. Though this may have been to cater to European sensibilities that may have embraced the poetic persona more readily, it suggests an ambiguity in Cohen's stage persona – the sense that both he and his marketing team were unsure how to position himself.

---

[28] Nancy Elrich, "Interview with Leonard Cohen," *Billboard* (August 8, 1970), in Simmons, *I'm Your Man*, 221.

[29] Mike Jahn, "I Have Been Satirized as Suicidal and Self-Indulgent," *New York Times* Special Features Syndicate (June 1973), in Burger (ed.), *Leonard Cohen*, 44.

[30] See Lebold, "Traitor and the Stowaway," 8.

In an attempt to reject his previous poetic image and fully embrace the rock image, Cohen recorded *Death of a Ladies' Man* with Phil Spector as producer in 1977, at the suggestion of Marty Machet, who managed both artists. No one was satisfied with the outcome. The mismatch between Spector's elaborate arrangements and Cohen's simple melodies and sophisticated lyrics was evident. An anecdote from the recording sessions perfectly encapsulates this. The wild-haired Phil Spector is said to have screamed, "This isn't punk rock! This is ROCK PUNK!," as the always sartorially elegant Cohen sat in the recording booth dressed in "a finely tailored dark-blue blazer and well-cut grey slacks," at odds with the ripped jeans and safety pins of the punk movement.[31]

The transformative mask of the anarchic rock star was not one that Cohen wore easily. It seemed so antithetical to his authentic self that it came across as a shoddy disguise and failed to fool his critics. The music journalists' suspicion of his true rock credentials was apparent in the December 1977 cover of French magazine *Rock & Folk*, which featured a caricature of an awkward-looking Cohen in an Elvis Presley stance beneath the dubious headline "Leonard Cohen, Rocker?" Cohen himself seemed exhausted by the pretense. The 1976 single "Do I Have to Dance All Night" expressed the effort that Cohen felt having to keep up with current trends, as he asks plaintively, "I'm forty-one, the moon is full ... I like you Mademoiselle/ But do I have to dance all night?" The persona of the rock & roll "Ladies' Man" was giving way to the popular conception of Cohen as a "Depressive Lothario."

Cohen's work always dwelt on themes of love and sex, but like the character in his songs, he became the barfly shooed from the inn at closing time, another woman whose name he would not remember on his arm, another night to fill with meaningless sex, another morning of regrets. The raucous "Don't Go Home with Your Hard-On" (*Death of a Ladies' Man*, 1977) belies the weariness of a man who – like Rimbaud – sat beauty on his knee and reviled it.[32] The "Depressive

---

[31] Harvey Kubernik, "What Happened When Phil Spector Met Leonard Cohen?," *Los Angeles Phonograph* (January 1978), in Burger (ed.), *Leonard Cohen*, 114.
[32] Arthur Rimbaud, *A Season in Hell and Other Poems*, trans. Norman Cameron (London: Anvil Press Poetry, 1994), 137.

Lothario" tells us he has "looked behind all of the faces/ That smile you down to your knees/ And the lips that say, 'Come on, taste us'" with a boredom that suggests his imperative to not go home with your hard-on is simply the practical fulfilment of another biological function. He goes on to imply that he tires of this "Ladies' Man" charade, but cannot shake the persona, as he is "chained to the old masquerade/ The lipstick, the shadow, the silicone." Songs such as "I Left a Woman Waiting" (*Death of a Ladies' Man*) depict a man with dead eyes, who takes an old lover to bed, "quick as dogs and truly dead." These lyrics are at once harrowing and evocative: the instant of pleasure, the emptiness afterwards.

The depression that plagued him throughout his life reared its head as he failed to sustain critical and commercial success and became an "avalanche that covered up [his] soul" ("Avalanche," *Songs of Love and Hate*). In his "Depressive Lothario" era, Cohen could sense the slow collision of his public and his private self, and the damage this wrought on his psyche. He knew that he could not survive the "joining" of public and private personae. His poetry collection *Death of a Lady's Man* included the heartbreaking plea, "I am ashamed to ask for your money ... but I need it to keep my different lives apart. Otherwise I will be crushed when they join."[33] It was time to change the mask.

HIGH PRIEST OF THE HEART

This sense of catastrophic self-collapse led Cohen to return with an intensity to the teachings of Zen Buddhism which he had flirted with periodically for solace since the 1970s. After his depression and anxiety came to a frightening climax during the 1993 world tour promoting *The Future* he retreated completely from public life. Previously he had frequently visited Mt. Baldy's Rinzai Zen Monastery for short periods of escape from his sometimes debilitating depression, but he now stayed for a prolonged and potentially permanent retreat. The next five years were spent studying at the feet of his friend and master, Roshi Kyozan Joshu

---

[33] Leonard Cohen, "The Price of This Book," *Stranger Music: Selected Poems and Songs* (London: Jonathan Cape, 1993), 274.

Sasaki, where he subjected himself to the harsh discipline and the rigorous schedule of monastic life.

Cohen's long-standing interest in Buddhism aligned with his fascination for the negation of self – a theme he explored before fully committing himself to becoming a Buddhist monk. In the 1978 poetry collection *Death of a Lady's Man* Cohen used double-voicing and the clever deconstruction of the narrative voice to create a poetic persona which Stephen Scobie described as assuming "too many contradictory positions ever to be assimilated back into any coherent picture of a unified self."[34] For example in "Death to This Book," the author switches to writing in the detached third person about the "I" who wrote the poem, asking "does he really wish to negate his life and his work?" The poem borrows the style of Vladimir Nabakov's *Pale Fire*, but inverts it, with the detached third-person critic examining the poet's work. The stanzas switch from first person, to second person, and to the collective voice. This dissemination is itself an act of self-negation through which Cohen explores a multitude of selves and characters, while repudiating the stable core of a unified "self."

This loss of self was not to be feared. Buddhist philosophy teaches that self-negation and overcoming the ego are an essential component of enlightenment. Achieving the negation of self is "the means to cut through the illusions of existence as substantive reality" by eliminating the dualism between subject and object. Ironically, for such a prolific writer as Cohen, this dualism is intrinsic to the grammatical structure of most Western languages.[35] Cohen sought to achieve this self-negation through the exploration of self and other in his work, while simultaneously cultivating and projecting personae for public consumption. It was a theme that fascinated him throughout his life. In a 1964 poem, "What I'm Doing Here" (*Flowers for Hitler*), the narrator is an "I" addressing a collective community of "you." The selfhood of "I" is negated by its insistence that it is a "mirror" in a movie theater lobby, reflecting the

---

[34] Stephen Scobie, "Keynote Address: The Counterfeiter Begs Forgiveness: *Leonard Cohen* and Leonard Cohen," *Canadian Poetry: The Proceedings of the Leonard Cohen Conference*, no. 33 (fall/winter 1993), 14.
[35] Michiko Yusa, "D. T. Suzuki and the 'Logic of Sokuhi,' or the 'Logic of Prajñāpāramitā'," in *The Dao Companion to Japanese Buddhist Philosophy*, ed. Gereon Kopf (New York: Springer, 2019) 607.

other back to itself, yet it is positioned in opposition to the "you" as it rejects the community of the collective and waits in judgment "for each of you to confess."

The rejection of ego and the idea of self-negation are common themes throughout Cohen's work, and they became more important as his interest in Zen Buddhism grew. The 1984 volume of poetry, *Book of Mercy*, contains his staunchest rejection of ego and selfhood, while simultaneously exploring his own selfhood through the adoption of a collective character. The collective voice dismisses the quest for an immutable self, announcing as a Greek chorus of self-recrimination that "we thought we were summoned, the aging head-waiters, the minor singers, the second-rate priests. But we couldn't escape into these self-descriptions."[36] The speakers of these poems understand that their attempts to fashion an identity through the descriptors of their jobs, their religions, their talents, have failed. In this respect, Cohen may perhaps have been reflecting on his own failure to fashion a self-identity through the construction of his stage personae. This self-examination came years before his retreat to Mt. Baldy but can be seen as the nascent seeds of this fascination with self-negation and rejection.

Cohen's acceptance of the ethos of self-negation did not mean a rejection of his transformation into the characters within his songs and stories. Instead, he was able to become "not Leonard Cohen, not any figure of 'Leonard Cohen,' but the problematic, vacant, discontinuous, non-authorial 'author' who ... has repeatedly emptied himself out in front of us."[37] Descending from the cloistered atmosphere of Mt. Baldy, Cohen became a composite character. In the ultimate act of self-negation, Cohen subsumed himself into the collective, appearing at once the "lecherous sinner, wandering Jew, hopeless monk, Zen master, high priest."[38] He became the vessel for a multitude of selves, speaking in the collective voice as he addressed his audiences' anxieties and fears, allowing them to explore their relationship to death, sex, and religion, while maintaining the detachment of the spiritual sage.

---

[36] Leonard Cohen, *Book of Mercy* (London: Canongate, 2019), 17.
[37] Scobie, "Keynote Address," 21. [38] Lebold, "Traitor and the Stowaway," 13.

While Cohen released the album *Ten New Songs* in 2001, he was reticent about returning to live performances. In 2008, economic necessity persuaded the Montreal bard to embark on a world tour. The anxiety that had plagued his career had not abated. In a personal email to David Boucher, he confessed "second to last day of rehearsal. Must confess to some degree of anxiety."[39] He need not have worried. His audiences welcomed him with ecstatic fervor. Assuming the character of the "Holy Sage," the "High Priest of the Heart," the seventy-six-year-old impressed the crowds with his showmanship. Sharon Robinson, long-time collaborator and backing singer, recalled that he "believed in the most committed delivery of a song that he could do ... the fact that he was older and starting to look kind of frail, that became part of the story."[40] Cohen's advanced years added to the gravity of this new character. The rich texture of his deep and haunting voice, the iconic tailored suits and fedoras that made him seem like a "rat-pack Rabbi," all became part of the "High Priest of the Heart" persona.[41] He even played upon his advancing years by altering the lyrics of "I'm Your Man" to "I'll wear an old man's mask for you."[42]

With age came a hard-won wisdom which audiences perceived as the persona of a holy seer. Fans such as Elton John described these concerts as a "religious experience."[43] This persona united the multitude of selves that Cohen had presented over the years. He was a poetic priest, a sensual ascetic, a fashionable outsider in his own inimitable style. This mask – at once an audience projection and a reflection of the man himself – seemed to be the one he was most at ease with wearing.

Throughout his career Leonard Cohen created masks and personae both to enhance his art and to hide his private self. The series of masks Cohen wore were not just his own inventions but collaborative productions

---

[39] Email from Leonard Cohen to David Boucher, April 29, 2008.
[40] Andy Greene, "Sharon Robinson Reflects on Touring with Leonard Cohen," *Rolling Stone* (July 12, 2017), www.rollingstone.com/music/music-features/sharon-robinson-reflects-on-touring-with-leonard-cohen-194281/.
[41] Simmons, *I'm Your Man*, 557.   [42] Ibid.
[43] Andy Greene, "Elton John Still Wants to Make Hip-Hop Records," *Rolling Stone* (March 18, 2014), www.rollingstone.com/music/music-news/elton-john-still-wants-to-make-hip-hop-records-190560/.

of the media, the audience, and the man himself. Sometimes this resulted in an uneasy tension between the man and the mask, as seen in the middle years of his career as he struggled to find himself both personally and professionally. The final mask, the "High Priest of the Heart," was at once his own creation and an interplay with his audiences' expectations. Though Cohen could not always control how he was perceived in the media, his personae always served to augment his art and have become part of his lasting artistic legacy.

CHAPTER 22

How to Be an Aged Rock Star

David R. Shumway

In 2023, the pandemic having been declared over, we saw many acts out on the road, most touring for the first time since 2019 or earlier. While artists of all ages toured, some of those who received significant coverage in the press were artists over the age of sixty-five, including Bruce Springsteen, Dead and Company, the Eagles, Aerosmith, and many more. The Rolling Stones got a jump on the trend, touring Europe in 2022, but they made news in 2023 by releasing their first album of new material in eighteen years. What is notable is that these acts were generally treated without the previously standard remarks about nostalgia.[1] That popular music can have the lasting value routinely attributed to, say, novels or poems is still hard for many to comprehend, even though record companies have long recognized that their back catalogs have significant commercial value. The idea that popular music is subject to the iron law of fashion remains a commonplace, even though rock & roll remained popular with new generations for decades after its initial ascendence and despite the fact that rockers in their golden years sell out concerts and continue to produce new records. Leonard Cohen's late albums and tours perhaps were the beginning of this reassessment of aging rock stars.

But if older acts are getting more respect, they generally are not presenting themselves as old. Mick Jagger supposedly said, "I'd rather

---

[1] See, e.g., Mark Tracy, "Saying Goodbye to the Dead. (Again.)," *New York Times* (July 14, 2023), www.nytimes.com/2023/07/14/arts/music/dead-and-company-final-tour.html?smid=url-share.

be dead than singing 'Satisfaction' when I'm forty-five." He turned eighty in 2023, but he's still singing "Satisfaction." There is little in Jagger's performance or self-presentation that would clue you in to his age, though his heavily lined face does. Jagger remains remarkably spry, continuing to prance around the stage much as he did when he was in his twenties and thirties. Rock & roll has always been music for (and often by) youth, and it has not often represented the experience of aging with much sympathy. The Beatles' "When I'm 64," for example, imagines that moment of life in terms of physical decline and threatened loneliness, its premise being the assumption that the old are superfluous at best.

Perhaps because we continue to link popular records with the moment of their release, rock stars too seem frozen in time. While they cannot, of course, avoid physical evidence of aging, the experience of aging is not something typically acknowledged, much less addressed. Even Bob Dylan, who looks and moves like someone in his eighties, does not write from the perspective of an octogenarian. The older members of Dead and Company don't hide their ages, but they don't ask us to think about them either. The one clear exception to this pattern was Leonard Cohen. During the great resurgence of his career in 2008, when he was seventy-four, Cohen developed a persona I will call "Old Leonard Cohen" that foregrounded his age, while his songs often addressed concerns especially relevant to older people. In what follows, I want to explore that persona and its meaning for the culture.

Cohen, of course, had always been somewhat of an exception when it came to the identification of music and youth. When he recorded his first album in 1967, he was already thirty-three at a time when young people told each other not to trust anyone over thirty. And it wasn't just a matter of chronology. Cohen looked the part of an adult, wearing suits and short hair at a time when almost no one else in rock did. His songs did not directly appeal to youth, as, for example, the Who and Dylan did in "My Generation" and "The Times They Are a'Changin'." Yet Cohen early in his career had an audience of young people and within a few years began to perform live within the conventions of rock rather than folk.

Cohen was thus a rock star even though many would not classify his music as rock & roll.² Even though in the United States he was not among the most popular of stars, he still enjoyed the perquisites of the dominant form of celebrity. Indeed, his age diminished neither his sexual promise nor his hipness. Cohen's appeal was different from that of a Paul McCartney or Mick Jagger, but it was not completely unique. Indeed, Cohen looked similar to Dustin Hoffman (only three years younger), who in *The Graduate* played one of the iconic representations of 1960s youth (he was thirty when the film was released), a character whose combination of privilege and alienation bears similarity to Cohen. Paul Simon and Randy Newman were musical stars who were not conventionally sexy and presented themselves as a bit more "adult." Rock stars came in all shapes and sizes, and they were not all young.

Still, Cohen in the late 1960s seemed older than Simon or Newman. In his study *The Late Voice*, Richard Elliott has asserted that Cohen exhibited even on his first album an "early lateness," an ability "to convincingly articulate maturity through singing and/or writing while still young."³ Elliott is certainly correct that Cohen seemed mature compared with most of his peers in the late 1960s and early 1970s, and this did not have to do entirely with his actual age. As Sylvie Simmons put it, "Leonard always was old. He was old on first album – thirty-three, a decade older than the other singer-songwriters making their debuts."⁴ Anthony DeCurtis says of Cohen's first album, "Its ten songs were entirely contemporary and strangely outside time, ancient without seeming what we would now call retro."⁵ Cohen's appearance on that album underscores his relative maturity, his sepia-toned portrait presenting him in a white shirt and dark suit jacket with a serious expression on his face.

The lyrics on the first album were not regarded as bleak, but his next two albums were described that way. His songs have dealt with death

---

[2] I have argued that rock & roll is best understood not as a genre, but as a cultural practice that includes many musical genres. See David R. Shumway, "Rock & Roll as a Cultural Practice," *South Atlantic Quarterly* 90 (fall 1991): 753–69.

[3] Richard Elliott, *The Late Voice: Time, Age and Experience in Popular Music* (New York: Bloomsbury, 2015), 134, 31.

[4] Sylvie Simmons, *I'm Your Man: The Life of Leonard Cohen* (New York: Ecco, 2012), 522.

[5] Liner notes, *Songs of Leonard Cohen*, 2007.

repeatedly since at least 1974's *New Skin for the Old Ceremony*, which includes "Who by Fire," based on a Yom Kippur prayer that asks how people might die in the coming year. There's also a song titled "A Singer Must Die," making it clear that it is the singer's own mortality that is being evoked. For a period in the 1970s, he did attempt to present himself in ways that made him appear more youthful – sporting longer hair, for example – but that phase only lasted a short time. He seemed to double down on the dour and depressing, beginning with *Various Positions* in 1984, perhaps reflecting his own battle with depression. And yet Elliott is perhaps too quick to associate these serious matters with maturity. If it is true that pop music has long eschewed serious subjects beyond heartbreak, rock & roll had claimed seriousness before Cohen started recording. The culture often makes fun of adolescent anxieties about death and assumes that most young people believe they are immortal. Alas, the frequency of suicide among young people suggests otherwise. The songs of the singer-songwriters who would emerge just a few years after Cohen – such as James Taylor and Joni Mitchell – were often equally serious (see Chapter 6 above).

However, there is a moment when Cohen seems to have begun to embrace old age in a way that other popular musicians of his era did not. In 1988, when Cohen was in his fifties, he recorded "Tower of Song" on the album of that year, *I'm Your Man*, which begins "My friends are gone, my hair is gray/ I ache in the places where I used to play." Where most rock stars in their fifties did their best to appear to be in their thirties, Cohen seems to be already in this song adopting the voice of an older person. Ira B. Nadel calls it "the keynote work on *I'm Your Man*," and asserts that its concern is "the aging songwriter."[6] Interestingly, "Tower of Song" is full of self-deprecating wit, including the lines, "I was born like this, I had no choice/ I was born with the gift of a golden voice." The album *I'm Your Man* deals with such serious subjects as terrorism and AIDS, and includes the song "Everybody Knows," which is a kind secular litany of the world's problems. And yet it is Cohen's most upbeat album, and not just as a matter of tempo. Age, it seems, suited Cohen better than

---

[6] Ira B. Nadel, *Various Positions: A Life of Leonard Cohen* (New York: Random House, 1996), 249.

youth. "Tower of Song" aside, however, Cohen was not yet presenting himself as an old man, nor was he perceived that way. The press coverage of the period makes no mention of age or aging.

Cohen receded from public view during the 1990s after he took up residence at the Zen monastery at Mt. Baldy, California, in 1994. While he did release several albums and continued to publish books, he did not tour again until 2008. Thus, when Cohen appeared on a tour made necessary by the theft of most of his assets by his longtime business manager, the person in the limelight was not someone like Dylan or Springsteen, who had consistently been in the public eye. While the persona he presented was not entirely unfamiliar, his age defined him now in a way it hadn't previously. As Ann Powers observed of his Los Angeles concert in April 2009:

> the 74-year-old poet and chanteur represented for the wintery side of manhood, but his beatific smile revealed the little boy within. Within the pop world, Cohen has always been an elder statesman; he released his first album in 1967, at age 33, already a published poet and novelist. The fact that he's long projected a certain maturity has helped him as he's physically aged. The transformation doesn't seem as drastic.[7]

Or perhaps one should say that he embraced his age as a defining condition. In the key document of the 2008–09 tour, the *Live in London* album and DVD (2009), Cohen introduces himself in a way that immediately calls attention to his age. He tells the audience, "It's been a long time since I stood on a stage in London. It was about fourteen or fifteen years ago. I was sixty years old, just a kid with a crazy dream." The observation not only emphasizes the speaker is now in his seventies, but that he is not the same person that he was at sixty. It is acute in that the Cohen of the 1993 tour behind the album *The Future* seemed essentially the same as he always had: older, but only by degree. The Cohen of 2008 and later was someone distinctly elder, a senior citizen.

Most of the songs Cohen was performing during the late tours, then, were not new, but many of them fit well with the persona he had adopted.

---

[7] Ann Powers, review of Leonard Cohen at the Nokia Theatre, Los Angeles, *Los Angeles Times* (April 13, 2009), D.1.

There are many different components to this new self-presentation, but it begins with his appearance. In the London concert, Cohen is dressed in a dark, pin-striped suit, and he is wearing a fedora. There is no doubt that the suit is well tailored, but its style is retro, as of course is the hat. Cohen said in a 2008 interview, "I've been wearing a fedora for a long, long time," but then acknowledged that previously "I've never performed with a hat."[8] He had usually performed in suits, but he appears to be more formally dressed now. And because the general style of dress in most of the places he performed had become more informal, Cohen's formality made him look now more at odds with the current moment.

Cohen's dress is not so important to his image as an old man as is his physical appearance. Cohen attributed the idea that he wasn't handsome to Janis Joplin in "Chelsea Hotel No. 2," but photos over the years belied that. In 2008, however, he really is no longer handsome. His face is deeply lined, and the skin is blemished. His hair is not only gray but cut very short, and his hairline is receding. His hands, even more than his face, reveal his age. They are marked with "age spots," the skin appearing to be darker than his facial complexion. Moreover, there is something stiff-looking about his fingers, which do not seem nimble as he plays his guitar. Cohen's larger movements to some extent contradict these impressions. He literally skips onstage. And in the London concert, there are brief moments of dancing, which, however light-footed he appears then, do not undo the perception that his performance lacks movement.

Cohen's visual presentation makes it clear that he is not trying to hide his age, but what he says and sings call attention to it. In London, he tells the audience that his Zen teacher, Roshi Kyozan Joshu Sasaki, once said to him, "Excuse me, I forgot to die," and Cohen reports that he sometimes feels that way too. He lists the psychoactive drugs he has taken since he was sixty: "Since then I've taken a lot of Prozac, Paxel, Welbutrin, Effexor, Ritalin, Focalin. I've also studied deeply in the philosophies and the religions. But cheerfulness kept breaking through." This last line

---

[8] Leonard Cohen, interview by Brian D. Johnson, "Cohen Wore Earplugs to a Dylan Show," in *Leonard Cohen on Leonard Cohen: Interviews and Encounters*, ed. Jeff Burger (Chicago: Chicago Review Press, 2014), 540.

points to another aspect of Old Leonard Cohen: that he seems happier than when he was younger. His manner onstage suggests contentment, perhaps even relish in performing. What drugs and religious discipline could not provide, making music has. Or perhaps it was his study of Zen and Vidanta that lifted his depression (see Chapter 9 above), but in any case Cohen appears to illustrate the now widely reported fact that the elderly are typically happier than younger people. As Neil Strauss observed in *Rolling Stone*, "Compared to his last concert in [New York], during which he seemed like a grizzled old rabbi who'd accidentally wandered onstage, Cohen was a polished, dapper showman – perhaps because since then he has quit drinking before shows and smoking altogether."[9]

Of course, another aspect of Old Leonard Cohen is his voice, which has clearly aged. Liel Leibovitz asserts that it changed as early as 1971 with *Songs of Love and Hate*, when "something crushing had happened to Cohen's voice." Where on "Suzanne" his voice conveyed "a considerable degree of warmth" and created "small wells of emotion and empathy," now the songs are "sung coldly, with little feeling" and with an "acerbic tone."[10] Leibovitz seems to be speaking here more of performance style than the voice itself. Cohen spoke of changes in his voice as early as 1992, when he reports in an interview that his "voice has gotten very, very deep over the years," and the interviewer responds, "You actually sound like a different person on the earlier records."[11] Elliott observes, "Cohen's voice does change over the course of his career, more noticeably so than those of Bob Dylan or Neil Young."[12] Sometimes on these late recordings Cohen seems merely to be speaking rather than singing his lyrics, while at others there remains a melodic dimension to his performance, albeit with a smaller range than he had as a younger man. Certainly, the warmth that Leibovitz finds missing in 1971 has returned in these performances.

---

[9] Neil Strauss, "Leonard Cohen, down from the Mountain," *Rolling Stone* (March 19, 2009), 66–67.
[10] Liel Leibovitz, *A Broken Hallelujah: Rock and Roll, Redemption, and the Life of Leonard Cohen* (New York: W. W. Norton, 2014), 166–67.
[11] Leonard Cohen, interview by Paul Zollo, "Leonard Cohen: Inside the Tower of Song," *SongTalk* (April 1993), in Burger (ed.), *Leonard Cohen*, 280.
[12] Elliott, *The Late Voice*, 135.

Simmons describes Cohen's voice on the 2010 tour as "softer and rougher at the edges now, a little cracked," a change she suggests even from the 2009 performances.[13] Compared with Dylan's voice of the same era (on *Tempest*, for example), Cohen's voice is less rough and more polished, but certainly softer. Cohen gives the impression of trying to stay within the limits of his voice, while Dylan seems to strain against his. Cohen, in other words, seems to embrace his "late voice" just has he has embraced other aspects of his old age. Indeed, it could be argued, as Elliott implies when he notes that Cohen won the Canadian Juno Award for Male Vocalist of the Year for *The Future*, that his "late voice" is actually more pleasing than his younger one: "it is . . . worth highlighting that this newfound acceptance of his voice is recognition of an increased gravitas that came with age."[14]

There is another aspect of the later performances that complements, and perhaps is a partial explanation for, Cohen's more pleasing vocal performance. Cohen had toured regularly until the early 1990s, but he seemed never to be entirely at ease with it. Early in his career there were several incidents in which he left the stage in mid performance, having to be coaxed back to finish the show. During the 1993 tour, he reported later that he had been drinking three bottles of Château Latour before every concert because "he was very nervous."[15] In 2008, he was no longer drinking, which in itself may help account for the superiority of these performances. When he first realized that touring was the only solution to his financial difficulties, Cohen was "very apprehensive," according to Roscoe Beck, whom Cohen had asked to be musical director.[16] Cohen's solution was to rehearse for more than six weeks before the first concert, and this unprecedented preparation that Cohen and his band undertook for the tour may account for his lack of nervousness in performance. It may also account for the fact that "it sounded like nothing Leonard Cohen had previously produced."[17] While other older acts certainly acquitted themselves well on these late tours, it is doubtful that one could say of any of them that they sounded new. But that is exactly how

---

[13] Simmons, *I'm Your Man*, 504.   [14] Elliott, *The Late Voice*, 135.
[15] Johnson, "Cohen Wore Earplugs," 541.   [16] Quoted in Simmons, *I'm Your Man*, 482.
[17] Leibovitz, *A Broken Hallelujah*, 236.

Cohen and his band sounded. Old Leonard Cohen was performing as a new Leonard Cohen, the old songs transformed by new arrangements and by Cohen's singing of them. As Strauss put it in his review of the first US show at the Beacon Theater in New York, "he seemed to have entered the material again: vaguely pantomiming each song, changing inflections to more directly depict the romantic defeatism of his lyrics, singing in a smoother, less raspy bass than he has in years."[18]

Old Leonard Cohen seemed different in other ways too. It is striking how gracious and humble he is, unlike the typical rock star who expects the fans' adulation as his due. In the late tours, Cohen repeatedly expresses gratitude to the audience for their presence, and he gives every impression of feeling genuinely moved by the audience's attention. In London, he acknowledges the audience's sacrifices to be there, saying, "I understand many of you have undergone geographic and financial inconvenience." He acknowledges the audience's applause by doffing the fedora and bowing, gestures that in themselves seem to be of an older person. He told an interviewer in 2008, "this is every musician's dream, to stand in front of an audience and not have to prove your credentials, to come into that warmth. Of course, it creates other anxieties, because you really want to deliver. There's a lot to live up to. But it is quite a rare thing."[19]

As we have seen, Cohen had dealt with death from early in his career, and he began to write about aging in his fifties. He addressed these issues more explicitly later. In an interview broadcast on April 16, 2009, Jian Ghomeshi refers to something Cohen had told another interviewer in 2001, that he was in the third act of his life. Cohen responds,

> Well, the beginning of the third act seems to be very, very well written. But the end of the third act, of course, when the hero dies – each person considering himself the central figure of his own drama – that, generally speaking from what one can observe, can be rather tricky. My friend Irving Layton said it's not death that he's worried about – it's the preliminaries.

"As I get older," Cohen continued, "I like to hear stories of the elderly. I'm reading Irving Layton's poems now over again, especially the poems

---

[18] Strauss, "Leonard Cohen," 66–67. [19] Johnson, "Cohen Wore Earplugs," 545.

he wrote toward the end of his life, and they are deeply instructive, not in a pedagogic way but in some kind of information for which the heart is hungry."[20] By explicitly discussing these matters, Cohen refuses the illusion of eternal youth that other stars on later tours continued to maintain.

The albums Cohen released after he returned to touring also embrace old age. The very title of *Old Ideas* (2012) seems to emphasize the point, although the intended referent was probably the ideas that Cohen himself had been dealing with throughout his career.[21] The album cover depicts Cohen seated on a wooden chair on a lawn, dressed all in black except for a light-colored shirt. He's wearing a fedora and sunglasses, his head tilted slightly to his right. He looks like the septuagenarian he is, seeming thinner and frailer than he had onstage in London in 2009. Cohen and his photographer both cast dark shadows on the lawn. On the CD itself there's a drawing by Cohen of a nude woman next to a skull. The first cut on the album is "Going Home," a phrase which is certainly in this context a metaphor for death: "Going home/ Without my burden … Going home/ Without the costume/ That I wore." The song is a dialogue with a speaker who addresses Leonard as one who does his bidding, perhaps God, or perhaps another side of the singer himself who is divided between resisting and accepting death. Cohen's next release, *Popular Problems* (2014), pictured the star on the front cover with a cane, suggesting continuing decline in physical health. The first track, "Slow," tells us, "You want to get there soon/ I want to get there last," again in apparent reference to death. While the song proclaims, "It's not because I'm old," the denial of the cause is an embrace of the condition. Death is an even bigger concern on *You Want It Darker* (2016), an album released just a few weeks before Cohen's demise. All three of these late albums were critically well received, and they sold better in the United States than any of his previous releases. This shows that the public embraced Old Leonard Cohen in a way that it had not done the earlier personae.

---

[20] Leonard Cohen, interview by Jian Ghomeshi (2009), "TV and Radio Interview," in Burger (ed.), *Leonard Cohen*, 551–52.

[21] See "I'm Your Man," interview with Alberto Manzano, 1988, in Burger (ed.), *Leonard Cohen*, 222, where both Cohen and Manzano agree that he has been dealing with "old ideas" for a long time.

Cohen's late success is hard to overstate. Of the late tours, Simmons notes, "Leonard is playing to the biggest and most age-diverse audiences of his career, and every show was a sellout."[22] And she observes, "The Tour not only restored Leonard's lost funds, it improved on them considerably. But it also brought Leonard something more important: vindication as an artist."[23] This reception is quite different from that accorded to the performances of other older rockers late in life. While they range from respectful to dismissive, Cohen's reception was ecstatic. The standard take was not that "he has still got it," but that Cohen's art had achieved a new level of greatness.

Why does it matter that Cohen presented himself frankly and unapologetically as an old man? Because ageism is perhaps the last prejudice to remain socially acceptable. "Unlike all the bigotries now recognized as evils (among them sexism, racism, homophobia), 'ageism' has yet to become an everyday pejorative."[24] Cohen's performance and persona as Old Leonard Cohen can help us to understand aging and to defeat this prejudice. Aging may seem simple and even obvious, but, as Elizabeth Barry and Margery Vibe Skagen, observe, it "is grindingly linear – an inexorable process with no dramatic arc. Conversely, however, it is also bafflingly, unpredictably non-linear."[25] This paradox applies both to the subject's experience of aging, which Barry and Skagen emphasize, but for our purposes, more importantly, to the different way aging affects different people. The physical strength and stamina of the Rolling Stones and Bruce Springsteen as compared with the frailer Cohen illustrate this. While aging is inexorable, it doesn't happen at the same rate or in the same sequence to everyone. It used to be believed by many that something called "senility" was a predictable result of growing older. We now speak of "dementia," recognized as a symptom of various degenerative diseases, which, while more common among older people, does not affect all or perhaps even most. And yet the public's opinion of

---

[22] Simmons, *I'm Your Man*, 495. [23] Ibid., 510.
[24] Margaret Morganroth Gullette, *Ending Ageism, or How Not to Shoot Old People* (New Brunswick: Rutgers University Press, 2017), 1.
[25] Elizabeth Barry and Margery Vibe Skagen (eds.), "Introduction: The Difference That Time Makes," in their *Literature and Ageing*, NED-New edition (Rochester, NY: Boydell & Brewer, 2020), 1.

ex-President Biden (2021–25) suggests that many still assume that age equals cognitive decline, understood as meaning the loss of significant capacities. Cohen (and the other older rockers) demonstrate that this is a pernicious prejudice.

But if those stars who present themselves as unchanged by age help us to understand the condition of aging, they also contribute, however unintentionally, to the prejudice of ageism. Old Leonard Cohen embodies the idea that the old are valuable not despite their age, but because of it. Old Leonard Cohen addresses issues that especially pertain to those in later stages of life in popular songs. Those issues matter in principle to everyone, because everyone who lives long enough will face them. As he said of Layton's late poetry, Cohen's late performances provided "a kind of information for which the heart is hungry." Cohen's aesthetic and popular success in his eighth decade shows that creativity is not solely the property of the young. The point is that such lucky folks cannot be the standard. Sooner or later, everyone who lives long enough will experience physical decline, many, perhaps most becoming disabled in one or more ways. As Jane Gallop puts it, "there is ... a wide swath where the categories of disability and aging bleed into one another."[26] Theoretically, though not sufficiently in practice, we have learned that disability does not equal inability, and that it is both just and practical to recognize special needs. A society that is both neuro- and physically diverse is better than one that is not. Cohen's example shows that we should value, rather than disparage, the old because of what they can offer that the young do not.

What is significant about Cohen's embrace of old age is not that it reveals the limitations of that state, but that it makes its possibilities seem more widely available. Moreover, Cohen's self-presentation makes some of the relative advantages of old age apparent. Cohen's graciousness onstage was certainly not entirely new in 2008, but it was nevertheless striking. It fit with the underlying assumption of the late tours, which was that the star was living on borrowed time. The audience was just as grateful to have him with them as he was for their presence. Unlike late

---

[26] Jane Gallop, *Sexuality, Disability, and Aging: Queer Temporalities of the Phallus* (Durham, NC: Duke University Press, 2019), 5.

tours by some other older performers around the same time, the word "nostalgia" never came up with regard to Cohen's late performances. This in part may have to do with his image as a poet, since we don't regard older poetry as inherently nostalgic. It also certainly has to do with the large number of recent covers of his songs, "Hallelujah" and "Suzanne" of course, but also many others. Songwriters seem to have longer currency than do performers. The albums that appeared after the 2008 tour were regarded as significant contributions to his oeuvre, something that distinguishes him from pretty much everyone, save perhaps Dylan. But I think it is the fact that Cohen was not pretending to be someone from another era that made it impossible to attribute the appeal of these late performances to nostalgia. The performances themselves were undeniably great. The arrangements were often new, the ensemble outstanding, and the star himself obviously, as he said, caring enough to deliver. Finally, if Cohen was not handsome, he was charismatic and perhaps even sexy. He made being old very attractive.

CHAPTER 23

Covers

Six Hundred and Forty-Nine Broken "Hallelujah"s

Ray Padgett

I N THE COURSE OF RESEARCHING MY BOOK ON THE 1991 TRIBUTE album *I'm Your Fan: The Songs of Leonard Cohen* for Bloomsbury's "33 1/3" series, I encountered a Leonard Cohen fan in Finland named Jarkko Arjatsalo. Someone had mentioned to me that Arjatsalo tracked Cohen covers, so I shot him a quick email asking about it. He responded with an Excel spreadsheet detailing every single different Cohen cover he has collected. It ran to 98 pages of very small type cataloging 3,201 different versions of Cohen's songs. Scrolling through the spreadsheet can be daunting: 105 "Hey, That's No Way to Say Goodbye"s; 136 "Famous Blue Raincoat"s; 169 "Dance Me to the End of Love"s. Even a relatively recent and obscure song like "Here It Is" has seventeen different covers listed. Plus, Arjatsalo cautioned me that he only tracks covers released on physical media – vinyl, CD, etc. – so this massive spreadsheet represents only a small fraction of the Cohen covers out there.

Two songs appear more in his spreadsheet than any other. The first is "Suzanne," at 286 covers. For "Suzanne," many familiar names appear in the tiny type under the "Artist" column: Tori Amos, Joan Baez, Harry Belafonte, Nick Cave, Judy Collins – and we haven't even gotten through the "C"s yet. There are many obscure names, too. Short-lived English new-wave group the Flying Lizards do a bonkers spoken-word-and-synths "Suzanne." There's a thirty-person male choir called Conspiracy of Beards that does a fully a cappella "Suzanne."

Those 286 "Suzanne" covers, though, pale in comparison to the *most* covered song on the list. You already know what it is. With 649 separate entries on the spreadsheet, "Hallelujah" wins by a mile (or, given Cohen is Canadian, a kilometre). Listing the artists' names seems pointless. Think of a famous name, particularly one known for their vocal prowess – or someone who thinks they *should* be known for their vocal prowess – and the odds are decent they've sung their own broken "Hallelujah" at some point.

In the history of music, the "cover" as we know it today is a relatively new concept. People have been performing music composed by others more or less forever, of course, but no one in the 1800s was talking about their local orchestra's new "cover" of Ludwig Van Beethoven. The word first came into use in this sense in the 1940s. At the time, with a few household-name exceptions, many listeners bought records by song title, not artist. If someone wanted to play a recording of "Some Enchanted Evening" at home, they may not have cared whether Perry Como or Frank Sinatra or Bing Crosby or Ezio Pinza sang it. Pinza's was the "original" in this case, from the Broadway cast recording of *South Pacific*, making all the others "covers." But all those recordings came out within a few months of each other – as did, more to the point, many others by lesser-known names. The point was not, as it often is with covers today, to put one's own spin on it. It was to jump onboard a popular hit as quickly as possible with your own copycat recording.

The first mention of the word "cover" I found in the leading music-industry magazine *Billboard* comes in 1949. In a discussion of current country-music hits, *Billboard* writes, "The original disking of Why Don't You Haul Off and Love Me?, cut for King by Wayne Raney, has hit 250,000, and versions are now available on all major labels." They then continue on to another song: "Another King disk, Blues Stay 'Way From Me?, by the Delmore Brothers, is close to 125,000 in six weeks, and the other companies have just begun to cover the tune."[1]

Notice that they say other *companies* cover the tune, not artists. That ties into a phase from the previous sentence, "versions are now available on all major labels." If someone had a hit, other labels would quickly crank out their own versions sounding as close as possible to

---

[1] Bill Simon, "Indies' Surprise Survival: Small Labels' Ingenuity and Skill Pay Off," *Billboard* (December 3, 1949).

the hit version. How this practice became known as a "cover" is a little murky. Some sources say the word comes from a label "covering its bets" by releasing its own recording of a popular song. Others claim labels aimed to have their physical record literally "cover up" another version of the same song on a store's shelves. This style of copycat cover didn't last long. Though plenty of sound-alike covers proliferated (and still do), by the end of the 1960s an alternative goal of a cover emerged: to sound *different* from the original. Stevie Wonder didn't record "We Can Work It Out" as close as he possibly could to how the Beatles recorded it. He made it his own. If a listener went to a record store to buy "We Can Work It Out," they knew damn well whose version they wanted.

It was into this world that Leonard Cohen emerged as a songwriter. The trajectory of Leonard Cohen's musical career would look far different without covers. In fact, he might not have had much of a career in the first place. When the successful author and poet first began exploring branching out into music, a friend directed him to Judy Collins's literal doorstep. "All the singers with new songs would come to me, because I had the record contract and I could get them out," Collins told Cohen's biographer, Sylvie Simmons.[2] Cohen played her three new songs he had written. One she decided to record immediately: "Dress Rehearsal Rag." "Talk about dark," she told Simmons, "a song about suicide. I attempted suicide myself at fourteen, before I found folk music, so of course I loved it. We were desperately looking for something unusual for my album and when I heard 'Dress Rehearsal Rag,' that was it."[3] Her partner, who had been listening in on Cohen's performance, convinced her to try a second: "Suzanne." She released both songs on her 1966 album *In My Life*. "Suzanne" became a minor hit and helped launch Cohen's music career. It was the first of many covers that would bring his songs to wider audiences than his own recordings could reach.

---

[2] Sylvie Simmons, *I'm Your Man: The Life of Leonard Cohen* (New York: HarperCollins, 2013), 183.
[3] Ibid., 184–85.

Collins did not try to make her version sound just like the original. In this case, there *was* no original. Cohen had yet to release the song himself. Which leads to the tricky semantics that one sometimes encounters when talking about covers. Is Collins's "Suzanne" a cover? Or is hers the original version? To muddy the water further: Collins wasn't even the first artist to perform "Suzanne" beyond its writer. That would be the Stormy Clovers, out of Toronto, who played it live in concert and on Canadian television. They and Cohen shared a manager in Mary Martin, who, following the model of her old boss, Albert Grossman, in pairing up his clients Bob Dylan and Peter, Paul & Mary, ferried Cohen's songs to the Clovers to perform. Does that make *their* "Suzanne" in fact the original? Probably not: they never released a recorded version. A 1966 session went nowhere, and they disbanded in 1968 without ever having released a single or an album. Cohen didn't release his own recording of "Suzanne" until December 1967, over a year after Collins released hers.

Calling Cohen's version a "cover" seems silly, though. Saying a songwriter can "cover" his or her own song makes the term fairly meaningless. The more you try to pin down the exact definition of a cover, the more gray-area cases you discover. For instance, "someone performs a song written by someone else" seems a straightforward enough definition, right? Well, what about a song written explicitly for that performer? Many pop singers don't write their own material, but they do originate it. Madonna did not write "Like a Virgin" herself, but few would call it a "cover" of the songwriters-for-hire Tom Kelly and Billy Steinberg. Subsequent versions of "Like a Virgin" do get called Madonna covers, even though Madonna did not write it. Or what about a composition written before the dawn of recorded music? See again the silliness of talking about "covering" Beethoven, even though a new orchestra performance of Symphony No. 9 would fit the technical definition.

So, really, you could make a justification for calling a new version of "Suzanne" a Leonard Cohen cover, a Judy Collins cover, or, if you want to be especially contrary, a Stormy Clovers cover. Most people – myself included – would follow common sense and call any version of "Suzanne" a Leonard Cohen cover. But the definitional gray areas of covers are one reason they're interesting to think about.

If that first "Suzanne" from Collins helped launch Cohen's career, other covers propelled it along. At every step, artists covered his songs – and, in many cases, had more success than he did with his own versions. By the end of the 1960s, Leonard Cohen covers flooded the market by everyone from soul-belter Joe Cocker ("Bird on the Wire") to early rock hitmaker Dion ("Sisters of Mercy") to bluegrass giants Flatt & Scruggs ("Tonight Will Be Fine"). The list grew longer in the 1970s: Rita Coolidge, Jackie deShannon, Tim Hardin, Dave Van Ronk – and that's just for "Bird on the Wire." In the 1980s, singer Jennifer Warnes, hot off her Cocker duet hit "Up Where We Belong," released a covers record, *Famous Blue Raincoat*, that charted in the United States, the United Kingdom, and Canada. Collins was already up to ten different Cohen covers by then.

Notice that none of those artists I just listed are much younger than Cohen himself. As I wrote about in my "33 1/3" book, Cohen by the end of the 1980s was at risk of being seen, like many of his peers, as a has-been, destined to run out the remaining decades of his career touring the nostalgia circuit.[4] Once again, though, covers changed the trajectory of his career, in this case by bringing him a whole new fan base. A series of tribute albums, most notably *I'm Your Fan: The Songs of Leonard Cohen* in 1991, brought younger artists, and their younger audiences, to Cohen. On *I'm Your Fan*, R.E.M. covered "First We Take Manhattan," the Pixies covered "I Can't Forget," and Nick Cave and the Bad Seeds covered "Tower of Song," among many other bands that were then big in the college-rock world.

It would be the oldest artist on the album, though, whose cover would have the greatest impact. As Alan Light explores in his 2018 book, *The Holy or the Broken: Leonard Cohen, Jeff Buckley, and the Unlikely Ascent of "Hallelujah,"* John Cale decided to cover Cohen's obscure, fairly new song "Hallelujah" after hearing Cohen had performed it in concert.[5] The Velvet Underground cofounder wasn't the first to recognize the

---

[4] Ray Padgett, *I'm Your Fan: The Songs of Leonard Cohen* (New York: Bloomsbury Academic, 2020).

[5] John Cale and Brian Nankervis, interview by Harriet Lonnborn, ABC Radio Melbourne, 2010.

genius of "Hallelujah." Bob Dylan performed it live a couple times in 1988, but Cale didn't know that. He only knew the song from seeing Cohen himself sing it in concert. So, he faced a problem covering "Hallelujah": he didn't know the words. In a sign of the doldrums of Cohen's career then, his label had declined to release the album "Hallelujah" came off, *Various Positions* (1986), in the United States (a tiny indie put it out instead). Cohen faxed Cale pages and pages of verses. Cale selected a few – most different from those Cohen had used – and recorded a spare piano cover.

I'm Your Fan was a hit when it came out in September 1991, but hardly a sensation. And Cale's cover didn't make "Hallelujah" famous either – at least, not directly. But it served as a bridge to the cover that finally would. One day in 1992, Jeff Buckley, then an up-and-coming singer primarily known for being the son of folk hero Tim Buckley, was cat-sitting for some friends. Bored, he perused their record collection and pulled out *I'm Your Fan*. Cale's recording of "Hallelujah" knocked him out, just as Cohen's live performance had Cale. Buckley decided to perform the song, having never even heard Cohen's own version of it. He covered Cale's cover, using the same verses Cale had.

Buckley's recording was as spare as Cale's, with guitar subbing in for piano. The main difference, though, was his voice. Buckley's elegiac crooning established "Hallelujah" as a showcase for vocal emoting. This approach would define all the other covers that followed, far more than both Cohen and Cale's more understated takes (much less Dylan's strangled yelp). Thanks largely to Buckley's influence, by the turn of the century, "Hallelujah" was already on its way to surpassing "Suzanne" as Cohen's most-covered song. Rufus Wainwright's recording for the *Shrek* soundtrack exposed the song to another generation of listeners, and, a decade later, it became one of the most-performed songs on singing competition shows like *American Idol*.[6]

As "Hallelujah" has saturated the culture, Cohen fans have been quick to note the song's more incongruous and inappropriate appearances,

---

[6] Benjamin Solomon, "Which Songs Are Performed Most Often by Reality-Competition Contestants?," *Vulture, New York* (January 15, 2014), www.vulture.com/2014/01/reality-competition-songs-frequency-american-idol-voice-xfactor.html.

perhaps none more so than when a cover by Tori Kelly accompanied the fireworks concluding President Donald Trump's speech at the 2020 Republican Convention. That one even drew a rebuke from the Cohen estate, whose lawyer decried the Republican National Committee's "rather brazen attempt to politicize and exploit in such an egregious manner 'Hallelujah,' one of the most important songs in the Cohen song catalogue."[7] Does Donald Trump even know who Leonard Cohen is? Does it matter? Even more than "Suzanne," "Hallelujah" has fully transcended its author, almost entirely due to the covers.

Though "Hallelujah" looms large in the Leonard Cohen covers story, with "Suzanne" not too far behind it, the broader trend in Cohen covers is the breadth of the songs performed. Other songs with over 100 covers on Arjatsalo's spreadsheet include "Bird on the Wire," "Dance Me to the End of Love," and "Famous Blue Raincoat" – no real surprises in that bunch – but perhaps even more interesting is how many songs have one or two covers. The tail of Cohen covers is long. In fact, it's genuinely difficult to find a Cohen song someone *hasn't* covered. As an experiment, I thought of the most obscure original Cohen composition I could. I came up with "Do I Have to Dance All Night," a live 1976 single he never put on any album. Sure enough, I quickly found three covers: a German-language cover from 1977 by singer Thomas Vogel, a 2016 dreampop version by Georgia duo Powerkompany, and a ragtime version in Budapest by pianist Martin Kubetz from 2018. As a second experiment, I looked for covers from his 2019 album, *Thanks for the Dance*. I assumed that album would have a couple things working against it: a) that it's so recent, leaving little time for covers to build up; b) that the songs barely have vocal melodies, being mostly spoken-word poetry recitations; and c) that the album was completed posthumously, with Cohen's son, Adam, and others setting those poems to music after the singer was gone (so even calling these "Leonard Cohen songs" is a stretch). Nevertheless, I found at least one cover of every single track. There may be a Cohen composition out there no one has covered, but I have yet to find it.

---

[7] Brooke Seipel, "Leonard Cohen Lawyer Considers Legal Action after RNC Uses Song after Trump Acceptance Speech," *The Hill*, August 28, 2020, https://thehill.com/blogs/in-the-know/in-the-know/514238-leonard-cohen-lawyer-considers-legal-action-after-rnc-uses-song/.

I tried the same experiment a different way: not with songs, but with genres. Sure, there is a ton of sensitive singer-songwriter–type covers of Cohen's. Plenty in the obvious genres: folk, rock, country. With fairly well-known covers by the likes of Nina Simone ("Suzanne") and Roberta Flack ("Hey, That's No Way to Say Goodbye"), we can slot soul and jazz as standard fare too. But what about more niche or unexpected genres? Again, I came up short finding a genre in which Leonard Cohen hasn't been covered. Hip hop? That one's easy: it's on *I'm Your Fan* – David McComb of the Triffids and Adam Peters using Eric B. & Rakim as inspiration for their sample-heavy "Don't Go Home with Your Hard-On" ("We chose the song because it was not one of the holy songs," Peters told me; even the most ardent Cohen fan wouldn't mind if they messed around with it). Shoegaze? A classic: Jesus and Mary Chain's majestically loud "Tower of Song." There are Leonard Cohen covers in the genres of polka (Ronen Segall's accordion medley of four tunes), punk (Wild Fire's aggressive "Everybody Knows"), hell, even zydeco (Washboard Jo's "Almost Like the Blues"). Cohen took note of these cross-genre covers too. When a flamenco tribute album *Omega* came out in Spain in 1996, Cohen told a local newspaper, "I'm very touched that my songs are played in flamenco style. Nobody has performed my songs in this way before!"[8]

Take just one song by way of example: "Avalanche," which opens Cohen's third album, *Songs of Love and Hate* (1971). Without even digging too deep, there are fairly prominent covers in a wide array of genres. Most famous of all is perhaps the scorching garage-punk cover Nick Cave and the Bad Seeds put as the very first track on their very first album, using Cohen's song to announce themselves to the world. Cohen himself commented on that one: "I guess you could say Nick Cave butchered my song, 'Avalanche,' and if that's the case, let there be more butchers like that."[9] Jarvis Cocker joined electronic-music producers Boys Noize and Erol Alkan for a thudding, dancefloor-ready "Avalanche" in 2011.

---

[8] Jarkko Arjatsalo, "Omega," Leonard Cohen Files, www.leonardcohenfiles.com/omega.html.

[9] Steven Blush, *Seconds* (June–July 1993), quoted on leonardcohen.com, "Songs of Love and Hate" (March 19, 2021), s.v. "1. Avalanche," at www.leonardcohen.com/songs-of-love-and-hate.

Masked metal band Ghost released an ominous gothic-synth cover in 2018. The proliferation of Cohen covers becomes like Mad Libs at a certain point: "Find ____[genre] cover of ____[Leonard Cohen song]." You probably will.

Another sign of the breadth of Cohen covers is the number of artists who cover not just individual songs, but entire albums. *Songs of Leonard Cohen* seems to be the most popular to tackle. In 2012, UK music magazine *MOJO* commissioned a host of younger indie-rock and folk luminaries like Father John Misty, Bill Callahan, and the Low Anthem to tackle every track, the "Winter Lady" deep cuts right alongside the "Suzanne" classics. Two years prior, Beck had recruited friends from MGMT, Wolfmother, and other bands to do the same thing (their funk-rap "Master Song" defies description). Some look later than the debut album. A French singer-producer who goes by Red put out a strange experimental record covering every song off *Songs of Love and Hate*. A decade later, elsewhere in France, an indie-pop duo called Yules tackled the entire *I'm Your Man* (yes, they even covered "Jazz Police"). California songwriter Greg Ashley went so far as to recreate the album cover photo on his tribute to Cohen's little-loved Phil Spector collaboration, *Death of a Ladies' Man*, stripping the songs of their heavy Wall of Sound production to give it a bar-band direction.

What is it about Leonard Cohen's songs that they lend themselves to such a wide array of covers? Okay, they're good songs. We'll take that as a given. But plenty of artists writing "good songs" don't get covered nearly to the extent Cohen does. They certainly don't have covers change the course of their entire careers. Cohen has answered the question himself. When he played "Tower of Song" in concert on his final tours, the line "I was born with the gift of a golden voice" always elicited laughs and applause. The audience was in on the joke – namely, that he *wasn't* born with any such gift. His speak-singing style is mesmerizing to those who appreciate it, and few can deliver Cohen's words with the sincerity of the man himself. But, like Bob Dylan before him, such an idiosyncratic voice is not destined for Top 40 success. So, also like Dylan, his songs tend to reach wider audiences when they emanate from the mouths of more traditionally "pretty" singers. It's an amusing twist that, with "Hallelujah" especially, a man with a fairly limited vocal range wrote a song that many belters use to show off their pipes on *American Idol* and its ilk. A would-be pop star that actually sang like Leonard Cohen would be laughed off the TV stage. Their loss.

The trend of other singers making Cohen's songs more broadly palatable has continued even after his death. *You Want It Darker* (2016), the final studio album during Cohen's life, features him intoning more than singing, merely hinting at the melodies he's written. In October 2022, jazz singer Norah Jones recorded the album's penultimate track, "Steer Your Way," for the Blue Note Records tribute album *Here It Is: A Tribute to Leonard Cohen*. Jones has a history of popularizing unusual singers' work: her "Long Way Home" cover has three times as many Spotify streams as Tom Waits's original recording. It's too early to say as of this writing, but her "Steer Your Way" may well do the same for Cohen's song.

A second reason Cohen songs prove so irresistible to cover might be the rinkydink production on some (though by no means all) of the original recordings. Have you listened to the original "Hallelujah" recently? Not Cohen's many brilliant live renditions, but the *Various Positions* studio take. It drowns one of the greatest lyrics and melodies in the history of popular music in Muzak-level production. Tim Booth, the singer of popular Britpop band James, told me that the problem with that and other 1980s recordings was "rather tacky drum machines and synthesizer sound that nobody has bothered to work on . . . The production sounds dated, whereas somehow those sixties ones, they sound universal and eternal."[10] That makes it tempting to rescue the song from its original sonics. It wouldn't be just other artists attempting that either: Cohen himself would do it in later years, where his concert arrangements often bore little resemblance to the dated sound of the original recordings.

No one was more aware of how important covers were to Cohen's career than the man himself. For my "33 1/3" book, I spoke with Robert Kory, who started managing Cohen in 2008 after working for eight years as his lawyer. He remembers all the artists who would send Cohen their covers of his songs for his approval. Legally, they didn't need to; they just

---

[10] Tim Booth, original interview by Ray Padgett (2019).

wanted the master's blessing. "The covers were personally very, very gratifying to him," Kory said. "We talked about the covers, although he didn't like to pick favorites. On the other hand, he was deeply appreciative of both covers in English and also the translations because he saw it as keeping his music alive. He was grateful that so many artists thought his work was worth that attention."

Jarkko Arjatsalo, the man with the ninety-eight-page spreadsheet, agrees. In the last years of Cohen's life, Arjatsalo transitioned from a fan to something closer to a friend. He would periodically send Cohen mix CDs of covers he thought the songwriter would enjoy. Cohen seemed to appreciate them, but hardly gave detailed notes about what he liked or didn't about various interpretations. "He always very nicely thanked me when I sent him compilations of covers we had found, but never, ever said that this and that song are great or are really bad," Arjatsalo said. "He was a gentleman who certainly didn't want to say something negative about an artist who had covered his songs." He would say something positive on occasion, though. After McCombs and Peters covered "Don't Go Home with Your Hard-On" for *I'm Your Fan*, Cohen sent them a fax (it was 1991, after all). It featured a dot-matrix drawing of himself and a simple message: "Thanks for the song." Peters still has it framed. Fifteen years later, he cold-emailed an indie-rock band called Ravens & Chimes to compliment their cover of "So Long, Marianne."[11] Just a few weeks before his death in November 2016, Cohen wrote a note to Australian singer-songwriter Anita Lester to praise her cover of "You Want It Darker." "Basically it was saying that he felt as though we sung from the same primal wound – we were speaking from the same place," she told the *Sydney Morning Herald*.[12]

That line his manager mentioned in passing about "covers in English and also the translations" touched on one of the deepest meanings that covers held for Cohen. Arjatsalo says Cohen was particularly aware of the importance of these translated covers helping his words impact people who didn't speak fluent English. Among the few specific cover albums

---

[11] David Greenwald, "Buzz Bands," *Los Angeles Times* (June 12, 2008), www.latimes.com/archives/la-xpm-2008-jun-12-gd-musicbuzz-story.html.

[12] Michael Dwyer, "Sure, Men Liked Leonard Cohen. But, for Women, It Was Something Else," *Sydney Morning Herald* (October 30, 2020).

Cohen ever singled out for praise were a 1993 Norwegian-language tribute album called *Hadde månen en søster: Cohen på norsk*, and the aforementioned 1996 Spanish-language flamenco tribute, *Omega*. My favorite find researching the book was an entire 2008 tribute album, *In Frysk earbetoan oan Leonard Cohen: Cohen in het Fries*, that translated Cohen songs into Frisian, a language spoken in only a single Netherlands province by a few hundred thousand people. It's unclear whether Cohen himself ever heard that album, but, if he did, he certainly would have approved.

Upon Cohen's death in November 2016, covers became a forum for mourning. Tribute shows abounded in the months after his passing at venues around the world. The most prominent, organized by Cohen's son and producer, Adam, brought Sting, Elvis Costello, Lana Del Rey, and more to Montreal's Bell Centre arena. But just as important were the tribute nights at tiny venues, coffeehouses, and folk clubs around the world. I myself attended one at LIC Bar in Long Island City a few weeks after his passing. Some of the covers were good. Some were lousy. But, in that context, it didn't really matter. The occasion of artists, even ones most of the audience had never heard of, covering his songs provided an excuse for Cohen fans to come together and remember the man and the music.

One thing struck me during that Long Island City bar show: no one covered "Hallelujah." The song had apparently descended into such cliché that everyone avoided it. At one other tribute show I saw after his passing, at Music Hall of Williamsburg, someone *did* cover "Hallelujah" . . . but only instrumentally. Avoiding cliché required abandoning the famous lyrics altogether. A wise move, perhaps. The most prominent postmortem "Hallelujah" cover was widely mocked. Kate McKinnon performed the song in character as Hillary Clinton to open the *Saturday Night Live*'s first show after the 2016 election – and first show since Cohen's passing five days earlier. *SPIN* later called it "*SNL*'s worst idea,"[13] and former cast member Rob Schneider said it was the moment that killed the show.[14]

[13] Jordan Sargent, "SNL's Worst Idea Was Almost Not That Bad," *SPIN* (May 21, 2018), www.spin.com/2018/05/snl-kate-mckinnon-hallelujah-gq-interview/.

[14] Marianne Garvey, "Rob Schneider Says 'SNL' Was 'Over' after Kate McKinnon Performed 'Hallelujah' as Hillary Clinton," CNN Entertainment, September 3, 2022, www.cnn.com/2022/09/01/entertainment/rob-schneider-kate-mckinnon-hillary-clinton-saturday-night-live-snl/index.html.

Not everyone, though, considers singing "Hallelujah" a cliché. In the past twenty-four hours at the moment I'm writing this sentence, eighteen new "Hallelujah" covers have been uploaded to YouTube. One features a man playing the song on acoustic guitar in his bedroom in Hawaii. Another shows a thirteen-year-old girl playing it on a violin outside in Ukraine. There's a bespeckled hipster in Israel playing it on a chromatic harmonica, a teenage indie-rocker singing it alongside distorted electric guitar, a Black blues guitarist soloing through it on the streets of Sydney. One cover video even travels into a Spanish cathedral, for an opera singer who translated the song into his native tongue. Cohen would have approved of that one.

None of these new YouTube covers has more than a handful of views as of this writing. But what comes through in all of them is their sincerity. "Hallelujah" covers can seem so played-out to music nerds wondering, "Why not try 'The Law' or 'Samson In New Orleans'?" And the overwrought *American Idol*-style versions can make the jaded among us roll their eyes. But the beauty of covers in general, and Cohen covers in particular, is that they can expose these songs to people who've never heard *Various Positions* or might be put off by a gravelly voice that speaks as much as sings.

Cohen himself knew this as well as anyone. After the *I'm Your Fan* tribute album came out, Cohen told an interviewer, "I've never gotten over the pleasure of somebody covering one of my songs . . . Somehow my critical faculties go into a state of suspended animation when I hear someone's covered one of my tunes. I'm not there to judge it, just to say thank you."[15]

---

[15] Deborah Sprague, "Leonard Cohen and the Death of Cool," *Your Flesh* (spring 1992), reprinted in *Leonard Cohen on Leonard Cohen: Interviews and Encounters*, ed. Jeff Burger (London: Omnibus Press, 2014), 250.

CHAPTER 24

The Archives

"I Hope You're Keeping Some Kind of Record"

Robert de Young

A S LEONARD COHEN TOLD BIOGRAPHER IRA B. NADEL, the archive is the mountain, and the published work the volcano ... I didn't have a sense of who I was, or where I was going, or what the world was like, what women were like. The only thing I had a sense of is that I'm going to document this little life ... It's all here ... I did do what I set out to do which was to document my trip without any judgment on it. But my trip is here. There is no question about it.[1]

The Leonard Cohen archives, currently housed in the Family Trust offices in Los Angeles, are indeed an impressive and enormously comprehensive "mountain" of material reflecting and documenting Leonard's life and work. The threefold mission of the archives, as articulated by trustee Robert Kory, is preservation, scholarship, and exhibition. In addition to careful storage of the original notebooks, manuscripts, photos, video and sound recordings, correspondence, artwork, business records, and fan mail, these original assets are also being "preserved" through high-level digitization. The digital files are then organized on a digital management system called Starchive, also used for Bob Dylan's archives. Photos are normally scanned at 2,400 dpi, and all notebook pages and manuscripts are digitized at 3,000 pixels along the long side. One advantage of digitizing the archive is that scholars do not need to handle the original, sometimes fragile, material, or travel to the location where the original assets are housed to undertake research. Another is

---

[1] Ira B. Nadel, *Various Positions: A Life of Leonard Cohen* (London: Bloomsbury, 1996), 2–3.

that the digital archive with metadata on the Starchive platform enables searches and cross-referencing that traditional rare-book library housing and organization of archival material into boxes, folders, and items described in a finding guide do not. For example, a search in Starchive under "Chelsea Hotel" quickly locates related audio-files, photographs, manuscripts, notebooks, ephemera, video-files, and so forth. Files can then be downloaded in a range of formats or curated into a "collection" for a particular project. Once the digitization and metadata work is completed, Starchive effectively provides a "one-stop shop" for research on Leonard's life and work. As with the Dylan archive, the plan is to ensure that the Leonard Cohen archives continue to be a "living archive" on the Starchive platform by adding material from photographers, collectors, and personal and professional friends of Leonard's as it surfaces.

The third mission of the Cohen archive team is exhibition, and the first major one, "Leonard Cohen: Everybody Knows," was held at the Art Gallery of Ontario (AGO) in Toronto from December 10, 2022 to April 10, 2023. Beginning in March 2022, the team worked closely with the AGO curatorial staff in assembling materials for the exhibition.[2] The time frame for the preparation and curation of assets for this exhibition was very tight in terms of normal museum and gallery timelines. The "collections" function in Starchive enabled us to quickly assemble a group of more than 700 items, later refined, that we thought would be of interest to the AGO curatorial team. AGO curators were especially interested in Leonard's artwork, including watercolors, prints, and born-digital art, and the large number of self-portraits produced by Leonard, some of which are reproduced in *Book of Longing*. This exhibition was the first public exhibition of Leonard's archives.

NOTEBOOKS

Leonard's 243 notebooks are undoubtedly the core textual record of Leonard's work and his creative process, and span his entire career, from the mid 1950s – prior to the publication of his first volume of

---

[2] An illuminating and expressive catalog of the exhibition was produced: see Jim Shedden and Julian Cox (eds.), *Leonard Cohen: Everybody Knows: Inside His Archive* (New York: AGO, Delmonico DAP, 2022).

poetry, *Let Us Compare Mythologies,* in 1956 – through to a few months prior to his death in November 2016. The notebooks contain drafts of unpublished poems and songs, or drafts of songs and poems later published in various texts and albums, rather than more personal diary-style entries. In addition, most of the notebooks contain the names and phone numbers of people Leonard was in touch with at particular points in his life and career. A notebook that sheds light both on a period of Leonard's life and his published work is the one written in the Chelsea Hotel during 1967 (Notebook 11–15). From May until November 1967 Leonard was working in Columbia Studios in New York, initially with producer John Hammond, then briefly with David Crosby, and finally with John Simon, who is credited as the producer for his first album, *Songs of Leonard Cohen*, released on December 27, 1967. From comments in Notebook 11–15 – and from onstage statements during the 1972 tour in unseen film footage from our archives – we know that this is when Leonard first saw Nico, the chanteuse who sang with the Velvet Underground. According to Leonard's own statements, he was instantly smitten with Nico and immediately wrote "Winter Lady" for her. Notebook 11–15 contains a very witty, typically self-deprecating, real (or imagined) conversation with Nico about his unrequited love:

> NICO: Why don't you find some 16-year-old Madonna who resembles me?
> [LEONARD]: I already did that. I've been through the whole blonde adventure.
> [NICO]: Then what do you want with me? I'm wooden. Besides most of all I like to jerk off.
> [LEONARD]: So do I. If you ever get tired of jerking off alone, call me.
> In excellent humour as I left. The facets of my fraudery suddenly attractive if not actually heroic. Even Nico somewhat intrigued. Asked her to get heroin.

A few pages later Leonard notes another brief conversation in the Chelsea: "Jim caught me at the door: 'You wrote one of the most beautiful songs I've ever heard.' He actually knows a girl called Suzanne that is exactly like her." The "Jim" referred to is very likely to be Jim Morrison, the songwriter and front-man for the Doors, who was also in residence at the Chelsea during 1967 and had a brief liaison with Nico. Notebook 11–15 also sheds light on the origin of Leonard's poem "How We Used to Approach *The Book of Changes*: 1966," published in the 1972 volume, *The Energy of Slaves*. In keeping with what Stephen Scobie has aptly referred to as the stance of the "anti-poet"[3] throughout *The Energy of Slaves*, the speaker tells us he is "no singer, no musician, no master of anything." The poet goes on to beseech, "show me the way ... to possess what I long for ... to love and be loved by —."[4] The handwritten draft of this poem on page 159 of Notebook 11–15 is virtually identical to the published version, and even the line breaks are the same, but there is one very important difference. While Leonard chose to use a long dash after the published words "to love and be loved by," in the handwritten notebook the text reads "to love and be loved by Nico." In this instance, the notebook entry reveals the date of composition, which is sometime after April 1967, and a source of inspiration for the poem – his unrequited love for Nico.

Leonard's 243 notebooks were effectively his "library" as a writer, and they contain innumerable examples of the ways in which songs and poems are revised and developed over time, and it's evident there's a continuum between verse and song. I have documented elsewhere the development and changes to the text of "Thousand Kisses Deep," which first appears as a poem in Notebook 4–35 from 1994, is tried out as a song in 1996, endlessly rewritten throughout 1998, further modified as a song for the 2001 album *Ten New Songs*, recited as a poem during the world tours from 2008 to 2013, and finally revised for a Sony television commercial in 2011.[5] Another example is a hastily written two-line entry in Notebook 31–25 from 1984–85: "There is a crack in everything/ That's how the light gets in," which would not emerge in a song lyric

---

[3] Stephen Scobie, *Leonard Cohen* (Vancouver: Douglas & McIntyre, 1978), 157–63.
[4] Leonard Cohen, "How We Used to Approach *The Book of Changes*: 1966," *The Energy of Slaves* (London: Jonathan Cape, 1972), 65.
[5] Robert de Young, "Leonard Cohen's Archival Mountain and the Volcanic Eruptions of 'Thousand Kisses Deep'," in *Imperfect Itineraries: Literature and Literary Research in the Archives*, ed. Michael Paduano (Nancy: Éditions de l'Université de Lorraine, 2025 [forthcoming]).

until 1992 for the song "Anthem" on *The Future*. Similarly, as Leonard, Larry Sloman, and others discuss in the 2022 documentary *Leonard Cohen: Hallelujah, a Journey, a Song*, more than eighty rejected verses for "Hallelujah" are found across three different notebooks from the mid 1980s.[6]

Notebook TN1968 was written while Leonard was living in Franklin, Tennessee, usually living alone without Suzanne Elrod, in a relatively isolated cabin in the country, working on songs for this second album, *Songs from a Room*. Unlike most of the notebooks, TN1968 is more of a personal journal or diary about his daily thoughts and activities, and includes nearly eighty Polaroid photos that Leonard took, mainly of himself, and some photobooth strips. Not only are the majority of the Polaroids accurately dated in the text underneath or above the photos, but Leonard also describes the location of the photobooth used – for example, two photobooth strips pasted onto page 19 of the notebook identify the location as "The Post House Cafeteria on Commerce Street." This notebook also provides a fascinating connection with Leonard's creative work as a visual artist, and especially his self-portraiture, during the late 1990s and 2000s. On page 61 of TN1968, underneath two Polaroids glued to the page, Leonard writes "6am false faces," and a number of other photos have similar quips that foreshadow the self-portraits, many of them done on Leonard's Wacom tablet and Apple computer, published in the 2006 publication *Book of Longing*. Page 55 of Notebook TN1968 includes another rather startled self-portrait by Leonard, with the caption "return of the Polaroid Swinger,"[7] a note that identifies the model of Polaroid camera he was using but is also a sexual double entendre. Notebook TN1968 also contains the original Polaroid photo that was graphically treated for the cover of *Songs from a Room*, released the following year.

---

[6] *Hallelujah: Leonard Cohen, a Journey, a Song*, dir. Dayna Goldfine and Dan Geller (Sony Pictures Classics, 2022).

[7] This photo from the Tennessee notebook is reproduced in Shedden and Cox (eds.), *Leonard Cohen: Everybody Knows*, 8.

LOOSE MANUSCRIPT PAGES

Complementing the rich material to be found in the notebooks, Leonard's Los Angeles archives also contain more than 4,000 loose pages. An example of this is a group of six pages written from Montreal on one of his trips back there during his residence on the Greek island of Hydra during the mid 1960s. This group of pages describes his feelings about his sexual encounters with a Montreal model, "Dominique," praising her rather favorably in comparison with his intimacy with Marianne Ihlen. However, the vast majority of individual manuscript pages are unpublished drafts of songs and verse. Together with the pages in the Los Angeles archives, there are many important manuscripts in the 2003, 2004, and 2005 collections currently housed (but not publicly accessible) at the Thomas Fisher Rare Book Library at the University of Toronto. The archive team in Los Angeles are in the process of having these collections digitized, to be added with appropriate metadata to Starchive. The 2003 collection includes a lot of material related to the 1977 book, *Death of a Lady's Man*, including galley proofs with handwritten corrections and alternative artwork designed by Leonard for the cover. This material provides an insight again into Leonard's creative process in writing this collection, and there are some excellent connections (able to be interrogated through the variety of search functions on the Starchive platform) with Leonard's Notebook 27–16, which identifies on the front cover that it contains material written in Israel during 1973 and on Hydra in 1976 with the notation "the unfinished song D.O.A.L.M. notes." The last third of Notebook 26–16 is filled with page after page of prospective verses for the poem–song.

Together with a breakdown of the proposed content and pagination for *The Spice-Box of Earth* in 1961, the 2004 and 2005 manuscripts also contain handwritten drafts of many of the songs on the first three albums, including one of Cohen's best-loved songs, "Suzanne," which first appeared as a poem in the volume *Parasites of Heaven* published in 1966.[8] The poem was modified slightly for the 1967 album version: for example, in the poem "stay the night beside her" becomes "spend the night beside her" for the song, and "you have no gifts to give her" is

---

[8] Leonard Cohen, "Suzanne Takes You Down," *Parasites of Heaven* (Toronto: McClelland and Stewart, 1966).

more powerfully re-imagined in the song as "you have no love to give her." In the final refrain of the published text of the poem, "and you're sure that she can find you" becomes "and you know you can trust her." But the two loose and undated handwritten drafts of "Suzanne" currently housed in the Fisher Library seem to pre-date the published version of the poem. Both pages are written in green ink and have significantly different versions of the text, and one page is clearly a working draft with many proposed lines crossed out or edited. This page has verses in two columns with corrections, and towards the bottom of the page on the right-hand side Leonard is clearly still developing the thrice-repeated refrain of the poem–song:

> If you're too tired then you'll find
> she'll let you touch her body
> with your mind

And also:

> & when you know her bed
> was made a 1000 years ago
> the blankets come from Iceland
> and the sheets from Mexico
> & if you are thinking Suzanne is quick & kind
> If you are too blind
> She'll let you touch her with your mind

AUDIO. The audio archives in the collection include eleven complete concerts from the 1972 tour of the United Kingdom, Europe, and Israel, and in the Paris concert there is a hilarious moment when Leonard starts to sing "Suzanne" but then stops and confesses he's forgotten the words. This track is also found on a four-disc CD collection in the archive called *Cohen Sings Cohen*, which covers live performances from 1972 to 1993, and may have been being considered by Leonard (and/or Sony) for a live-album release sometime in the 1990s. Audience members in the front row and backup vocalists Jennifer Warnes and Donna Washburn start to call out the lyrics to Leonard, who is highly amused and thanks them. He then launches into a spontaneous song:

> C'mon Suzanne don't leave me now
> Been waiting for you a long, long time
> You know a lot has happened since I wrote that song for you babe
> Ah yes, I'm the man who wrote Suzanne [big audience laugh]
> A thousand years ago
> Yes, I'm the man who wrote Suzanne 100 years ago
> Yes, I'm the man who wrote Suzanne 100 years ago.[9]

Leonard's spontaneous, parodic version of the song still echoes the "1,000 years ago" motif from a handwritten draft written at least some seven years earlier. Once all the loose manuscript material in the Los Angeles office and the material housed in the Thomas Fisher Library is digitized and imported with metadata into Starchive, it will be possible for future Cohen scholars to map more accurately Leonard's creative process in the crafting of individual poems, songs, and albums.

CORRESPONDENCE AND FAMILY DOCUMENTS

Leonard's archives in Los Angeles also contains more than 1,100 pages of personal correspondence (fan mail is housed separately), some 3,000 files of business records, and nearly 3,000 documents related to family. The collection includes letters from Joan Baez, telegrams from Joni Mitchell, postcards from Allen Ginsberg, and in the Thomas Fisher Rare Book Library, letters from Patti Smith. Leonard kept an enormous amount of material related to his family history, and this includes photographs and letters his father, Nathan, sent back to his family from Europe during World War One.

The Leonard Cohen Family Trust has already acquired some additional material to add to the existing correspondence, the most significant being

---

[9] The eleven complete concerts of the 1972 tour in the United Kingdom, Europe, and Israel that are in the archives have been curated as a two-disc collection of the best performances, together with two bonus discs of the final concert in Jerusalem. This is to be contained in the first retrospective Leonard Cohen box set, produced by Robert de Young and Steve Berkowitz, who has produced all of the *Bob Dylan Bootleg Series* for Sony and Dylan's management. The more than twenty-two hours of unseen footage has been used to make a new film, directed by Robert de Young, and is to be included as a BluRay in the box set. Unfortunately, there is no definite release date at this time.

twenty-seven letters sent from Leonard to Marianne Ihlen, the woman he was in a relationship with during the early 1960s on Hydra. Marianne's son, Axel, auctioned fifty letters at Christie's in mid 2019, and the decision was made to bid for twenty-seven of the most important ones. Leonard's letters to Marianne date from 1960 through 1972, and one, dated February 23, 1967, provides a detailed account of his first historic stage performance in New York at a benefit for the WBAI radio station on February 22, 1967. Leonard had been invited onstage by Judy Collins, whose own recording of "Suzanne" on her album *In My Life* had been released in November 1966. In this letter Leonard writes:

> Judy Collins introduced me to the audience, over 3000 people, and they seemed to know who I was, mostly because of "Suzanne." I stepped up to the mike, hit a chord on my guitar, found the instrument had gone completely out of tune, tried to tune it, couldn't, decided to sing anyhow, couldn't get more than a croak out of my throat, managed four lines of "Suzanne," my voice unbelievably flat, then I broke off and said simply, "Sorry, I just can't make it," and walked off the stage, my fingers like rubber bands, the people baffled and my career in music dying among the coughs of the people backstage. Judy went out and did some more songs while I stood numbly in the wings while a curious happiness seemed to overtake me: I had failed, I had really failed, there is something so beautiful about total failure, it really made me drunk. I found myself walking on stage again & I managed to squeeze Stranger ["The Stranger Song"] out of my throat. The people love a failure, & I know they loved me for those minutes & suffered with me & let me be their bravest selves ... Everybody backstage very sorry for me & they couldn't believe how happy I was, how relieved I was that it had all come to nothing.

PHOTOGRAPHS, PHOTO ALBUMS, AND ARTWORK

There are over 1,700 photos in the archive, ranging from the early 1920s through to Leonard's death in 2016. An additional 500 photos are contained in photo albums such as the ones belonging to Leonard's sister, Esther. Because the Leonard Cohen Family Trust wants to ensure that the archive continues to be a "living archive," other photographers such as Hazel Field, who was friends with Leonard from the mid 1970s, and his next-door neighbor, and various European photographers are being contacted to make the digital archive on the Starchive platform as comprehensive as possible. The photos have been scanned at high resolution (2,400 dpi, some at 1,200 dpi) so that they can be reproduced for future exhibitions and publications, and interrogated in great detail. The success of this decision to digitize at high resolution was immediately observable in the AGO exhibition, which included a brooding, 20-foot, wall-size blow-up of a 1972 photobooth strip Leonard took of himself.

Many of the photos in Leonard's archive are the basis for his self-portraiture developed from the mid 1990s, and they reflect his creative fascination with art and technology as tools for self-examination. The archive contains many photobooth strips from the early 1960s, including the one used on the cover of his first 1967 album *Songs of Leonard Cohen*, credited to "machine." It is also clear that during the early 1960s Leonard was actively engaged in taking photographs. For instance, on the camping trip to the Laurentians with his girlfriend, Annie Sherman, and Irving and Aviva Layton, Leonard took a series of photos of Annie, and the proof sheets of those photos (including some intimate ones) are in the archive.

The 1967 Notebook 11–15, written while Leonard was staying at the Chelsea Hotel, illustrates that Leonard was interacting with Nico and others from Andy Warhol's Factory. Warhol had been using a Polaroid camera since the early 1960s to document life at the Factory and the artists, drag queens, and guests who were drawn to the scene there and associated performance venues such as Max's Kansas City. There is no doubt that Leonard was exposed to Warhol's use of the Polaroid as a means of immediately documenting his artistic life. I noted above that Leonard owned a Polaroid "Swinger" model – first released in 1965 – which was used to take the large number of self-portraits included in the 1968 Tennessee notebook. As AGO Chief Curator Julian Cox has observed,[10] whereas an artist like Andy Warhol used the camera to document his life and environment (and sometimes himself as well),

---

[10] Robert de Young, telephone conversation with Julian Cox, Chief Curator, Art Gallery of Ontario (AGO), May 11, 2023.

for Leonard the camera was essentially an instrument used to further his interest in self-examination. The Tennessee notebook provides very clear evidence of this, and the vast majority of the eighty or so photographs glued onto the pages are self-portraits. Later, in the mid 1980s, Leonard was using a color Polaroid SX-70, and the archives contain half a dozen or so of the "out-takes" from the early 1980s when Leonard was trying to capture a self-portrait to be used for the cover of the *Various Positions* album, released in December 1984.

We are fortunate that Leonard's final assistant, Kezban Ozcan, donated around 2,000 of her candid photographs of Leonard taken with her iPhone. Because Kezban was on various legs of Leonard's 2008–13 World Tours, this collection includes candids from soundchecks, backstage, and the like. But her collection also contains a wonderful miscellany of Leonard at home in Los Angeles, with friends, his children and grandchildren, his Zen master, Roshi Kyozan Joshu Sasaki, and other people close to him. Important too, these provide a visual record of some of Leonard's home recordings with Patrick Leonard for his final album, *You Want It Darker*, released on October 17, 2016, just weeks before his death.

According to Aviva Layton, a close friend of Leonard's from the late 1950s until his death, Cohen's publishers, McClelland and Stewart, decided to provide an early Apple Mac computer in the mid 1980s for their most important writers.[11] Irving Layton wasn't interested in using his, but Aviva has a photograph of herself and Irving with Leonard proudly sitting in front of his new computer. The collection of floppy discs from the late 1990s in the archives provides clear evidence that, while Leonard was writing drafts of verses and songs in his notebooks, he was also writing extensive drafts of poem–songs such as "Thousand Kisses Deep" on his Mac. Leonard's artwork from this period again indicates the extent to which he embraced new technology to develop and extend the range of possibilities for creative expression. Many of these born-digital self-portraits – frequently with witty captions – find their way into the 2006 publication, *Book of Longing*. The collection includes more than 230 original works of art.

---

[11] Personal conversation with Aviva Layton, May 12, 2023.

ROBERT DE YOUNG

AUDIO AND VIDEO ARCHIVES

If the 243 notebooks provide a centerpiece for Leonard's creative writing process for verse and song, the audio and video archives provide insight into Leonard's work as a recording artist. For instance, during the June 5, 1967 recording sessions with producer John Hammond, Leonard recorded various takes of a song called "Jewels on Your Shoulder," later reworked as the song "Take This Longing," which appears on the 1974 album, *New Skin for the Old Ceremony*. The date of these recordings confirms the interpretation that the song was written about his unrequited love for Nico during 1967 while he was in residence at the Chelsea Hotel and in contact with her. Another reference to Nico is found in a story Leonard told onstage at a concert in Vienna on April 10, 1972 (in unseen footage from the 1972 tour) after an audience member calls out a request for him to sing "Winter Lady":

> That's a curious thing with that song, "Winter Lady," but I forgot how to play it [audience laughter]. I came into a bar one night in New York city, it was at the Dom in Saint Mark's Place, and there was a girl singing behind the bar, and I walked past the maître d'hôtel and I just stood there and watched her for about half an hour, and then I retired to an obscure table at the corner of the bar, and I wrote that song "Winter Lady," and I sang it for her and I recorded it the next night, and I never sang it again. There is another song for another girl who wasn't singing in a bar [more laughter]. This woman goes by the name of midnight lady, and some ladies you can sing their songs for once and you dare not sing them again, and some ladies insist that you repeat your song over and over again. This song is for those of the latter category. [Leonard then launches into singing "Lady Midnight" from his second album, *Songs from a Room*][12]

Throughout 1967 Andy Warhol had transformed the Dom in Saint Mark's Place into an avant-garde venue for his Exploding Plastic Inevitable multimedia show, featuring the Velvet Underground and Nico. Nico was also performing by herself at the Dom, accompanied by

---

[12] This audience interaction in which Leonard recounts the background to his writing of "Winter Lady" is included in Robert de Young's film of Leonard's 1972 tour in the forthcoming box set.

a young Jackson Browne on guitar.[13] Leonard recorded the first takes of "Winter Lady" on September 8, 1967, so presumably he saw Nico, who apparently didn't like the song, sometime shortly before then. The audio and video archives also shed light on the development of songs, and multiple versions from recording sessions provide an insight into Leonard's creative practice. A twenty-four-track version of "Closing Time" recorded in March 1992, some eight months before the version on *The Future*, is radically different. Not only are the lyrics different, but Leonard's vocal performance is less jaunty, closer to the mic, and much darker.

Overall, the Leonard Cohen archives and the organization of the digital files on the Starchive platform will provide a powerful resource for scholars, musicologists, and journalists, and for fans, for decades to come. The digitally preserved archive, digitized at high resolution, also enables the Leonard Cohen Family Trust to engage in further exhibition and publication of previously unseen and unheard material from this extraordinary and comprehensive record of the artist's work.

---

[13] See also Sylvie Simmons, *I'm Your Man: The Life of Leonard Cohen* (New York: Ecco, 2012), 155ff.

Further Reading

WORKS ON LEONARD COHEN

Bird on a Wire. Dir. Tony Palmer. The Machat Company, 1975; restored version released 2010.

Boucher, David. *Dylan and Cohen: Poets of Rock 'n' Roll.* London: Continuum, 2004.

Boucher, David, and Lucy J. Boucher. *Bob Dylan and Leonard Cohen: Deaths and Entrances.* New York: Bloomsbury, 2021.

Burger, Jeff, ed. *Leonard Cohen on Leonard Cohen: Interviews and Encounters.* Chicago: Chicago Review Press, 2014.

Burnham, Clint. "How Postmodern Is Cohen's Poetry?" *Canadian Poetry: Studies, Documents, Reviews* 33 (fall/winter 1993): https://canadianpoetry.org/volumes/vol33/burnham.html.

Cohen, Leonard. Acceptance Speech at Induction into the Rock & Roll Hall of Fame. March 10, 2008, "Induction of Leonard Cohen," www.youtube.com/watch?v=t9IZfiHEgd8&t=35s.

— Interview. *Songwriters on Songwriting*, ed. Paul Zollo. 2nd ed. New York: Da Capo Press, 2003.

— Interview by Terry Gross. "The 'Serious' Sounds of Leonard Cohen." *Fresh Air*, NPR, April 29, 1986, www.npr.org/1986/04/29/101067264/the-serious-sounds-of-leonard-cohen.

Cox, Julian, and Jim Shedden, eds. *Leonard Cohen Everybody Knows: Inside His Archive.* New York: AGO, 2023.

DeCurtis, Anthony. "No Mercy: Leonard Cohen's Tales from the Dark Side." In his *Rocking My Life Away: Writing about Music and Other Matters.* Durham, NC: Duke University Press, 1998, 87–93.

Deshaye, Joel, and Kait Pinder. *The Contemporary Leonard Cohen: Response, Reappraisal and Rediscovery.* Waterloo, Ontario: Wilfrid Laurier University Press, 2023.

Devlin, Jim. *Leonard Cohen: In Every Style of Passion.* London: Omnibus, 1996.

Devlin, Jim, ed. *In His Own Words, Leonard Cohen.* London: Omnibus, 1998.

de Young, Robert. "Leonard Cohen's Archival Mountain and the Volcanic Eruptions of 'Thousand Kisses Deep'." In *Imperfect Itineraries: Literature and Literary Research in the Archives*, ed. Michael Paduano. Nancy: Éditions de l'Université de Lorraine, 2025, forthcoming.

Díaz-Cintas, Jorge, and Francis Mus. "Recontextualizing Nouvelle Vague Cinema in Québec: Leonard Cohen, Subtitler of Claude Jutra's *À Tout Prendre.*" *Babel* 70, nos. 1–2 (February 29, 2024): 277–303.

Dorman, Lorraine, and Clive Rawlins. *Leonard Cohen: Prophet of the Heart.* London: Omnibus, 1990.

Elliott, Richard. *The Late Voice: Time, Age and Experience in Popular Music.* 1st ed. New York: Bloomsbury, 2015.

Footman, Tim. *Leonard Cohen: Hallelujah: A New Biography.* New Malden, UK: Chrome Dreams, 2009.

Freedman, Harry. *Leonard Cohen: The Mystical Roots of Genius.* London: Bloomsbury, 2021.

Friedman, Matti. *Who by Fire: Leonard Cohen in the Sinai.* New York: Spiegal and Grau, 2022.

Hallelujah: Leonard Cohen, a Journey, a Song. Dir. Dayna Goldfine and Dan Geller. Sony Pictures Classics, 2022.

Girard, Philippe. *Leonard Cohen: On a Wire.* Trans. Helge Dascher and Karen Houle. Montreal: Drawn and Quarterly, 2021.

Gitlin, Todd. "Grizzled Minstrels of Angst: Leonard Cohen and Bob Dylan, Forever Old." *The American Scholar* 71, no. 2 (spring 2002): 95–100.

Glazer, Aubrey. *Tangle of Matter & Ghost: Leonard Cohen's Post-Secular Songbook of Mysticism(s) Jewish & Beyond.* Boston: Academic Studies Press, 2017.

Gnarowski, Michael, ed. *Leonard Cohen: The Artist and His Critics.* Toronto: McGraw-Hill, 1967.

Grierson, Tim. "How Leonard Cohen's Music Turned *McCabe & Mrs. Miller* into a Masterpiece." *Rolling Stone* (November 14, 2016), www.rollingstone.com/tv-movies/tv-movie-news/how-leonard-cohens-music-turned-mccabe-mrs-miller-into-a-masterpiece-107637/.

Holt, Jason, ed. *Leonard Cohen and Philosophy: Various Positions.* Chicago: Open Court, 2014.

Hutcheon, Linda. "Leonard Cohen and His Works." In *Canadian Writers and Their Works*, ed. Robert Lecker et al. Fiction Series, vol. X. Toronto: ECW Press, 1992 [1980].

Irwin, Colin. *Leonard Cohen: Still the Man.* London: Flame Tree Publishing, 2015.

Kubernik, Harvey. *Leonard Cohen: Everybody Knows.* London: Omnibus Press, 2017.

Ladies and Gentleman, Mr. Leonard Cohen. Dir. Donald Brittain and Don Owen. National Film Board of Canada, 1965.

Lebold, Christophe. "I'm the Little Jew Who Wrote the Bible: Leonard Cohen's Holy Hoaxes/A Reconfiguration of the Devotional Poet for the Age of the Mass Media." In *Literature and Spirituality in the English Speaking World*, ed. Katie Birat and Zaugg Brigitte. Berne: Peter Lang, 2014, 133–44.

Leonard Cohen, The Man Who Saw the Angels Fall. Toronto: ECW Press, 2024.

"The Traitor and the Stowaway: Persona Construction and the Quest for Cultural Anonymity and Cultural Relevance in the Trajectories of Bob Dylan and Leonard Cohen." In *Journal of the International Association for the Study of Popular Music*, 1, no. 2 (2011): 1–17.

Leibovitz, Liel. *A Broken Hallelujah: Rock and Roll, Redemption, and the Life of Leonard Cohen.* New York: W. W. Norton, 2014.

Leonard Cohen Files, The. www.leonardcohenfiles.com.

Lerner, Eric. *Matters of Vital Interest: A Forty-Year Friendship with Leonard Cohen.* New York: Da Capo, 2018.

Light, Alan. *The Holy or the Broken: Leonard Cohen, Jeff Buckley and the Unlikely Ascent of "Hallelujah."* New York: Atria, 2012.

Murray, Nick. "How Pop Culture Wore Out Leonard Cohen's 'Hallelujah,'" *New York Times* (September 19, 2016), www.nytimes.com/2016/09/20/arts/music/leonard-cohen-emmys-hallelujah.html.

Mus, Francis. *The Demons of Leonard Cohen.* Ottawa: University of Ottawa Press, 2020.

Nadel, Ira B. *Various Positions: A Life of Leonard Cohen.* New York: Random House, 1996.

Ondaatje, Michael. *Leonard Cohen.* Toronto: McClelland and Stewart, 1970.

Pally, Marcia. *From This Broken Hill I Sing to You: God, Sex, and Politics in the Work of Leonard Cohen.* London: T&T Clark, 2021.

Posner, Michael. *Leonard Cohen, Untold Stories: The Early Years,* vol. I. New York; London: Simon & Schuster, 2020.

Leonard Cohen, Untold Stories: From This Broken Hill, vol. II. New York: Simon and Schuster, 2021.

Leonard Cohen, Untold Stories: That's How the Light Gets In, vol. III. New York: Simon and Schuster, 2022.

Rae, Ian. *From Cohen to Carson: The Poet's Novel in Canada.* Montreal: McGill-Queen's University Press, 2008.

Rasky, Harry. *The Song of Leonard Cohen: Portrait of a Poet, a Friend, and a Film.* Oakville, Ontario: Mosaic Press, 2001.

Reynolds, Anthony. *Leonard Cohen: A Remarkable Life.* 2nd ed. New York: Omnibus Press, 2012.

Scobie, Stephen. "Keynote Address: The Counterfeiter Begs Forgiveness: *Leonard Cohen* and Leonard Cohen," *Canadian Poetry: The Proceedings of the Leonard Cohen Conference,* no. 33 (fall/winter 1993).

Leonard Cohen. Vancouver: Douglas & McIntyre, 1978.

"Leonard Cohen, Phyllis Webb, and the End(s) of Modernism." In *Canadian Canons: Essays in Literary Value,* ed. Robert Lecker. Toronto: University of Toronto Press 1991, 57–69.

Scobie, Stephen, ed. *Intricate Preparations: Writing Leonard Cohen.* Toronto: ECW Press, 2000.

Simmons, Sylvie. *I'm Your Man: The Life of Leonard Cohen.* New York: HarperCollins, 2012.

Wolfson, Elliot R. "New Jerusalem Glowing: Songs and Poems of Leonard Cohen in a Kabbalistic Key." *Kabbalah: A Journal for the Study of Jewish Mystical Texts* 15 (2006): 103–52.

SECONDARY WORKS

Atwood, Margaret. *Survival: A Thematic Guide to Canadian Literature.* Toronto: McClelland and Stewart, 1972.

Cameron, Laura. "'A Strange Gestation': Periods of Poetic Silence in Modern Canadian Creative Careers," PhD thesis, McGill University, 2015.

FURTHER READING

Cohen, Ronald D. *Rainbow Quest: The Folk Music Revival and American Society, 1940–1970.* Urbana: University of Illinois Press, 2002.

Cohen, Ronald D., ed. *"Wasn't That a Time!": Firsthand Accounts of the Folk Music Revival.* Metuchen, NJ: Scarecrow Press, 1995.

Collins, Judy. *Trust Your Heart: An Autobiography.* New York: Fawcett Crest, 1989.

Denning, Michael. *The Cultural Front: The Laboring of American Culture in the Twentieth Century.* New York: Verso, 1996.

Deshaye, Joel. *The Metaphor of Celebrity: Canadian Poetry and the Public, 1955–1980.* Toronto: University of Toronto Press, 2013.

Douglas, Susan J. *Where the Girls Are: Growing up Female with the Mass Media.* New York: Random House, 1995.

Filene, Benjamin. *Romancing the Folk: Public Memory and American Roots Music.* Chapel Hill, NC; London: University of North Carolina Press, 2000.

Frith, Simon, Will Straw, and John Street, eds. *The Cambridge Companion to Rock and Pop.* Cambridge: Cambridge University Press, 2011.

Hutcheon, Linda. *The Canadian Postmodern: A Study of Contemporary English–Canadian Fiction.* Toronto: Oxford University Press, 1988.

James, David. *Rock'n'Music: Cinema's Dance with Popular Music.* Oxford: Oxford University Press, 2016.

Joshu, Sasaki Roshi. *Buddha Is the Center of Gravity.* San Cristobal: Lama Foundation Press, 1974.

Tathagata Zen. Los Angeles: Rinzai-Ji Press, 2014.

Lorca, Federico Garcia. *The Collected Poems: A Bilingual Edition.* Rev. ed. New York: Farrar, Straus, and Giroux, 2002.

Marcus, Greil. *Mystery Train: Images of America in Rock 'n' Roll Music.* 6th ed. New York: Plume, 2015.

Moore, Meido. *The Rinzai Zen Way: A Guide to Practice.* Boulder, CO: Shambhala, 2018.

Petrus, Stephen, and Ronald D. Cohen. *Folk City: New York and the American Folk Music Revival.* Oxford: Oxford University Press, 2015.

Rosenberg, Neil, ed. *Transforming Tradition: Folk Music Revivals Examined.* Urbana: University of Illinois Press, 1993.

Shumway, David R. "The Emergence of the Singer-Songwriter." In *The Cambridge Companion to the Singer-Songwriter,* ed. Katherine Williams and Justin A. Williams. Cambridge: Cambridge University Press, 2016, 11–20.

Rock Star: The Making of Musical Icons from Elvis to Springsteen. Baltimore: Johns Hopkins University Press, 2014.

Warner, Simon. *Text and Drugs and Rock 'n' Roll: The Beats and Rock Culture.* New York; London: Bloomsbury, 2014.

Yaffe, David. *Reckless Daughter: A Portrait of Joni Mitchell.* New York: Farrar, Straus, and Giroux, 2017.

Index

1967 Arab–Israeli War, 271

Adorno, Theodor, 33, 38
Aerosmith
   "Sweet Emotion," 115
"After the Sabbath Prayers," 127
"Ain't No Cure for Love," 70
Aix-En-Provence Music Festival, 318
"Alexandra Leaving," 146
Alkan, Erol, 347
"All There Is to Know about Adolf Eichmann," 39
"Almost Like the Blues," 32
Alpert, Richard, 250–51
Altamont Festival, 258
Altman, Robert, 195
Alvarez, Al, 38
   The New Poetry, 38
"Amen," 159
American Graffiti, 115
Amos, Tori, 243–44
   Strange Little Girls, 243
Anderson, Sandra, 266
"Anthem," 19, 22, 57, 58, 61, 110, 118, 120, 121, 130, 161, 190, 357
Anthology of American Folk Music, 86
Arendt, Hannah, 39
Arjatsalo, Jarkko, 340, 350
Art Gallery of Ontario, 354
Art of Worldly Wisdom, The, 200
Auden, W. H., 50, 224
"Avalanche," 67, 109, 110, 111, 157, 322, 347

Baez, Joan, 360
Ballad of the Absent Mare, 69, 190
Ballet of Lepers, A, 26, 183
Balsekar, Ramesh, 149

Barry, Elizabeth, 337
Barton-Fumo, Margaret, 198
Basquiat, 207
Baudelaire, Charles, 189
Beat movement, 189, 267
Beatles, The, 112, 147, 289, 342
   "When I'm 64," 328
   "Hello-Goodbye," 147
   Magical Mystery Tour, 255
Beautiful Losers, 2, 20, 39, 49, 83, 143, 152, 173, 175, 184, 185, 253–54, 315
   preface to Chinese translation, 188
Beck, 122, 348
Beck, Roscoe, 190, 334
"Beneath My Hands," 36
Berlin Alexanderplatz, 199
Berlin, Irving, 52
   "Always," 52, 119
   "White Christmas," 119
Berry, Chuck, 112
Best of Leonard Cohen, The, 170, 286, 292, 297
Beverly Hills Cop, 121
Beware of a Holy Whore, 198
Bible, the
   Amos, 154
   Exodus, 154
   Genesis, 134, 154
   Revelation, 151
Big Thief, 110
Bill Haley
   "Rock around the Clock," 115
Billboard, 341
Billie Holiday
   "Strange Fruit," 113
Bird on a Wire, 142, 228, 237, 305–9
"Bird on the Wire," 21, 66, 92, 169, 276, 308, 344, 346

INDEX

"Bleistein with a Cigar," 34
"Boogie Street," 146, 234
Bon Jovi, Jon, 60
Book of Longing, 2, 24, 46, 140, 148, 174, 187, 193, 263, 354, 357, 363
Book of Mercy, 23, 36, 39, 45, 126, 128, 140, 155, 157, 201, 324
Booth, Tim, 349
"Born in Chains," 54, 280
Boucher, David, 86, 91–92
Bourgois, Christian, 42
Bowie, David, 73, 114, 313
  Blackstar, 112
boygenius, 61, 110, 118
Boys Noize, 347
Brautigan, Richard
  Trout Fishing in America, 254
Breaking the Waves, 205–6
Bridgers, Phoebe, 118
Brittain, Donald, 19, 301–5
Broomfield, Nick, 310
Brown, Jackson, 365
Bruce Springsteen, 337
Bruce, Lenny, 116
Brunet, Alain, 180
Brusq, Armelle, 310
Buckley, Jeff, 181, 207, 210, 345
Buckmaster, Paul, 67
Buckskin Boys, The, 15, 81, 97, 214
Burke, Alexandra, 59
Burroughs, William
  Naked Lunch, 254
"Butcher, The," 66
Byrds
  Younger than Yesterday, 255
Byron, Lord, 231–32
  "We'll Go No More A-Roving," 174

Cale, John, 4, 9, 117, 181, 206, 207, 344–45
Callahan, Bill, 121, 348
"Came So Far for Beauty," 69
Canadian Jewish Chronicle, 175
Canadian Jewish Times, 152
"Captain, The," 203
Carlil, Brandi, 59
Carson, Anne
  Glass, Irony, and God, 172
  Plainwater, 172
Castro, Fidel, 268
Cave, Nick, 109, 111, 116, 118
Celebration, 36
Chappet, Marie-Claire, 245

Charles, Ray, 45
  The Genius Sings the Blues, 45
Chatterton, Thomas, 29
"Chelsea Hotel #2," 18, 21, 37, 67, 106–7, 121, 199, 227, 243, 260–61, 275, 332
Chilton, Alex, 114
Citizen Kane, 114
Clarkson, Adrienne, 83
Clift, Charmian, 251
"Closing Time," 208, 365
Cobain, Kurt, 61, 110, 117
Cocker, Jarvis, 347
Cocker, Joe, 344
Cohen, Adam, 23, 27, 72, 122, 272, 346
Cohen, Doron, 161
Cohen, Esther, 274
Cohen, Leonard
  amphetamine use, 254
  and communists, 269
  as Canadian Dylan, 87–90, 167
  at home when in Montreal, 219
  Buddhism, 141, 281
  celebrity, 295
  changing voice, 333
  covenantal theology, 153–56
  depression, 142, 145
  father's death, 30–31
  Montreal references in, 213–16
  notebooks, 354–57
  ordained as Zen monk, 140
  rock star, 329
  self-negation, 323–24
  sex symbol, 294
  syncretistic impulse, 135
  voice, 245–47
  Zen and Judaism, 133
Cohen, Lyon, 126, 152
Cohen, Nathan B., 30, 31
Cohen, Ronald D., 84
Cohen, Tzvi Hirsch, 152
Collins, Aileen, 16
Collins, Judy, 9, 21, 50, 67, 84, 94, 98, 100–1, 224, 238, 245, 254, 289, 311, 342, 361
  Maid of Constant Sorrow, 99
  Trust Your Heart, 238
  Wildflowers, 85, 98
Collins, Sarah A., 246
Columbia University, 269
"Come Healing," 60, 129, 160, 162
Concrete Blond, 116
confessional poetry, 102–3
Consolations (Love Is an Art of Time), 202

INDEX

Conspiracy of Beards, 340
Corso, Gregory, 252
Costello, Elvis, 226
"cover," meaning and history, 341–42
Cox, Julian, 362
Creeley, Robert, 16
Crosby, David, 355
Cuba, 20, 269–70, 292
"Cuckold's Song, The," 37, 38, 43, 181

Dabrowski, Stina, 152
Dacus, Lucy, 61
Damrosch, David, 183
"Dance Me to the End of Love," 69, 144, 237, 340, 346
"Darkness," 280
Dazed & Confused, 115
De Mornay, Rebecca, 18, 23, 72
Dead and Company, 328
Dear Heather, 71, 174, 176, 231, 266
Death of a Ladies' Man, 22, 68, 143, 195, 201, 223, 233, 298, 299, 321
"Death of a Ladies' Man," 298, 348
Death of a Lady's Man, 40, 175, 272, 299, 322, 323, 358
DeCurtis, Anthony, 329
Del Rey, Lana, 67, 110, 121
"Democracy," 6, 117, 159, 226, 266
Denning, Michael
  The Cultural Front, 112
Depeche Mode
  "Enjoy the Silence," 115
Dery, Mark, 116
Deshaye, Joel, 286, 295
Devlin, Jim, 307
"Different Sides," 280
"Disturbed This Morning," 131
Ditchburn, Anne, 201
Djwa, Sandra, 86, 89, 189
"Do I Have to Dance All Night," 321, 346
"Don't Go Home with Your Hard-On," 68, 321, 347, 350
"Don't Pass Me By," 155
Doors, The, 356
Dorman, Lorraine, 151
Douglas, Susan J.
  Where the Girls Are, 237
Dragland, Stan, 42
Drake, 211
"Dress Rehearsal Rag," 60, 67, 85, 178, 342
Dubro, Alec, 319
Dudek, Louis, 15, 35, 167, 287

Dylan, Bob, 3, 32, 47, 51–53, 68, 77, 78–79, 87–90, 94, 96, 98, 99, 104, 110, 114, 120, 196, 204, 223, 224, 226, 242, 256, 289, 290, 292, 293, 299, 309, 311, 313, 315, 319, 328, 334, 339, 345, 348
  "The Times They Are a'Changin'," 328
  Blood on the Tracks, 100
  Bringing It All Back Home, 98, 301
  Highway 61 Revisited, 98, 167, 301
  John Wesley Harding, 91
  "My Back Pages," 99

Eitzel, Mark, 56
Elder, Bruce, 200, 202–4
"Elegy," 29, 30, 31, 45
Eliezer, Israel ben, 127
Eliot, T. S., 29, 33
  "Burbank with Baedeker: Bleistein with a Cigar," 34
  Four Quartets, 46
  "Tradition and the Individual Talent," 29
Elliott, Richard, 330, 333, 334
  Late Voice, The, 329
Elrich, Nancy, 320
Elrod, Suzanne, 18, 28, 227, 272, 273, 297, 306, 357
"End of My Life in Art, The," 143
Energy of Slaves, The, 32, 40, 143, 173, 201, 295, 296, 301, 318, 356
Engle, Paul, 285
Eric B. & Rakim, 347
"Every Pebble," 144
"Everybody Knows," 6, 58, 70, 115, 116, 118, 121, 159, 210, 330, 347
Everybody Knows (exhibition), 354

Faggen, Robert, 168, 301
"Faithless Wife, The," 193
"Famous Blue Raincoat," 67, 106, 110, 181, 237, 243, 340, 346
Fassbinder, Rainer Werner, 198–99
Father John Misty, 348
Favourite Game, The, 28, 31, 39, 41, 103, 168, 182, 184, 214, 221, 235, 268, 286, 287, 316, 318
Fear of Fear, 199
Felix, Julie, 85
Fenton, James, 50
Ferlinghetti, Lawrence, 267
Field, Hazel, 362
Fields, Danny, 267
"Final Examination," 32

INDEX

"First We Take Manhattan," 70, 116, 145, 344
Flack, Roberta, 347
Flame, The, 2, 26, 46, 168, 183, 184, 192
Flatt & Scruggs, 344
Flowers for Hitler, 18, 32, 37, 38, 41, 131, 189, 286
Flying Lizards, The, 340
Folk, 38
Footman, Tim, 81
Franca, Celia, 201
Francis Mus
   Demons of Leonard Cohen, The, 172
Freedman Company, 14
Friedman, Matti, 27
   Who by Fire, 27–28
Frith, Simon, 319
Fulford, Robert, 49
"Future, The," 58, 151, 205, 207, 231, 266, 277, 278, 280
Future, The, 23, 52, 57–58, 61, 69, 70, 71, 72, 117, 130, 159, 204, 322, 331, 334, 365

Gallop, Jane, 338
Garcia Lorca, Federico, 111, 121, 178, 191–94, 230, 268, 275
   "The Faithless Wife," 263
Gateless Gate, The, 144
Gaye, Marvin, 223
Genet, Jean, 189
Ghomeshi, Jian, 335
Ghost, 348
Ginsberg, Allen, 68, 223, 233, 250, 252
   Howl, 250
Girard, Philippe, 212
Glam, 114
Glass, Philip, 122
Glastonbury Festival, 119, 259
Glazer, Aubrey, Rabbi, 212–13, 216, 218, 219
Godard, Jean-Luc, 204
"Going Home," 37, 149, 171, 181, 336
Goldstein, Richard, 289
   Poetry of Rock, The, 294
Graduate, The, 196, 329
Greece, 268, 273–74
Greenstein, Michael
   Third Solitudes, 179
Greenwich Village, 267
Greil Marcus
   Mystery Train, 113
Greyson, N. David, 38

Gross, Terry, 236
Grossman, Albert, 50, 343
Grubbs, David, 121
"Guests, The," 190, 201
Guevara, Che, 268
Guitar Player, 52
Guthrie, Woody, 78, 85
Guttman, Freda, 16, 18, 264
"Gypsy's Wife, The," 202

Hadde månen en søster: Cohen på norsk, 351
Haight-Ashbury, 253, 257
Halbertal, Moshe, 172
"Hallelujah," 2, 4, 9, 23, 28, 45, 50, 52, 53, 58–60, 61, 62, 69, 71, 110, 111, 117, 118, 120, 127–28, 162, 181, 206–7, 210, 214, 222, 225, 230, 233, 237, 244, 311, 340, 345, 346, 348, 349, 351, 352
   covers, 344–46
Hallelujah: Leonard Cohen, a Journey, a Song, 27, 221, 310
Hammond, John, 21, 92, 113, 288, 355, 364
Harris, Michael, 302, 304
Harrison, Noel, 87
Havana, 269–70
Heap, Imogen, 207
"Heart with No Companion," 129, 144, 203
"Hellenist, The," 36
Henahan, Donald, 319
"Here It Is," 340
Here It Is: A Tribute to Leonard Cohen, 349
Herzog, Werner, 199
"Hey, That's No Way to Say Goodbye," 64, 228, 340
Hilton, Lisa, 240
hippies, 257
Histoire de la littérature québécoise, 185
"Hitler the Brain Mole," 38
Hoffman, Dustin, 329
Holiday, Billie, 113
"How to Speak Poetry," 40
"How We Used to Approach *The Book of Changes*: 1966," 356
Howe, Irving, 102
Hutcheon, Linda, 173, 190
Huxley, Aldous
   Doors of Perception, The, 250
Hydra, 6, 18, 20, 21, 29, 82, 85, 120, 138, 251, 253–54, 272, 288, 305, 310, 358

I Am a Hotel, 4, 201–2
"I Came So Far for Beauty," 28

"I Have Not Lingered in European Monasteries," 35
"I Have Two Bars of Soap," 36
"I Left a Woman Waiting," 322
I'm Your Fan: The Songs of Leonard Cohen, 116, 344–45, 352
"I'm Your Man," 23, 208, 232, 325
I'm Your Man, 18, 23, 37, 56, 69, 70, 115, 116, 117, 144, 159, 170, 239, 277, 309, 330, 348
"I've Stepped into an Avalanche," 39
Ian, Janis, 100
I-Ching, 138
"If I Didn't Have Your Love," 155
"If It Be Your Will," 116, 128, 162, 203–4
Ihlen, Marianne, 18, 20, 105, 228, 288, 294, 297, 305, 306, 358, 361
Il Divo, 53
Illyes, Gyala, 274
In Frysk earbetoan oan Leonard Cohen: Cohen in het Fries, 351
"In My Secret Life," xiii, 146
Iowa Writers' Workshop, 285
"Irving and Me at the Hospital," 174
"Isaiah," 36
Isle of Wight Festival, 94, 258–60
Israel, 22, 27, 28, 126, 175, 270, 271, 293, 296, 358
Issermann, Dominique, 18, 23, 311

"Jazz Police," 348
Jesus, 152–53, 156–64
Jesus and Mary Chain, 347
"Joan of Arc," 54
John, Elton, 325
Johnston, Bob, 21, 22, 66, 92, 93, 307, 308
Johnston, George, 251
Jolson, Al, 293
Jones, Norah, 349
  "Long Way Home," 349
Joplin, Janis, 18, 21, 67, 227, 258, 260–62
Joyce, James, 49, 118, 290
  Ulysses, 229
Jutra, Claude
  À tout prendre (Take It All), 185

Kagan, Ruth Gan, Rabbi, 59
Kaleidoscope, 92
"Kanye West Is Not Picasso," 190
Keats, John, 29
  "Ode to a Nightingale," 169
Keightley, Keir, 93

Kelly, Tom, and Billy Steinberg
  "Like a Virgin," 343
Kelly, Tori, 346
Kerouac, Jack, 252
  On the Road, 250
King, Carole, 299
  "Will You Love Me Tomorrow," 237
Kingston Trio, 93
Kirshner, Mia, 118
Klein, A. M., 35, 38, 175–77, 185
  Hath Not a Jew, 176
  Hitleriad, 176
  Portrait of the Poet as Landscape, 177
  The Rocking Chair and Other Poems, 176
  The Second Scroll, 175
Kloman, William, 289
Klonitzky-Kline, Solomon, Rabbi, 34, 126, 152
Komrij, Gerrit, 42
Kory, Robert, 349, 353
Kraftwerk, 199
Krasner, Lee, 240
Kristofferson, Kris, 66, 227
Kubernik, Harvey, 255
Kubetz, Martin, 346

L Word, The, 208
LaBelle, Patti
  "New Attitude," 121
Ladies and Gentlemen, Mr. Leonard Cohen, 19, 119, 177, 197, 213, 286–88, 301
"Lady Midnight," 364
"Land of Plenty," 146
lang, k.d., 120
Lang, Penny, 86
"Last Dance at the Four Penny," 127
"Last Year's Man," 63
Layton, Aviva, 362, 363
Layton, Irving, 15, 35, 49, 127, 155, 172, 174, 177, 287, 302, 335, 362
Leary, Timothy, 250
Leary, Timothy, Ralph, Metzner, and Richard Alpert
  The Psychedelic Experience, 250
Lebold, Christophe, 320
Ledbetter, Huddie (Lead Belly), 78
Leibovitz, Liel, 104, 333
Lenker, Adrianne, 110
Lennon, John, 226
Leonard Cohen – Hallelujah in Moll, 311
Leonard Cohen: I'm Your Man, 173
Leonard Cohen: Spring 1996, 310

INDEX

Leonard, Patrick, 363
Lerner, Eric, 19, 27, 28
   Matters of Vital Interest, 27
Lerner, Yafa, 16
Lester, Anita, 247–48, 350
Let Us Compare Mythologies, 16, 18, 29, 30, 32, 33, 35, 36, 39, 49, 138, 167, 185, 187, 213, 286, 300, 315, 355
Lewis, Juliette, 117
Lewy, Henry, 69
Light, Alan, 207
   Holy and the Broken, The, 52, 310, 344

Man with the Golden Arm, The, 64
McGill University, 81, 167, 212, 287
McKinnon, Kate, 351
McLuhan, Marshall, 178
Meeropol, Abel
   "Strange Fruit," 113
"Memories," 68, 202, 225
Metzner, Ralph, 250–51
MGMT, 348
Miller, David, 53
Mitchell, Joni, 3, 69, 85, 97, 107, 108, 114, 121, 169, 170, 225, 226, 228, 299, 360
   Blue, 100, 107, 108, 171
   "Both Sides Now," 101
   "Case of You, A," 101, 121, 171
   "Circle Game, The," 101
   Cohen's influence on, 100–2
   "Gallery, The," 101
   Ladies of the Canyon, 100
   "Rainy Night House," 101
   "River," 106, 107
   "That Song about the Midway," 101
Mojo, 348
Montreal, 3, 4, 17, 20, 26, 27, 34, 35, 82, 86, 101, 120, 126, 152, 163, 170, 171, 172, 179, 184, 186, 213–16, 253, 287, 358
Montreal Moderns, 173
"Morning Song," 168
Morrison, Jim, 355
Mus, Francis, 42
   The Demons of Leonard Cohen, 188
"My Mentors," 131

Nabakov, Vladimir
   Pale Fire, 323
Nadel, Ira, 98, 176, 292, 307, 330, 353
   Various Positions, 167, 301
Nashville, 20, 21, 44, 92, 98
National Rifle Association (NRA), 265

Natural Born Killers, 23, 55, 117, 204–5
Ndegeocello, Meshell, 67
Nelson, Paul, 298
"Nevermind," 127, 132, 208
Nevermind, 116
New Skin for the Old Ceremony, 55, 67, 95, 143, 226, 260
New York, 17, 20, 21, 22, 83–84, 86, 87, 89, 98, 168, 267, 289, 355, 361
Newman, Randy, 100, 121, 329
Newport Folk Festival, 100
Nichols, Mike, 196
Nick Cave and the Bad Seeds, 344, 347
Nico, 22, 90, 225, 233, 263, 355, 356, 362, 364
"Night Comes On, The," 131
Night Music, 117
"Night of Santiago, The," 121, 193–94, 263
Nirvana, 112
Nyro, Laura, 100

O'Hara, Frank, 37
O'Brien, Robert, 157
O'Connor, David, 309
OC, The, 207
Old Ideas, 25, 54, 71, 149, 162, 336
Oldham, Will, 121
Omega, 347, 351
"On The Sickness of My Love," 40
Ondaatje, Michael, 176, 187, 315
"One of Us Cannot Be Wrong," 63, 227
"Overheard on Every Corner," 295
Owen, Don, 19
Ozcan, Kezban, 363

Padgett, Ray
   I'm Your Fan, 344
Palmer, Tony, 307
   Bird on a Wire, 295
Papadopoulos, Georgios, 273
Papandreou, Georgios, 273
Parasites of Heaven, 39, 110, 172, 358
Paris, 53
Parliament-Funkadelic (P-Funk), 114
"Partisan, The," 91, 92, 98, 179, 187, 190, 298
Pennebaker, D. A.
   Don't Look Back, 307
People's Song Book, The, 15, 81, 82, 91, 98
Peters, Adam, 347, 350
Petrus, Stephen, 84

INDEX

Pinza, Ezio
    "Some Enchanted Evening," 341
Pixies, The, 116, 344
Plath, Sylvia, 38, 107
    "Daddy," 38
Pleshoyano, Alexandra, 168
Pop, Iggy, 112, 227
Popular Problems, 25, 266, 336
Porter, Cole
    "Every Time We Say Goodbye," 106
Posner, Michael
    Leonard Cohen: Untold Stories, 305
Pound, Ezra, 16, 33
Powerkompany, 346
Powers, Ann, 331
Presley, Elvis, 113
Prince, 224
Project Sigma, 276
Puissance de la parole, 204
Pulp Fiction, 118
Pump Up the Volume, 115–17, 210
Pynchon, Thomas
    Gravity's Rainbow, 254

R.E.M., 344
Rae, Ian, 185
Rasky, Harry, 309
Ravens & Chimes, 350
Ravvin, Norman, 35
Rawlins, Clive, 151
Ray Padgett
    I'm Your Fan, 340
Recent Songs, 62, 69, 91, 143, 190
Red, 348
Reed, Lou, 22, 66, 111, 114, 225
Reid, Malcolm, 186
Remnick, David, 51
Reznor, Trent, 55, 117
Richard Hell and the Voidoids
    "Love Comes in Spurts," 116
Richler, Mordecai, 185
Rimbaud, Arthur, 29, 63, 189, 275
Rinzai Zen, 139
"Rites," 30
Robinson, Sharon, 18, 24, 72, 121, 146, 239, 271, 325
rock stardom, 293, 296
Rolling Stone, 99, 290
Rolling Stones, The, 327, 337
Rollins, Sonny, 117
Rosenberg, Neil, 90, 94
Rosenfarb, Chava, 35

Rosengarten, Morton, 317
Rosenthal, M. L., 102, 107
Roszak, Theodore, 249
    The Making of a Counter Culture, 250
Rousseau, Jean-Jacques
    Confessions, 264
    The Social Contract, 264
Ruddy, Jon, 54
Rush, Tom, 100
    Circle Game, 100
    "No Regrets," 100
Rushdie, Salman, 48, 50, 56

Sabrina Carpenter, 110
Sainte-Marie, Buffy, 86, 189
San Francisco, 251, 268
Sasaki, Kyozan Joshu, Roshi, 24, 138, 262, 299, 332
Saturday Night Live, 351
Schmidt, Arthur, 317
Scobie, Stephen, 173, 301, 323, 356
Scott, F. R., 15–16, 167
    "Villanelle for Our Time," 174
Seeger, Pete, 78, 95
"Seems So Long Ago, Nancy," 92
Segall, Ronen, 347
Seidel, Frederick, 37
Selected Poems: 1956–68, 21, 291, 294
Shaar Hashomayim, synagogue, 14, 171
Shakespeare, William
    Julius Caesar, 101
Shapiro, Gary, 313
Sherman, Annie, 18, 362
Shimabukuro, Jake, 52
Shirelles, 237
Shrek, 197, 206–8, 221
Shumway, David R., 289, 293
Siemerling, Winfried, 176
Simmons, Sylvie, 30, 54, 81, 91, 97, 110, 171, 253, 286, 288, 293, 316, 317, 329, 334, 337, 342
    I'm Your Man, 30, 239
Simon & Garfunkel, 196
Simon, John, 94, 355
Simon, Paul, 99, 256, 329
Simone, Nina, 241, 347
Sinatra, Frank, 119
"Sing Another Song, Boys," 67
"Singer Must Die, A," 276, 330
singer-songwriters, 79
"Sisters of Mercy," 51, 56, 64, 143, 318, 344
Skagen, Margery Vive, 337

INDEX

Slater, Christian, 115
Sloman, Larry, 311, 357
"Slow," 336
Smith, Patti, 111, 360
"So Long, Marianne," 32, 60, 92, 105, 108, 199, 228, 229, 230, 274, 297, 306
"Smokey Life, The," 144
Solway, David, 266
"Song for Abraham Klein," 177
"Song of the Hellenist, The," 33
Songs from a Room, 18, 21, 62, 66, 69, 91, 92, 98, 106, 142, 228, 229, 291, 318, 357
Songs from the Life of Leonard Cohen, 309
Songs from the Road, 25
Songs of Leonard Cohen, 2, 4, 6, 21, 45, 56, 62, 63, 65, 66, 77, 92, 98, 182, 186, 195, 200, 214, 255, 256, 257, 289, 290, 303, 309, 316, 317, 348, 362
Songs of Love and Hate, 62, 66, 67, 70, 93, 106, 113, 114, 120, 157, 233, 305, 319, 333, 347, 348
Sopranos, The, 119
Spector, Phil, 22, 68, 201, 223, 321, 348
Spice-Box of Earth, The, 20, 35, 127, 172, 175, 286, 301, 358
Spin Alternative Record Guide, 114
Starchive, 353–54
Steer Your Way, 349
Steinberg, M. W., 175
Stevens, Wallace, 224, 229
Stipe, Michael, 116
Stone, Oliver, 204
Stone, Sly, 114
Stormy Clovers, The, 84, 343
"Story of Isaac, The," 92, 106, 134
Stranger Music: Selected Poems and Songs, 184, 186
"Stranger Song, The," 111, 195–96, 279
Strauss, Neil, 333, 335
"Style," 39
Succession, 110
"Suzanne," 21, 50, 54, 64, 85, 86, 87, 92, 101, 105, 120, 143, 152, 162, 163–64, 171, 199, 205, 206, 213, 216, 224, 237, 238, 241, 242, 244, 254, 274, 275, 294, 298, 333, 340, 342–44, 345, 346, 348, 358, 359, 361
Söderlind, Sylvia, 42

"Take This Longing," 18, 188, 193, 364
"Take This Waltz," 36, 191, 193, 204, 230
Take This Waltz (film), 208

Taylor, James, 97, 108, 242–43
"Fire and Rain," 105, 106, 242
James Taylor, 100
Sweet Baby James, 100
Taylor, Johanna, 245
"Teachers," 92, 132, 200, 276
Tel Aviv, 296
Ten Bulls, The, 144
Ten New Songs, 18, 24, 62, 63, 71, 72, 121, 145, 146, 149, 159, 325, 356
Tennessee, 306, 357
Tennessee Notebook, 265
Testa, Bart, 202
Thanks for the Dance, 27, 72, 234, 263, 346
"That Don't Make it Junk," 279
"That's No Way to Say Goodbye," 297
"These Heroics," 36
"This Marriage," 272
Thomas Fisher Rare Book Library, 358
Thomas, Anjani, 18, 24, 72, 311
Thomas, Dylan, 32, 267, 275
"Thousand Kisses Deep, A," 63, 146, 356
Timberlake, Justin, 60
"To a Teacher," 175
"Tom Dooley," 93
"Tonight Will Be Fine," 344
Toronto, 172, 201, 211, 343
"Tower of Song," 9, 23, 55, 58, 64, 98, 116, 233, 245, 330, 331, 344, 347, 348
"Travelling Light," 150
"Treaty," 54, 164
Trehearne, Brian, 214–16, 217
Triffids, The, 347
Trochi, Alexander, 276
True Detective, 197, 208
Trump, Donald, 346
"Twelve O'Clock Chant," 301
Tyler, Steven, 115

"*Un Canadien errant*,"91, 186, 190

Vallese, Joe, 243
Various Positions, 9, 23, 61, 69, 144, 145, 201, 204, 301, 305, 311, 312, 330, 345, 349, 352, 363
Vedanta, 24, 149
Vega, Suzanne, 56, 235, 248
Velvet Underground, The, 111, 117, 199, 344, 355
"Heroin," 111
Velvet Underground and Nico, The, 364
Verdal, Suzanne, 104, 179, 241, 255, 294

INDEX

Vertus, Aisha C., 218
Vogel, Thomas, 346
von Trier, Lars, 205

Wainwright, Rufus, 120, 181, 345
"Waiting for the Miracle," 117, 121, 140, 145
Waits, Tom, 349
Walkowitz, Rebecca, 189
Warhol, Andy, 90, 362
Warnes, Jennifer, 67, 72, 188, 239, 296, 309, 344, 359
   Famous Blue Raincoat, 344
   "Up Where We Belong," 344
Washboard Jo, 347
Washburn, Donna, 296, 359
Watts, Alan
   Way of Zen, The, 250
"We Shall Not Be Moved," 309
Weil, Simone, 202
"Welcome to These Lines," 295
Westmount, 13, 14, 80, 185, 212
Wexler, Barrie, 265, 271
"What I'm Doing Here," 323
Whatley, Jack, 241
White, Barry, 115
"Who by Fire," 55, 117, 133, 298, 330
Wieseltier, Leon, 55
Wild Fire, 347
Wilde, John, 265
Wilde, Oscar, 314

"Wilf and His House," 33
Williams, Hank, 98, 112
Willner, Hal, 56
"Window, The," 158
"Winter Lady," 348, 364
Wisse, Ruth R., 94
Wolfmother, 348
Wonder, Stevie, 342
Woodstock Festival, 258
Woolf, Virginia, 230
Wordsworth, William, 29
Wright, Robert A., 88

Yaffe, David, 100, 102
Yetnikoff, Walter, 69, 121, 312
Yom Kippur War, 270, 271
"You Are Right, Sahara," 46
"You Have Loved Enough," 146
"You Know Who I Am," 161, 292
You Want It Darker, 25, 55, 72, 112, 151, 152, 164, 171, 190, 234, 280, 336, 349, 363
"You Want It Darker," 32, 63, 134, 135, 247, 248
Young, Izzy, 99
Young, Neil, 47, 114, 169, 170
   "Helpless," 170
Yules, 348

Zollo, Paul, 241, 246